AMERICAN FAMILIES

GARLAND LIBRARY OF SOCIOLOGY
VOLUME 30
GARLAND REFERENCE LIBRARY OF SOCIAL SCIENCE
VOLUME 1015

GARLAND LIBRARY OF SOCIOLOGY

PETER W. COOKSON, JR., *Series Editor*

AMERICAN FAMILIES
ISSUES IN RACE AND ETHNICITY

EDITED BY
CARDELL K. JACOBSON

GARLAND PUBLISHING, INC.
NEW YORK AND LONDON
1995

Library of Congress Cataloging-in-Publication Data

American families : issues in race and ethnicity / edited by Cardell K. Jacobson.
      p.   cm. — (Garland library of sociology ; vol. 30) (Garland reference library of social science ; vol. 1015)
    Most of the papers in this volume were originally presented at a conference held at Brigham Young University.
    Includes bibliographical references and index.
    ISBN 0-8153-1959-2 (alk. paper)
    1. Minorities—United States—Family relationships—Congresses. 2. Family—United States—Congresses. I. Jacobson, Cardell K., 1941–   .
II. Series. III. Series: Garland reference library of social science ; v. 1015.
E184.A1A63444 1995
305.8'00973—dc20   95-20273
                                                CIP

Printed on acid-free, 250-year-life paper
Manufactured in the United States of America

Series Editor's Preface

The Garland Library of Sociology is proud to include Cardell K. Jacobson's new book, *American Families: Issues in Race and Ethnicity*, in its evolving series of top flight sociological studies. Now more than ever, there is a need for publishing sociological research that addresses the critical issues of our era. Clearly, our society is undergoing very rapid cultural, political, social, and economic change; social science can help illuminate the future by carefully examining the present. It is our hope that the books published in this series will reach not only professional sociologists but all those readers who are deeply concerned about the present condition of society and the future direction of our culture. Society can be analyzed as a series of problematics that result in considerable human suffering; we ought to face these problems with courageous realism. One of the strengths of sociology is that it seeks to uncover potential solutions to social problems without resorting to sentimentality or illusory wishful thinking. Empiricism and tough-mindedness are more likely to lead to enlightenment than the expression of good feelings. Thus, the role of the Garland Library of Sociology is to bring to the public those books that will advance our thinking and propel us to engage more actively in the resolution of those contradictions and dilemmas that keep our society from reaching its potential.

Contents

Introduction and Overview

Cardell K. Jacobson

The racial and ethnic diversity of the American population has long been one of its most salient features. Few Americans grow up without some contact with members of other racial or ethnic groups. Moreover, in a racially conscious society one's own racial or ethnic membership is a significant part of one's identity. Thus, one's identity influences one's interactions with members of other groups and individual's behaviors in a myriad of situations and ways that reflect group membership.

At the same time, the crucible of racial and ethnic identity is the family. Identities, including racial and ethnic ones, are formed, nurtured, and harbored in the family. Kith and kin, our extended relationships, establish identity and influence our lives in innumerable ways.

The strength of family and racial identities persist despite how little we differ from each other genetically. As Hoffman (1994:4) has noted, "Our society is obsessed with race and confused by it." Hoffman calculates that genetics accounts for only about 0.2 percent of the difference between any two randomly chosen people on Earth. And only 6 percent of that difference results from differences between racial groups. In other words, Hoffman (1994:4) states, "race accounts for a . . . minuscule .012 percent difference in our genetic material."

Yet humans are incredibly obsessed with race. Note the recent controversy over possible racial IQ differences that has been generated by Charles Murray and Richard J. Herrnstein's recent book entitled *The Bell Curve* (1994).

Despite America's obsession with race, race and ethnicity are defined far less by genetics than by social prescriptions. Americans

1

often think of race in a tripartite sense: caucasians or caucasoid, Negroid, and Mongoloid. Yet the very term race lacks a clear scientific definition. Furthermore, the common triple-race category system is completely unworkable when one considers the plethora of groups that defy classification under such systems. Consider, for example, the Polynesian and Melanesian islanders, the Ainu of Japan, Eastern Indians, the aborigines of Australia, American Indians, and the Khoisan (bushmen) of Africa. Even anthropologists have trouble placing these groups within, or as subsidiary categories of the three main groups. In fact, anthropologists themselves appear to be moving away from racial classification systems and the notion that "true races" exist (Littlefield et al., 1982). Furthermore, early history and prehistory reveals a constant intermixing of countless groups. Scientists are agreed, however, that all peoples belong to one species. But there are no true races.

Even in the United States, a highly racially conscious society, substantial intermixing has occurred. The same is true of all countries with significant minority groups. Substantial intermarriage and intermixing has occurred. Estimates of the black gene pool that is originally of white origin for blacks living in the United States usually range from 20 to 30 percent (Shreeve, 1994; Pettigrew, 1964). Obviously more intermixing has occurred in societies where race is less salient such as in Puerto Rico and Brazil. Offspring from such unions have mixed identities. Highly racially conscious societies such as the United States sometimes force such individuals to adopt one identity. But any classification system is quite arbitrary and hides the vast commonalities that we all share as humans. The vast majority of human variation occurs within human groups, and not between them.

The criteria humans use to classify "others" are fickle, illusory, and literally only skin deep. Jared Diamond (1994) has recently noted that racial classifications on the basis of body chemistry would make as much sense as classifications on skin and eye color, hair form, lip thickness, or other commonly used criteria. Classifying groups on the basis of resistance to malaria, lactose intolerance, or genetic distinctiveness makes as much sense as skin color. Yet each of these criteria would result in different classification systems and all of them would be radically different from any current classification system in use.

Despite the difficulty of classifying racial and ethnic groups, racial and ethnic identities remain strong. Even if the social-economic status of minorities in the United States were equal to that of white Americans, most Americans are sufficiently race conscious that group identity would remain strong, and strongly influence perceptions, attitudes, and behaviors. This is the sense in which race and ethnicity are used by social scientists. While acknowledging that pure races and ethnic groups do not exist, we must also concede that most Americans and other peoples of the world have a basic understanding of ethnic groups. Most individuals have little difficulty in supplying a racial or ethnic designation when asked by pollsters, census takers, or others who inquire about their background. But race and ethnicity are socially constructed characteristics, not biological ones. And though family patterns may vary from group to group, they result from cultural and social phenomena.

Though substantial differences continue to exist between groups, researchers generally agree that attitudes about racial and ethnic groups have softened in the United States over the past few decades (Schuman et al., 1985; Firebaugh and Davis, 1988). The family structure differs in various racial and ethnic groups and earnings income and educational differences are substantial. Even when we compare just married couples, to eliminate some of the structural differences in the various ethnic groups, these differences persist. Some of these differences are presented in the following figures.

Figure 1 presents the mean earnings income of married men, by various racial and ethnic groups, in the 1990 1 percent Public Use Microdata Sample of the United States Census (PUMS). White married males made slightly higher than the national average for married men; they had an average income of $34,673. But two groups of males, Japanese Americans and Asian Indians who live in the United States, had earnings that were substantially higher than the national and white male averages. The success of these latter two groups can, in part, be explained by their extraordinary educational success (see Figure 2). Over two-thirds of the married Asian Indians living in the United States have completed college. Comparable figures for white American men and Japanese American men were 26.1 percent and 44.3 percent respectively (see Figure 2). But education is not the only explanatory

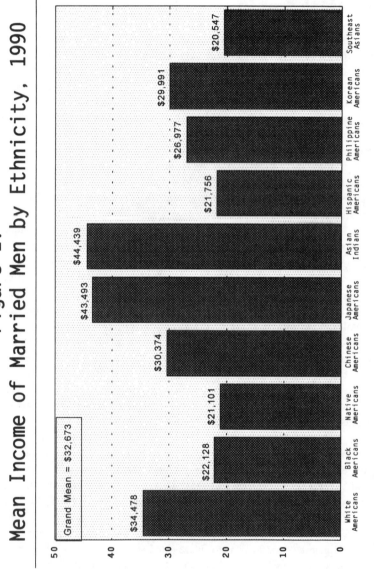

Figure 1.
Mean Income of Married Men by Ethnicity, 1990

Source: 1% Public Use Microdata Sample, U.S. Census, 1990

Figure 2.

Percent of Married Men Completing High School and College by Ethnicity

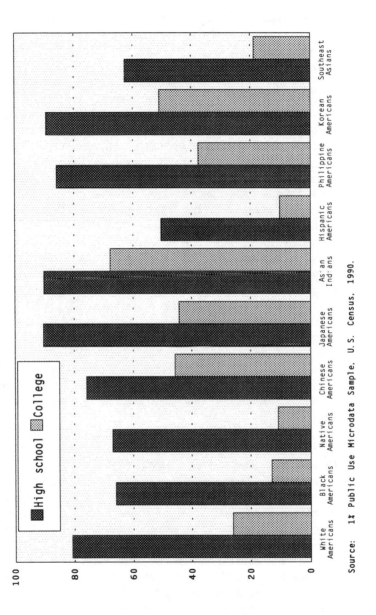

Source: 1% Public Use Microdata Sample.   U.S.   Census.   1990.

variable. Otherwise, the Chinese American, Japanese American, Korean American, Asian Indian, Philippine American, and Korean American males would all make more than white American males since their educational levels are higher than the white males' education level. Furthermore, the earnings of married Asian Indians husbands are only slightly higher than those of the Japanese American husbands, but their educational levels are much higher. Selective migration to the United States and cultural factors have obviously been factors in producing these earnings and educational differentials.

At the same time that these minority husbands have done well economically, other groups have not. Most Americans are aware that black American households are less likely than other households to be two-parent households. But when we examine only couples, the earnings of black American husbands still fall far short of the national average. Figure 1 shows that husband's earnings from four racial and ethnic groups are quite close: black Americans, Native Americans, Hispanic Americans, and Southeastern Asians (Vietnamese, Hmong, Cambodians, Laotians, and Thais). The married males from these four groups all have earnings incomes between $20,500 and $22,200. The earnings of married Philippine American, Korean American, and Chinese American men are higher than the poorer groups, but are still below the national average. The educational levels of the four lowest groups are somewhat different, but all are substantially below the other groups. Again, we should note that these averages and differences would be much different if we considered all males or even those who have children.

Different disparities are evident for ethnic wives in the United States. Figure 3 presents the earnings of women for the same racial and ethnic groups. Two striking observations are apparent from Figure 3. First, married women make substantially less than married men. While the average of the earnings for married men in this 1 percent census sample was $32,673, the average for women was $11,777. This discrepancy is large because many married women don't work outside the home. Others are more likely than married men to work only part-time. If we were to examine only married women who work full-time, their earnings levels would be much closer to that of the married males. A second observation from Figure 2 is that the earnings disparities for ethnic women are smaller than for their husbands. Hispanic wives report the lowest earnings though Native American wives have only

Figure 3.
Mean Income of Married Women by Ethnicity, 1990

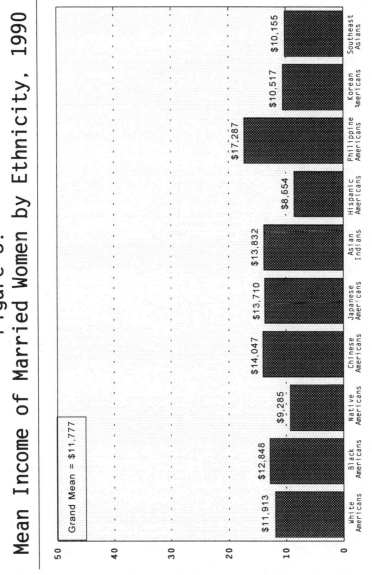

Source: 1% Public Use Microdata Sample,   U.S.   Census,   1990

slightly higher ones. The Philippine American wives report the highest earnings, but the earnings of several other groups are close to theirs. Five groups report earnings that are higher than those of white American wives, and this includes black American wives. The other groups are Chinese American, Japanese American, Asian Indian, and Philippine American married women. Obviously, the educational, income and cultural dynamics of these families influence these figures. For example, black American wives have long worked, more than white American wives, to bring family incomes into a middle-class range (see Schaefer, 1990; chapter 9).

The educational differences of these racial and ethnic married women are presented in Figure 4. As with the husbands, graduation rates from high school vary less than do the graduation rates from college. And again, as with the men, the college graduation rates of several ethnic groups are higher than that of white married women. The cultural and educational factors again explain some of the earnings differentials for ethnic married women, but not all of them. Age, English proficiency, and numerous other variables also contribute both to the richness of ethnic variability in American life and to the earnings and educational differences we have discussed thus far.

Examining and explaining these and other family patterns is the task of this volume. The publication is a collection of articles on ethnic families in the United States. The authors are social scientists, primarily sociologists. Most of the papers were originally delivered as part of a conference held at Brigham Young University in Provo, Utah.

CURRENT STATUS OF SPECIFIC ETHNIC FAMILIES

Most groups receive attention in several articles, but the first section of articles generally provides an overview of particular groups. The first chapter on African Americans is authored by Robert Staples who has written dozens of articles and books on the black family. In this paper he briefly reviews the history of the black family in the United States and describes the conditions that black families face today.

In a comprehensive chapter W. Parker Frisbie and Frank D. Bean from the Population Research Center at the University of Texas-Austin

Figure 4.

Percent of Married Women Completing High School and College by Ethnicity

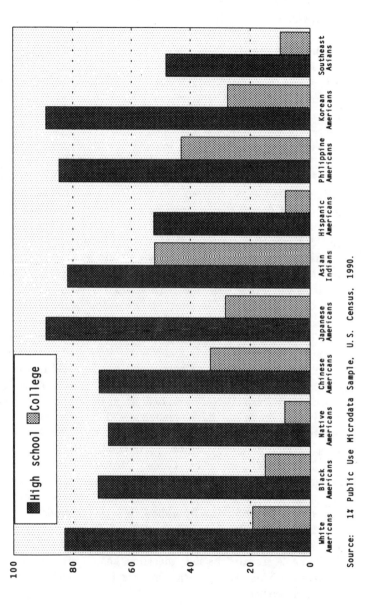

Source: 1% Public Use Microdata Sample, U.S. Census, 1990.

describe Hispanic Americans. They utilize data from the 1990 census to provide a wide variety of information on the Latino family. They close their chapter with a discussion of the "familial paradox." Havingdocumented the multiple disadvantages (such as low income and educational levels) that Latino families experience in the United States,they show that the high rates of familism persist in the Latino communities. Thus, despite pressures on the families, Latino families fare reasonably well in maintaining marital and family stability. They suggest that a "cultural buffer" may insulate these families from the devastating effects that other low-income, single-head-of-household families experience.

Federal law prohibits the government from collecting data on religious groups. Since Jews are considered a religious group, the government does not collect data on them. Other national surveys are seldom sufficiently large to obtain information on small groups. Thus, few data sets have much information about Jews in the United States. Actually Jews in the United States are both an ethnic group and a religious group. In his chapter Vivian Klaff utilizes data from the National Survey of Religious Identification to examine trends in the Jewish community. He couches his discussion in the context of the historical trends that have taken place over the last several decades.

Two articles focus on Native Americans. Jay Stauss, director of the American Indian Studies program at the University of Arizona, is member of the Jamestown Klallam tribe that regained tribal status in 1982. Stauss reminisces about his own experience growing up with his extended family in the Northwest to illustrate the strengths of the Indian family. He contrasts these strengths with the "social problems" approach taken by many non-Indians to tribal life. He believes there is hope for the future of American Indian families.

The second article by Cardell Jacobson focuses on Native American fertility. While Native American fertility has long been above the national average, it has actually been below that of African Americans. Utilizing data from the Public Use Microdata samples of the 1990 census Jacobson shows that the fertility trends of recent cohorts of blacks and whites, as well as Native Americans, have been declining. Age, marital status, education, and poverty status appear to explain much of the higher-than-average fertility rate for the Native American women.

Various authors have examined assimilation using both an assimilationist perspective and emergent ethnicity perspective. While the earlier model assumes that ethnic Americans must give up their own culture to assimilate American culture, the latter perspective argues that ethnic groups in the United States emerge with a new identity that combines elements of both cultures. Vivian Klaff's paper on Jewish families in the United States examines this question as do three articles on Asian families in the United States.

In the first of these three papers Yan Yu examines the patterns of work and family of three generations of Chinese American families. Cultural explanations have usually been offered to account for the success and work ethic of these families. Yu follows a few authors who have offered an alternative explanation, a structural explanation. She also describes several different types of Chinese American families in the United States and notes that the Chinese American family continues to change in response to ongoing structural changes.

Trina Hope and Cardell Jacobson discuss the history of the Japanese in the United States and examine the structural assimilation of Japanese Americans. They, perhaps more than any other ethnic group, have integrated into American society. As noted earlier, they along with Asian Indians living in the United States have extremely high education and income levels. And they, along with Jews, show an increasing rate of outmarriage, a strong indicator of integration and assimilation.

The notion that all Asian groups are following a similar path of integration into American society is further dispelled by Carolyn Jew. In her article she shows the tremendous variety that exists in the group many Americans refer to as a "model minority." Economically several new Asian groups fall far short of the more successful Asian groups. Their economic conditions are much more equivalent to those of black Americans, though their family conditions are much different. Though they appear to value education as highly as the older Asian groups, their educational and economic levels are currently far below the older groups. And Carolyn Jew argues that some of the children from these new groups may not be taking the same path to success that the older Asian American groups did.

PARENTING AND SOCIALIZATION
IN ETHNIC FAMILIES

The authors in the second section of this book discuss several parenting and socialization issues that affect minority families. Three papers are based on qualitative data while three others are based on quantitative data. Vânia Penha-Lopes and Carol Ward and her co-authors show how the contributions to family life of two groups have been underestimated. These families may be contributing more than traditionally thought. Using in-depth, qualitative interviews with black men who are not living in traditional two-parent families, Penha-Lopes shows how black men are quite involved in the rearing of their children.

Likewise, Carol Ward, Gregory Hinckley, and Kae Sawyer, using in-depth interviews with Northern Cheyenne women, analyze the adaptations that three generations of Northern Cheyenne women have made to changing social and economic conditions on the reservation. They argue that while all three generations have expanded their roles to include nontraditional work, the middle generation has expanded these roles the most. At the same time, they have looked to their cultural heritage to meet their identity and spiritual needs and have been at the forefront of the "cultural recovery" processes.

Kathleen Bahr and Howard Bahr are also interested in the role women, particularly grandmothers, play in the transmission of culture. Using qualitative data, the Bahrs show how the influence of grandmothers among the Apache has declined with the advent of television and VCRs and Anglo education.

In the first of the three quantitative papers, Marilou Blair and Sampson Blair use data from the National Survey of Families and Households to examine child care usage by whites and blacks. White mothers are more likely to utilize daycare centers while black mothers are more likely to use kin as child care providers. They also find that increased complexity of child care arrangements negatively affects maternal attitudes and behaviors.

Katherine McDade compares the attitudes of several racial and ethnic groups in the Seattle area about child socialization. The attitudes of the Native American parents are quite different from Asian, African, Caucasian, and Hispanic American parents. Many of the differences can be interpreted as resulting from cultural differences in child socialization. Many Native American groups delegate much of the childrearing to members of the extended family rather than to the parents specifically.

Monica Griffin Scruggs reverses the analysis in her chapter "African American Households and Community Effects on Economic Deprivation." Rather than take the family as the dependant variable that is affected by the community, she examined the effects of the household structures, community structures such as percentage of the aged in an area, and education, have on the economic outcomes for families. These effects, especially the effect for single-parent families loom large in her analyses.

INTERRACIAL DATING, MARRIAGE, AND STABILITY

The third section of the book deals with interracial dating, interracial marriage from both the black and white perspective, and marital stability of interracial and inter-ethnic couples. While university campuses are generally considered to be good places for whites, blacks, and other minorities to meet, Larry Williams, Kenneth Clinton, and Lisa Wyatt show that dating across racial and ethnic lines is not always easy. Gathering data from a Texas State University, they show that a lot of self-segregation occurs on campus. And while black students may have their own fraternity and sorority, they are often still excluded from the Greek societies to which many of the white students belong. Finally they find that the Hispanic students feel they have more opportunities to date than the black students feel they do. Indeed they find that a third of the black students do not date at all.

The second and third papers in this section both use data from the General Social Survey collected annually by the National Opinion Research Center at the University of Chicago. The paper by Yanick St. Jean and Robert Parker assesses the reactions of black females toward black/white marriages. The authors find that those black females who have fewer contacts with whites are more likely to approve of laws banning intermarriage.

The paper by Wilson and Jacobson examines white approval or disapproval of interracial marriage between blacks and whites. The results suggest that those who approve of such marriages tend to be men, the young, those with professional or business occupations, the college educated, and the less religious. Education, age and religion are the strongest indicators of those who favor or oppose laws against racial intermarriage.

Many analysts have used exchange theory to examine interracial marriages. In this type of analysis, the authors usually explain that white women from working-class or lower-class backgrounds and middle-class black men "exchange" whiteness for social class mobility. In their chapter on marital stability of black/white marriages, Chan and Smith take a somewhat different approach. They examine stresses on interracial marriage from a status-inconsistency perspective. This theory argues that status inconsistent people experience conflicting expectations from various people. Thus, a black middle-class person may be treated (or mistreated) on the basis of his or her race, rather than on social class. People who have such mixed statuses may experience more stress than others do. Examining interracial couples from this perspective, Chan and Smith find that some interracial couples experience more marriage failures than same-race couples.

EDUCATIONAL AND FAMILY STRUCTURE ISSUES

The final section of the book examines other family-related issues. The Aguirre and Hernandez paper focuses on the contextual and structural factors that affect the educational levels of the Chicano family. They suggest that the contextual factors of parental acculturation, parental teaching styles, and mother's role will affect educational outcomes. They also suggest that contextual factors such as achievement motivation, self-concept and prosocial behaviors will also effect academic achievement for the Chicano population.

One vestige of past discrimination in housing is that many middle-class African Americans continue to live in lower-class neighborhoods. In previous decades middle-class African Americans were excluded from better housing by both legal and illegal activities. Janet Hope examines some of the effects this residential segregation continues to have on the academic performance and educational aspiration of middle-class African Americans. Neighborhood continues to have an effect after the effects of several other variables are controlled statistically. Thus, she titles her piece "The Price They Pay for the Places they Live."

Albrecht and Clarke present an interesting and anomalous finding about single African American mothers. Most researchers have found that the children of single mothers have significantly higher chances of dying within the first month after birth (neonatal mortality). Examining all births from Florida for one year, Albrecht and Clarke found that, unlike children of single white and Hispanic mothers, the children of single black mothers actually had better chances of living than did the children of black mothers who were married. They suggest that informal family support structures, especially through extended families, may actually provide more support for single black women than they do for married black women. Furthermore, these arrangements have become quite normative in parts of the black community.

Finally, Gabe Wang, Stephen Bahr, and Anastasios Marcos examine the racial and ethnic differences in three important family-related predictors of substance abuse among adolescents. Though they did not find family cohesion to be directly related to adolescent substance abuse they did find it to be strongly related to both educational commitment and the number of drug-using friends. These two variables were, in turn, related to the rate of substance abuse. Wang, Bahr, and Marcos suggest that drug-use variations by ethnic group can be explained in terms of social context in which the individuals find themselves. Close friendships with drug-using friends do not have the same effect for those who live in an environment where drug use is common, and strong family cohesion may not shield adolescents where drug use is common.

REFERENCES

Diamond, Jared. 1994. "Race Without Color." *Discover* 15:83-89.

Firebaugh, Glenn, and Kenneth E. Davis. 1988. "Trends in Antiblack Prejudice, 1972-1984: Region and Cohort Effects." *American Journal of Sociology* 94:251-272.

Hoffman, Paul. 1994. "The Science of Race." *Discover* 15:4.

Littlefield, Alice, Leonard Lieberman, and Larry T. Reynolds. 1982. "Redefining Race: The Potential Demise of a Concept in Physical Anthropology." *Current Anthropology* 23:641-647.

Murray, Charles, and Richard J. Herrnstein. 1994. *The Bell Curve.* New York: The Free Press.

Pettigrew, Thomas F. 1964. *A Profile of the Negro American.* Princeton, NJ: D. Van Nostrand.

Schaefer, Richard T. 1990. *Racial and Ethnic Groups* (Fourth Edition). Glenview, Illinois: Scott, Foresman.

Schuman, Howard, Charlotte Steeh, and Lawrence Bobo. 1985. *Racial Attitudes in America.* Cambridge, MA: Harvard University Press.

Shreeve, James. 1994. "Terms of Estrangement." *Discover* 15:57-63.

The Current Status

of

Racial and Ethnic Families

Socio-Cultural Factors
in Black Family Transformation:
Toward a Redefinition of Family Functions

Robert Staples

For the last 30 years there have been concerns about the black American family—where it is going, and what the implications are for other problems in society. Before discussing its current status we need to discuss its history. While it may not add very much to our understanding of where it is today, it is important that we understand where it has been historically. We know that the blacks in this country came primarily from the continent of Africa, a continent which at that time, some four or five centuries ago, was highly patriarchal, but like many patriarchal societies it was very stable. There was no such thing as divorce and relatively little nonmarital sex, and what existed was institutionalized and controlled by tribes or communities of elders. These patterns and values were brought to the United States. Unfortunately, under slavery the black family ceased to exist as a legal entity.

A family is, in many ways, a legal entity as well as a social one. The slave had no legal right to a family; the slave family's functions consisted of those which the slave master mandated. There are many claims about what happened to the family of slaves, and those claims are not all consistent with one another. One claim is that the family was destroyed for black Americans during slavery because the roles of the husband and the father were institutionally obliterated. Others claim that simply for economic reasons slave owners did not destroy families, because in order for slavery to be an efficient economic system, it was important to keep families intact. Happy workers were thought to be generally more productive workers.

At any rate, recent evidence has indicated that the post-slavery black family structure was essentially similar to that of white

Americans of that period. This was the period between 1865-1925. About 75 percent of all black families were what one historian calls "simple nuclear families" (Gutman, 1976). Only during the second and third quarters of the 20th century, during a time of massive immigration and also urbanization, did the black family begin to disintegrate. Thus after about 1925 the black family began to face problems brought about by immigration and urbanization. Blacks no longer had the folk culture that had kept them together under the most adverse conditions in the rural South. Hence, we saw several new phenomena: children being raised by mothers, welfare dependency, juvenile delinquency, and some educational failures. But such breakdowns have to be viewed in context: only 10-15 percent of all black families in the period between 1930 and 1950 experienced these problems. In fact, around 1950, the black and white American families were remarkably similar in terms of their structure, if socioeconomic status differences of the two groups were taken into account.

In 1965 the notorious and much-read Moynihan report (Moynihan, 1965) was published. Officially entitled "The Negro Family: The Case for National Action," the report was written by Moynihan who at that time was the Assistant Secretary of Labor, and who later became the senior senator from the State of New York. Moynihan's major thesis was that the root of the problems of the black community was not economic but rather the deterioration of the black family. Since Moynihan was an important government official, the report seemed to imply a change in direction of government policy toward blacks and black American families in the United States. It was 1965, much of the South was still segregated, and blacks, of course, were at the bottom of the caste line according to the Moynihan report. The black family structure was out of line with the white American family structure. Furthermore, approximately 22 percent of all black families were headed by women—a "black matriarchy," in Moynihan's words. These families were dominated by women simply because there was no one to challenge them for power and control. The men obviously were not part of these families, but Moynihan claimed that even when men were present, they were weak and spineless; the women basically ruled the roost, and as a result produced ineffective, effeminate, and, by implication, homosexual males. He based many of his conclusions on rather flawed research evidence supplied to him by two sociologists (Blood and Wolf, 1960).

Additionally, he noted that 23.6 percent of all births to black women were out of wedlock, approximately one out of four. As a result, he said that this had led to welfare dependency and educational failures, and again to spineless men. In fact, many people cannot believe, or simply do not know, what Moynihan's solution was to the "problem." Moynihan recommended that black men go someplace where men could be men. At that time, he believed that place to be the United States military. Of course, the black man also had a fairly high chance of being killed if he joined the army at that time, since many men in the military were serving in Vietnam. Some claim he has subsequently been vindicated; the figures he cited in 1965 have grown increasingly worse, so that by 1992, according to the latest figures I have, 60 percent of black births were out of wedlock. If this has been the basic reason for lack of black achievement, the problem has gotten worse. But these same figures are now also higher for white families: 22 percent of out-of-wedlock births for white women, and approximately 26 percent of white women heading families with children. What are we then to say about the white American family in 1992? Sociologists have debated the question for years: "Is the family the engine that drives the car, or is it the car that is being driven by the engine?" In other words, does the family determine the economic status of individuals, or does the economy determine the structure of a family?

Let us now examine what is happening in black families in the 1990s. First, let us understand the variations within black subgroups in the United States; the black family in the United States is not a monolithic unit. Approximately 35 to 40 percent of black families would be considered middle class, depending on what definition is used. Most successful black Americans are not just those who are highly educated; gender plays a factor. Success is also not just socioeconomic status; it actually turns out to be marital status. If you are a black married couple in the United States, as Martin Luther King Jr. might have said, "You have reached the promised land." We actually find that black married couples in the northeastern part of the United States have a median income of approximately $43,000 a year, about parity with white married couples in that same geographic area of the country. Relatively few of the children of black married couples will be poor. In comparison to single-parent households, in which 65 percent of the children are poor, only 18 percent of the children in married couple households are poor, again a figure very comparable to that for white American families. What blacks essentially need in order to achieve equality is to be married. Obviously, one of the results of being married is that, particularly for black families, they have two incomes. The problem with black Americans, of course, is that one of the consequences of the travail of the 30 years since the Moynihan report was published is that approximately 40 percent of black adults over the age of 16 are married. This low figure represents one of the steepest declines, certainly in the western industrialized world, for a particular racial group. Only a third of black women over the age of 16 are currently married and living with a spouse. Thus, the fairly positive economic state for blacks, in terms of marital status, applies to only about 40 percent of the black American population. Yet despite these positive results, the poverty rate has increased by 3 percent among black married couples in the last two to three years.

Another key indicator of variations within the black community is gender. Approximately 85 percent or 90 percent of college-educated black males with an income of more than $25,000 a year are married and live with their spouse. Again, the unfortunate part is that black males are currently only about one-third of all the blacks enrolled in college, and they represent even a smaller percentage of those who will graduate from college. But, reasonably well-educated black males have no shortage of eligible and desirable mates, and they will have a fairly stable marital life.

Black women, who are two-thirds of the black college graduates, on the other hand, find themselves in a much different situation. Maybe half, or perhaps only 25 percent of them will find comparably educated black men who are available for marriage. Several years ago, I was struck by a 1978 figure, and I don't think it has changed. I was looking at educational levels and marital status of college graduates. I happened to look at the column for black women between the ages of 35 and 54, who had five or more years of college who had not been formerly married. The census bureau listed about 15,000 blacks in that category. One might assume that those black women would also like to marry a black male with similar characteristics. I looked at the column for black males that had the same characteristics. The census bureau did not list any. In other words, the ratio of black women to black men, who had five or more years of college who hadn't been formerly married, and were between the ages of 35-54, was 100:0. I knew that technically this was an error, because I was in that category. The Census Bureau told me that because of statistical variance, it had calculated that the number was less than 500. That meant that at best, according to Census Bureau statistics, there were about 15,000 black women in that particular category and 499 black males—a dismal marriage pool if they wished to marry within the race. And of course approximately 97 percent of all black American women do marry within the race. Thus gender is an important variable, for it (1) determines your chances of finding a sufficient number of people in the marriage pool, and (2) if you get married, as these 15,000 women have done and get divorced, it determines in large part your chances of getting remarried. And if you wish to have a marriage of socioeconomic equals, you are looking at very low prospects for black American women who have graduated from college.

Another factor, of course, is socioeconomic status in general. What we find is that middle-class black families also have problems. We don't really hear about problems of black middle-class families, because much of the concern over black American families is distorted in the media. There are these problems, but they are not problems of an economic nature, and therefore the government is not concerned. One of the problems is the downward mobility for many black middle-class families in the sense that they are simply not able to transmit their class status to their children in the way that many white families do. Black women must also deal with the problem of a declining marriage pool which forces women, in many cases, to marry down. These marriages have the highest divorce rate—at least they did in the past—of almost all marriages. So, the divorce rate for black women in middle-class marriages is fairly high and remarriage rate is very low, simply because of the low numbers and sex ratios in the marriage pool. We also know that the marriage pool is reduced even further by other kinds of behavior or statuses, such as high rates of interracial marriages by the middle-class blacks. Even the highest rate of homosexuality also appears to be in that group, although we are not really sure because data are so unreliable on homosexuality.

So the problem of the middle class is in many ways a problem of gender. Gender brings about other kinds of behavior less closely associated with the middle class. For instance, *Newsweek* published figures showing that even among black women who earned more than $75,000 a year, approximately one out of five had a child out of wedlock, one of the most famous examples being a TV news anchor in Boston. Again, this is a function of gender, although it is also a function of socioeconomic status, because the inability of many black men to rise up to the level of black women creates this low number in the marriage pool.

These are, in a nutshell, some of the key factors, but what about the explanations? As has been already mentioned, there is a demographic relationship and imbalance in sex ratios. Approximately 46 percent of black men, for a number of reasons, are not in the civilian labor force. Between the ages of 20 and 30, almost 25 percent are in jail, on probation, or on parole. The mortality rate in that same age range is about five times higher for black men than for black women. The largest cause of death is homicide, the second largest accidents, the third largest suicide, and the fourth largest, a cause that just basically came into existence in the 1980s—AIDS. As of 1992, 46 percent of those who died from AIDS were either black or Latino males. It is little wonder that for black women the out-of-wedlock birthrate is about 70 percent, simply because there are no men who are able to meet the basic requisites of being employed, drug-free, and able to carry out the normative functions of husbands and fathers.

This situation does not exist to the same extent in the white community. Black males are eight times more likely to be in prison than white males, about eight times more likely to die from homicide than white males, about eight times more likely to be out of the labor force. And even those who are in the military are often not in places where they can carry on functional marriages, because they are often stationed in places like Somalia, the Philippines, Spain and elsewhere abroad.

We must look closely at these social causes that bring about such demographic relationships. We also must consider, and this we do not often do, the social and cultural factors. Seventy-five percent of births being out of wedlock is not all socioeconomic or even demographic. High rates of out-of-wedlock births are also beginning to appear, as I have already pointed out, among middle-class whites. What we also need to understand is that the increase among whites has been considerably greater than among blacks. In fact, if blacks had increased their rates of divorces, out-of-wedlock children, and single-parent households at the same rate as whites, they would now be beyond 100 percent. That is, there would be no black married couples in the United States.

Because they were at a higher level in the beginning, their percentage is now larger, but the rate of increase is smaller.

Some of these factors are social and cultural, and it is not always popular to talk about them. Among them is the change in sex roles. It is simply much easier to maintain a stable family in a patriarchy. Thus, at this point of transition when we are striving for gender equity, families are under stress. The tensions, disagreements, and dissonance that occur at a time when we are trying for this noble goal are having a very disruptive effect on the family. This is, of course, by no means an endorsement of patriarchy; it simply points out what should be a fairly clear-cut fact: it is easier to have order in a dictatorship than in a democracy.

The media and the role models available to us through the media have essentially made non-marital sex, and even anti-marriage attitudes, normative in this country. I can hardly think of a well-known celebrity in a conventional marriage who is living the normative lifestyle of husbands and wives as we have traditionally defined it. Most of them, and certainly the more visible ones, often have children out of wedlock, are cohabitating, and are certainly in agreement with permissive attitudes towards sex and even drugs. This eventually has an impact on the most impressionable sector of the black population, the youth, as well as on the white population. It is among that population where we have the largest number of out-of-wedlock births and the most sexually active population. As long as society, which really has no choice in a democracy, allows this sort of media impact of role models, who are entertainers and other prominent people, including those in the highest levels of government, the message is that this is desirable behavior.

There is a combination of factors for black Americans. The most imminent and decisive factor still tends to be the economic one, but it is also cultural, which means that it is beginning to have an impact on the middle class as well as the lower class.

What is the 'solution'? I am not sure we really know. We assume that a two-parent household is preferable to a single-parent household, and I would add to that a two-parent household in which husbands and wives are in a loving and caring relationship may be more preferable to a single parent household in which the woman has to struggle with all sorts of roles; in that case, a two-parent household is preferable. The significant thing about this whole debate about two-parent versus one-parent households has to do with the subtle problems that ostensibly come from the one-parent household: educational failures, crime, delinquency, welfare dependency, etc. We have never really been able to sort this out, simply because most single-parent households (and this is particularly true of black single-parent households) actually have about 40 percent of the income available to them that black married couple households have. Thus we are looking at two groups with very different resources, and when we talk about crime, when we talk about educational failures and welfare dependency caused by female heads of households, we also know that those are the poorest households. And until we have carefully constructed studies which can show that, with socioeconomic status controlled, we are still going to have these problems, we cannot really direct all the blame or responsibility to the one- or two-parent structure of such households.

Moreover, remember that when we talk about certain factors like crime, it is one of the easiest things in the world to say that crime in this country is primarily a function of its definition and its enforcement. Certainly, like everyone else, I would prefer to have the criminal that comes into the bank and robs it and kidnaps all the customers put behind bars. He is in many ways, a much greater threat to my safety and well-being than the white-collar criminal who manages to steal millions through the use of a computer. On the other hand, the person who robs the bank generally gets only $1000 to $2000. The white-collar criminal who generally has access to the computer through what we call "human capital," "credentials,"—a degree, job experience, good recommendations—steals a lot more. They both commit crimes, but essentially we punish the crimes of the poor, we enforce the law against the poor, and of course the poor are less likely to have a defense, because they are less likely to be able to afford a good lawyer who can get them off. We really do not want to talk about crime as coming from these one-parent families because obviously, the white-collar criminal comes from a more privileged family that is likely to be a two-parent family. We must consider which is the worse crime. Certainly in terms of magnitude, the white-collar criminal gets away with more.

Educational problems are widespread in society. They are no longer unique to the lower class. They exist in the suburbs; that is why we have initiatives to establish vouchers so that everybody can go to private schools, except for the most intransigent students, who will be left in the public schools, along with their teachers, who I would suggest should arm themselves and not worry about teaching.

So, we are at this point where we have to consider all American families in the overall context of American society, and the family's function in society. Certainly many of its traditional functions are no longer carried out in most of the United States. Statistically, probably only 18 percent of Americans belong to what we would consider the traditional American family, that is, a two-parent family in which the wife stays at home and the parents have approximately 1.8 children. That family is a small minority nowadays. We will have to go beyond these traditional models and figure out a niche, a role, a function, for families in American society. The black American family, in a sense, is in the vanguard of these changes. We will not know whether these changes are positive or negative until the economic basis of these family structures has been reduced or eliminated. Until that time, we have to remember the words of John Donne who once wrote, "Never send to know for whom the bell tolls." If we do not get a grip on these problems and get credible and workable solutions, the answer will have to be, "The bell will toll for me and for thee."

REFERENCES

Blood, Robert, and Donald Wolf. 1960. *Husbands and Wives: The Dynamics of Married Living*. New York: The Free Press.

Gutman, Herbert. 1976. *The Black Family in Slavery and Freedom, 1750-1925*. New York: Pantheon.

Moynihan, Daniel Patrick. 1965. *The Negro Family: The Case for National Action*. Washington, DC: Office of Policy Planning and Research. U.S. Department of Labor.

Newsweek, 1993. "Endangered family." August 30, pages 17-29.

The Latino Family
in Comparative Perspective:
Trends and Current Conditions[1]

W. Parker Frisbie and Frank D. Bean

Two decades ago, Brigitte and Peter Berger published a volume, entitled *The War over the Family* (1974), which graphically delineated highly conflicting perspectives on family structure and relationships. A decade later, Thornton and Freedman called attention to the fact that many of the most divisive issues that have arisen in the United States, ranging from specific debates over abortion rights and sex education to more general philosophical differences over the appropriateness of government intervention in individual activities, "have focused directly on central aspects of the family" (1983:3). With the passing of another 10 years, it appears that the debate has become no less vitriolic. The intensity of interest is scarcely surprising. The family has long been recognized as the primary agent of socialization in society, while households[2] may be viewed as staging areas in which the tangible and intangible resources required by family members are gathered and distributed. Thus, it is to be expected that family structure and composition will be major determinants of the health and economic well-being of individuals, and remaining current in our knowledge of conditions and trends characterizing the family therefore continues to be a crucial enterprise for scholars and policy-makers alike.

Media accounts seem to reflect the popular notion that the traditional family "is going out of style" (Glick and Norton, 1977:3), but there is a difference of opinion among scholars whether over time there has been a serious weakening of the family as a social institution (Bean and Tienda, 1987:Chapter 6; see also Espenshade, 1985; Westoff, 1983). Depending on one's perspective and which indicators are emphasized, there may be cause for either optimism or dismay. However,

29

if one considers the shifts in the demographic profile of the American family that have occurred over the past several decades, including a slackening of marriage and remarriage rates, a decline in the proportion of married couple households, increases in the proportion of persons never marrying, and soaring rates of marital disruption, nonmarital births, and children residing in one-parent families (Lugaila, 1992; Eggebeen and Lichter, 1991), there seems little doubt that the foundations of traditional family life have been severely shaken.

Among the most compelling reasons for continuing interest in these matters are persistent race and ethnic differentials in family structure and in measures of the well-being of individuals associated with those differentials. Sandefur et al. (1992:103) report that:

> *Not living with both parents at age 14 has negative consequences for children's high school graduation regardless of whether the child lives with a single parent, a parent and stepparent, or neither parent; . . . and the effects of family structure and changes in family structure . . . persist after controlling for income and social psychological attributes of the adolescent. . . .*

In a test of three competing theoretical models using data from the National Survey of Families and Households, Wu and Martinson (1993) have demonstrated that growing up in a nonintact family significantly increases the risk of a premarital birth, especially among white and Hispanic women, "even at long durations after a change in family situation" (1993:228). Further, in a recent study limited to whites and blacks, Eggebeen and Lichter produced an array of findings strongly implicating family structure as a determinant of childhood poverty, including the following:

> *1) child poverty rates would have been one-third less in 1988 if family structure had not changed since 1960; (2) changing family structure accounted for nearly 50 percent of the increase in child poverty since 1980* (1991:801).

These authors conclude that racial variation in family structure acted to exacerbate the already substantial differences between the poverty rates of black and white children. In addition, something of a "polarization" of poverty appears to be emerging due to family size differences between poor and more affluent households (Eggebeen and Lichter, 1991).

Along with the widespread recognition that changes of major proportions have occurred in family and household structure, it is important also to realize that trends have been neither monotonic nor monolithic. For example, the upsurge in divorce that began in the 1960s had, by the late 1970s, reached levels that implied "that about one of every three white children and two of three black children born after marriage will experience a parental marital dissolution by age 16" (Thornton and Freedman, 1983:8). But divorce rates subsequently leveled off and, in fact, diminished slightly in the 1980s, while the rates of first marriage and remarriage, which had dropped precipitously as the risk of divorce rose, showed little change in the 1980s (Lugaila, 1992). Nor has the trend in child poverty been a consistent one. The poverty rate for children, which stood at around 27 percent in 1959, was cut nearly in half (to 14 percent) by 1969, increased alarmingly to over 22 percent in 1983, only to fall to below 20 percent by 1988 (Bianchi, 1990:14).

RESEARCH ON THE LATINO FAMILY: A SUMMARY

In light of the growing recognition of the influence exercised by basic family and household structural characteristics such as size, headship, household composition,[3] and marital status on the socioeconomic conditions and prospects of America's families, and of the clear and persistent racial/ethnic divergence in these relationships, the importance of this conference on "Racial/Ethnic Families in the United States" is self-evident. What might not be palpable is the significance of research that focuses specifically on Latino families. As noted by Bean and Tienda, this topic

> . . . *attract(s) particular interest in the case of Hispanics for whom family and kin relationships have been argued to assume greater importance than is the case among non-Hispanic whites. Because Hispanic groups are composed of relatively recent immigrants from less developed countries, they might be expected to adhere more closely to traditional patterns of marriage, family, and household behavior* (1987:179).

Empirical evidence is mixed with respect to the question of whether Latinos, in fact, are more familistic in their orientation than other groups (Bean and Tienda, 1987; Frisbie et al., 1985). Nonetheless, "the extent to which Hispanics exhibit demographic behaviors consistent with familistic orientations not only is interesting in its own right, but also may have implications for . . . further advances in socioeconomic achievement" (Bean and Tienda, 1987:179) as well as for the welfare of this population as indicated by measures as diverse as poverty levels, prevalence of marital disruption (Frisbie, 1986) and rates of infant mortality (Forbes and Frisbie, 1991; Williams et al., 1986).

The volume of research relevant to marital and family characteristics among Latinos has grown significantly in recent years (e.g., Bean and Tienda, 1987; Castro Martin and Bumpass, 1989; Frisbie, 1986; Frisbie and Kelly, 1986; Lugaila, 1992; Mutchler and Frisbie, 1987; Schick and Schick, 1991). Unfortunately, few studies of substantial longitudinal depth have compared specific Latino populations, although it is clear that demographic, economic, and social characteristics of the Mexican origin, Puerto Rican, Cuban, and other Hispanic populations differ significantly (Bean and Tienda, 1987; Angel and Worobey, 1991). One reason for this gap in our knowledge is the difficulty in achieving consistency in identification of Latinos over long periods of time due to the changing definitions employed by the Census and other data collection entities (Hernandez et al., 1973; Bean and Tienda, 1987).

THE LATINO FAMILY: 1960-1990

Objectives of the Research

The general objective of the present analysis is to investigate over time, and in comparative perspective, family and household conditions experienced by Latinos. The following specific questions suggested by findings and gaps in previous research will be of particular interest: (1) Have the characteristics which distinguished Latino families from their non-Latino white counterparts ("Anglos") around the middle of the century (e.g., Bean and Tienda, 1987; Grebler et al., 1970) persisted into the 1990s? (2) Has the diversity observed among Latino groups in this regard narrowed or widened in recent years and to what extent have

Latino family trends paralleled those observed among Anglos and blacks? (3) Has the economic inequality that typified specific Latino populations in various degrees over the past 20 years (Bean and Tienda, 1987) persisted, and to what degree do such disparities vary by family structure? (4) Are the changes in family/household patterns that have led some observers to argue that a decline in the importance of the family has occurred in the United States as representative of Latino groups as they are of Anglos?

In order to address these questions, we trace family and household trends beginning in 1960 and extend previous analyses by including data from the 1990 census enumeration. In so doing, we will also be interested in accumulating evidence regarding whether Latinos exhibit a more familistic orientation than other racial and ethnic groups.

By applying ethnic identifiers developed for the study of Latinos in Bean and Tienda's 1980 census monograph (1987), it is possible to document and evaluate trends in family and household characteristics over the past 30 years.[4] We draw heavily on the U.S. Census Bureau's 1990 Public Uses Microdata Sample (PUMS-A, 1%) to extend the work of Bean and Tienda, and supplement this source with other information where this is available and relevant.

Household Size and Composition

Current information on basic demographic characteristics suggests that Latino families have followed the general pattern of decline in husband-wife households, with a concomitant rise in the prevalence of other family households (largely female headed), and non-family households (Table 1, first panel). In 1960, the proportion of Latino husband-wife families varied narrowly between 68 and 76 percent, figures quite similar to the Anglo percentage (76.4). In both 1980 and 1990, the largest relative number of husband-wife families was found among Mexicans and Cubans, but the percentage of such families had declined to three-fifths of all households by 1990. Of the Latino groups, only the Puerto Rican population is characterized by a distribution in which the number of couple-headed households falls below 50 percent, but even the 1990 figure (44.0 percent) exceeds by almost 10 percentage points the fraction found among non-Latino blacks.

In the three decades covered by our data, non-Latino whites and Cubans registered only minor increases in the "other family" category.

Table 1

Latino Household Size and Composition, 1960-1990

PERCENTAGE DISTRIBUTION

Ethnic Group	Husband-Wife Families				Other Families				Nonfamilies			
	1960	1970	1980	1990	1960	1970	1980	1990	1960	1970	1980	1990
Non-Latino White	76.4	70.8	63.0	58.3	9.4	9.5	10.1	11.0	14.3	19.6	26.9	30.7
Mexican	75.9	70.7	66.1	60.7	14.0	16.4	17.9	23.5	10.1	12.9	16.0	15.8
Puerto Rican	71.8	62.2	48.7	44.0	17.8	24.5	31.5	34.9	10.5	13.3	19.8	21.1
Cuban	72.1	74.4	65.7	59.2	13.3	13.2	14.1	16.4	14.6	12.4	20.2	24.4
Central/South Am.	68.0	64.1	56.8	54.8	14.5	18.8	23.6	26.5	17.5	17.1	19.6	18.7
Other Latino	75.7	70.6	58.1	50.5	10.3	13.4	16.7	23.7	14.0	16.0	25.2	25.9
Non-Latino Black				34.6				36.1				29.3

table continues

Table 1 (continues)

MEAN HOUSEHOLD SIZE

Ethnic Group	Husband-Wife Families				Other Families				Nonfamilies			
	1960	1970	1980	1990	1960	1970	1980	1990	1960	1970	1980	1990
Non-Latino White	3.7	3.6	3.3	3.1	2.9	3.0	2.8	2.8	1.4	1.1	1.2	1.2
Mexican	4.9	4.6	4.4	4.5	3.9	3.8	3.7	4.0	1.2	1.2	1.3	1.5
Puerto Rican	4.4	4.2	4.0	3.8	3.7	3.8	3.6	3.6	1.2	1.2	1.2	1.2
Cuban	3.7	3.8	3.5	3.4	3.0	3.2	3.0	3.1	1.1	1.2	1.2	1.2
Central/South Am.	3.9	3.9	4.0	4.2	3.2	3.3	3.4	3.8	1.3	1.2	1.3	1.5
Other Latino	3.5	4.1	3.7	3.7	3.7	4.0	3.3	3.5	1.2	1.3	1.2	1.3
Non-Latino Black				3.7				3.5				1.2

Source: Bean and Tienda, 1987, Table 6.7; U.S. Bureau of the Census, 1990 PUMS-A 1% Sample.

In striking contrast is the trend for Puerto Ricans among whom the proportion of other families doubled (from 17.8 percent in 1960 to 34.9 percent in 1990). Less spectacular, but still sizable increases occurred among most other Latino populations. Between 1960 and 1990, rather prominent gains in the proportion of non-family households (on the order of 10 to 12 percent) characterized all groups, except for Mexicans and Central/South Americans. It should be noted that the income distributions presented below suggest that the processes underlying changes across these groups may be different. To illustrate, both Cubans and Anglos are comparatively affluent populations, and thus their members are more likely to be able to "purchase privacy" and to live outside an extended family setting. In the less affluent Puerto Rican and black populations, individuals may find it necessary to "double-up" in order to acquire even minimally acceptable housing.

The consistent decline in Anglo household size across all household types is not mirrored in the Latino population (Table 1, second panel). The three largest Latino groups (Mexicans, Puerto Ricans, Cubans) experienced a reduction in the average number of persons per husband-wife household over the entire 1960-1990 period, but there was a small increase among Mexicans over the last decade, and over the entire time interval both Central and South Americans and other Latinos recorded increases. Indeed, Central/South American mean household size grew rather consistently across all household types, perhaps reflecting the influx of new immigrants. At *all* points in time, Mexicans have the largest average family size, which is a function of the higher fertility of this group, as well as of increments due to immigration.

The implications of the findings with respect to household composition and size for the issues addressed by the current research seem relatively straightforward. The previous finding of considerable diversity across the several Latino subgroups is once again documented. And while the larger family size and greater concentration of certain Latino groups, particularly Mexicans, in husband-wife families[5] is consonant with the view that these groups are characterized by a more familistic orientation, the continued increase in the percentage of other families (most of which are female-headed households with children) at the expense of the traditional husband-wife arrangement, supports the conclusion reached earlier by Bean and Tienda that whatever familistic forces are operating, "they apparently are not strong enough to ward off the forces making for these increases in families without fathers" (1987:191).

Nuptiality

In investigations of the extent to which the propensity to marry varies by race and ethnicity, it is necessary to take into account the fact that differences in age structure strongly influence between-group differences in marital status distributions. Accordingly, we follow Bean and Tienda (1987:Chapter 6) in focusing on the proportions of 25-year-old persons who have ever married. For both males and females, the trend is one of secular decline for most of the subpopulations (Table 2).

Table 2

Percentage of 25-Year-Olds Ever Married,
by Sex and Ethnicity, 1960-1990*

| | Males | | | | Females | | | |
Ethnic Group	1960	1970	1980	1990	1960	1970	1980	1990
Non-Latino White	71.4	74.0	59.1	46.0	86.8	85.6	73.7	63.4
Mexican	65.6	75.2	66.0	50.7	84.9	82.8	79.6	66.0
Puerto Rican	67.7	75.2	58.6	43.3	79.8	82.4	67.4	54.0
Cuban	77.8	75.9	60.0	51.6	88.9	74.4	72.2	62.8
Central/South Am.	38.9	65.9	59.9	41.0	71.4	79.6	72.8	56.2
Other Latino	50.0	75.3	60.1	37.9	66.7	83.1	74.4	59.3
Non-Latino Black				30.9				36.2

*Based on persons.
Source: Bean and Tienda, 1987, Table 6.2; U.S. Bureau of the Census, 1990
    PUMS-A 1% Sample.

Between 1960 and 1970, save for a small decline in the case of Cubans, male propensity to marry increased moderately to substantially (with the increase being particularly striking in the case of Central and South American and other Latino males, among whom the percent married was quite low in 1960). By 1980, however, the trend toward delay of marriage was fully evident, so that by 1990, only Mexicans and

Cubans reported a majority of 25-year-old males who had ever married. It is interesting that a sharp recent decline (15.3 percent between 1980 and 1990) occurred among both Mexican males for whom the likelihood of being married was greatest, and among Puerto Rican men who were characterized by the lowest proportion ever married in 1980. Although quite low by historical standards, the 1990 Latino percentages are considerably higher than the 30.9 percent of non-Latino black males who had ever married.

Although, across time and ethnic group, females are much more likely than males to have ever married by their twenty-fifth birthday, the within-ethnic-group temporal pattern for females tends to parallel the male trend, including the marked curvilinear slope observed among Central and South American and other Latino males. As was the case with males, the propensity of black females to marry lags rather far behind the rates for the other racial/ethnic groups in 1990 (Table 2).

All of this is consistent with the steady increase in the median age at marriage for both males and females which emerged in the United States in the mid-1970s and the venerable tendency (at least a century old) for the average male age at marriage to exceed that of females by two to three years (see Eshleman, 1988:259). More important for present purposes, it may be observed that, while the propensity to marry clearly differs among Latinos and between Latinos and non-Latino whites and blacks, there are relatively few notable ethnic differentials in either proportions married or trends in those proportions.

Fertility

The fertility of Mexican American women has, for quite some time, exceeded that of most other racial or ethnic groups in this country (Bean and Marcum, 1978; Rindfuss and Sweet, 1977). One explanation for the higher fertility of this group is that, net of influences such as age structure and marital patterns, Mexican Americans may "adhere more closely than non-Hispanic whites to familistic norms and values, that is, to give overriding importance to collective needs of the family as opposed to individual needs" (Swicegood et al., 1988:18; see also Bean et al., 1977; Murillo, 1971). This culturally-based explanation clearly is not capable of accounting for all of the variation in Mexican American fertility, and, in fact, may well be inferior to conceptual models based on economic factors as related to costs of child-bearing

(Bean and Tienda, 1987: Chapter 7). Nevertheless, the number of children born is obviously a key aspect of family structure, and regardless of the precise direction of the relationship, it seems certain that higher fertility dampens opportunities for economic advancement if only because scarce, or at least limited, resources must be spread more thinly as the number of children borne increases.

Data are available that permit comparison of children ever born for some groups of Latino women with non-Latino whites and blacks over the entire 1960-1990 period (Table 3), along with a less inclusive comparison by age of mother over the same time interval (Table 4). As Table 3 shows, Mexican women, age 15-44, have higher fertility than any other racial or ethnic groups being considered at each of the four points in time, followed at some distance by Puerto Rican and non-Latino black women. Inspection of the fertility ratios in Table 3 makes it clear that the differentials between Latino and Anglo women did not diminish over time, but rather tended to increase slightly or moderately (in the case of Puerto Ricans) in magnitude. Much the same observation can also be made from the percentage change scores that trace the fertility declines that typified the 1970-80 and 1980-90 intervals. All of the groups evidenced something of a "birth dearth" during the 1970s, with continuing, albeit smaller, declines in the 1980s.

Fertility is highest among Puerto Ricans in the teen and young adult ages, but for ages 25-34 and 35-44, the number of children ever born is highest among Mexican women at each of the four points in time (Table 4). To illustrate, 15-24 year-old Puerto Ricans report 657 children born in 1970. This cohort would be 25-34 years old in 1980, at which point Mexican American fertility had come to exceed Puerto Rican fertility by over 100 children per 1000 women, and by 1990, the gap (for those 35-44 years old) had widened to almost 400 births per 1000. Examination of fertility by age of mother yields additional insights into ethnic trends, but does not alter the general conclusions (1) that between 1960 and 1990 fertility has dropped significantly for all groups, and (2) that except for Cubans, Latino women have fertility levels which exceed those of non-Latino white women (Table 4).

Table 3

Mean Number of Children Ever Born
per 1000 Women Aged 15-44, 1960-1990

Ethnic Group	Mean Number Children Ever Born per 1000				% Change 1960- 1970	% Change 1970- 1980	% Change 1980- 1990
	1960	1970	1980	1990			
Non-Latino White	1712	1589	1232	1176	-7.2	-22.5	-4.5
Mexican*	2290	2114	1715	1620	-7.7	-18.9	-5.5
Puerto Rican	1855	1938	1662	1515	4.5	-14.2	-8.8
Cuban	na	1310	1069	1063	na	-18.4	-0.6
Other Latino†	na	1719	1355	1336	na	-21.2	-1.4
Non-Latino Blacks	2016	1862	1575	1461	-7.6	-15.4	-7.2
	Fertility Ratios						
Non-Latino White	1.00	1.00	1.00	1.00			
Mexican*	1.34	1.33	1.39	1.38			
Puerto Rican	1.08	1.22	1.35	1.29			
Cuban	na	0.82	0.87	0.90			
Other Latino†	na	1.08	1.10	1.14			
Non-Latino Blacks	1.18	1.17	1.28	1.24			

*In 1960, refers to the Spanish surname population of the five Southwestern states.

†Includes Central and South American as well as Other Latino.

na not available

Source: Bean and Tienda, 1987, Table 7.1; U.S. Bureau of the Census, 1990 PUMS-A 1% Sample.

Table 4

Mean Number of Children Ever Born per 1000 Women Aged 15-44
Latino Women, by Age, 1950-1990

Ethnic Group	15-24 Years				25-34 Years				35-44 Years			
	1960	1970	1980	1990	1960	1970	1980	1990	1960	1970	1980	1990
Non-Latino White	515	347	262	257	2190	2100	1383	1232	2419	2891	2523	1853
Mexican*	694	492	528	520	2950	2760	2105	1914	3834	4222	3646	2825
Puerto Rican	770	657	548	535	2302	2507	1986	1718	2873	3240	3202	2435
Cuban	na	238	192	169	na	1622	1189	1143	na	1932	2033	1674
Other Latino†	na	476	337	346	na	2168	1567	1480	na	3041	2640	2179

*In 1960, the identifier is the Spanish surname population of the five Southwestern states.
†Includes Central and South American as well as Other Latino.

Source: Bean and Tienda, 1987, Table 7.2; U.S. Bureau of the Census, 1990 PUMS-A 1% Sample.

The Elderly and Their Living Arrangements

As changing fertility, mortality, and immigration patterns have led to the "graying of America," a vast amount of research on the potential impact of this demographic trend for the economy and public welfare has been conducted. However, empirical studies of the household structure of specific Latino groups have been nearly non-existent (but see Mutchler and Frisbie, 1987).

In the U.S., the ability to live independently tends to be seen as highly desirable among all adult age groups, so that, when possible, privacy will be purchased and household headship maintained (Beresford and Rivlin, 1966; Gordon et al., 1981). In this context, Mutchler and Frisbie note that racial/ethnic differentials could affect residential patterns of elderly persons in at least three ways:

(1) Due to different fertility, mortality, and migration patterns, racial/ethnic groups may differ in number of "available kin" with whom to share housing.

(2) Due to differences in employment and income patterns, minority elderly may have fewer resources on which to draw . . . . The sharing of households may be perceived as more "cost effective" among these groups (Moon, 1983).

(3) Due to differences in norms and expectations developed historically in the U.S., as well as in country of origin, minority group families may favor certain forms of householding to a greater or lesser extent than the majority population (1987:7).

Since Latinos are characterized by high fertility, high levels of immigration to the U.S. (Bean and Tienda, 1987), and mortality rates that are similar to those of Anglos (Schoen and Nelson, 1981; Bradshaw et al., 1986; Rosenwaike and Bradshaw, 1989; Forbes and Frisbie, 1991; Frisbie et al., 1992), and since these minority populations have fewer economic resources than do Anglos (Bean and Tienda, 1987), it is logical to suppose these conditions would reinforce whatever tendency that might already exist toward the formation of multigenerational households as a result of a more familistic Latino culture.

As one would expect based on the fertility differentials previously discussed, except for Cubans, the age structure of the Latino population is relatively young. In 1988, the median age for Latinos was 25.5, as compared to 32.9 for the population not of Hispanic origin, with Mexican Americans having the lowest median (23.9) and Cubans by far the highest (38.7). The proportion of the Latino population aged 65 and older ranges from lows of 3 to 5 percent for most groups, to a high of 13.1 percent for Cubans (Schick and Schick, 1991:7).

Table 5 displays living arrangements across six mutually exclusive household types for the several Hispanic groups, as compared with non-Latino whites and blacks in 1990. The category "Householder" includes

Table 5

Living Arrangements of the Population Age 65 and Older, by Ethnicity, 1990

	Percentage with each Living Arrangement					
Ethnic Group	Householder*	Alone	With Child	With Other Relative	With Non Relative	Institution
Non-Latino White	58.6	29.5	2.8	2.7	1.0	5.4
Mexican	58.7	19.3	9.8	7.3	2.0	3.0
Puerto Rican	53.1	26.2	9.9	5.8	2.5	2.5
Cuban	52.1	18.4	11.7	13.0	2.6	2.1
Central/South Am.	35.1	18.0	22.8	15.7	7.3	1.1
Other Latino	54.5	26.4	7.8	6.3	2.2	2.8
Non-Latino Black	52.1	31.1	5.0	4.9	2.2	4.7

*Includes household heads and spouses of heads.

Source: U.S. Bureau of the Census, 1990 PUMS-A 1% Sample

the spouses of household heads, as well the head of household, which along with those living alone[6] define those elderly who live independently. The category "With Child" refers to those elderly who live in a household headed by adult offspring.

The modal living arrangement of persons 65 and older is clearly that of householder. While Mexican Americans and Anglos are most likely to be in such an arrangement, relative concentrations range narrowly between 52 and 59 percent for all groups, with the exception of Central and South Americans (Table 5). Living alone is also a fairly common occurrence, especially among non-Latino whites and blacks. A major difference can be seen in regard to the proportion of the elderly who live with other family members. The proportion of Anglos living with their adult children or some other relative is only 5.5 percent, a total lower than the figure for either of these arrangements taken separately for any of the Latino groups. For example, slightly over 17 percent of older Mexican Americans live with some other relative (9.8 percent with an adult child), and nearly 40 percent of the Central and South American elderly reside in such a household. The reasons for the rather exceptional pattern found among Central and South Americans is unclear, but it is plausible that the explanation may reflect an adaptation forced by recent heavy immigration.

Even if a wide number of options exists with respect to availability of kin and economic resources, the age structure within elderly populations will have an impact on living arrangements. The data in Table 6 shed some light on this matter by dividing the elderly population into the "young old" (65-74 years of age) and the "old old" (75+), and then comparing sex- and ethnic-specific ratios with non-Latino white males and females as the base of the calculations. In Table 6, categories of living arrangements are reduced to three: (1) independent living (combines the householder and alone categories), (2) living with relatives (combines living with children and other relatives) and (3) institutionalization.[7]

In 1990, regardless of age or sex, elderly members of minority groups are, in every instance, less likely than Anglos to be living independently (Table 6). Although the differences are typically more modest in the case of males compared to females, for elderly Central and South Americans of both sexes, the probability of living independently is much below that for any other group. Extended family households which include dependent elderly persons are substantially more

Table 6

Ratios of Selected Living Arrangements*
by Age, Sex, and Ethnicity, 1990

	Males 65-74 Living Arrangements			Males 75+ Living Arrangements		
Ethnic Group	Living Independently	Living with Relative	Institution	Living Independently	Living with Relative	Institution
Non-Latino White	1.00	1.00	1.00	1.00	1.00	1.00
Mexican	0.92	4.23	1.07	0.84	4.07	1.03
Puerto Rican	0.93	3.73	0.47	0.87	3.34	0.86
Cuban	0.92	4.64	0.87	0.82	5.61	0.30
Central/So. Am.	0.75	10.27	0.60	0.57	9.56	0.26
Other Latino	0.95	2.36	1.13	0.95	2.66	0.47
Non-Latino Black	0.92	2.45	2.07	0.93	2.10	0.99
	Females 65-74 Living Arrangements			Females 75+ Living Arrangements		
Non-Latino White	1.00	1.00	1.00	1.00	1.00	1.00
Mexican	0.87	3.66	0.50	0.84	2.84	0.43
Puerto Rican	0.89	3.15	0.69	0.82	2.89	0.41
Cuban	0.77	5.28	0.13	0.66	4.12	0.42
Central/So. Am.	0.57	8.17	0.19	0.49	5.37	0.21
Other Latino	0.87	3.32	1.00	0.92	2.26	0.41
Non-Latino Black	0.95	1.83	1.06	0.96	1.67	0.70

*"Living Independently" combines the categories Householder and Alone, and "Living with Relative" combines the categories Living with Child and Other Relative as shown in Table 5. "Institution" is based directly on the Institution category in Table 5. The Alone category in Table 5 includes a small number of elderly living in group quarters but who are not institutionalized.

Source: U.S. Bureau of the Census, 1990 PUMS-A 1% Sample.

common among Latinos, with blacks occupying an intermediate position. The high point of the range is found among Central and South Americans who, depending on age and sex, are from five to 10 times more likely to live with relatives than are non-Latino whites, but each of the other groups of Latino elderly are at least twice, and usually three to four times, as likely to reside with relatives compared to their Anglo counterparts. Finally, residence of the Latino elderly in nursing homes and other institutions tends to be a far less common occurrence than it is among non-Latino whites and blacks.

In accentuating the importance of intergenerational ties for the Mexican American population, Maldonado argues that "the aged, regardless of physical and mental capacity, will continue to be a part of the extended family" (1975:214). The results displayed in Table 6 suggest that Maldonado's conclusion might be generalizable to Latinos in general. Further, the finding by Mutchler and Frisbie (1987) of no significant interaction effect involving household status, race/ethnicity, and income implies that the effect of race/ethnicity on the living arrangements of the elderly is similar across broad categories of economic status and thereby makes a cultural interpretation a bit more plausible. But, as important as the *consequences* of these striking ethnic differences in living arrangements of the elderly may be for family life and resource allocation, it is not possible to conclude that the *cause* of the differentials displayed in Tables 5 and 6 is rooted in cultural variation. At this juncture, all that can be said definitively is that, regardless of how the "ideal" arrangement might be conceived in different populations or cultures, maintenance of an independent household at advanced ages is a more realistic expectation for Anglos than for Latinos.

Income Attainment

Even though households are no longer the primary production units in modern societies, they constitute staging areas in which resources are gathered and distributed to family members. Consistent with previous analyses (Davis et al., 1983; Bean and Tienda, 1987), a comparison of mean household income (in 1989 dollars; see Table 7) shows that Latinos lag behind the Anglo majority. Only Central/South Americans and Other Latinos in 1960 and 1970 and Cubans, from 1970 forward, begin to approach the average income of non-Latino white households.

Table 7

Mean Household Income by Ethnicity: 1960-1990*
Latino Women, by Age, 1950-1990

Ethnic Group	1960	1970	1980	1990	Percent Change 60-70	Percent Change 70-80	Percent Change 80-90	Ratio to Non-Latino White 1960	1970	1980	1990
Non-Latino White	26082	33510	35218	38951	28.5	5.1	10.6	1.00	1.00	1.00	1.00
Mexican	19086	25210	27370	28554	32.1	8.5	4.3	0.73	0.75	0.78	0.73
Puerto Rican	17743	23371	21582	25876	31.7	-7.7	19.9	0.68	0.70	0.61	0.66
Cuban	21782	30112	32386	36377	38.2	7.6	12.3	0.84	0.90	0.92	0.93
Central/South Am.	23623	30057	28460	33096	27.2	-5.3	16.3	0.91	0.90	0.81	0.85
Other Latino	23781	30013	30296	31563	26.2	0.9	4.2	0.91	0.90	0.86	0.81

table continues

Table 7 (continued)

Ethnic Group	1960	1970	1980	1990
Dollar Difference from Non-Latino White				
Non-Latino White	0	0	0	0
Mexican	6996	8299	7848	10397
Puerto Rican	8339	10139	13636	13075
Cuban	4300	3398	2832	2574
Central/South Am.	2458	3453	6758	5856
Other Latino	2301	3497	4924	7388

*In 1989 dollars

Source: Bean and Tienda, 1987, Table 6.13; U.S. Bureau of the Census, 1990 PUMS-A 1% Sample

Trends in household constant dollar income show substantial shifts over time, reflecting economic cycles as well as group-specific variation. All groups experienced substantial income growth during the 1960s, led by a 38.2 percent increase among Cubans. The recession of the 1970s appears to be reflected in the much smaller and, in the case of some groups, negative constant dollar income change during that decade. During the 1980s, all groups except Mexicans enjoyed gains in average household income that exceeded the performance of the previous decade. However, as the second panel of Table 7 demonstrates, the constant dollar difference between majority and minority populations generally widened over time, although Cubans consistently improved their relative position in the 30 years from 1960 to 1990, and two more Latino groups (Puerto Ricans and Central/South Americans) managed to narrow the gap between 1980 and 1990. Perhaps most striking is the finding that the changes just delineated scarcely altered the ratio of minority to Anglo income. Throughout the 1960-1990 interval, Mexican and Puerto Rican income averaged roughly three-fourths and two-thirds, respectively, of that achieved by Anglos. Over the same time period, Cuban household income rose steadily from 84 percent to 93 percent of the Anglo average, while the remaining Latino groups evidenced changes that were comparable in magnitude, but different in direction; e.g., Central/South American and Other Latino household income ratios declined from the 90th percentile to the mid- to low-80th percentile range.

Because household income is so heavily affected by size of family, for many purposes, it is more instructive to compare mean per capita household income—i.e., the average number of dollars available to each member of the household. Here we are able to present information only for 1990 (income as of 1989), but are able to expand the comparison to include non-Latino blacks. As should be anticipated from the data on household size (Table 1) and fertility (Tables 3 and 4) discussed previously, the picture is much more dismal from the standpoint of per capita household income (Table 8). This is particularly true in the case of Mexican Americans for whom the per person income available within households was only $9155, barely half the amount enjoyed by Anglos ($17,615). Puerto Ricans and blacks fare only modestly better than Mexicans in this regard, with income ratios of 56 to 57 percent. Even among Cubans, the per capita income ratio reaches only 81 per-

Table 8

Mean Per Capita Household Income by Ethnicity, 1990

Ethnic Group	Income in 1989	Dollar gap from non-Latino white income	Ratio to non-Latino white income
Non-Latino White	17615	0	1.00
Mexican	9155	-8460	0.52
Puerto Rican	9820	-7795	0.56
Cuban	14289	-3326	0.81
Central/South Am.	11134	-6481	0.63
Other Latino	12544	-5071	0.71
Non-Latino Black	10057	-7558	0.57

Source: U.S. Bureau of the Census, 1990 PUMS-A 1% Sample

cent in 1990 (Table 8), as compared to the 93 percent figure that emerged in overall mean household income tabulations (Table 7).

In general then, inequality has been highly persistent over time when indexed in terms of either absolute or relative mean household income. On a household per capita basis, the situation is even less encouraging, especially in regard to Mexican Americans, Puerto Ricans, and blacks, in whose households every man, woman, and child must make do with income that averages only 50 to 60 percent of that available to non-Latino whites.

POVERTY AND PUBLIC ASSISTANCE AMONG FEMALE-HEADED FAMILIES AND CHILDREN

The feminization of poverty (Garfinkel and McLanahan, 1986; Wojtkiewicz et al., 1990) has long been a topic of great concern. Similarly, the deterioration of the economic well-being of children, as documented by Preston (1984) and others, that has occurred in connection with "stark economic changes" and secular alterations in family structure, has assumed ever-greater import in the national agenda (Eggebeen and Lichter, 1991:801). Recent data continue to show huge racial/ethnic disparities in the case of both women and children. For example, in 1990, nearly half of ever-married Puerto Rican female-headed families lived in poverty;[8] among the never-married, the figure is in excess of 70 percent (Table 9). For both comparisons, Puerto Ricans are substantially worse off than blacks. These figures contrast

Table 9

Percent of Female-Headed Families* in Poverty
by Nuptiality and Ethnicity, 1990

Ethnic Group	Ever-married percent in poverty	Never-married percent in poverty
Non-Latino White	20.0	33.9
Mexican	41.0	54.3
Puerto Rican	48.5	71.6
Cuban	26.6	24.8
Central/South American	29.8	31.3
Other Latino	40.0	55.4
Non-Latino Black	37.1	59.0

*Excludes subfamilies

Source: U.S. Bureau of the Census, 1990 PUMS-A 1% Sample

sharply with those reported for the non-Latino white population where poverty rates reach one-fifth and one-third of ever-married and never-married female heads, respectively. Among Latinos, Cuban and Central/South American female-headed families are relatively well off, and in fact, are somewhat advantaged compared to Anglos when families headed by never-married women are considered. The Mexican and other Latino distributions are quite similar to each other (poverty rates around 40 percent for families headed by ever-married females and around 55 percent for families headed by never-married women). Except for Cubans, poverty risk is typically much greater for families with never-married female heads.

In general, the most vulnerable groups are also the ones most likely to be receiving public assistance, but there is often a considerable disparity between poverty and likelihood of receiving public assistance. Only in the case of Puerto Rican families headed by *ever-married* women is the proportion receiving public assistance (43.4 percent) roughly comparable to the proportion below the poverty line (48.5 percent, see Table 10). However, for Puerto Rican families with a *never-married* fe-

Table 10

Percent of Female-Headed Families* Receiving Public
Assistance by Nuptiality and Ethnicity, 1990

Ethnic Group	Ever-married receiving public assistance	Never-married receiving public assistance
Non-Latino White	12.4	22.5
Mexican	26.0	33.2
Puerto Rican	43.4	56.1
Cuban	16.7	19.3
Central/South American	14.4	13.7
Other Latino	28.1	37.4
Non-Latino Black	23.6	39.9

*Excludes subfamilies

Source: U.S. Bureau of the Census, 1990 PUMS-A 1% Sample

male head, the relative numbers receiving public assistance lag behind the poverty percentage by 15 points. Similarly, while 41 percent of Mexican families with ever-married female heads are in poverty, only about one-fourth receive public assistance. Least apt to be recipients are Anglos, Cubans and Central/South Americans, with Mexicans, Other Latinos, and blacks occupying intermediate positions.

Two out of every five Puerto Rican children reside in families below the official poverty line—almost identical to the risk experienced by black children. The proportions of Puerto Rican and black children who exist in conditions of deep poverty—i.e., children in families whose income is more than 50 percent below the official cutoff point (see Eggebeen and Lichter, 1991)—are about 21 percent and 23 percent, respectively (Table 11). By contrast, the percentages of children in the other racial/ethnic groups who are in deep poverty range from 4.2 percent of non-Latino white children to 12.4 percent of Mexican children.

Table 11

Percentage of Children* in Poverty[†] by Ethnicity, 1990

Ethnic Group	Official poverty	Deep poverty
Non-Latino White	10.5	4.2
Mexican	32.1	12.4
Puerto Rican	41.3	20.8
Cuban	20.1	10.1
Central/South American	21.5	8.2
Other Latino	28.2	12.0
Non-Latino Black	40.3	23.1

*Children under 18 years of age in families, i.e., related to head by blood, marriage, or adoption.
[†]Official poverty refers to the government-defined money income cutpoint. Deep poverty includes those more than 50 percent below the official poverty line.
Source: U.S. Bureau of the Census, 1990 PUMS-A 1% Sample.

Slightly less than one-third of Mexican children are in poverty according to the official definition. Overall, as might be anticipated based on the income figures discussed above, the smallest probability of impoverishment accrues to Anglo children. Cuban, Central/South American and Other Latino children enjoy some advantage when compared to Mexican, and especially Puerto Rican children, but are at a palpable disadvantage vis-à-vis Anglos.

The data in Table 12 are clearly consistent with Eggebeen and Lichter's conclusions regarding the association between family structure

Table 12

Percentage of Children* in Poverty[†]
by Family Type and Ethnicity, 1990

| | Family Type | | | |
| | Couple-Headed | | Female-Headed | |
Ethnic Group	Official poverty	Deep poverty	Official poverty	Deep poverty
Non-Latino White	6.3	2.0	38.8	19.1
Mexican	24.4	7.9	62.8	30.6
Puerto Rican	18.8	7.4	69.0	37.3
Cuban	10.4	4.1	58.3	33.5
Central/South Am.	15.3	5.4	47.0	20.2
Other Latino	16.4	4.9	58.7	30.0
Non-Latino Black	15.1	5.5	64.2	39.8

*Children under 18 years of age in families, i.e., related to head by blood, marriage, or adoption.
[†]Official poverty refers to the government-defined money income cutoff point. Deep poverty includes those more than 50 percent below the official poverty line.

Source: U.S. Bureau of the Census, 1990 PUMS-A 1% Sample

and child poverty. For example, except for Anglos (38.8 percent) and Central/South Americans (47.0 percent), well over half of all children in female-headed families live below the official poverty line, and deep poverty typically characterizes the situations of 30 percent or more of children in most of the Latino groups. By contrast, in families with both father and mother present, official poverty rates never exceed 25 percent and deep poverty rates, without exception, remain at single-digit levels.

The data in Table 12, when compared to those in Table 11, also reveal that child poverty is more characteristic of Mexican Americans than Puerto Ricans, once family structure is controlled. The figures in Table 11 show Puerto Ricans with the greatest prevalence of child poverty. However, Table 12 makes it clear that this pattern results from the extremely high proportion of female-headed households among Puerto Ricans. When this variable is controlled, Mexicans show a higher prevalence of child poverty in couple-headed families.

Infant Mortality

Given that "infant mortality is the most widely used measure of health in a population" (Becerra et al., 1991:217), that the care of infants vests so substantially in the family, and that only a small amount of research has focused on infant mortality differences among specific Latino national origin groups (Hummer et al., 1992:1055), an examination of Latino family conditions would scarcely be complete without consideration of this topic. One of the most dramatic findings from the fast-growing literature in this area is that Mexican American infant mortality rates are quite similar to, and often lower than, Anglo rates (Rogers, 1984; Selby et al., 1984; Williams et al., 1986; Cramer, 1987; Powell-Grainer, 1988; Eberstein et al., 1990, NCHS, 1990; Forbes and Frisbie, 1991; Frisbie et al., 1992).[9] This finding, in the context of the much higher level of risk factors to which Mexican American infants are subject, may be seen as an "epidemiologic paradox" (Markides and Coreil, 1986). Table 13 presents information on several factors that have commonly been found to be implicated in infant mortality risk, including birth weight, which is far and away the most powerful predictor of survival chances during the first year of life (McCormick, 1985; Kleinman and Kessel, 1987; Scribner and Dwyer, 1989). The prevalence of low-weight births varies little across the

Table 13

Latino Reproductive Behavior, 1987*

| | Percentage Distribution of Characteristics | | | |
Ethnic Group	Births parity 4 and higher	Births to unwed mothers	Late or no prenatal care	Births of low birth weight[†]
Non-Latino Whites	7.7	13.9	4.1	5.6
Mexican	18.1	28.9	13.0	5.7
Puerto Rican	11.8	53.0	17.1	9.3
Cuban	5.5	16.1	3.9	5.9
Central/South Am.	11.4	37.1	13.5	5.7
Other Latino	11.7	34.2	9.3	6.9
Non-Latino Black	14.1	63.1	11.6	12.9

*Data from 23 reporting states and District of Columbia. (Encompasses approximately 90 percent of all Latino origin births.)

[†]Less than 2500 grams.

Source: "Advance Report of Final Natality Statistics, 1987," *Monthly Vital Statistics Report*, National Center for Health Statistics, Vol. 38, No. 3, 1989.

racial/ethnic groups, with the notable exception of blacks among whom this problem has been well-documented (Buehler et al., 1987; Kleinman and Kessel, 1987). However, except for Cubans, Latino infants, compared to Anglos, would seem to be at greater risk of death based on a set of maternal characteristics which include higher parities, proportion of births to unwed mothers, and inadequate prenatal care. Indeed, Mexican American infants evidence a greater disadvantage than every other group, including non-Latino blacks, with respect to parity, and lag behind most groups in regard to adequacy of prenatal care.

Recent data demonstrate that a high-risk profile does not translate into higher mortality for any of the three largest Latino populations. Mexicans, Puerto Ricans, and Cubans are all characterized by levels of infant mortality that are modestly lower than those observed among Anglos, and substantially below the rates for black infants (Table 14).

Table 14

Latino Infant Mortality, 1987*

| | Infant Mortality Rates, 1987 | | |
Ethnic Group	Infant mortality < 1 year	Neonatal mortality < 28 days	Postneonatal mortality 28-364 days
Non-Latino Whites	8.4	5.2	3.1
Mexican	7.6	4.9	2.7
Puerto Rican	7.3	4.3	2.9
Cuban	7.5	4.1	3.4
Other Latino	9.2	5.8	3.4
Non-Latino Blacks	16.5	10.3	6.3

*Rates per 1000 live births. Data from 18 reporting states and District of Columbia. (Encompasses approximately 80 percent of the Latino population.)

Source: "Advance Report of Final Mortality Statistics, 1987." *Monthly Vital Statistics Report*, National Center for Health Statistics, Vol. 38, No. 5, 1989.

One reason for the unlikely combination of low mortality with a high risk profile may be that a more familistic orientation among Latinos eventuates in "a higher regard for parental roles" (Williams et al., 1986:390). Rumbaut and Weeks (1991) go even further to suggest that immigrants to the U.S. from Mexico and Southeast Asia may be characterized by a "salutogenic" (as opposed to "pathogenic") cultural heritage which discourages unhealthy behaviors, but that this cultural buffer becomes attenuated over time. In particular, "despite the varying backgrounds that immigrants bring to the United States, exposure to American culture seems to lead successive generations to acquire unhealthful behavior over time" (Rumbaut and Weeks, 1991:102).

The evidence seems clear that Mexican origin, and perhaps other Latino, women are more likely than others to avoid behaviors that jeopardize positive pregnancy outcomes. Supportive of this line of reasoning is a body of research showing that Hispanic women have lower rates of consumption of alcohol and drugs, such as marijuana and cocaine, and practice better nutrition than their non-Hispanic counterparts (see Moss and Carver, 1991 for a summary). In addition, Mexican origin women are less likely to engage in cigarette smoking (Rogers and Crank, 1988), and the less acculturated among them are less apt to be smoking currently (Scribner and Dwyer, 1989:1264).[10] However, while this pattern of conduct may be characterized as cultural in a broad sense, it is not at all certain that the roots of this "salutogenic" life-style lie in a set of norms and values that are more familistic in orientation. Our own data on household and family structure over the past three decades are quite mixed in this regard. In any case, in the context of the socioeconomic and demographic characteristics and trends examined here, the pregnancy outcomes experienced by Latino families constitute a remarkable high point.

CONCLUSIONS

This paper has examined patterns of family/household structure and behavior in Latino populations of the United States, focusing on the broad themes of whether the diversity in demographic patterns that has so often been found representative of these groups (Bean and Tienda, 1987) continues to characterize their family patterns, and whether any differences in comparison to non-Latino whites can be explained by cultural factors, broadly speaking. While the answer to the first question can definitely be answered in the affirmative, the results do not reveal a clear-cut answer to the second. The movement away from marriage and toward forms of more individualistic behavior over the past thirty years which has been so prominent among non-Latino whites, as epitomized by sharply increasing proportions of persons living in non-family situations, has not been nearly so characteristic of Latino groups. Some observers might argue that this is due to a greater emphasis on familistic norms and values in these groups. Latinos, on the other hand, have experienced more substantial increases than have Anglos in the number of persons living in non-couple families. Most of the latter are single women living with children. This is not consonant with the hypothesis of a stronger emphasis on the family.

The retreat from conventional marriage and family patterns, including rising rates of marital disruption, declining proportions of persons in couple-headed families, and a diminishing propensity to marry, has been shown to be linked to child poverty and to the associated racial/ethnic disparities in the economic well-being of children (Eggebeen and Lichter, 1991). It is ironic, therefore, that child poverty is so widespread among Mexican Americans—note especially the higher proportions of impoverished children in couple-headed households (Table 12)—the group that in recent years has been characterized by the highest proportion of husband-wife families (Table 1), a relatively slow retreat from marriage (Table 2), and low rates of divorce and separation (Frisbie et al., 1985; Frisbie, 1986). To whatever degree a more familistic orientation distinguishes Mexican Americans from other groups, any benefits derived apparently do not eventuate in substantial economic benefits. A possible explanation of the high prevalence of poverty among Mexican American children may be that the higher fertility of this group (Tables 3 and 4) requires that resources, which otherwise might constitute the basis for socioeconomic advancement, be diverted to the support of children. However, as we saw in the case of mortality (Table 14), rewards of a strictly economic nature are not the only benefits that may derive from the family situation of Mexican Americans.

It is important to elaborate on the latter finding because it appears that, just as in the case of the paradoxical combination of high risk factors and low mortality observed among Latinos (especially among Mexican Americans; see Markides and Coreil, 1986), certain Latino populations are typified by family characteristics that are surprisingly favorable in the context of disadvantageous economic and demographic conditions. To illustrate what might be termed a "familial paradox" paralleling the "epidemiologic paradox," we focus on the Mexican population (for whom the accumulation of empirical evidence is considerably greater than for other Latino groups) as compared to the

Anglo population. In Table 15, a summary of selected findings for Mexican Americans and Anglos from previous tables is presented, supplemented with additional data from other sources. Without doubt, Mexican Americans have a decidedly high risk profile with respect to numerous economic and demographic indicators. Their mean household income in 1990 was less than three-fourths that of Anglos, and the gap is widening as shown by the constant dollar increase for Anglo households (10.6 percent) between 1980 and 1990, which was two and one-half times the 4.3 percent increase achieved by Mexican households. Further, on average, individuals within Mexican households have access to only about half as much income as their Anglo counterparts. Mexican American poverty rates are often two to three times higher than Anglo rates, a situation exacerbated by higher fertility, which, in turn, is realized under riskier conditions related to less adequate prenatal care.

Despite this high risk profile, Mexican Americans fare at least as well as Anglos in regard to pregnancy outcomes, including birth weight and infant mortality rates, and are more likely than Anglos to have maintained marital and family stability into the 1990s. Families with both spouses present are slightly more prevalent among the former, and non-family households are much less commonly observed. Indeed, in recent years, the proportion of non-family households has increased more than twice as rapidly among Anglos as among Mexicans. As mentioned previously, the 1990 census data do not allow precise analyses of the prevalence of marital disruption. However, information available from the 1980 enumeration shows that, unlike Anglos, a majority of Mexican American households have never been disrupted from any cause, whether divorce, separation, or death of spouse (Frisbie and Kelly, 1986). Narrowing attention to divorce and separation, we find that only 22.7 percent of ever-married Mexican American females had ever experienced marital disruption in 1980—substantially less than the proportion of Anglo women (31.6 percent) who had ever experienced divorce or separation (Frisbie and Opitz, 1985).

Unfortunately, the reasons for the "familial paradox," i.e., for the greater than expected stability of Mexican American marriages and families, remain indeterminate. However, it has been suggested that, if in fact, Mexicans are characterized by a more familistic orientation emphasizing strong kinship ties, including the marital bond, then a

Table 15

A Familistic Paradox?
Comparisons of the Mexican Origin and Anglo Populations,
Circa 1990

Economic & Demographic Conditions		Family & Health Conditions	
Mean Household Income		**Husband-Wife Families**	
M/A ratio	0.73	Mexican	60.7%
1980-90 change:		Anglo	58.3%
Mexican	4.3%	**Non-Family Households**	
Anglo	10.6%	Mexican	15.8%
M/A mean per capita ratio	0.52	Anglo	30.7%
Poverty		Change 1960-90:	
Ever-married female heads:		Mexican	5.7%
Mexican	41.0%	Anglo	16.4%
Anglo	20.0%	% increase 1960-90:	
Never-married female heads:		Mexican	56.4%
Mexican	54.3%	Anglo	114.7%
Anglo	33.9%	**Never-Disrupted HH***	
Children:		Mexican	54.9%
Mexican (official poverty)	32.1%	Anglo	49.0%
Anglo (official poverty)	10.5%	**Ever-Disrupted Marriage**[†]	
Mexican (deep poverty)	12.4%	Mexican women	22.7%
Anglo (deep poverty)	4.2%	Anglo women	31.6%
Fertility & Reproductive Behavior		**Odds of Marital Stability**	
M/A fert ratio (women 15-44)	1.38	**Within Education Categories**[†]	
CEB per 1000 (women 35-44)		Mexican women (0-7 education)	1.458
Mexican	2825	Mexican women (8-11 ed.)	0.834
Anglo	1853	Mexican women (12+ ed.)	0.823
Births parity 4 and higher:		Anglo women (0-7 education)	1.106
Mexican	18.1%	Anglo women (8-11 ed.)	0.857
Anglo	7.7%	Anglo women 12+ ed.)	1.058
Inadequate prenatal care:		**Low Birth Weight (1987)**	
Mexican	13.0%	Mexican	5.7%
Anglo	4.1%	Anglo	5.6%
		Infant Mortality Rate (1987)	
		Mexican	7.6
		Anglo	8.4

*Abstracted from Frisbie and Kelly (1986) based on 1980 data for the United States.
[†]Abstracted from Frisbie and Opitz (1985) based on 1980 data for 5 southwestern states only. All other data from previous tables.

"cultural buffer" may act to ameliorate the impact of forces that tend to promote marital instability (Murillo, 1971; Frisbie et al., 1978). Such an interpretation is obviously analogous to the notion that a "salutogenic" culture may promote healthy behaviors and help lower mortality among Mexican Americans (Rumbaut and Weeks, 1991). If we assume that more highly educated Mexican Americans are also more acculturated, then the finding that the odds of marital *stability* decline monotonically as educational level increases among Mexican American women, while among Anglo women the often noted curvilinear association is observed,[11] supports a cultural explanation (Table 15).

Inasmuch as educational level is, at best, an indirect indicator of the degree of acculturation, alternative measurement strategies are necessary. Language variables have frequently been considered key indicators of cultural attachment and identification (Lopez and Sabagh, 1978). One attempt in this direction that has been made by the present authors (using 1980 census data) employs Spanish use as a predictor of marital stability among Mexican Americans, Puerto Ricans, and Cubans, controlling for other more conventional determinants such as age, age at first marriage and education. Our results relevant to the cultural hypothesis were mixed, but highly suggestive was the emergence of a martial status/language use/education interaction effect such that the odds of marital *stability* were highest for ever-married women characterized by a combination of the lowest educational level and highest Spanish use.

Obviously, English proficiency is also a human-capital resource in the quest for upward social mobility (Mirowsky and Ross, 1984), and thus our preliminary analysis may well confound cultural and economic effects. Hence, we turned to nativity as yet another indicator of acculturation (or lack of it) and found that the odds of marital stability were nearly 40 percent greater for first-generation females, and almost 60 percent greater for first-generation males, as contrasted to their U.S.-born counterparts. Unfortunately, collinearity problems prevented nativity and language use from being included in the same models, and it is certainly plausible that selectivity of migration might partially account for the findings with respect to nativity.

Given the ambiguity remaining, what, if anything, can we say about the "familistic paradox"? In all candor, we must agree with Rumbaut and Weeks that we still contend with "a black box of cultural variability" (1991:103) that requires more investigation before it can be unlocked. Nevertheless, we believe the evidence is now sufficient to go beyond a simple recognition that Latino cultural differences are phenomena that warrant tolerance, to conclude that there may well be elements of their cultural heritage that buttress the health and stability of Latino families.

Finally, it is important to emphasize that data on Latino groups which provide a basis for longitudinal comparisons of family/household patterns are increasingly affected by the presence of immigrants in the samples studied. Often these immigrants exhibit substantially different characteristics (Bean et al., 1984) than do the native-born members of these populations, which, in turn, means that comparisons among groups and over time will be affected by differences in the proportion of immigrants present. We have not tried to control for this because of our interest in describing general household/family trends and because we have often focused on the consequences of these patterns (e.g., their relationship to child poverty), regardless of the reasons for differences in between-group household/family composition. It is of interest to document these consequences on their own terms. Further, our results on increasing percentages of non-couple families could not derive from an increasing presence of immigrants in any case, since immigrants are not characterized by such patterns to begin with. Nonetheless, future research on Latino families and households should give consideration to the importance of nativity in explaining the results obtained.

NOTES

[1] The authors gratefully acknowledge support provided for portions of this research by grants from the Andrew W. Mellon Foundation, the National Institute of Child Health and Human Development, and the State of Texas Advanced Research Program.

[2] Given the nature of census data and definitions, all families are households, but not all households contain families. Where census data underlie the analyses presented, the term "family" denotes persons related by blood, marriage, or adoption who co-reside, while "household" simply refers to any persons who co-reside.

[3] That is, whether households consist of married couple families, other types of families or nonfamily members.

[4] The basic identifier of Hispanics in 1980 was the Spanish origin, self-identification item, supplemented by data on ancestry and Spanish language use. Since the self-identification item was available only in the 5 percent sample in 1970, and not at all in 1960, identification of Hispanics in 1960 and 1970 was based on information on nativity, parentage, surname, and state of residence. Details regarding the comparability of these methods of classification and the means of distinguishing specific Hispanic groups are found in Bean and Tienda (1987:Appendix A).

[5] Another useful indicator would obviously be the proportion of ever-married persons who have ever experienced marital disruption due to divorce or separation. Unfortunately, unlike earlier enumerations, the 1990 census did not include items asking whether persons had been married previously and whether first marriage was broken by divorce or widowhood. Hence, it is not possible either to replicate for 1990 the calculations of Bean and Tienda (1987) or previous computations by other authors who report that prevalence of marital disruption among Mexican Americans and Cuban Americans is similar to, and often lower than, that among Anglos (Frisbie et al. 1985; Frisbie, 1986).

[6] The "Alone" category also contains a very small number of persons 65 and older who live in institutions, but are not themselves institutionalized. Such persons are likely to be employees of the institutions.

[7] For simplicity, the living with non-relative category (Table 5) is omitted from Table 6.

[8] A number of unresolved issues surround the measurement of poverty, including the question of whether poverty indexes should be calculated on an absolute or relative basis (Eggebeen and Lichter, 1991). In the case of female-headed families, we rely on the government's official definition of poverty as reflected in census tabulations. In our assessment of poverty among children, we draw on both the official measure and on what Eggebeen and Lichter (1991) refer to as "deep poverty" as defined in Tables 12 and 13.

[9] Except possibly for areas along the U.S.-Mexico border, low levels of infant mortality among Mexican Americans cannot be accounted for by underreporting of infant deaths (cf. Forbes and Frisbie, 1991).

[10] By contrast, smoking appears to be higher among Puerto Rican young adults than among either non-Latino blacks or whites (Moss and Carver, 1991:6).

[11] The finding of a higher probability of marital instability among those who drop out of the educational system prior to achieving the next level of certification has been termed the "Glick effect" after the scholar most prominent in calling this relationship to the attention of the research community (Glick, 1957).

REFERENCES

Angel, Ronald J. and Jacqueline L. Worobey. 1991. "Intragroup differences in the health of Hispanic children." *Social Science Quarterly* 72 (2):361-378.

Bean, Frank D., Harley L. Browning, and W. Parker Frisbie. 1984. "The sociodemographic characteristics of Mexican immigrant status groups: Implications for studying undocumented Mexicans." *International Migration Review* 18 (Fall):672-691.

Bean, Frank D., Russell L. Curtis, and John P. Marcum. 1977. "Familism and marital satisfaction among Mexican Americans: The effects of family size, wife's labor force participation, and conjugal power." *Journal of Marriage and the Family* 39:759-776.

Bean, Frank D., and John P. Marcum. 1978. "Differential fertility and the minority group status hypothesis: An assessment and review." Pp. 189-211 in Frank D. Bean and W. Parker Frisbie (eds.), *The Demography of Racial and Ethnic Groups*. New York: Academic Press.

Bean, Frank D., and Marta Tienda. 1987. *The Hispanic Population of the United States*. New York: Russell Sage Foundation.

Becerra, Jose E., Carol J. R. Hogue, Hani K. Atrash, and Nilsa Perez. 1991. "Infant mortality among Hispanics: A portrait of heterogeneity." *Journal of the American Medical Association* 265 (2):217-221.

Beresford, John C. and Alice M. Rivlin. 1966. "Privacy, poverty and old age." *Demography* 87:1360-1383.

Berger, Brigitte and Peter L. Berger. 1974. *The War over the Family: Capturing the Middle Ground*. New York: Anchor Press/Doubleday.

Bianchi, Suzanne M. 1990. "America's children: Mixed prospects." *Population Bulletin* 45 (1):2-41.

Bradshaw, Benjamin S., W. Parker Frisbie, and Clayton W. Eifler. 1986. "Excess and deficit mortality due to selected causes of death and their contribution to differences in life expectancy of Spanish surnamed and other white males—1970 and 1980." In *Report of the Secretary's Task Force on Black and Minority Health*, Vol. 2. Washington, DC: U.S. Government Printing Office.

Buehler, James W., Joel C. Kleinman, Carol J.R. Hogue, Lilo T. Strauss, and Jack C. Smith. 1987. "Birth weight-specific infant mortality, United States, 1960 and 1980." *Public Health Reports* 102 (2):151-161.

Castro Martin, Teresa and Larry L. Bumpass. 1989. "Recent trends in marital disruption." *Demography* 26 (1):37-51.

Cramer, James C. 1987. "Social factors and infant mortality: Identifying high-risk groups and proximate causes." *Demography* 24:299-322.

Davis, Cary, Carl Haub, and Joanne Willette. 1983. "U.S. Hispanics: Changing the face of America." *Population Bulletin* 38:1-43.

Eberstein, Isaac W., Charles B. Nam, and Robert A. Hummer. 1990. "Infant mortality by cause of death: Main and interaction effects." *Demography* 27 (3):413-430.

Eggebeen, David J. and Daniel T. Lichter. 1991. "Race, family structure, and changing poverty among American children." *American Sociological Review* 56 (6):801-817.

Eshleman, J. Ross. 1988. *The Family* (5th edition) Boston: Allyn and Bacon.

Espenshade, Thomas J. 1985. "Marriage trends in America: Estimates, implications, and underlying causes." *Population and Development Review* 11:193-245.

Forbes, Douglas and W. Parker Frisbie. 1991. "Spanish surname and Anglo infant mortality: Differentials over a half-century." *Demography* 28 (4):639-660.

Frisbie, W. Parker. 1986. "Variations in patterns of marital instability among Hispanics." *Journal of Marriage and the Family* 48 (February):99-106.

_____, Frank D. Bean, and Isaac W. Eberstein. 1978. "Patterns of marital instability among Mexican Americans, Blacks and Anglos." Pp. 143-163 in Frank D. Bean and W. Parker Frisbie (eds.), *The Demography of Racial and Ethnic Groups*. New York: Academic Press.

_____, Douglas Forbes, and Richard G. Rogers. 1992. "Neonatal and postneonatal mortality as proxies for cause of death: Evidence from ethnic and longitudinal comparisons." *Social Science Quarterly* 73 (3):535-549.

_____ and William R. Kelly. 1986. *Marital Instability Among Hispanics*. Final Report. National Institute of Child Health and Human Development. National Institutes of Health.

_____ and Wolfgang Opitz. 1985. "Race/ethnic and gender differentials in marital instability: 1980." Paper presented at the annual meeting of the Population Association of America. Boston, March.

_____, Wolfgang Opitz, and William R. Kelly. 1985. "Marital instability trends among Mexican Americans as compared to blacks and Anglos." *Social Science Quarterly* 66 (3):585-601.

Garfinkel, Irwin and Sara S. McLanahan. 1986. *Single Mothers and Their Children: A New American Dilemma*. Washington, DC: The Urban Institute.

Glick, Paul C. 1957. *American Families*. New York: Wiley.

_____ and Arthur J. Norton. 1977. "Marrying, divorcing, and living together in the U.S. today." *Population Bulletin* 32(5):2-39.

Gordon, Michael, Brendan Whelan, and Richard Vaughn. 1981. "Old age and loss of household headship: A national Irish study." *Journal of Marriage and the Family* 43:741-747.

Grebler, Leo, Joan W. Moore, and Ralph C. Guzman. 1970. *The Mexican American People: The Nation's Second Largest Minority*. Glencoe, IL: Free Press.

Hernandez, Jose, Leo Estrada, and David Alvirez. 1973. "Census data and the problem of conceptually defining the Mexican American population." *Social Science Quarterly* 53 (4):671-687.

Hummer, Robert A., Isaac W. Eberstein, and Charles B. Nam. 1992. "Infant mortality differentials among Hispanic groups in Florida." *Social Forces* 70 (4):1055-1075.

Kleinman, Joel C. and Samuel S. Kessel. 1987. "Racial differences in low birth weight." *The New England Journal of Medicine* 317 (12):749-753.

Lopez, David E. and Georges Sabagh. 1978. "Untangling structural and normative aspects of the minority status-fertility hypothesis." *American Journal of Sociology* 83 (6):1491-1497.

Lugaila, Terry. 1992. "Households, families, and children: A 30-year perspective." *Current Population Reports. Population Characteristics*. P-23-181. Washington, DC: U.S. Government Printing Office.

Maldonado, David J. 1975. "The Chicano aged." *Social Work* 20:213-216.

Markides, Kyriakos S. and Jeannine Coreil. 1986. "The health of Hispanics in the southwestern United States: An epidemiologic paradox." *Public Health Reports* 101 (3):253-265.

McCormick, Marie C. 1985. "The contribution of low birth weight to infant mortality and childhood mortality." *The New England Journal of Medicine* 312 (32):82-90.

Mirowsky, John and Catherine E. Ross. 1984. "Language networks and social status among Mexican Americans." *Social Science Quarterly* 65 (2):551-564.

Moon, Marilyn. 1983. "The role of the family in the economic well-being of the elderly." *The Gerontologist* 23:45-50.

Moss, Nancy and Karen Carver. 1991. "Explaining racial and ethnic differences in birth outcome: The effect of household structure and resources." Paper presented at annual meeting of the Population Association of America, Denver, CO.

Murillo, Nathan. 1971. "The Mexican American family." Pp. 97-108 in Nathaniel N. Wagner and Marsha J. Haug. *Chicanos: Social and Psychological Perspective*. St. Louis: Mosby.

Mutchler, Jan E. and W. Parker Frisbie. 1987. "Household structure among the elderly: Racial/ethnic differentials." *National Journal of Sociology* 1 (1):3-23.

National Center for Health Statistics. 1990. "Advance report of final mortality statistics, 1988." *Monthly Vital Statistics Reports* 39 (7) Supplement.

Powell-Grainer, Eve. 1988. "Differences in Infant Mortality among Texas Anglos, Hispanics, and Blacks." *Social Science Quarterly* 2 (2):452-467.

Preston, Samuel H. 1984. "Children and the elderly: Divergent paths for America's dependents." *Demography* 21 (4):435-457.

Rindfuss, Ronald R. and James A. Sweet. 1977. *Postwar Fertility Trends and Differentials in the United States*. New York: Academic Press.

Rogers, Richard G. 1984. "Infant mortality among New Mexican Hispanics, Anglos, and Indians." *Social Science Quarterly* 65 (3):876-884.

_____ and John Crank. 1988. "Ethnic differences in smoking patterns: Findings from NHIS." *Public Health Reports* 103 (4):387-393.

Rosenwaike, Ira and Benjamin S. Bradshaw. 1989. "Mortality of the Spanish surname population of the Southwest: 1980." *Social Science Quarterly* 70 (3):631-641.

Rumbaut, Ruben G. and John R. Weeks. 1991. *Perinatal Risks and Outcomes Among Low-Income Immigrants*. Final Report prepared for The Maternal and Child Health Research Program. Rockville, MD: Department of Health and Human Services.

Sandefur, Gary D., Sara McLanahan, and Roger A. Wojtkiewicz. 1992. "The effects of parental marital status during adolescence on high school graduation." *Social Forces* 71 (1):103-121.

Schick, Frank L. and Renee Schick. 1991. *Statistical Handbook on U.S. Hispanics*. Phoenix: Oryx Press.

Schoen, Robert and Verne E. Nelson. 1981. "Mortality by cause among Spanish surnamed Californians, 1969-71." *Social Science Quarterly* 62 (2):259-274.

Scribner, Richard and James H. Dwyer. 1989. "Acculturation and low birthweight among Latinos in the Hispanic HANES." *American Journal of Public Health* 79 (9):1263-1267.

Selby, Maija L., Eun Sul Lee, Dorothy M. Tuttle, and Hardy D. Loe. 1984. "Validity of the Spanish surname infant mortality rate as a health status indicator for the Mexican American population." *American Journal of Public Health* 74:998-1002.

Swicegood, Gray, Frank D. Bean, Elizabeth Hervey Stephen, and Wolfgang Opitz. 1988. "Language usage and fertility in the Mexican-origin population of the United States." *Demography* 25 (1):17-33.

Thornton, Arland and Deborah Freedman. 1983. "The changing American family." *Population Bulletin* 38 (4):2-43.

Westoff, Charles F. 1983. "Fertility decline in the West: Causes and prospects." *Population and Development Review* 9:99-104.

Williams, Ronald L., Nancy J. Binkin, and Elizabeth J. Clingman. 1986. "Pregnancy outcomes among Spanish-surname women in California." *American Journal of Public Health* 76 (4):387-390.

Wojtkiewicz, Roger A., Sara S. McLanahan, and Irwin Garfinkel. 1990. "The growth of families headed by women: 1950-1980." *Demography* 27 (1):19-30.

Wu, Lawrence L. and Brian C. Martinson. 1993. "Family structure and the risk of a premarital birth." *American Sociological Review* 58 (2):210-232.

The Changing Jewish Family: Issues of Continuity

Vivian Z. Klaff

DEMOGRAPHIC BACKGROUND TO THE JEWISH POPULATION

An issue receiving a considerable amount of attention in recent years is the question of how people identify themselves in terms of race, ethnicity and religion. The increasing heterogeneity of American society has led to a proliferation of models of integration either calling for the absorption of immigrants into the "mainstream" culture or calling for the recognition of diversity and the retention of "ethnic" identification (Klaff, 1980). Furthermore, demographic data indicate that the racial and ethnic composition of the U.S. has altered dramatically over the past few decades (Archdeacon, 1983; Jasso and Rosenzweig, 1990) both from differentials in natural increase as well as immigration.

Evidence for the changing demographic structure of religious groups is much more difficult to obtain due to the paucity of national data on religious affiliation of the population. Because of the principle of separation of church and state no data on religion are collected in any of the federal data collection systems, including the decennial census of population and housing (Good, 1959). Thus while much has been written on the sociodemographic characteristics of racial and ethnic groups, (Bean and Frisbee, 1978; Lieberson and Waters, 1988) the analysis of nationally representative religious subgroups lags behind.

This paper examines the sociodemographic background of the Jewish population in the 1990's and then focuses on a critical issue facing the Jewish family and the community as a whole, namely, religious intermarriage. The context to this issue lies in recent observations about the direction in which the Jewish population is moving in its continuing attempt to integrate into American society.

A Brief History

In the year 1654 a ship arrived from Brazil, bringing a small group of Jews to America. The history of Jewish settlement in these early years is colorful and interesting, but it was not until the later part of the 19th century that large numbers of Jewish immigrants entered the United States. A review of the early settlement history can be found in Gartner (1974). Prior to about 1720 most Jews were predominantly Spanish-Portuguese (Sephardim). After 1720 the population grew through immigration from Central and East Europe. In 1880 the population was estimated at about 250,000, less than 0.5 percent of the population and of predominantly German origin. By the early 20th century, due to rapid immigration from Eastern Europe they had become a significant minority group, numerically and culturally. In 1924, the year of the implementation of the second and most rigid of the Quota Acts which restricted the flow of immigrants, the Jewish population stood at about 4.5 million and reached what was probably its highest proportion in the U.S. population (approximately 4 percent). By the 1990's the Jewish population of the U.S. was a small minority, ranging in size between 2 and 3 percent of the total population. These estimates depend on the data collection process and on who is defined as Jewish.

The Process of Social Integration

The history of Jewish settlement in the U.S. is rich in experiences and culture. The Jews were introduced into a society which encouraged religious de jure (by law) freedom. In reality, however, the Jews were caught between an assimilationist model of integration which encouraged the absorption of new immigrants into the mainstream "Anglo" culture and a fairly deep-seated de facto prejudice against outsiders by the dominant culture (Gordon, 1964). By the 1990's evidence suggests that the Jewish population had overcome most of the obstacles to entry into the mainstream culture. The community now faces a new problem which reflects a basic conflict in American society today. This is the conflict between assimilation and pluralism. Assimilation is defined as integration based on narrowing the differences between the Jewish culture and the general evolving American cultural environment. Pluralism describes groups retaining a strong identity which is separate from but resides within the diverse community of cultures of the American population.

In the context of these models of integration, the history of the Jewish population in the course of the 20th century reflects a somewhat paradoxical situation. On the one hand the Jewish community had established an extensive and complex set of social and organizational institutions. On the other hand individual families worked energetically to adapt and integrate into the economic and cultural segments of the society. Families exhibited surprising ability to overcome the prejudice and anti-Semitism standing in the way of social and economic advancement (Hertzberg, 1989).

Two opposing viewpoints have been expressed concerning the current and future demographic and sociological paths to be taken by American Jewry, with a number of positions in between. In their extreme form these perspectives may be referred to as the "optimists" and the "pessimists." The optimists are characterized by those who feel that while changes are indeed occurring, these changes are for the better of the community and are leading to a revitalization of the Jewish population (Goldscheider, 1986; Silberman, 1985). The pessimists, on the other hand, see changes in demographic patterns leading to a reduction in the size of the population and increasing assimilation as eroding the cultural base of the community. Cohen (1988) characterizes the "assimilationists" as those who see considerable erosion through assimilation. This also results in at least temporary polarization of American Jewry. The "transformationists," on the other hand, are those who see change as leading to the cultural revival of the community, with the revival taking different but positive forms. Each of these groups bases its conclusions on different conceptualizations of how the changes affect the community and on different interpretations of statistical trends. There is also a middle position. The less extreme representation of the assimilationist and transformationist positions may share some common ground.

This paper examines an aspect of the process of change which leans more to the assimilationist side of the equation. A review of the socioeconomic conditions of the Jewish population reveals that functionally and structurally they have been very successful (Featherman,

1971; Mueller, 1980). But just as individuals have achieved this goal, the Jewish community finds itself in jeopardy on a number of fronts. The very act of success in integrating into the social and economic framework of the majority society has lead to the weakening of community affiliation in religious, familial and cultural areas. A quote from Kosmin and Lachman (1993:41-42) gives insight to the problem as viewed by the Jewish institutional leadership:

> *In 1954, when the American Jewish community celebrated the tercentenary of Jewish settlement in North America, it was discovered that the descendants of only one of the 23 Sephardic Jews (originally from Spain and Portugal) who in 1654 arrived in New Amsterdam from Recife, Brazil, were themselves Jewish; the other immigrant descendants have all intermarried and assimilated into the Protestant majority. American Jews have obviously had greater difficulty in maintaining and perpetuating their own values and religious commitments in the free marketplace of the New World.*

Sociologists routinely refer to the family as the primary agency of socialization. Alba in a study of ethnic identities notes that "*The taproot of ethnic identity nestles in families*" (Alba, 1990:164). In modern industrialized societies such as the U.S., the functions of the family have been narrowing as family functions are taken over by other institutions such as the schools, the church and the state. The issue of group continuity thus takes on increasing importance within the family. The family is central to Jewish social organization. To quote Cohen:

> *Understanding changes in the family and how those changes influence the expression of Jewish commitment is crucial for understanding the prospects for Jewish continuity. It is in and around the family that some of the most crucial interactions between Jews take place (1988:21).*

"Identity" is important as an ascribed characteristic of the individual. It is in the setting of the family that the child has the early cultural and behavioral experiences which define and promote feelings of belonging and self-consciousness. The American educational system is designed to "assimilate" students of different racial, ethnic and religious backgrounds to a common-school tradition stressing the normative culture. Thus, in situations where parents feel that this process does not adequately provide for the needs of children from different backgrounds, or works against the retention of ethnic traditions which are viewed as positive, the family remains the key institution for perpetuating group identity. While other functions are being carried out in other social spheres, the self-consciousness of "who I am" remains an activity which in formative years is nurtured in the family. Conversely, in situations where the continuity of a particular cultural or ethnic tradition is not important to the parents, this too influences the children's perspective on how they view their cultural heritage.

Data on Religion

The U.S. has no official religion and separation of church and state is guaranteed by the First Amendment to the Constitution. In addition, due to large-scale immigration from a wide range of cultures, the religious environment is extremely diverse. The religious pluralism which developed allows individuals to theoretically choose between dozens of religious denominations. A recent study, referred to as the National Survey of Religious Identification (NSRI), asked a series of questions about religious identification and produced one table containing over 60 different religious "groups," although only 13 of these comprised of at least 1 percent of the total adult population. (Kosmin and Lachman, 1993:15-17). Despite the fact that sociologists have recognized the importance of religion as a critical variable in understanding social behavior there are no official governmental statistics collected on religion. This makes it very difficult to develop a national profile of the size, composition and distribution of religious groups.

In Table 1 we have constructed data from a variety of sources at different points in time to attempt to determine the pattern of religious affiliation for the major groups. It must be noted that the data comes from sources which use different definitions and strategies of data collection.

In terms of religious affiliation and identification the U.S. has from the earliest immigration to current times been overwhelmingly Christian. The U.S. has generally been regarded as a predominantly Protestant nation numerically and ideologically. Although the framers of the Constitution declined to establish a State religion, being Protestant

Table 1

Religious Composition of the USA

	1957 US Abstract	1977 GSS	1990 GSS	1990 NSRI
Protestant	66.5	68.5	60.4	60.1
Catholic	26.5	21.0	27.8	26.2
Jewish	3.0	2.3	2.1	2.2
Other	1.0	1.3	2.1	3.3
None	3.0	6.9	7.6	8.2
Total	100%	100%	100%	100%

Source:
  A)   U.S. Statistical Abstract
  B)   General Social Survey, 1977
  C)   General Social Survey, 1990
  D)   National Survey of Religious Identification, 1990

became synonymous with the dominant culture. The NSRI 1990 survey found that 86 percent of persons surveyed considered themselves to be Christian. In 1990 the largest groups were Protestant (60 percent) and Catholic (26 percent). The Jewish population was estimated at between 2 and 3 percent. Compared to the 1957 CPS data, by 1990 the Protestant population had decreased by about 6 percent (from 66 to 60) and the Catholic population remained approximately the same. Gains were made by other religions (from 1 to 3 percent) and by those professing no religion which increased from 3 percent to 8 percent.

Demographic factors influencing the size of a religious group are birth rates, death rates and levels of immigration. Sociological factors influencing size include levels of in and out conversion; assimilatory losses out of a religion due to intermarriage, and general secularization passed on to future generations. The Jewish population is clearly influenced by both these demographic and sociological factors. Up until the

1970's very little was known about the national characteristics of the Jewish population. In 1970 a national survey of Jewish population was conducted (Lazerwitz, 1978). This study had a number of methodological weaknesses with regard to sample selection and it was not until the National Jewish Population Survey (NJPS) was conducted in mid-1990 that a comprehensive profile of a randomly selected national Jewish population was available to researchers for comparative analysis.

Beginning in 1989 a three-stage national survey was conducted encompassing about 125,000 households representing all religious groups in the United States. After ascertaining the religion of correspondents, screening was extended to identify those households in which the respondents did not report their religion as Jewish but which contained any persons (including the respondent) who "considered" themselves Jewish, who were raised Jewish, or who had a Jewish parent. A list of households with the appropriate inclusion criteria was prepared and 3665 households qualified for inclusion in the next survey stages; 59 percent on the basis of religion; 27 percent on the basis of having one or more members who considered themselves Jewish; 4 percent through having at least one member raised Jewish; and 11 percent through having at least one member with a Jewish parent.

The final data set was collected through random digit dialed (RDD) telephone interviews with a national sample survey of 2441 households drawn from a qualified universe of households containing at least one person identified as currently or previously Jewish. The survey interviews collected information about every member of the household, summing to 6514 individuals living in these households. A number of these individuals are not themselves Jewish, reflecting the mixed composition of the households in the Jewish sample. As a result of this complex screening system and examination of the survey it was determined, by weighting from the Stage I sample, that there were 8.1 million people living in 3.2 million household units that could be defined as a Jewish household. A detailed explanation of the methodology and sample design of the 1990 NJPS survey can be found in Kosmin et al. (1991), and Goldstein (1992).

The data produced the Jewish identity constructs shown in Table 2. Alternative typologies could be created from these data so that other analysts, if they wish, can create a "Jewish population" in keeping with their particular ideology or purpose. The typologies reflect a principal feature of Jewishness, namely that it is an amalgam of ethnicity and

Table 2

Jewish Identity Constructs:
Based on NJPS Survey

	Jews by Rel **JBR**	Core **J** **CJP**	Total Jewish Ethnic	Total
BJR: Born Jews (Religion Judaism)	4,210	4,210	4,210	4,210 [51.3%]
JBC: Jews by Choice (converts)	185	185	185	185 [2.3%]
JNR: Born Jews w/no Rel (Secular)		1,120	1,120	1,120 [13.7%]
JCO: Adults of J parents w/other current Rel			415	415 [5.1%]
JCOR: Kids - 18 raised w/other Rel			700	700 [8.5%]
GA: Gentile Adults living with Jews				1,350 [16.5%]
Total in sub-groups	4,395	5,515	6,840	
Total population in 3.2 million qualified Jewish Households				8,200
Percent of Total:	53.5%	67.3%	83.2%	100%

Note: Numbers are in thousands. The population estimates are based on a sample of 2,441 households which contain 6,514 individuals.

religion, and America allows for choice about one's religio-ethnic identity. For the purposes of this general analysis I make a conceptual distinction between two types of Jewish populations; a Core Jewish population and a peripheral population. The Core Jewish Population (CJP) is an aggregate which reports no non-Judaic religious affiliation. It is comprised of three identities: those who currently report their adherence to Judaism, both Born Jews and Jews by Choice (BJR, JBC), as well as those Born Jews without a current religion (JNR). This group, represented by the first 3 rows in Table 2, comprise 66 percent of the 8.2 million persons living in 3.2 million Jewish defined households. Of the 3.2 million household units: 57 percent were composed entirely of members of the Core (entirely Jewish in current composition). An additional 27 percent were mixed with at least one person belonging to the Core, but these households also included at least one person who was non-Jewish at time of survey. Finally 16 percent had no Core Jews but qualified because one or more of the household members were of Jewish descent even though currently professing another or no religion.

SOCIAL AND DEMOGRAPHIC CHANGES IN THE JEWISH POPULATION

Demographic Change

In the 1990's a key concern of many religious communities is the numerical size of the population and continuity as a viable religious community. Different religious groups have been affected by a specific combination of these factors leading to their increase or decline as a group. For example, Canevin (1912), a Catholic Bishop of Pittsburgh, employed a demographic perspective to show that among Catholics, losses through death, emigration and religious withdrawal were compensated for by births, immigration and religious conversion. While many of the larger religious groups may have population downturns due to specific conditions, the groups as a whole have not been in any danger of any serious demographic decline. Smaller religious groups, however, are often exposed to population declines.

A number of factors have over the years led to changes in the Jewish population. Some have argued that the demographic changes are leading to a weakening of both the size of the Jewish population and the degree of affiliation to the established Jewish community. American Jewry, according to Goldstein (1992) has "progressively weakened demographically as a result of low fertility, high intermarriage, significant dispersion, and assimilatory losses." This is not, however, a universally held opinion. In this section of the chapter I briefly examine the basic sociodemographic changes occurring in the Jewish population, and in the next section I examine the household structure with particular focus on the social dynamics of assimilation and intermarriage.

Finally I will return to the controversy between the optimists and pessimists on the future "position" of the Jewish population in the context of U.S. diversity. Since almost the entire Jewish population may be defined as white, by race, the referent group when comparing this group to the U.S. population will be the white population. To examine the parameters of the changing Jewish population we will first examine the demographic variables and then will focus on the socio-logical variables.

Fertility, mortality and migration are the three components of the demographic equation which determine the changes in population size of a group from one time period to another. Birth rates in the U.S. declined over the course of the 20th century to a low point in the mid 1930's, increased to a high point in the late 1950's (the baby boom) and have declined again to a fertility rate which has been below re-placement level for the past two decades. According to DellaPergola (1980) the limited evidence available suggests that Jewish fertility has consistently been the lowest among the religious and ethnic subgroups identified. Similar data are reported by Bogue (1985:660) based on analysis of the General Social Survey data from NORC. Bogue noted that Jewish women have fewer children than White Protestant or Catho-lic women. Despite the biblical injunction of the Old Testament to "be fruitful and multiply," the Jewish fertility in the U.S. for many decades has tended to be lower than the general population. The 1970 Jewish population study estimated the Jewish total fertility rate (TFR) to be about 2.4, which was slightly lower than the TFR for the white U.S. population in that year. The TFR is the average number of children, on the average, born to women at the end of their childbearing. In 1990 the TFR for the white population was 1.8 compared to 1.7 for the Jewish population (based on the NJPS data). This figure drops to about 1.5 children per woman when we examine only the Core women.

The NJPS data also show that the older cohorts have more child-ren on average than the younger cohorts, and in the older cohorts the non-Core women have considerably higher numbers of children than the Core. The differences tend to be much lower in the younger cohorts. For example, 37.5 percent of the non-Core women aged 51-64 have had 3 or more children compared to 14 percent of the Core women. In contrast, 5 percent of non-Core women aged 25-40 have had 3 or more children compared to 6.1 percent of the Core women aged 25-40. This suggests that the fertility of Jewish Core women has been low for some time with the reductions in younger cohort non-Core women leading to the narrowing of the fertility gap for non-Jewish women living in a household with a Jewish respondent. The general conclusion is that below replacement level fertility among Jewish women has now become a fairly stable trend.

Life expectancy at birth has increased consistently over the course of the 20th century. There are fairly marked differences in mortality rates across sex, race and other ethnic and religious subgroups. The pattern of Jewish mortality has followed that of the U.S. white population reasonably closely in terms of life expectancies. Jews exhibit a higher crude death rate, however, due to the age structure of the Jewish population.

The U.S. population is aging. One can interpret this trend as a loss of the more traditional members from active participation in community affairs as the proportion of the population over the age of 65 increases. In 1900 the U.S. median age was 23. This increased to 26 in 1930, to 29 in 1960 and was 33 in 1990. The Jewish population of the U.S. reflects an extreme example of this aging population with the median age in 1990 at 37 years as compared to 34 for the total U.S. white population. Declining fertility, increased life expectancy, and generally lower levels of immigration have resulted in a growing proportion of older persons. This clearly has dramatic consequences for the demographic and social environment of the Jewish population and community organizations.

The overall conclusion is that the Jewish Core group is aging at a level above that of the general population. The cause can be found in lower fertility rates, improved health conditions, and declines in traditional immigrant groups who would strengthen the community base at younger ages. In addition those Jews who assimilate and opt out of the community as a result of intermarriage or selection of another religion are generally from the younger members of the community.

Lowered fertility combined with an aging population, and an increasing level of assimilation is likely to lead to a decline in the population. Based on the age structure data and fertility data available from the survey it is possible to estimate the future population trends from current parameters. Using the age structure for the 1990 Jewish and white populations we projected the natural rate of growth (excluding migration) of the populations for the next 40 years. The results are presented in Table 3. In general we see that while the white population reflects a slight increase over the period (4.9 percent by 2010 and 3.6 percent by 2030) the Jewish Core population is projected to decline over the period by 12.5 percent in the year 2030. By the year 2030 the median age for the Core population is projected to be close to 45 compared to 42 for the USA white population.

Table 3

Age Structure Characteristics for Jewish Core and White U.S., 1990 and Projected to Year 2030.

Population (Thousands)	1990	2010	2030	% Change 1990-2010	% Change 1990-2040
USA White Population, 1990					
Total	199,684	209,376	206,861	4.9	3.6
Male	97474	102,836	100,875		
Female	102,210	106,541	105,987		
0-4	13,649	12,119	11,472	-1.1	-15.9
5-14	26,469	24,973	23,740	-5.6	-10.3
15-64	131,714	141,264	125,182	7.2	-5.0
65+	27,852	31,020	46,468	11.4	66.8
Jewish Core Population, 1990					
Total	5,396	5,155	4,719	-4.5	-12.5
Male	2,683	2,517	2,287		
Female	2,712	2,637	2,431		
0-4	390	264	220	-32.1	-43.5
5-14	632	513	480	-18.9	-24.1
15-64	3,446	3,551	2,795	-3.1	-18.8
65+	926	825	1,222	-10.9	-31.9

The third component of the demographic equation is migration. In the context of the demographic equation we refer to migrants as those persons who enter or leave the boundaries of a specifically defined area. The demographic history of the Jewish people in the U.S. revolves around patterns and levels of immigration. During the decades surrounding the turn of the century, Jewish migration was a substantial component of total immigration into the country, while in more recent decades Jewish immigration has declined to an insignificant number (Kass and Lipset, 1982). Evidence suggests that despite the recent immigration of Russians and Israelis, the proportion of Jews in the immigrant pool in the 1990's is fairly small. Thus the infusion of Jewish immigrants cannot be considered to be a compensating factor for fertility declines.

An additional factor influencing the character of the Jewish population is the location of the population. The U.S. is a highly mobile society. During the 1980's, every year on the average about one in five persons moves residence and about 12 percent of the population moves to a different city or county. The Jewish population forms part of a subpopulation with characteristics which make them highly mobile (Goldstein, 1990). Over time the Jewish population has dispersed territorially, with considerable consequences for communal and organizational structures (Newman and Halvorsen, 1979; Jaret, 1978, Goldstein, 1982, 1992). In particular Goldstein's analysis of the NJPS data (1992) points out that considerable regional redistribution of the Jewish population has occurred. In an examination of residential distribution patterns of Jews I have stated:

> *The overall summary points to the Jewish trend of decentralization at an ever-increasing rate combined with the tendency to relocate in areas that are Jewish in character. Thus, although clustering or residential segregation persists, it continues in a diluted form. Concentration does not necessarily reflect isolation, and Jews living in what might be termed a Jewish environment in the suburbs are nevertheless exposed to physical and cultural contact with other groups.* (Klaff, 1991: 149).

There is also evidence that the intermarriage rates of members of smaller religious groups vary inversely with the size and geographic concentration of the group in the community (Rosenthal, 1968; Thomas, 1972). Support for this conclusion comes from McCutcheon who finds evidence for support of the propinquity hypothesis, that physical proximity affects the rates of intermarriage (McCutcheon, 1988). As Jews become more dispersed and live in increasingly less

Jewish environments and join social groups with fewer Jews as members, the likelihood of an interfaith marriage increases.

SOCIAL CHANGE: THE ISSUE OF INTERMARRIAGE

In summary, lowered fertility, declining immigration and higher internal mobility, and the aging of the population are powerful demographic influences on the structure of the Jewish population. In addition to the demographic conditions which characterize the Jewish population, a number of social and psychological factors impact the Jewish population. Among these are intergenerational increases in educational levels; the attainment of middle class professional occupations; the reduction of prejudice and discrimination; the secularization of the U.S. religious environment in general and of Judaism in particular; and the assimilation into the dominant social structure and culture resulting from declines in institutional prejudice and discrimination toward Jews both individually and as part of a community.

Both the assimilationist and transformationist perspectives generally agree that levels of marriage between Jews and non-Jews are increasing. The disagreement lies in the interpretation of the data. For the assimilationists, intermarriage is viewed as an indicator of the degree of assimilation which occurs between members of different racial, ethnic or religious groups. It can also be seen as a means by which intermarried couples increase the potential for further assimilation in the next generation. For the transformationists intermarriage has a number of implications, including the integration of the in-marrying spouse through conversion, thus adding to the numerical size of the group and the assumption that certain levels of contact with the new group are developed and maintained by the in-marrying spouse.

While a number of studies have dealt with intermarriage between racial and ethnic groups (Lieberson and Waters, 1988), very little recent national data are available for religious intermarriage. As a result the NJPS study is an important data source on Jewish intermarriage. It should be noted that census data show that the overall trend is toward increasing ethnic intermarriage for white groups in the U.S., and the rate is increasing with each generation (Alba, 1986). We are not able, however, to compare levels or rates with the NJPS studies due to the lack of religion as a variable in the census data.

It should be noted that there is a definite symbolic and conceptual difference in the meaning of ethnic versus religious intermarriage. Ethnic intermarriages often involve the blending of symbolic commitments which are not intrusive enough to interfere with the marriage or the socialization of children. Unless there are serious conflicts related to the ethnic groups involved, there is usually an acceptance by the couple for the other member's ritual and cultural norms. As pointed out by Alba (1990:17) with regard to religious intermarriage:

While there are pressures to agree on a single religious identity for a family, especially when it comes to the religious upbringing of children, there appear to be no similar pressures in inter-ethnic marriages, as witness the frequently divergent ethnic identities of spouses and low level of concern with children's identities.

Historically the rates of Jewish outmarriage in the U.S. were extremely low up to the 1950's. Intermarriage has been increasing steadily, however, and is now a major factor in the American-Jewish experience. This is viewed by a large segment of the community leadership as having serious implications for group continuity in the next generation. Mayer (1989:252) captures a popular response to the recent evidence of increasing intermarriage by stating that:

The rapid growth in the incidence of intermarriage among America's Jews has compelled the Jewish community to raise profound questions about its own future under conditions of unprecedented freedom and general wellbeing.

The evidence of increasing intermarriage is quite compelling. Based on 1957 Current Population Survey (CPS) data for the total U.S. population, Glick (1960) concluded that 94 percent of marriages were endogamous by religion. He further calculated that if the couples had been randomly assigned to marriages without regard to the religion of their marriage partner, only 56 percent of the marriages would have been to a spouse of the same religion (endogamous). For example, based on the 1957 CPS, 91 percent of Protestants were in-married as compared to an expected endogamous measure of 53 percent when calculated on the random assignment of marriages. For Catholics the percent endogamous was 78 percent (as compared to 26 percent with random assignment) and for Jews the percent endogomous was 93 percent (as compared to 2 percent with random assignment). The evidence points to the fact that intermarriage occurs much more readily among Protestants and Catholics than between Jews and Christians, but that Jews in particular married out at far lower levels than would have been expected by their representation in the population. Using data from the GSS surveys in the mid 1970's, Glenn (1984) demonstrated that Protestants were 84 percent endogamous, Catholics 62 percent and Jews 80 percent. In comparison to other religious groups, inmarriage is seen to be very high in the Jewish religion, in spite of its small proportion of the total population and consequent high exposure to opportunity for exogamous marriage.

The 1970 NJPS study reported that 8.1 percent of Jews were married to non-Jews and also that there was an increase in the level of intermarriage with younger marriage cohorts. In 1970 about 2 percent of those marrying before 1925 were outmarried as compared to 29 percent of those marrying between 1965 and 1970. In the 1990 NJPS the outmarriage was measured in terms of the religious identification of the current marriage partner of anyone who was born Jewish and was now married irrespective of current Jewish identity. In order to examine the level of intermarriage in the 1990 NJPS survey we extracted a separate file of 1462 married couples and created a variable with two categories:

(1) respondents who were born Jewish and were married to a Jewish-born spouse.

(2) a Jewish respondent or spouse married to a non-Jewish respondent or spouse.

It should be noted that this essentially represents couples who are defined as Core by virtue of the fact that at least one person in the marriage would have to be classified as a Core Jew in order to be included in the married couples file. As such married couples, both not being Jewish but living in a home with a Jewish respondent were excluded from this married couple data set. The resulting dataset (INTMAR) comprised 1139 couples.

The resulting categorization is shown in Table 4. Panel A in Table 4 shows that 31 percent of the Jewish-born married population were married to a spouse who was not born Jewish. There is clearly a trend toward greater intermarriage over time. The 31 percent intermarriage is considerably larger than the 7 percent reported from the 1957 CPS, the 8 percent reported in the 1970 NJPS and the 15 to 20 percent reported by Bogue for the mid-1970 years.

Table 4

Percent Intermarried by Year of Marriage

| | \multicolumn{5}{c}{Year of Marriage} |
	Before 1965	1965-1974	1975-1984	1985-1990	Total
(A) Individuals					
Endogamous J-J	91	73	51	47	69
Intermarried J-O	9	27	49	53	31
Total	100%	100%	100%	100%	
(N)	(686)	(317)	(455)	(296)	(1754)
(B) Households					
Endogamous J-J	84	57	34	31	55
Intermarried J-O	16	43	66	69	45
Total	100%	100%	100%	100%	100%
(N)	(371)	(201)	(339)	(225)	(1136)

We also see that intermarriage rates increase quite considerably for younger marriage cohorts. Panel A of Table 4 shows 9 percent of the pre-1965 marriage cohort were intermarried compared to 53 percent of those marrying between 1985 and 1990. Since 1985 more than half of born Jews who marry have chosen a non-Jewish spouse who did not convert. In only 5 percent of the cases do the spouses convert (to become Jews by Choice). Thus the majority of all new Jewish households formed in the U.S. in recent years involved a non-converted non-Jewish spouse.

Household data are presented in panel B of Table 4. Here we look at households rather than individuals. We see from the table that 45 out of every 100 households are intermarried households. This compares with 31 percent of Jewish married individuals who are in an intermarried household. Again as with individuals, families established in more recent years are much more likely to be intermarried households. While only 16 percent of households established before 1965 consisted of a born Jew with a non-Jewish spouse, this percentage increased to 69 for those families established between 1985 and 1990. Thus, in less than one third (31 percent) of the households are there children who are exposed to parents who were both born into the Jewish religion.

Not only are intermarriage rates increasing, but NJPS survey finds an increasing acceptance of intermarriage. This acceptance is even stronger if the non-Jewish spouse is prepared to convert to Judaism. When respondents in married households were asked if their child were considering marrying a non-Jewish person, how they would feel about this, 45 percent of the endogamous household respondents stated they would accept or be neutral and 18 percent said they would support this choice. Of the intermarried households 46 percent would be neutral or accepting and another 49 percent stated they would support the marriage. Years of marriage did not seem to matter very much. When asked how they would respond if the future spouse agreed to convert to Judaism, by far the majority of both endogamous and intermarried household respondents would accept or be favorable to the marriage.

While attributing causality is very difficult with the cross sectional data available in the NJPS survey, it is nevertheless possible to demonstrate some relationships between critical variables. There is a definite relationship between the religious denomination of the respondent in each household and intermarriage. As shown in Table 5 about 88 percent of the endogomous households belong to one of the four recognized denominations as compared to 66 percent of the intermarried households. Intermarrieds are particularly strong in the Reform denomination which has a much more liberal nontraditional focus.

Table 5

Current Religious Affiliation of Household,
By Marriage Type

	Endogamous	Intermarried	Total
Religious affiliation	J-J	J-O	Total
Conservative	44	19	33
Orthodox	10	1	6
Reform	33	44	38
Reconstructionist	1	2	1
Secular	4	10	7
Other, including combinations of above	8	24	15
Total	100%	100%	100%

It is not surprising that there is direct relationship between denominational origins and the likelihood of intermarriage—the more religious the person, the less the rate of intermarriage. The difference is particularly evident in recent years and likely results from increasing secularization and assimilation into the mainstream culture. This data suggests that intermarried couples are more likely to be less traditional in their religious affiliation and has implications for the cultural continuity of the group.

Consequences of Religious Intermarriage

The NJPS data show a link between one generation and the next and allow us to evaluate the issue of "group continuity." This section looks at two subsets of the NJPS "INTMAR" dataset:

(1) the married couples dataset where the respondent was Jewish (N=1149 couples).

(2) a subset of children living in these married couple endogamous and intermarried homes where the respondent was Jewish (N= 1019 children up to age 18).

Using the married couple data set we examined six behavioral items related to Jewish continuity by marriage cohort and marriage type. In Table 6, the items listed are: 1) percent who said the household contributed to a Jewish cause in the past year; 2) percent who said a member of household was affiliated with a temple or synagogue; 3) percent who said that someone in the household celebrated the Israel Day of Independence; 4) percent who said the household lights candles on Friday night usually or all the time; 5) percent who said that the household celebrates the Passover Seder at home usually or all the time and 6) percent who said that the household respondent fasts on Yom Kippur, the day of atonement. On all of the items, for each marriage cohort, the intermarried couples had a lower percentage who were affiliated with the Jewish community or participated in cultural activities. It is also interesting to note that among the endogamous couples, the younger marriage cohorts demonstrate lower levels of community participation and tend to level off their level of cultural commitment. While the change in group identity is clearly stronger for endogamous couples, that level of identification appears to vary, depending on the particular activity. This has a number of implications for the transference of cultural traditions from one generation to the next through education.

One of the major issues related to group continuity and identity is the education, and particularly the religious socialization of children in families. These are the children living in the 1149 households contained in the INTMAR subset. As Lieberson and Waters point out in their study of racial and ethnic groups in the U.S.:

> *A homogeneous nuclear family, along with a homogeneous extended family, is more able and likely to pass on to offspring the ethnic feelings, identification, culture and values that will help to perpetuate the group* (Lieberson and Waters, 1988: 165).

Findings by Alba, based on analysis of white American ethnics, conclude that parents who are in endogamous marriages are more likely

Table 6

Cultural Identity by Year of Marriage and Marriage Type
Data File: Respondents N = 1149 couples

Cultural Variables	Before 1965		1965- 1974		1975- 1984		1985- 1990		Total	
	JJ	JO	JJ	JO	JJ	JO	JJ	JO	JJ	JO
% who contributed to a Jewish cause in the past year	83	39	82	42	74	43	65	31	79	39
% of households affiliated with a synagogue or temple	57	20	76	27	64	25	32	19	59	23
% of households where someone celebrated Israel's Day of Independence	23	4	35	7	34	12	21	7	27	9
% of households who light Friday night candles usually or all the time	26	5	33	6	37	11	31	10	30	9
% of households who celebrate Passover usually or all the time	80	30	87	48	89	59	85	52	83	51
% of respondents who fast on Yom Kippur (the day of Atonement)	62	21	75	35	72	41	75	38	68	37

Note: JJ = Endogamous Household; JO = Intermarried Household

than others to want their children to identify with their ethnic group:

> *Parents' own ethnic identity status and the subjective importance they attribute to ethnicity stand out as powerful determinants of their desires for their children to identify. . . .* [and] *Parents with several ethnic experiences are highly likely*

to want their children to identify ethnically; parents with less experiences, much less so (Alba, 1990:190-191).

Two indices of Jewish education were created, each consisting of three categories: Index R_EDUC is the amount of Jewish education received by the respondent (Jewish parent) of the child and index K_

Table 7

Current Religious Affiliation by Marriage Type
by Level of Formal Jewish Education of Respondents

Current Religious Affiliation of Children	No Formal Education		1 - 4 Years of Formal Education		5 or more years Formal Education	
	JJ	JO	JJ	JO	JJ	JO
Jewish	98	40	95	39	100	52
Catholic	--	8	--	8	--	12
Protestant	--	13	--	9	--	5
Other religion	--	15	2	17	--	17
None	2	21	3	24	--	12
N/A	--	5	--	2	--	3
Total %	100	100	100	100	100	100
N =	52	171	113	203	467	143

Note: JJ = Endogamous Household; JO = Intermarried Household

EDUC is the amount of Jewish education received by the child. For each index the categories are: (a) no formal education, (2) one to four years of Jewish education and (c) five or more years of education. As we see in Table 7, of those children living in endogamous households almost all were being raised as Jews independent of amount of Jewish education received by the respondent in the house. In intermarried households 40 percent of children with respondents having no Jewish education were being raised as Jews compared to 52 percent of those where respondents had received five or more years of education. While education does seem to have some effect, it seems the main difference lies between endogamous and intermarried households.

Table 8 examines the relationship between intermarriage and formal Jewish education for both respondents (R_EDUC index) and children (K_ EDUC index). The table demonstrates that about a quarter of respondents in married couple households received no formal Jewish education, with intermarried respondents having slightly less exposure to education (28 percent compared to 20 percent). With regard to the

Table 8

Level of formal Jewish education	Formal ed. of respond by marriage type			Formal ed. of children living in household		
	JJ	JO	Total	JJ	JO	Total
% no formal Jewish education	20	28	24	8	72	59
% 1-4 yrs formal Jewish education	38	38	38	29	13	27
% 5+ yrs formal Jewish education	42	34	38	63	15	14
Total %	100	100	100	100	100	100
N	584	510	1094	434	565	999

Note: JJ = endogamous household; JO = intermarried household

children, respondents report that about two thirds of children aged 15-18 have received no formal Jewish education, and the lack of education is considerably greater for intermarried households (72 percent) than endogamous households (8 percent). While it is clear that the children have not completed their potential Jewish education, the trend suggests that children living in endogamous homes are receiving more formal Jewish education than their Jewish (respondent) parent, and children living in intermarried homes are receiving considerably less formal Jewish education than their Jewish (respondent) parent.

The conclusion based on the above data suggests that while both intermarriage and Jewish education have an influence on the cultural environment in which children are raised, intermarriage seems to be the predominant factor. This confirms the analysis carried out by Lipset (1994) in an examination of the influence of formal Jewish education on group continuity. Lipset used a number of different measures of Jewish education as dependent variables in a series of regression analyses. Examining influences on the dependent variable (education) he concluded that the most important influence was the extent to which respondents came from fully Jewish families:

> *The most powerful factor affecting the dependent variable in virtually every model is intermarriage. . . . Clearly, a cohesive Jewish family unit is vital in increasing the probability that a respondent secures some form of religious training* (Lipset, 1994:29).

In order to test the different environment in which children are being raised, we looked at a number of behavioral and attitudinal variables associated with the socialization and social consciousness of children. We examined the patterns in these variables for children living in endogamous and intermarried households, controlling for the formal Jewish education status of the Jewish respondent in the household (R_EDUC). As previously demonstrated there appears to be a declining influence of cultural transmission with years of marriage as intermarriage increases, but in this section we did not control for years of marriage. Table 9 presents the results for 8 items which examine aspects of the cultural environment to which children in endogamous and intermarried households are exposed. All data refer to the characteristics of the respondent in the married couple household. The table was constructed as follows:

> * Cell A (JJ-Yes) represents the percentage of children who live in endogamous households where the respondent has had at least five years of formal Jewish education
>
> * Cell B (JJ-No) represents the percentage of children who live in endogamous households where the respondent has had no formal Jewish education

* Cell C (JO-Yes) represents the percentage of children who live in intermarried households where the respondent has had at least five years of formal Jewish education

* Cell D (JO-No) represents the percentage of children who live in intermarried households where the respondent has had no formal Jewish education

For example, row Q1 is the percentage of households affiliated with a synagogue or temple. Thus 64 percent of children who live in endogamous households with no respondent having formal Jewish education have families who belong to a synagogue or temple. Two items deal with community affiliation, affiliation with a synagogue or temple and volunteering to work for a Jewish organization. Two items deal with the link to Israel, expressed through visits to Israel and celebration of Yom Haatzmaut, the Israeli national Day of Independence. Four items reflect ritual commitment to Judaism in the form of lighting candles on the Sabbath, attending a Passover Seder (traditional ritual meal on the first and second night of the Passover festival), lighting candles on Channukah and fasting on Yom Kippur, the day of Atonement.

In Table 9 we see that 77 percent of JJ-Yes children are affiliated with a synagogue or temple as compared to 64 percent of JJ-No children followed by 40 percent of JO-Yes and 24 percent of JO-No. While the level of volunteering is lower in general, the same pattern exists as for the synagogue membership.

Similar trends are found when respondents were asked about the families' participation in a Passover Seder. Almost all children living in JJ-Yes households are exposed to the Seder as compared to 46 percent living in JO-No households. In fact, reviewing the complete table we note that the same pattern exists for each of the 8 variables. The highest level of cultural connection is for the JJ-Yes group, followed by JJ-No, JO-Yes and JO-No.

Table 9

Exposure of Children to Cultural Environment in Households
with Differing Levels of Respondents' Formal Jewish
Education and Marriage Type of Household

Cultural Variables	A JJ-Yes	B JJ-No	C JO-Yes	D JO-No
% of households who belong to a synagogue or temple	77	64	40	24
% of households where respondent has volunteered for a Jewish organization	51	33	21	11
% of respondents who have never visited Israel	47	23	20	9
% households where no one celebrates Israel's Day of Independence	49	23	14	5
% of households who light candles on Friday night usually or all the time	49	37	19	7
% of households who celebrate Passover usually or all time	99	85	70	46
% of households who light candles on Channukah usually or all the time	98	83	76	51
% of respondents who fast on the day of Atonement (Yom Kippur)	86	65	53	2

The next table (Table 10) contains 3 items which refer to respondents' attitudes to Jewish friends and neighborhood. The table was constructed in similar fashion to Table 9 where cell A is JJ-Yes, cell B is JJ-No, cell C is JO-Yes and cell D is JO-No. Q1 (row 1) asked respondents what proportion of their closest friends were Jewish and

Table 10

Exposure of Children to Cultural Environment in Households with Differing Levels of Respondents' Formal Jewish Education and Marriage Type of Household

Cultural Variables	A JJ-Yes	B JJ-No	C JO-Yes	D JO-No
% of respondents who state that "most or almost all" close friends are Jewish	72	62	15	13
% of respondents who state that the neighborhood is "somewhat or very Jewish"	54	39	17	20
% of respondents who state it is "somewhat or very important" that neighborhood has a Jewish character	71	65	42	28

the data are the percentage who responded "most or almost all." Q2 (row 2) asked about the Jewish character of the respondents' neighborhood, and the data are the percentage who responded that the neighborhood was "somewhat or very Jewish in character." Q3 (row 3) asked respondents how important it is that the neighborhood have a Jewish character and the data are the percentage who responded that it was "somewhat or very important." We note that in all three situations children who live in endogamous households are exposed to parents who have considerably higher levels of "identity" with a Jewish environment than those living in intermarried households, independent of the respondents' Jewish education. In summary it seems that there is a fair amount of evidence to suggest that children growing up in an intermarried household do, on average, receive some measure of exposure to Jewish culture, but that this level is considerably below that received by those living in endogamous households.

If we follow the argument that those respondents with lower levels of exposure to Jewish education are more likely to intermarry and that children in intermarried families are generally less likely to be exposed to the cultural environment, the data show that the process of intermarriage, independent of education, is a powerful instrument of assimilation. This supports the point made by Alba that parents who are in endogamous marriages are more likely than others to expose their children to an environment which encourages group continuity.

SUMMARY AND CONCLUSION

The analysis carried out in this paper points to the fact that both demographic and sociological changes are occurring in the Jewish population. Demographically the Jewish population is aging as fertility levels remain below replacement level and as the number of Jewish immigrants decline both in absolute and relative terms. Sociologically, as the Jewish community and the family have increasingly integrated into the mainstream culture, the issue of qualitative group continuity has become of central concern. While there is evidence to suggest that certain qualitative components of Jewish life amongst the most committed sections of the community are gaining strength, the data presented in this paper point to a general weakening of the Jewish identity of the average family as levels of intermarriage increase. In response to the evidence of increasing intermarriage some researchers have noted that the impact of intermarriage will depend on the extent of conversion to Judaism of the non-Jewish spouse and on the extent to which children of interfaith marriages are raised as Jews. The NJPS data clearly demonstrate that the "Jewish" component of the social environment in which Jewish children are raised is declining both for the endogamous and the intermarried households. With demographic and assimilative cultural pressures on the Jewish family, the issue of strategies of adaptation to be developed by the community leadership assumes great importance. The social demographer can point to the trends, but the community leader needs to make decisions on how to adapt. For example, should efforts be made to combat conditions conducive to intermarriage or to encourage intermarried households to maintain a connection with the community? Is education sufficient to counter the numerous pressures placed in individuals to break from the group? No matter what the answer, this small and highly visible subgroup on the American ethnic mosaic faces a series of critical challenges as we enter the 21st century.

REFERENCES

Alba, Richard D. 1990. *Ethnic Identity: The Transformation of White America*. New Haven, CT: Yale University Press.

Alba, Richard D. and Reid M. Golden. 1986. "Patterns of ethnic marriage in the United States." *Social Forces* 65:202-223.

Archdeacon, Thomas J. 1983. *Becoming American: An Ethnic History*. New York: Free Press.

Bean, Frank and Parker Frisbee. 1978. *The Demography of Racial and Ethnic Groups*. New York: Academic Press.

Bogue, Donald. 1985. *The Population of the United States: Historical Trends and Future Projections*. New York: Free Fress.

Canevin, Regis. 1912. "An examination, historical and statistical, into losses and gains of the Catholic church in the United States from 1790 to 1910." Pp. 380 in Charles Nam (ed.), *Understanding Population Change*. Itasca, IL: F.E. Peacock Publishers, Inc.

Cohen, Steven. 1988. *American Assimilation or Jewish Survival?* Bloomington, IN: Indiana University Press.

DellaPergola, Sergio. 1980. "Patterns of American Jewish Fertility." *Demography* 17:261-273.

Featherman, David L. 1971. "The socioeconomic achievement of white religio-ethnic sub-groups: Social and psychological explanations." *American Sociological Review* 36:207-222.

Gartner, Lloyd P. 1974. "Immigration and the formation of American Jewry, 1840-1925." Pp. 31-50 in Marshall Sklare (ed.), *The Jew in American Society*. New York: Behrman House, Inc.

Glenn, Norval D. 1984. "A note on estimating the strength of influence for religious endogamy." *Journal of Marriage and the Family* 46: 725-728.

Glick, Paul. 1960. "Intermarriage and fertility patterns among persons in major religious groups." *Eugenics Quarterly* 7:31-38.

Goldscheider, Calvin. 1986. *Jewish Continuity and Change: Emerging Patterns in America*. Bloomington, IN: Indiana University Press.

Goldstein, Sidney. 1982. "Population movement and redistribution among American Jews." *Jewish Journal of Sociology* 24:5-23.

_____. 1990. "Jews on the move: Implications for American Jewry and for local communities." *Jewish Journal of Sociology* 32:5-30.

_____. 1992. "Profile of American Jewry: Insights from the 1990 National Jewish Population Survey." Pp. 77-173 in *American Jewish Yearbook, 1992*, Vol 92. New York: American Jewish Committee.

Good, Dorothy. 1959. "Questions on religion in the United States census." *Population Index* 25:3-16.

Gordon, Milton. 1964. *Assimilation in American Life: The Role of Race, Religion and National Origins*. Fairlawn, NJ: Oxford University Press.

Hertzberg, Arthur. 1989. *The Jews in America: Four Centuries of an Uneasy Encounter*. New York: Simon and Schuster.

Jaret, Charles. 1978. "The Impact of Geographic Mobility on Jewish Community Participation: Disruptive or Supportive." *Contemporary Jewry* 4 (Spring/Summer):9-21.

Jasso, Guillermina and Mark R. Rosenzweig. 1990. *The New Chosen People: Immigrants in the United States Census 1980 Monograph Series.* New York: Russell Sage Foundation.

Kass, Dora and Seymour M. Lipset. 1982. "Jewish immigration to the United States, from 1976 to the present: Israelis and others." Pp. 272-294 in M. Sklare (ed.), *Understanding American Jewry.* New Brunswick, NJ: Transaction Books.

Klaff, Vivian Z. 1980. "Pluralism as an alternative model for the human ecologist." *Ethnicity* 7:102-118

_____. 1991. "Models of urban ecology and their application to Jewish settlement in Western cities." In R. Dotterer, D.D. Moore, and S. Cohen (eds.), *Jewish Settlement and Community in the Modern Western World.* Toronto, Selinsgrove: Susquehanna University Press.

Kosmin, Barry A. et al. 1991. *Highlights of the CJF 1990 National Jewish Population Survey.* New York: Council of Jewish Federations.

Kosmin, Barry and Seymour P. Lachman. 1993. *One Nation Under God: Religion in Contemporary American Society.* New York: Harmony Books.

Lazerwitz, Bernard. 1978. "An estimate of a rare population group: The U.S. Jewish population." *Demography* 15:389-394.

Lieberson, Stanley and Mary C. Waters. 1988. *From Many Strands: Ethnic and Racial Groups in Comtemporary America.* New York: Russell Sage Foundation.

Lipset, Seymour M. 1994. *The Power of Jewish Education.* Los Angeles: Wilstein Institute, University of Judaism.

Mayer, Egon. 1989. "Intermarriage and modern Jewish family life in the United States: A research perspective." Pp. 246-252 in C. Diamant (ed.), *Jewish Marital Status*. New Jersey: Jason Aronson, Inc.

McCutcheon, Allan. 1988. "Denominations and religious intermarriage: Trends among white Americans in the twentieth century." *Review of Religious Research* 29:213-217.

Mueller, C.W. 1980. "Evidence on the relationship between religion and educational attainment." *Sociology of Education* 53:140-152.

Newman, W.M. and P.L. Halvorsen. 1979. "American Jews: Patterns of geographic distribution and change, 1952-1974." *Journal of the Scientific Study of Religion* 18:183-193.

Rosenthal, Erich. 1968. "Jewish intermarriage in Indiana." *Eugenics Quarterly* 15:277-287.

Silberman, Charles E. 1985. *A Certain People: American Jews and Their Lives Today*. New York: Summit Books.

Thomas, J. L. 1972. "The factor of religion in the selection of marriage mates." in M.L. Barron (ed.), *The Blending American: Patterns of Intermarriage*. Chicago: Quadrangle Books.

Reframing and Refocusing American Indian Family Strengths

Joseph (Jay) H. Stauss

INTRODUCTION

I grew up on the Olympic peninsula. That means that I grew up on some reservation, and some off-reservation rural areas in western Washington. What I remember most about growing up is the experiences on the "Indian side" of the family. We had clambakes every weekend. Uncle Ike, Uncle Bob, Uncle Dan, Uncle Howard—I had more uncles than I knew what to do with, and more cousins than I could count. It wasn't until later I found out that a lot of those folks weren't related to me by blood, but they were related through an extended family network that is very different from the way non-Indians see extended families. We had our socials on the beach every Saturday and that is where stories were told.

I grew up with my Grandma Kimball and spent many evenings with her. She was a very special person in my life. My given name is Joseph Harry after a grandfather and an uncle, and I wondered how I was nicknamed Jay. No one would tell me. I kept pestering Grandma Kimball to tell me. Finally she told me in the way that she usually did. She told me a story. It's a story I later heard in Snoqualmie and Snohomish and some of the other tribes up there. So it isn't a story that has particular relevance just to the Jamestown band, S'Kalallam.

She told me that long before there were people on the earth, the animals ruled the earth. They talked with each other and they would talk with the plants and all other "living" things. There was a force, a life force, throughout the entire world. The animals in the Pacific Northwest had great give-aways which were later to be called potlatches by humans when they came on the earth. Those give-aways really established a social rank and a prestige among the animals. Of course, the animal that had the most prestige was the Bear. The Bear had many give-aways in different seasons.

There was a pesky bird called a Bluejay (there are a lot of them in the Northwest) and these little birds spend all their time badgering everyone. They're loud, obnoxious, and they chase after everyone. They don't want to work. They try to get things the easy way.

Anyway, the Bear had a great give-away and at this give-away there were many gifts. There was a lot of food, but someone forgot to bring the lard, or the fat. In the Northwest, in traditional times, you simply didn't eat any kind of food without being able to dip it into lard or fat.

The Creator had, of course, given the Bear his own special song. Like the Bear, all of the tribes in the state of Washington have power that comes through song. The power comes from one's own song, and it is owned by that individual. So the Bear began to dance around the fire and sing his song. As he danced and sang, out of the rolls of fat around this Bear, lard started to drip out. Then all of the other animals came forward and received lard from the Bear.

Well, the Bluejay was there and he was watching all this. Of course the Bluejay, who had very little prestige, had never done a give-away. So he set about badgering people, trying to get them to help him pull together enough gifts and enough food to have a give-away, and he called for a give-away in the spring. Everyone came, simply because a Bluejay had never had this kind of social gathering before, and everyone was interested to see what would happen. The Bluejay had set all this up, with much singing and dancing. Then Bluejay laid out the food, and someone noticed that there was no lard available. The Bluejay immediately began to dance around the fire and sing the Bear's song. And of course, the animals knew that this was not the thing to do. They disappeared into the woods. The wind came up and held the Bluejay over the fire, and then set him back down.

And Grandma Kimball told me, "Now if you look at a bluejay, you will notice that the feet are black. And that's the charred black from the fire. And you'll notice they always hop, they never walk anywhere." That was the story she told me when I asked her why I was nicknamed Jay. I felt that it wasn't very flattering.

I didn't know until much later in life, when I began studying American Indian families, that I had grown up in one. In fact, I had no idea I belonged to an American Indian family until I failed the 7th grade. My non-Indian aunt from Missouri came and plucked me out of the family and moved me. And then, in discussions with her, I began to realize that I was in an Indian family. I found out that, for me, growing up in an Indian family meant:

> *Your mother is an alcoholic. And you have never seen your father. And you know that you've grown up in the Indian Shaker Church. And all your uncles are alcoholics, and those clambakes that you go to on the weekends are really places where people just get drunk.*

So I began to see the differences between an Indian family and a non-Indian family. Later, when I contrasted these views with the stories I had heard as I grew up, moving around on the reservations in the Northwest and attending other Indian socials, I began to see life in an Indian family as strength, not weakness.

My education continued. I got into graduate school and began to look at the research literature, and again I learned that I belonged to a dysfunctional family, by definition, because it was an Indian family. I contrasted this view with the reality of my Grandma Kimball. She prayed every day; she knew important things. She knew more than any educated person I'd ever known. And she did not go to any formal school. Yet Grandma Kimball knew things that happened in the family before they happened. I'll never forget the time I was living with her in her simple house. She had an outhouse and a house with no running water. She didn't have any of those kinds of amenities. One day I was sitting by the wood stove and there was a knock at the door, a very clear, sharp knock. I remember it. She went to the door and opened it; there was no one there. Grandma Kimball shut the door, and then she turned around and announced to no one in particular that Uncle Harry was dead. In fact, Uncle Harry had died.

I'll never forget her breakfasts. I never had a better breakfast than fried mush and toast and coffee. Grandma Kimball fixed it every day. These were Indian family strengths, my family strengths. In sharp contrast, I learned later in life that many people felt they were not strengths at all, but rather severe weaknesses. Those are all the ideas I bring to the study of American Indian families. Thus my interest is in family strengths and not weaknesses.

Several years ago I reviewed the literature on American Indian families and made some recommendations for doing applied research in this area. I concluded that:

> *The dominant focus for studying the American Indian has been a search for social problems! More specifically, a search for abhorrent behavior that could be quantified and thus indicate deviation from the norm of white, middle-class America* (Stauss, 1986:290).

Here in the mid-1990s the social problems focus still prevails, and research on Indian families continues to be a neglected area. The Euro-American trend has always been to study Indian social problems—teen pregnancy, alcoholism, suicide, etc.—and ignore Indian family strengths. There are many reasons for the persistence of the social problems focus, but the most important is the way social scientists are trained and funded. In addition, neither tribal councils nor other influential political or disciplinary bodies have identified American Indian family strengths as a research priority. Today, as in 1986, I would call for a brief 250-year moratorium on research which focuses on how American Indian families deviate from the white norm (Stauss, 1986:348).

The area of Indian family research also awaits application of a significant interdisciplinary effort. We need theoretical and conceptual approaches that will highlight paradigms that will focus attention on "what works" in Indian families, on what is "native," "Indian," "traditional," or adaptative about Indian family life, rather than on what is "non-white" and "problematic."

This paper brings together ideas from various literatures—education, political science, law, family studies, and sociology—in an attempt to refocus and reframe the area of Indian family strengths.

I repeat several conclusions from my earlier article:

1. Tribal diversity prevents us from generalizing family strengths to all Indian families.

2. Existing theoretical frameworks and social science family concepts have only limited value in organizing and extending this area of study.

3. The issues of tribal sovereignty, who is an Indian, research protocol on Indian reservations, and respect for spiritual privacy must be adequately dealt with by the scientist conducting research among Indian families.

We must be cautious when we generalize about American Indian "families" because the diversity of culture and variety of structural forms, including extended family, kinship, and band, does not permit a universally applicable definition. Here, I use "Indian family" as an umbrella term—just as we do "Indian" to denote over 650 tribes, bands, and groups across America. There is an abundant literature (see for examples, Snipp, 1989 or Robbins, 1984) on tribal diversity, illustrating the mistakes made by generalizing across tribal groups on any single issue. No member of any tribal group—when asked for an opinion—presumes to speak for all Indians, or even all members of one's own tribe or group.

Only in an interdisciplinary and holistic framework can this topic be properly approached. Discussions of American Indian families cannot be divorced from the interwoven nature of spirituality, politics, and economics in Indian country. Too often disciplinary barriers have artificially impeded creative approaches which might have provided new paths across the old, well-worn trails. In most discussions of Indian families, the old, well-worn road winds through very desolate territory, highlighting families shattered and destroyed by alcoholism, adoption, drugs, poverty, and racism. I focused on these social problems myself earlier in my career. These days, I regularly set aside papers and media messages about high Indian teen suicide rates, the problems facing Indian single mothers, or incidents of Indian child sexual abuse. I believe that it is time to turn our attention, and indeed our actions, toward why and how Indian families have survived against great odds and how they have persevered in ways that kept their cultural integrity intact—changed, yes—but still facilitating tribal identity in Indian children and power across tribal communities.

FAMILY STRENGTHS
AND FAMILY ETHNICITY DEFINED

Recent introductory texts in family studies usually discuss family strengths. Key concepts include healthy communications, affirmation, respect, trust, spiritual wellness, tradition, and ritual. Many of these concepts, such as spirituality and family history, may be particularly salient for Indian families. However, I am wary of simply applying a list of Euro-American family strengths to Indian families. That approach has been tried in the study of values, the most common topic for the comparison of Indian and non-Indian populations. Typically there are comparisons of values about family formation, status/role of age groups, and orientation to individuality and group identity. There are often discussions of Indian-other differences in theoretical polarities such as extended vs. nuclear family, respect for age vs. youth orientation, giving vs. saving, cooperation vs. competitiveness, and so on. The empirical evidence on significant value differentials is mixed and does not support the generality of these values or behavioral traits across either Indian or non-Indian cultures.

Two areas in the literature report Indian and non-Indian differences. One is social work and the other is personnel administration. Social workers and human service personnel have been concerned with learning about culturally-based behavioral differences. In particular, they have recognized that methods of discussing an individual's problems vary by ethnic group. In addition, the literature on interviewing and personal presentation has analyzed behavior such as eye contact, characteristics of the handshake, response time for answers, and so on.

All of this literature taken together provides a fairly generalizable set of behavioral characteristics distinguishing natives and non-natives. While I strongly believe differences between Native Americans and other groups exist with respect to certain values and behaviors, there are also significant tribal, age, urban, regional, and gender differences which severely limit the generalizability of apparent ethnic differences. A more fruitful avenue of investigation involves the area of "family ethnicity," which goes beyond the comparison of single characteristics and to a more substantial discussion of patterns and contexts of family strengths. Family ethnicity has been defined as *"the sum total of our ancestry and cultural dimensions, as families collectively identify the core of their being"* (McAdoo, 1993:ix).

McAdoo identifies unique family customs, proverbs and stories, celebrations, foods, and religious ceremonies as important for maintaining family ethnicity, and stresses significant heritage stories such as how one's ancestors came to America. She further discusses the difficulties of raising children to have ethnic pride, and the difference between self-concept and ethnic identity (McAdoo, 1993:4-8). The characteristics McAdoo identifies as important are all significant for American Indians. However, the Indian heritage is more likely to be represented in tribal origin accounts than in the romanticized stories of European immigration and manifest destiny.

Native American self-concept and national (not ethnic) pride stem from origin stories which place them in America forever, and not from any story about traversing an ice bridge, or in any way "coming to America."

Senese (1991) highlights this crucial contrast:

Fundamental differences exist between indigenous peoples whose traditional time on the land extends back for thousands of years. Tribal teaching and tradition count this continent as the birthplace of the souls of their people. Along with this comprehension comes culture structures which are radically different in terms of land use, sharing and ownership, as well as in human interaction (p. 159).

Indians and non-Indians share some family strengths, but the similarities often are overshadowed by major differences. Indian family strengths are sacred, cultural, and political—all at once. Non-Indian family strengths, based on European cultures, may also be sacred, cultural, and political, but in different ways. Furthermore, the special relationship Indians have with the federal government through lands held in trust and treaty rights creates and nurtures land-related family strengths which are fundamentally different from those of Euro-American families.

THEORETICAL IMPLICATIONS

The most recent scholarly review of family theories relevant to American Indians (and other racial/ethnic groups) is found in a chapter by Dilworth-Anderson and others (1993) entitled "Reframing Theories for Understanding Race, Ethnicity, and Families." These authors call for a reassessment of family theory with an eye to:

(1) restructuring assumptions and values to reflect ethnic reality; (2) creating new ways of thinking about ethnic minority

*families to enhance culturally relevant conceptual frameworks
on the family; and, (3) reframing existing theoretical perspectives and ideologies to explain and predict family phenomena among these families (p. 627).*

Dilworth-Anderson et al. (1993: 640-641) further argue that the
life course perspective is the most promising approach to studying
"minority families." This is a dynamic inter-disciplinary perspective
which can respond in a positive way to culturally diverse groups. They
suggest that "kin scripts" may be a fruitful way to study Indian families. Indeed, all research about Indian families ought to begin with
attention to the extended family or kin group.

EXTENDED FAMILY
AS A FRAME OF REFERENCE

Some researchers have classified Indian families as traditional and
non-traditional, or traditional and modern. One purpose of such di-
chotomies is to emphasize the key function of the traditional extended
family group in creating ethnicity and connecting children with an
Indian identity. While controversy exists about how effective contemporary Indian families are at fostering Indian identity and preserving
traditional cultures, Indian families do rely significantly more than non-
Indian families on a widespread extended family network.

Herring (1989) identifies three types of Indian families with regard
to their retention of American Native core values:

*(a) the traditional group, which overtly adheres to culturally de-
fined styles of living; (b) a non-traditional, bicultural group that
seems to have adopted many aspects of non-American Native styles;
and (c) a pan-traditional group that overtly struggles to redefine
and reconfirm previously lost cultural styles (p. 6).*

Herring's typology followed that of Red Horse et al. (1978:9), who
also identified traditional, bicultural, and pan-traditional family types
and stressed the importance of extended families in maintaining selected
cultural constants. A related typology offered by Miller (1981:179)
identified four orientations to Native culture: traditional, transitional,
bicultural, and marginal.

Herring's conclusion about the importance of the extended family is characteristic of this literature:

The American Native extended family is the primary social, economic, and political unit. The American Native family structure contains unique perspectives on the roles of women and grandparents in its child-rearing styles. Most of these perspectives are shared by traditional, non-traditional, and pan-traditional family lifestyle patterns (Herring, 1989:11).

CONCEPTUAL IMPLICATIONS FOR INDIAN FAMILY RESEARCH

The traditional conceptual boundaries between education, family studies, social work, and literature blur and indeed, disappear when the focus is on Indian family strengths. For example, Deloria (1991:14) introduces the concepts of power and place as central to Indian education. However, these ideas are also directly related to Indian family strengths. Relational bonding (Red Horse, 1980:462-467), balance and harmony (Miller, 1981:84), and other Indian values such as generosity, sharing, and respect are also important dimensions of Indian family dynamics. Deloria's (1991) key ideas are important for understanding Indian education in America, because they tie Indian family strength concepts together:

Keeping the particular in mind as the alternate reference point of Indian knowledge, we can pass into a discussion of some of the principles of the Indian forms of knowledge. Here power and place are dominant concepts—power being the living energy that inhabits and/or composes the universe, and place being the relationship of things to each other. It is much easier, in discussing Indian principles, to put these basic ideas into a simple equation: power and place produce personality (Deloria, 1991:14).

Deloria is writing about the differences between traditional Indian education and Euro-American education, which he characterizes as indoctrination. He distinguishes between Indian education, which focuses on the particular, and non-Indian education, which focuses on general laws. In a universe, where all things have life, Indian people have a personal and sacred relationship with the cosmos, which does not demand an explanation using scientific generalizability or the development of general laws. Although Deloria is writing about education, he provides a simple equation—power and place = personality—which dramatically summarizes Indian family strengths. Indian families are the context in which individuals (personalities) come to embrace power and place and personalities result from power and place.

A second set of important concepts are found in the Indian family strengths literature. Several Indian authors have identified concepts which are fruitful to the study of Indian family strengths, including relationship bonding (Red Horse, 1980), nature and harmony (Miller, 1981), and balance and spirituality (Light and Martin, 1986).

Light and Martin (1986:1) identify respect, generosity, and harmony within the context of spirituality as American Indian family strengths. In one of the few studies providing empirical data, they found that, compared to the general population, Indian women had high scores on esteem and communication. They concluded that:

> *From our results, it appears that helping systems that function within families and personal relationships are based on mutual respect. These positive relationships appear to serve as a foundation of strength for Indian people* (86:4).

None of the authors who introduced these concepts of basic family strengths defined them. Here I will make a preliminary attempt to define these concepts and to tie them directly to Deloria's prescription for traditional education.

Relational bonding is a core behavior which is built on widely shared values such as respect, generosity, and sharing. Relational bonding occurs every day, on a continual basis, with a large number of "relatives" within the extended family (which is much larger than the Euro-American notion of extended family). Indeed, relational bonding is the responsibility of all tribe, band, clan, and kin group members.

Harmony and balance are both family and community responsibilities—sometimes sacred, sometimes more widely shared in a ceremonial way. To have harmony and balance in life, a person must put community and family needs above individual achievements.

Power and place cannot be separated. Family and community are one in relationship to the land:

> *(a) The earth (cosmos) is holy, not profane; (b) all of the cosmos is alive and all communications with the natural world are spiritual; (c) all native people have a special responsibility for maintaining the balance and "sustaining harmonious relations within the whole natural world"; (d) there are natural cycles that sustain life and everything in the natural world cannot be explained; there is a continuous dialogue with nature* (Suzuki and Knudtson, 1992:15-20).

All of these concepts belong together in an interdisciplinary framework. All contribute to the strength of Indian families.

The tribal community, extended family, and immediate physical environment provide each Indian family member with the opportunity to interact daily in spiritual ways that shape each individual personality and sustain their identity, power, and place in the world.

Relational bonding through extended family and community interaction ensures support for maintaining both individual and group harmony and balance. Respect, generosity, and sharing are the basic ingredients of relational bonding. Knowledge and maintenance of a personal and sacred relationship with cosmic life-forces and, in particular, the immediate physical environment are paramount to sustaining family strengths. These are the concepts important to the study of Indian family strengths. They are the core concepts important to any traditional education.

SUMMARY

I have reviewed many economic development plans from reservations, and they typically identify low self-concept or self-esteem as a major problem among Indian youth. This is not just low self-esteem in the Euro-American, scientific sense, but the manifestation of a native self that does not include an understanding and reverence for the spiritual world, a family that is not supportive of speaking the heritage language, or a community that does not stress the responsibilities of being a member of that group.

The research focus on "social problems" of Native American families will not change until tribal resources are concentrated inward, toward building tribal education. Family strengths are not a policy or resource priority across America right now. The same is true in Indian country. When tribal councils talk about education they focus on providing funds for their children to attend Euro-American schools. When they talk about meeting the needs of families, they try to provide services to combat social problems from within a Euro-American framework. Instead, tribal efforts must start with families, not the formal school system. They must provide opportunities for elders and youth to learn about power and place in their family and community, increase opportunities for relational bonding, and not try to separate the spiritual or sacred from political, cultural, or family experiences.

Strong families should be brought together to lead by example and share their strengths with others. Tribal leadership should provide elders a physical location and materials to promote language, knowledge of the land, and spiritual lifeways.

I see a time, perhaps ten generations from now, when tribes have strengthened families because essential and sufficient elements of sovereignty have been restored. Sovereign tribal groups will hold as their highest priority facilitating family strengths which build on language, oral history, relationship to the land, spirituality, and all aspects of native society which serve to provide a shared vision of place and power. When this time comes to pass, traditional Indian education will be enacted through strengthened extended families whose members emphasize harmony, balance, spirituality, and relational bonding in everyday interaction with youth; and Indian families will no more be models of social problems, but of wellness.

REFERENCES

Deloria Jr., V. 1991. *Indian Education in America*. Boulder, CO: The American Indian Science and Engineering Society.

Dilworth-Anderson, P., et al. 1993. "Reframing theories for understanding race, ethnicity, and families." Pp. 627-646 in P. G. Boss, et al. (eds.), *Sourcebook of Family Theories and Methods*. New York: Plenum Press.

Dinges, N. G., Yazzie, M. L., and Tollefson, G. D. 1974. "Development intervention for Navajo family mental health." *Personnel and Guidance Journal* 52 (6):390-395.

Farris, C. E. 1976. "American Indian social worker advocates." *Social Casework* 57 (October):494-503.

Good Tracks, J.B. 1973. "Native American non-interference." *Social Work* 18 (6):30-35.

Havighurst, R.J. 1957. *Education Among American Indians: Individual and Cultural Aspects in the Annals.* Philadelphia, PA: The American Academy of Political and Social Science.

Herring, R.D. 1989. "The American Native family: Dissolution by coercion." *Journal of Multicultural Counseling and Development* 17 (1):4-13.

Light, H.K., and Martin, R.E. 1986. "The Native American family." Pp. 325-363 in C.H. Mindel et al. (eds.), *Ethnic Families in America* (3rd ed.). New York: Elsevier.

McAdoo, H.P. (ed.). 1993. *Family Ethnicity: Strength in Diversity.* Newbury Park, CA: Sage Publications.

Medicine, B. 1981. "American Indian family: Cultural change and adaptive strategies." *The Journal of Ethnic Studies* 8 (4):12-13.

Miller, D. 1981. "Alternative paradigms available for research on American Indian families: Implications for research and training." Pp. 79-91 in F. Hoffman (ed.), *American Indian Family: Strengths and Stresses.* Isleta, NM: American Indian Social Research Development Associates, Inc.

Red Horse, J.G. 1980. "Family structure and value orientation in American Indians." *Social Casework* 61 (8):462-467.

Red Horse, J.G., R. Lewis, M. Feit, and J. Decker. 1978. "Behavior of urban American Indians." *Social Casework* 59 (February):67-72.

Robbins, S.P. 1984. "Anglo concepts and Indian reality: A study of juvenile delinquency." *Social Casework* 65 (4):235-241.

Senese, G.B. 1991. *Self-Determination and the Social Education of Native Americans*. New York: Praeger.

Snipp, C.M. 1989. *American Indians: The First of This Land*. New York: Russell Sage Foundation.

Stauss, J.H. 1986. "The study of American Indian families: Implications for applied research." *Family Perspective* 20 (4):337-352.

Suzuki, D., and Knudtson. 1992. *Wisdom of the Elders*. New York: Bantam Books.

An Analysis of Native American Fertility in the Public Use Microdata Samples of the 1990 Census

Cardell K. Jacobson

Native Americans have long had a substantially higher than average fertility. The fertility rates of most tribal groups in the United States and Canada have fallen, however, over the past few decades (Sweet, 1974; Trovato, 1981, 1987; Broudy and May, 1983; Thornton, Sandefur, and Snipp, 1991). This paper examines some of the trends and factors associated with Native American fertility rates.

These higher than average fertility rates are evident in the Native American population as recently as the 1990 census. Data on the number of children ever born (CEB) to ever-married women are presented in Figure 1. In a sense, this graph should be read backwards, from right to left, since the data are presented by age cohorts and the youngest cohorts are on the left side of the graph. Clearly Native American women (including Alaskan Native women) have had and continue to have higher rates of fertility than both African American and white American women. The differences have begun to decrease, however. The younger cohorts of all three groups have much closer fertility rates. Ethnicity affects fertility, however, and more analysis is required to more fully understand how Native American fertility compares to that of white and African American women.

Additional information about Native American fertility rates can be obtained from more detailed examination of census data. Data from both the 1980 and 1990 censuses are presented in Table 1. Table 1 presents the mean number of children ever born to Native American women and White-American women of childbearing ages at the begin-

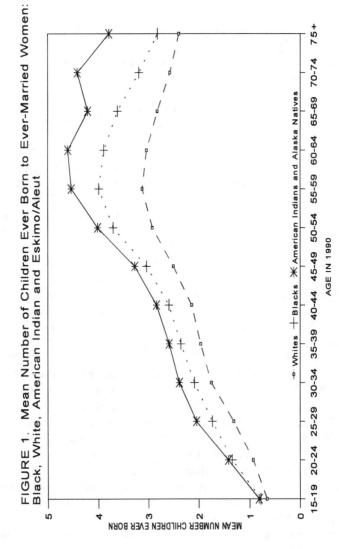

FIGURE 1. Mean Number of Children Ever Born to Ever-Married Women: Black, White, American Indian and Eskimo/Aleut

Source: Public Use Microdata Samples from 1990 Census.

Table 1

Mean Number of Children Ever Born
to Native American and White Women Aged 15 to 44

	American Indian*		White		U.S.	
	1980	1990	1980	1990	1980	1990
Married and non-Married						
15-24 Yrs of Age	0.53	0.54	0.27	0.25	0.32	0.31
25-34 Yrs of Age	2.01	1.90	1.40	1.25	1.48	1.33
35-44 Yrs of Age	3.46	2.48	2.54	1.87	2.64	1.96
Married Only						
15-24 Yrs of Age	1.22	1.28	0.79	0.84	0.86	0.88
25-34 Yrs of Age	2.25	2.22	1.62	1.54	1.69	1.59
35-44 Yrs of Age	3.61	2.66	2.67	2.08	2.77	2.13

*Includes Eskimo and Aleut. The 1980 data are from Thornton, Sandefur, and
Snipp (1991); 1990 data are from the 1 percent Public Use Microdata
Samples of the 1990 Census.

ning and end of the 1980s. It also includes both those who have been
married and those who have not.

The higher fertility rates for Native American women are again
evident. The second panel of Table 1 shows that Native American women who are married have somewhat higher rates of fertility than do
white American and all married women in the United States. Note,
however, that differences are somewhat larger for the older women.
Married Native American women aged 35-44 in 1990 had, on average,
.58 more children ever born than comparable white women while
Native American women 15 to 24 years had .44 more children. These
reflect the trends shown in Figure 1.

The first panel of Table 1 also shows the census figures for married
and non-married women. The overall number of children ever born is
lower in this portion of the table because most single women do not
have children. But the differences between young Native American wo-

men and young white American women are larger. The number of children ever born to Native American women aged 15-24 is roughly double the number of children that comparably aged white women had.

Furthermore, the number of children ever born to Native American women between the ages of 15 and 34 did not decline from 1980 to 1990. The number of children declined only for those Native American women between the ages of 35 and 44. The decline for women in this older group was substantial, however. They gave birth to approximately one less child than similarly aged Native American women had a decade earlier.

Two conclusions are evident from the data presented thus far. First, Native American fertility has declined over the past several decades. Secondly, the decline in Native American fertility appears to have stopped. Younger cohorts of Native American women (aged 15-34) are now having as many children as Native American women their age did a decade ago. Nevertheless, this rate is about 50 percent higher than that of white American women in 1990.

Numerous variables are related to the number of children women bear and these can be examined to see if they affect the fertility rates of Native American and other racial and ethnic groups. One source of information about such variables is the National Survey of Family Growth (NSFG—see U.S. Department of Health and Human Services, 1990). We shall examine these variables as possible explanations of the higher Native American fertility rates.

The National Center for Health Statistics has sponsored four cycles of the NSFG. Each cycle obtained data from a national probability sample of approximately 8,000 American women aged 15-44. The last two cycles were collected in 1982 and 1988. Several analyses of the NSFG data sets have examined racial differences (see for example, Mosher and Pratt, 1990; Forrest and Singh, 1990; Mosher, 1990; Goldscheider and Mosher, 1991; Miller and Heaton, 1991). The focus, however, has usually been on blacks and whites, and sometimes Hispanics. Data on the Indian samples in these surveys have received little, if any, attention.

Generalizing from these data must be done carefully. The response rates were excellent, in the high 70s, and the samples are good probability samples. The samples did not, however, include women from all parts of the country, and though the sample included Native American women, the representativeness of this subsample is unknown. But the surveys provide suggestive information about variables affecting Native American fertility. Much of this information is taken from Jacobson and Harris (1994).

Native American identity in the surveys was ascertained by self-report and included both those who have only Indian ancestry and those who have mixed ancestry. Despite various other attempts to measure Native American identity, this self-report item remains the most acceptable and best overall measure (see Snipp, 1989:61).

Being in the labor force generally depresses the rate of child bearing, but having children also induces some women to remain home with their children. These contradictory forces may balance out. The percentage of Native American women working in the 1982 NSFG sample was somewhat lower than for women from the other groups, but by 1988 the percentage was not substantially different. This parity may be a function of the sampling process. The NSFG relied more on urban sectors than on rural ones and unemployment among rural Indian groups is notoriously high. Thus, these labor force participation rates may not acurately reflect the experience of Native American women living in rural areas or on reservations.

A second possible explanation of the differences in fertility rates of Native American and white American women is sterility. Most women who are sterile are voluntarily so for contraceptive reasons. Many have had the number of children they want and they practice contraception, including one member of the couple being sterilized surgically. Some women are involuntarily sterile, however. In the NSFG data Native American women do not report substantially higher rates of either voluntary or involuntary sterilization. The total percentage for Native American women in 1988 was 34 percent compared to 33 percent for white American women (see Jacobson and Harris, 1994).

Marital status is also related to the number of children women bear because of the normative expectations that childbirth should occur within marriage. Native American women are substantially less likely to marry than other American women are. According to the 1990 census data, only 32 percent of all Native American women were currently married compared to 47 percent of all American women, and 54 percent had never married compared to 39 percent of all American women. These differences reflect the younger age of the Native American population, so we should expect a larger percentage of the Native American women to be unmarried. However, younger cohorts of Native American women also do not marry as early or frequently as most other American women. Only 50 percent of Native American women between 25 and 34 years of age were married in 1990 compared to 64 percent of the white women of the same age. And 32 percent of the Native American women of the same age had never married compared to 25 percent of the white women.

Age is closely related to fertility for several reasons. First, older women are more likely to have completed childbearing and many young women, especially unmarried young women, have yet to begin their families. At the same time, older women are less likely than younger women to be fecund. Younger cohorts have also experienced a decline in the number of children desired and normative pressures for a large number of children have weakened. Finally, older women are less likely to be well educated and, in most populations, education suppresses the mean number of children ever born. The educational levels of the Native American women are lower than the levels of other women in the United States (Jacobson and Harris, 1994; Snipp, 1989).

Generally those who begin sexual activity early, marry young, and have children while young. They also tend to have more children. The two NSFG surveys show that Native American women engage in sex somewhat earlier than white and Hispanic women do (16.8 years old for Native American women compared to 18.0 for white and Hispanic women according to data from the NSFG in 1988). And Native American women conceive their first child at a younger age (19.7) compared to white (21.2) and Hispanic women (20.1) according to the NSFG (see Jacobson and Harris, 1994). The Native American mean age for these two variables is close to the mean for African American women. Having sex and beginning childbearing at these younger ages probably account, in part, for the higher rates of childbearing among the Native American women. Unfortunately the census does not include these variables and we cannot include these variables in any examination of the census data.

Some women voluntarily choose to have no children, but the rate of voluntary childlessness is low and Native American women do not differ substantially from other American women in this regard (Jacobson, Heaton, and Taylor; 1988). Likewise, voluntary abortions may affect the number of children ever born, but Native American women do not appear to have substantially different rates of abortion than do African American, white American or Hispanic women. This was true in both the 1982 and 1988 cycles of the NSFG. Thus, differential rates of abortion are not likely to explain any differences in the fertility rates of Native American and other American women.

Some women have a harder time than others carrying a pregnancy to full term without spontaneously aborting or miscarrying. The proportion of Native American women who have had a spontaneous abortion or stillborn birth is roughly 50 percent higher than the other groups. Approximately 40 percent of the Native American women have miscarried or had a stillborn child compared to about a quarter of other American women (Jacobson and Harris, 1994). This difference is probably attributable to the poorer prenatal care and access to healthcare in general that Native Americans have. The effect of this variable, however, is to decrease the Native American fertility rate and bring it closer to that of other American women. Thus, it will not explain the higher rates of fertility for the Native American women.

Socioeconomic status may also be related, independent of education, to Native American fertility. Generally studies have found that people of lower socioeconomic status tend to have somewhat larger families (Snipp, 1989). Two measures of socioeconomic status will be included in the analysis of the 1990 census data: poverty status and annual family income.

Finally, Native Americans in rural areas have traditionally had larger families than those in urban areas and those living on or near reservations have higher rates than other Native Americans (Snipp, 1989). Although the PUMS data do not have information on reservation status of Native American women, they include information on whether they live in metropolitan or non-metropolitan areas and this variable will be included in the analysis of the 1990 PUMS data.

In summary, we can examine several variables as they affect Native American fertility. In the analysis which follows we will examine the effects on fertility of age, education, marital status, poverty status, family income, and metropolitan versus non-metropolitan area.

Table 2 presents the results of the analysis. All of the variables are significantly associated with Native American fertility, even when the others are controlled statistically. As might be expected, age and marital status are clearly the factors more closely associated with childbirth among Native American women. The Eta for each of these variables is quite high and remains high when the other variables are included in the analysis (the Betas). As we indicated earlier, age is a strong predictor of the number of children ever born for a number of reasons: the ideal number of children for earlier cohorts in the United States was higher, older women are more likely to have completed their childbearing, younger women are less likely to have started their family, and older women usually have less education which is also related to the number of children women have.

Marital status continues to have strong effects on childbearing. Though some Native American women have children out of wedlock, the rate does not seem to be increasing (see Table 1).

As expected, education has a suppressing effect on the number of children ever born for Native American women. And despite its association with age and marital status, education actually has a stronger effect when age and marital status are controlled statistically (Beta = .15 compared to .08 for the Eta). College graduates, on the average, are likely to have only about half as many children as Native American women with less than a high school education, and this is true when age and marital status, poverty status, income, and area location have been controlled statistically.

In the NSFG, the suppression effect of education on fertility was essentially the same for Native American women as for other American women (-.14 for the 1982 and 1988 surveys combined). Thus, for each year of education completed by both Native American and other American women, the number of children ever born decreases by about .14 (see Jacobson and Harris, 1994).

Family income was not strongly related to Native American fertility in the PUMS data (see Table 2), but poverty status was, even when income was controlled statistically. Those with lower incomes, and particularly those below the official poverty line were likely to have more children than other Native American women.

Why those below the poverty line are likely to have more children is not clear, but this result may have something to do with where they live. Those who live in non-metropolitan areas have slightly higher birth rates than those in metropolitan areas. Those on reservations have traditionally had higher birth rates (Snipp, 1989), but the metro, non-metro categories probably do not pick up all the variation from location. Thus, poverty status is significantly related to Native American fertility in these 1990 census data as is the metro-non-metro status.

Table 2

Mean Number of Children Ever Born to Native American
and Eskimo/Aleut Women,
Age 15-44, by selected Variables[1]

Variable	N	Mean No. of children	Eta	Adjusted for other variables	Beta
Age:			.51		.39**
15 to 24	1,965	0.55		0.82	
25 to 34	2,000	1.98		1.86	
35 to 44	1,652	2.59		2.41	
Marital Status:			.49		.33**
Never married	2,207	0.64		0.99	
Separated/wid/div	992	2.33		1.90	
Married	2,418	2.32		2.17	
Years Education Completed:			.08		.15**
Less than 12	2,006	1.58		1.91	
High school (12)	1,695	1.83		1.67	
Some college	1,601	1.66		1.48	
College grad. (16)	227	1.22		0.94	
More than 16	88	1.53		1.00	
Poverty Status:			.11		.17**
<50% official poverty level	927	1.91		2.15	
50% to 100% of pov. level	854	1.95		1.99	
Above poverty level	3,836	1.53		1.47	
Area:			.08		.07**
Metropolitan statistical area	2,722	1.53		1.53	
Non-metropolitan area	2,895	1.78		1.78	

Table 2 (continued)

Variable	N	Mean No. of children	Eta	Adjusted for other variables	Beta
Annual Family Income Levels:			.11		.04*
Less than $10,000	1,350	1.90		1.68	
$10,000 to $19,999	1,280	1.72		1.72	
$20,000 to $29,999	996	1.65		1.70	
$30,000 to $39,999	750	1.52		1.64	
$40,000 to $49,999	466	1.58		1.62	
$50,000 to $75,999	526	1.42		1.53	
$75,000+	249	1.19		1.47	
Grand mean = 1.66; R=.621; R^2=.386					

[1] Multiple Classification Analysis based on 1990 Census Public Use Microdata Samples.

* Beta significant at .05 level (computed on adjusted scores only).

**Beta significant at .01 level or higher.

CONCLUSION

Native American fertility has been declining over the past several decades and the last decade is no exception. From an analysis of census data, however, the decline appears to have stopped for younger cohorts. The only decline in the 1980s was for Native American women over the age of 35 and once they pass out of their childbearing years, Native American fertility may not decline further. Native American fertility is, however, lower than that of Hispanic or African American women (see Jacobson and Harris, 1994).

These higher fertility rates for Native American women also remain when the data from the NSFG were adjusted for several intervening variables that could affect the rate. Increased education usually suppresses childbearing and that is evident with these PUMS data.

Rates of sterility, frequency of abortion and percent of voluntary childlessness do not appear to affect Native American fertility any more than they do other groups. The rate of miscarriage and stillbirth is significantly higher for Native American women, indicating poorer health care may suppress the fertility rate. Early age at first sexual experience and first conception, on the other hand, probably increase the number of children born to Native American women.

If Native American women raise their educational levels close to those of white women, reduce their poverty status, and if they begin to postpone sexual intercourse and age at first conception, their fertility rates could well approach those of white American women. From the analysis done here, this does not appear to be happening at present, however, and is not likely to occur in the near future.

REFERENCES

Broudy, David W. and Phillip A. May. 1983. "Demographic and epidemiologic transition among the Navajo Indians." *Social Biology* 30:1-16.

Forrest, Jacqueline Darroch and Susheela Singh. 1990. "The sexual and reproductive behavior of American women, 1982-1988." *Family Planning Perspectives* 22:206-214.

Goldscheider, Calvin and William D. Mosher. 1991. "Patterns of contraceptive use in the United States: The importance of religious factors." *Studies in Family Planning* 22:102-115.

Jacobson, Cardell K. and Mark A. Harris. 1994. "Native American fertility: An analysis of data from the national surveys of family growth." *Family Perspectives* 27:485-492.

Jacobson, Cardell K., Tim B. Heaton, and Karen M. Taylor. 1988. "Childlessness among American women." *Social Biology* 35:186-197.

Miller, Brent C. and Tim B. Heaton. 1991. "Age at first sexual intercourse and the timing of marriage and childbirth." *Journal of Marriage and the Family* 53:719-732.

Mosher, William D. 1990. "Contraceptive practice in the United States, 1982-1988." *Family Planning Perspectives* 22:198-205.

Mosher, William D. and William F. Pratt. 1990. "Contraceptive use in the United States, 1973-88." *Advance Data from Vital and Health Statistics of the National Center for Health Statistics,* Number 182.

Snipp, C. Matthew. 1989. *American Indians: The First of This Land.* New York: Russell Sage.

Sweet, James A. 1974. "Differentials in the rate of fertility decline: 1960-1970." *Family Planning Perspectives* 6:103-107.

Thornton, Russell, Gary D. Sandefur, and Matthew C. Snipp. 1991. "American Indian fertility patterns: 1910 and 1940 to 1980." *The American Indian Quarterly* 15:359-367.

Trovato, Frank. 1981. "Canadian ethnic fertility." *Sociological Focus* 14:57-74.

_____. 1987. "A macrosociological analysis of Native Indian fertility in Canada: 1961, 1971, and 1981." *Social Forces* 66:463-485.

U.S. Department of Health and Human Services. 1990. *National Survey of Family Growth, Cycle IV, 1988.* Hyattsville, MD.

Patterns of Work and Family:
An Analysis of the Chinese American
Family Since the 1920s

Yan Yu

According to the 1990 census, 65.9 percent of Chinese Americans (16 years or older) were in the labor force, approximately 35.8 percent of them involved in managerial and professional occupations, and 31.2 percent in technical occupations (U.S. Bureau of the Census, 1993). The percentage of Chinese women's labor force participation in the United States was also high in 1990 when more than half of Chinese women (59.2%) worked for pay.

One may question the impact of higher labor-force participation upon family life of Chinese Americans. Does the Chinese American family continue to be "a stable family unit," with low rates of divorce and illegitimacy (Huang, 1981). Does it maintain "close ties between generations," with low rates of juvenile delinquency; "economic self-sufficiency"; and "conservatism" (Glenn, 1983)—a slow pace of cultural assimilation? Does Chinese women's labor force participation alter family power arrangements between husbands and wives? How do occupational patterns of Chinese Americans, both men and women, affect their family patterns?

In this chapter, the Chinese American family refers to the family after 1920; both parents and children live in the United States rather than in China. In other words, the Chinese sojourner family is not included in this paper (men who left their wives and children in China and worked to support their families in the United States). By family patterns, I refer to family economic well-being, family size, family relations (including husband-wife and parent-child relationships), family

functions, such as production, consumption, socialization, and education, and family residence.

The purpose of this paper is to examine the relationship between
work patterns and family organization among Chinese Americans after
1920 through reviewing sociological research. First, I focus on two
different perspectives in the explanation of the Chinese American
family. Second, I review the changes in occupational patterns of
Chinese Americans before and after the 1960s in the United States and
the resulting changes in family patterns due to different work patterns.
Finally, I show how the relationship between occupational patterns of
Chinese Americans and their family patterns is best explained through
a combination of structural and cultural perspectives.

CULTURAL AND STRUCTURAL PERSPECTIVES ON THE CHINESE AMERICAN FAMILY

The cultural perspective of the Chinese American family focuses
on the unique cultural and social characteristics which the Chinese
brought to the United States and the influence of these differences on
assimilation into American society (Li, 1977; Glenn, 1983). According
to this perspective, the Chinese were treated badly, regarded as
"strange, exotic and different," at their initial arrival in the United
States (Glenn, 1983). The 1882 laws excluded the Chinese from citizenship and prevented them from bringing over spouses and children.
Under such circumstances, family characteristics such as a stable unit,
close parent-child relationships, economic self-sufficiency, and the low
rates of divorce and juvenile delinquency are likely to be interpreted in
terms of specific aspects of traditional Chinese culture. The family in
Chinese culture is a very important unit, which focuses its energy on
the importance of raising male heirs to carry on the lineage (Pascoe,
1989), qualifies persons socially, and stabilizes the society. Parents may
sacrifice their individual happiness for the sake of a stable and intact
family. Divorce is disgraceful to the whole family kinship network.
Such factors may explain why the divorce rate among Chinese American families is low. Another aspect of Chinese culture concerns parental control over children, especially the father's control. Strict and
severe parental control over children might make Chinese children do-
cile and obedient to their parents, and this explains the low rate of
juvenile delinquency in the Chinese American family.

Glenn (1983) does not agree with this purely cultural analysis. She provides an alternative explanation for these characteristics of the Chinese American family. Low divorce rates are caused by the fact that "spouses are forced to stay together by the lack of economic options outside of family enterprises." Low delinquency rates may be caused by the lower number of adolescents in the whole Chinese population before the 1960s. In this setting, the local community is able to control adolescents (Glenn, 1983). Glenn (1983) clearly attempts to use structural perspectives to explain some characteristics of the Chinese American family, but her emphasis is on the change of family patterns among Chinese Americans rather than on a historical interplay of Chinese American occupational and family patterns. In this paper, I build on her structural explanation by providing evidence for the relationship between work and family patterns among Chinese Americans.

Because the Chinese American family lives in American society instead of in Chinese society, we must examine the social, political, and economic conditions of American society at the macro level and address their effects on the family patterns of Chinese Americans at the micro level. In light of my historical review, I argue that structural perspectives outweigh cultural perspectives in the explanation of the changes in the Chinese American family. Structural perspectives, however, interact with cultural perspectives, and the Chinese American family is constantly undergoing change in a culture that differs from traditional Chinese culture.

SMALL FAMILY BUSINESSES AMONG CHINESE AMERICANS

The 1960s were a turning point for Chinese Americans' work patterns. Between the 1920s and the 1960s, the dominant work pattern of both male and female Chinese Americans was to start with their own small family business and work without wages (M. Wong, 1988; Glenn, 1983; Huang, 1981; Bonacich, 1973). Participation in small, family-run businesses among early Chinese Americans was due to occupational restrictions caused by racial discrimination, the language barrier, and limited private capital (M. Wong, 1988; Glenn, 1983; Huang, 1981; King and Locke, 1980; Bonacich, 1973).

In the early period of Chinese immigration to the United States, Chinese immigrants were treated as scapegoats, due to "the heated economic competition with white railroad and mine workers, especially when Irish miners began to dominate the west coast" (Huang, 1981). Many Chinese immigrants, withdrawing from the competitive and discriminatory labor market, explored other occupations which other immigrants were not eager to perform. Ultimately, the Chinese were forced to confine their economic activities to certain less desirable fields of a noncompetitive nature, notably small family businesses, such as laundries, restaurants, groceries, and other small shops (King and Locke, 1980). Statistics supplied by the United States Census of 1940 showed that 84 percent of the gainfully employed Chinese in New York City were in restaurant or laundry work.

The 1960s were a period of turmoil for Americans, and they could be considered a turning point for Chinese Americans, both demographically and economically. The Chinese population in the United States increased rapidly after 1965; by 1980 it had overtaken the Japanese to become America's largest Asian population (Tsai, 1986). The phenomenal increase of the Chinese population between the 1960s and the 1980s owed to a combination of two factors. First, during his administration, President Kennedy invoked the provisions of existing legislation and permitted 15,000 Chinese to enter the United States as "parolees." Second, the 1965 Immigration Act eased restrictions on Chinese immigration. According to Immigration and Naturalization Service data, between 1965 and 1989, more than 850,000 Chinese immigrants entered the United States, and 54 percent entered between 1980 to 1990 (U.S. Bureau of the Census, 1993).

According to the 1990 census, over half of all Chinese (52.4 percent) in the United States still lived in the West; but, an increasing number had settled in the Northeast and the Midwest (35 percent). Only about 12 percent of Chinese resided in the South. The 1990 census also indicated that the Chinese population was primarily urban. They gathered in some major U.S. metropolitan cities, such as San Francisco, New York, Los Angeles, Chicago, and Seattle. This urban gathering provided them a very good business location and many potential customers.

Many immigrants after 1965 brought high skills and intellectual attainments (Chen, 1980), which were instrumental in many changes in the business establishment of the Chinese, and also among additional family members, who were potential laborers in the business. To control the admission of skilled or unskilled foreign workers, the 1965

Immigration Act instituted requirements for labor certification (Chen, 1980); the result was an increase in a new type of Chinese immigrants: men and women with high skills and educational attainments.

In addition, discrimination against Asian Americans weakened greatly, even though it did not cease. Many college-educated Chinese Americans were able to enter white-collar occupations and industries formerly barred to them. As a result, work patterns of Chinese Americans started to shift from family businesses to paid professional and technical jobs. In 1970, family-run laundries and food stores began to fade as traditional Chinese enterprises.

Some Chinese Americans, especially new immigrants (those who immigrated from China after 1965), still preferred to run family firms for the sake of flexibility, independence, and greater economic efficiency (B. Wong, 1987). Both the form and content of Chinese American family-run businesses, however, began to change. After the 1960s, family businesses are increasingly run by a core group of family members, with some outside employees, or by a core group composed of family members with a labor boss and his staff. The restaurant business, which used to be the dominant occupation for Chinese Americans before the 1960s, has become one of the basic components of Chinatown's enclave economy (Zhou, 1992).

Also, between 1920 and 1965, family businesses featured little separation between work and family life, because families lived and worked in the same establishment. After 1965, family businesses have had a clearer division between work and family life. Higher profits allow Chinese American business owners to buy houses that are separate from their workplace.

Participation in Paid Work

Currently, Chinese Americans are over-represented in three groups of occupations: engineering and technology, education at all levels, and health. The most spectacular increase had been in the professional and technical field, rising from 2.8 percent in 1940 (Sung, 1976) to 34 percent in 1990 (U.S. Bureau of the Census, 1993). Even though a lessening of inequality has allowed some Chinese Americans to move into the white-collar jobs, some now face barriers to promotion. Cabezas et al. (1989), in an empirical study of barriers to upward mobility for Asian Americans in the San Francisco Bay area, find that company-related barriers like shrinking opportunities for advancement and lack of education/training programs, racism, and language difficulty are serious barriers to upward mobility for the Chinese Americans.

On the other hand, many new immigrants who have a language handicap or no skills are generally forced to take low-paying jobs as dishwashers or janitors. Many are engaged in low-status blue-collar and service jobs (King and Locke, 1980; Tsai, 1986). According to the 1990 census, 20.3 percent of foreign-born Chinese Americans were engaged in service and labor, while only 13.5 percent of American-born Chinese were in the same occupations.

Chinese American Women in the Labor Force

The high rate of Chinese American women's participation in the labor force implies that Chinese American men's paychecks alone cannot support the whole family. Since many Chinese American men are working for average pay, or even low pay, Chinese American women are increasingly participating in the labor force; over half of them work outside the home. The 1980 census shows that a full 61 percent of those living with husbands were in the labor force (Amott and Matthaei, 1991). As Sung (1976) states, obtaining employment does not seem to be a difficulty for Chinese women; the problem is the type of job and the pay.

Tsai (1986) classifies Chinese American women's work as three types. The first type is low-paying work, which refers to the jobs in the garment industry of America's Chinatowns. Working conditions in most garment shops are very poor, lacking adequate fire exits, toilet facilities, and ventilation. A large number of women continue to work in their homes after the shops close for the day. The second type is high-paying work—professionals, such as professors, doctors, dentists, pharmacists, business managers, accountants, librarians, and lab researchers. During the past two decades, thousands of Chinese American women have completed higher degrees, which qualifies them for better-paying jobs.

According to Tsai (1986), however, the majority of Chinese American women, like the men, belong somewhere between these two types. In 1980, almost one-third of Chinese American women held college degrees, and almost one-third of employed Chinese American women held a managerial, administrative, or professional position.

However, positions and earnings are not always equivalent to the educational achievement. Chinese American women receive less monetary return for education than do whites (Amott and Matthaei, 1991). Chinese women are still subject to discrimination both as Chinese and as females.

I have described the transition of Chinese Americans' work, from unpaid small family business before the 1960s to paid professional and technical work and service after the 1960s. Does the transformation of work patterns among Chinese Americans, from unpaid to paid, affect their family patterns? The following section addresses the question of the impact of structural changes on the Chinese American family.

The Small-Producer Family

Two types of Chinese American families emerged from two types of work patterns of Chinese Americans: the small-producer family before the 1960s, and the dual-wage earner family after the 1960s (M. Wong, 1988; Glenn, 1983; Huang, 1981). In this section I focus on the family patterns associated with these work styles. I first examine the family pattern of the small-producer family before the 1960s.

The 1930 law allowed Chinese merchants to bring their wives to the United States; more and more wives of Chinese merchants reunited with their husbands, and a new type of family emerged during this period. This family type, the small producer family, consisted of the immigrant and first-born generation American-born family functioning as a unit of production (M. Wong, 1988; Glenn, 1983). All family members, including children, worked without wages in small family businesses such as laundries, restaurants, and grocery stores.

The family was closely connected with business; the family was the unit of production; and the family's living quarters were located above or behind the shop. In this way, the workplace and home were geographically combined. Taking advantage of the combination of work place and living place, Chinese American family members worked extremely long hours every day, even on holidays, so that the business could be profitable.

In this type of family, both the husband-wife and parent-child relationships tended to become more equal than in traditional Chinese family relationships (B. Wong, 1988; M. Wong, 1988; Glenn, 1983). Because wives worked as hard as their husbands in family businesses, husbands were no longer expected to be the only decision-maker for the family. Instead, men were expected to consult with their wives on major decisions.

Parent-child relationships in this type of family were very close. Because working place and living place were combined, children had close contact with their parents. Parents in the small-producer family emphasized their children's education as much as in the traditional Chinese family. Thus children occupied their time by working with their parents, studying, and taking care of younger siblings.

Unlike the traditional type of the small-producer family, the new small-producer family after 1965 is characterized by a separation between work and family life; the work setting is segmented from the living quarters. Children usually are no longer involved in their parents' work but are cared for by nannies. Children in these families are likely to have less time with their parents at home; furthermore, the lack of communication between parents and children is becoming a problem in this type of small-producer family.

The Dual-Earner Family

The second type of the Chinese American family, the dual-wage-earner family, can be further divided into two types: the ghetto Chinese American family, and the professional Chinese American family (M. Wong, 1988; Glenn, 1983). In the ghetto Chinese American family, work and family tend to be separate from each other. The parent-child relationship is not as close as it used to be in the small-producer family before the 1960s. Parents do not have as much time with their children as in the past because of different jobs and job schedules—one parent may have a regular shift (i.e., sweatshop), and the other parent the swing shift (i.e., restaurant). M. Wong (1988) vividly described the life-style of this type of family:

> *Penetrate, if you can, into the crowded tenements, and you will find families of four, five, and six living, working, playing, and sleeping in a single room. Pots, pans, and food must be taken to a community kitchen shared with other families. Privacy is a sometime thing. These facts speak for themselves: for all its gaiety, good humor, and indomitable spirit, this area suffers from wide-spread poverty, high unemployment, sub-*

standard and overcrowded housing, inferior public services
and facilities, and resulting grave health problems. (p. 248)

Clearly, high unemployment and low-paid work make it difficult for Chinese Americans to move out of Chinatown. Under such circumstances, the absence of a close-knit family life and the bad social conditions of Chinatown are blamed for the high rate of crime and juvenile delinquency during the 1960s and 1970s (Glenn, 1983).

The professional Chinese American family, on the other hand, tends to live in white neighborhoods and to have little connection with Chinatown. Although 30,000 Chinese Americans are still engaged in the family-run restaurant business, they are able to separate their working place from their living place and buy houses in good neighborhoods (Sung, 1976). For example, in Los Angeles, many wealthy Chinese American professionals and businessmen live in America's first suburban Chinatown, Monterey Park. In 1960 it was occupied by 85 percent whites and only 3 percent Asians (Takaki, 1989). By 1988, 50 percent of the 61,000 residents in Monterey Park were Chinese Americans, most of them from Hong Kong and Taiwan. It came to be called "Little Taipei," and sometimes "Chinese Beverly Hills."

In the professional Chinese American family, both husbands and wives work for pay. Commonly, when the children start off to school, the mothers start off to work. In this type of family, a mother needs to strive for marriage, family, and career on a more equitable basis.

In order to meet these challenges, many Chinese American women marry at a later age. In 1970, 68.6 percent of women aged 20 to 24 years were single, compared to only 36 percent of white American women (Sung, 1976). An astonishingly large proportion of Chinese women maintained their single status until they reached age 30 or older. Chinese American women also try to meet challenges by postponing children. According to Sung (1976), 45.9 percent of married Chinese women at ages 20 to 24 had no children at all in 1970. At the age of 25 to 29, almost one-third were still childless, whereas the same percentage of white females already had two children in 1970. Thus, the professional Chinese American family size is smaller than the traditional Chinese family size, and is becoming still smaller (Sung, 1976). Clearly, the traditional Chinese cultural preference for a big family and early marriage can be weakened and influenced by the family's economic conditions.

With regard to husband-wife relationships in the professional Chinese American family, M. Wong (1988) believes:

> . . . *the economic position of the husband and wife as co-breadwinners and/or their high socioeconomic position lends itself to a mutual sharing of responsibility and authority in the decision making of most aspects of family life, although the wife usually assumes the role of helper rather than equal partner* (p. 249).

Thus the high rate of Chinese American women's participation in the labor force does not necessarily change the power distribution between husbands and wives. Although many Chinese American women work for pay outside the home, they are still regarded as a *helper* of their husband rather than an *equal partner* with their husband (M. Wong, 1988).

I attribute this unequal power distribution between husbands and wives to two main reasons, which interact. Structurally, most Chinese American women are engaged in lower-paying work than Chinese American men (Woo, 1985). As a result, women's paychecks can only *help* the economic well-being of the family. Women's income is not the major financial resource of the family. Clearly, women's low earning power determines their low position in the family.

Culturally, traditional Chinese family ideology is still reflected in the power distribution between husbands and wives. According to traditional family ideology, men are supposed to support the whole family and have power over women, whereas women are responsible for bearing children and caring for all family members. This ideology does not fade at their departure from mainland China. It is still seen in the modern Chinese American family.

The parent-child relationships in professional Chinese American families are emotionally closer than in ghetto families, even though they are not as close as in the small producer family. To most Chinese, family education means discipline by the father. They believe that the father, as a disciplinarian figure, should constantly "watch over" his children, especially preteenagers and teenagers, if he wants his children to turn out well. Even though both parents work outside the home, they intend to find time to talk to their children. The quantity of time spent with children in the professional family is probably less than in the small producer family, but its quality can be higher, since parents and children are both busy working in the small producer family and hardly have time to talk to each other.

Education and Family

Parents in the small producer family are very interested in providing a college education for their children, and at the same time transmitting Chinese culture and values to them. Sanchirico (1991) researches a sample of Chinese residing in Washington, D.C. He finds that families in small businesses transmit high aspirations to the next generation, thereby promoting their offspring's educational achievement. He admits the importance of traditional values in promoting Chinese Americans' educational attainment, but he suggests that participation in small businesses has been an especially important channel of intergenerational educational mobility among Chinese Americans.

Children's education is also emphasized in the professional Chinese American family. On the one hand, parents believe that in order to stay in the United States permanently and comfortably, education is a very important way to mobilize upward, economically and socially. On the other hand, education has always been stressed in traditional Chinese culture. Successful children are the Chinese parents' dream. For these reasons, Chinese American parents often work hard and live frugally. They make it known to children that education will determine economic well-being.

SUMMARY AND CONCLUSION

The 1960s mark a transition in both the work patterns and family patterns of Chinese Americans. Before the 1960s, the occupational patterns of Chinese Americans were mainly unpaid family-run business, due to racial discrimination, language limits, and less capital. After the 1960s racial discrimination against Asian Americans has weakened, thanks to the Civil Rights Movement and Affirmative Action, more and more educated Chinese Americans are able to find average or even high-paying jobs. As a consequence, the work patterns of Chinese Americans have changed from unpaid to paid. Accordingly, their family patterns are changing quickly.

Before the 1960s, the dominant family type of the Chinese American was the small-producer family, the product of the small family-run business. After the 1960s, the dominant family type of Chinese Americans switched to the dual-wage earner family, the product of the shift of work patterns from unpaid to paid. Along with the development of family types among Chinese Americans, family relationships, family functions and family economic well-being have changed greatly.

My analyses have shown that family patterns of Chinese Americans at the micro level may reflect work patterns at the macro level in American society. Work patterns influence many aspects of the Chinese American family, including family income, family size, family residence, family functions and family relationships since the 1920s. Evidence has shown that the purely cultural analysis is not adequate to explain the changes in family patterns. The combination of cultural and structural perspectives is necessary to fully understand the Chinese American family.

With the enactment of the Chinese Student Protection Act of 1992 (Public Law No. 102-404),[1] which allowed over 70,000 Chinese students, including their families, to obtain permanent residence in the United States in June 1993, the patterns of the Chinese American family will likely continue to change in response to the macro-level changes. The future of the Chinese American family will continue to evolve, develop, and adapt structurally and culturally in American society.

NOTE

[1] According to the Independent Federation of Chinese Students and Scholars, the Chinese Student Protection Act of 1992 (Act S1216) was officially passed by President Bush in 1993. Since then, this act has become Public Law No. 102-404.

REFERENCES

Amott, Teresa L. and Julie A. Matthaei. 1991. *Race, Gender, and Work: A Multicultural Economic History of Women in the United States*. Boston: South End Press.

Bonacich, Edna. 1973. "A theory of middleman minorities." *American Sociological Review* 38:583-594.

_____. 1972. "A theory of ethnic antagonism: The split labor market." *American Sociological Review* 37:547-559.

Cabezas, Amado, Tse Ming Tam, Brenda M. Lowe, Anna S. Wong, and Kathy Turner. 1989. "Empirical study of barriers to upward mobility for Asian Americans in the San Francisco Bay area." In G.M. Nomura, R. Endo, S.H. Sumida, and R.C. Leong (eds.), *Frontiers of Asian American Studies: Writing, Research, and Commentary*. Washington: Washington State University Press.

Chen, Jack. 1980. *The Chinese of America*. San Francisco: Harper & Row, Publishers.

Glenn, Evelyn Nakano. 1983. "Split household, small producer and dual wage earner: An analysis of Chinese-American family strategies." *Journal of Marriage and the Family* 45:35-46.

Huang, Lucy Jen. 1981. "The Chinese American family." Pp. 115-141 in C. Mindel and R. Habenstein (eds.), *Ethnic Families in America*. New York: Elsevier.

King, Haitung and Frances B. Locke. 1980. "Chinese in the United States: A century of occupational transition." *International Migration Review* 14:15-42.

Li, Peter S. 1977. "Fictive kinship, conjugal tie and kinship chain among Chinese immigrants in the United States." *Journal of Comparative Family Studies* 8:47-63.

Pascoe, Peggy. 1989. "Gender systems in conflict: The marriages of mission-educated Chinese American women, 1874-1939." *Journal of Social History* 22:631-652.

Sanchirico, Andrew. 1991. "The importance of small-business ownership in Chinese American educational achievement." *Sociology of Education* 64:293-304.

Sung, Betty Lee. 1976. *A Survey of Chinese-American Manpower and Employment.* New York: Praeger Publishers.

Takaki, Ronald. 1989. *1939—Strangers From a Different Shore: A History of Asian Americans.* Canada: Little, Brown Company Limited.

Tsai, Shih-Shan Henry. 1986. *The Chinese Experience in America.* Bloomington and Indianapolis: Indiana University Press.

U.S. Bureau of the Census. 1993. *We the American. . . Asians.* U.S. Department of Commerce: Economics and Statistics Administration.

Wong, Bernard. 1988. *Patronage, Brokerage, Entrepreneurship and the Chinese Community of New York.* New York: AMS Press.

_____. 1987. "The Chinese: New immigrants in New York's Chinatown." In N. Foner (ed.), *New Immigrants in New York.* New York: Columbia University Press.

Wong, Morrison G. 1988. "The Chinese American family." Pp. 230-257 in C. Mindel, R.W. Habenstein, and R. Wright, Jr. (eds.), *Ethnic Families in America.* New York: Elsevier.

Woo, Deborah. 1985. "The socioeconomic status of Asian American women in the labor force." *Sociological Perspectives* 28:307-338.

Zhou, Min. 1992. *Chinatown.* Philadelphia: Temple University Press.

Japanese American Families:
Assimilation over Time

Trina L. Hope and Cardell K. Jacobson

When discussing racial and ethnic groups in America, Asians, especially Japanese Americans, are often noted as exceptional due to their educational, occupational, and financial success. Japanese Americans are often touted as the ideal minority group, showing *"reverence for hard work, achievement, self-control, dependability, manners, thrift, and diligence. . . entirely congruent with American middle class perceptions"* (Kitano, 1976:52). Like other minority groups, however, Japanese faced a history of prejudice, discrimination, and, most noteworthy, internment. This chapter will briefly discuss the history of Japanese immigration to the United States and the evacuation of Japanese Americans during World War II. The main focus of the chapter will be an exploration of assimilation of Japanese Americans using education, occupation, income, and other measures of structural assimilation.

IMMIGRATION

Most early Japanese immigrants (Issei) came from the farming class in Japan, which was the Japanese equivalent of America's middle class. Most had at least eight years of formal schooling, and a respect for the benefits and importance of education. In the early 1880s, there were fewer than 150 Japanese in America, most of whom were students who would return to Japan. Further immigration of young Japanese males to Hawaii and the West Coast began in 1885. From 1890 to 1900 about 22,000 Japanese immigrated to the United States, primarily to California. As Kitano (1976) notes, the timing was not good for Japanese; they were in *"the wrong country, the wrong state, [at] the wrong time"* (p. 15). Anti-Asian sentiment was strong, and California had just solved its "Chinese Problem" by passing anti-Chinese legislation. The hostility towards the Chinese, who had emigrated earlier, was transferred to the Japanese immigrants.

Early Japanese immigrants were barred from many jobs in urban settings and were forced to concentrate in industries like canning, mining, logging, railroad, and agriculture. Since most of the Issei had come from farming families in Japan, it was not surprising that many gravitated towards agriculture. These immigrants experienced some success due to the unity and cohesion of the Japanese community, which enabled them to pool money and resources. As Kitano (1976) stated, the relative success of these new immigrants did not go unnoticed by the majority population, and beginning in 1913, a series of anti-Japanese laws were passed.

In 1913 a California Alien Land Bill, the Webb-Heney Bill, was passed. This bill attempted to drive Japanese out of agriculture by limiting to three years the amount of time Japanese could lease land. It also stipulated that lands already owned or leased could not be bequeathed to subsequent generations. In spite of the Webb-Heney Bill and similar laws, Japanese immigration continued. Between 1910 and 1920, 20,000 immigrants came to the U.S., providing much-needed agricultural labor during WWI. As with any surplus labor source, however, when the war was over and Americans returned looking for work, anti-Japanese sentiments also returned. In 1920, the amended Alien Law deprived Japanese of the right to lease agricultural land. Furthermore, they were ineligible for permanent citizenship, were forbidden the use or ownership of power engines, and forbidden from hiring white girls as employees. Japanese inheritance of land was made illegal and the standard fishing license fee was raised from $10 to $100 a year for Asians. Alien Land Laws also prohibited Issei from owning land.

In 1908, the United States and Japan came to a "Gentleman's Agreement," in which Japan agreed to stop emigration and the United States agreed to ease harsh treatment of Japanese already here. Between 1908 and 1924 Japanese immigration slowed, and in 1924 national immigration laws established quotas for various countries; Japan's quota was zero. Immigration from Japan between 1924 and 1962 essentially stopped. Hostility towards Japanese immigrants came to a dramatic head following Japan's attack on Pearl Harbor.

EVACUATION

Immediately following the attack on Pearl Harbor, 2,192 Japanese were rounded up and arrested by the FBI. With the exception of some Quaker groups and the ACLU, no groups publicly opposed the treatment of the Japanese. In January of 1942, the first of a series of orders by U.S. Attorney General Francis Biddle established areas along the Pacific Coast requiring removal of all enemy aliens from these areas. On Feb 19, 1942, President Roosevelt signed Executive Order 9066 which (1) designated military areas where military commanders could exclude persons, and (2) authorized the building of "relocation" camps to house those affected (Kitano, 1976:72). The result was the in-ternment of more than 100,000 Japanese—both citizens and aliens— from the West Coast. More than 110,000 of the 126,000 Japanese in the United States were evacuated, including those with as little as one-eighth Japanese heritage. Two-thirds were United States citizens. They were relocated to California, Arizona, Idaho, Wyoming, Colorado, Utah, and Arkansas, giving up their homes, businesses, and lives as Americans to live in camps surrounded by barbed wire and guarded by armed Military Police.

Most Japanese cooperated with the evacuation, and only 2,300 of the evacuees requested that they be sent to Japan. In December of 1944, the Supreme Court ruled that detention of United States citizens was unlawful, and on January 2, 1945 the commander of the War Relocation Authority announced the revocation of the West Coast exclusion. The camps closed by the end of 1945 and termination of the program occurred by June of 1946. Most of the Japanese returned to the West Coast following internment, and attempted to put their lives back together. In spite of this history of discrimination and internment, Japanese Americans have emerged as one of the most successful minority groups in the United States.

ASSIMILATION OF JAPANESE AMERICANS

Assimilation and its relation to ethnicity can be examined in several ways. For purposes of this paper, we shall focus on structural assimilation. Structural assimilation links ethnicity to economic and political relationships (see Fendrich, 1983; Hechter, 1975, 1978; Bonacich and Modell, 1980). From this approach, the more minority groups resemble the majority in terms of economic and political life, the more assimilated the group is. As Fugita and O'Brien (1991) discuss, theorists in this perspective also argue that "*as ethnic group members assimilate and become more dispersed throughout the organizational and institutional structures of society, they will be less likely to have common class interests and therefore be less cohesive in their ethnicity*" (p. 20).

A perspective that challenges this idea of a zero-sum relationship between structural assimilation and the retention of ethnicity is the Emergent Ethnicity perspective (Handlin, 1951; Reitz, 1980). This theory rests on the idea that ethnicity and ethnic identification change in response to changing structural conditions. Fugita and O'Brien (1991) argue that there are important cultural elements in the persistence of ethnicity. For Japanese Americans, involvement in the Japanese American community persists despite high levels of structural assimilation. Fugita and O'Brien conclude that structural assimilation does not always result in the destruction of group cohesiveness. Though loss of cohesiveness was true of many European immigrants, Japanese immigrants came "*with a sense of peoplehood and experience[d] non familial social organization. . . [giving them] a distinct advantage over groups that were principally familistic and village-oriented*" (Fugita and O'Brien, 1991:182). Levine and Rhodes (1981) also argue that community still exists among Japanese Americans.

Japanese Americans have names for each generation. Issei are the first generation, who immigrated from Japan, followed by the Nisei, Sansei, and Yonsei. Research shows each generation becoming more assimilated into American culture. Most Sansei, for instance, do not read or speak Japanese but have an interest in their ethnicity (Levine and Rhodes, 1981). Succeeding generations show a trend toward more assimilation. For our analysis, we will focus on measures of structural assimilation and will review the trends over time using 1990 census data.

MEASURES OF STRUCTURAL ASSIMILATION

Education

The primary avenue to success for upwardly mobile minority groups is education. Japanese immigrants came to America with a cultural orientation that valued education. Levine and Rhodes' study of

Nisei in the 1970s showed that 57 percent of them had more than a high school education, compared to 20 percent of all Americans. The 1980 census data showed 96 percent of Japanese Americans age 25-29 had graduated from high school. Eighty-eight percent of Japanese American males and 82.5 percent of Japanese American females aged 45-54 had graduated from high school. These percentages are higher than those of whites, blacks, or Hispanics, and the highest among all Asian groups aged 25-29. By 1990, over 44 percent of married Japanese American males were college graduates.

Occupation

Data from a three-generational study of Japanese Americans by the Japanese American Research Project (JARP) at UCLA show that the first generation Issei were concentrated primarily in agriculture (45 percent). Another 28 percent were managerial/proprietors in mostly ethnic businesses (Levine and Rhodes, 1981). With each generation, Japanese Americans have moved out of agriculture into the professional occupations. In the JARP sample, Rhodes and Levine found 5 percent of Issei, and 33 percent of Nisei to be professionals, and three-fourths of Sansei were aspiring to professional occupations (half already were professionals). By 1960, the percentage of Japanese Americans in professional occupations equaled that of whites (15 percent). In 1980 census data, 28 percent of Japanese Americans were in professional, technical, or managerial occupations. Comparable percentages for whites and blacks were 24 percent and 14 percent respectively.

Earnings Income

Since Japanese Americans attain high levels of education and are well represented in the professions, their incomes should reflect this success. In 1980, the median earnings of a full-time Japanese American worker was $16,829, with 4.2 percent of families below the poverty level (compared to $15,572 and 7 percent for whites, and $11,327 and 26.5 percent for blacks). As with occupation and education, Japanese Americans' earnings exceed those of whites and blacks. Some research, however, has suggested that in spite of their high levels of education, Japanese Americans get less return in terms of earnings for their education (Wong, 1974).

Other measures of structural assimilation include outmarriage and region of country. Each successive generation of Japanese Americans has outmarried at higher rates. In 1972, Levine and Rhodes found that 50 percent of Sansei were marrying non-Japanese, and they predict that the overall exogamy rate for Sansei may reach 60 percent. Living outside California or Hawaii is also seen as another measure of assimilation, since these two states comprise 37.5 and 33.5 percent of Japanese Americans, respectively (1980 census).

A last issue we can address is the relationship between some of these variables and integration. Levine and Rhodes found that Japanese Americans who were younger, more successful in terms of education, occupation, and income, and living in areas of less Japanese American concentration, were more integrated into American culture and less involved in the Japanese American community. It is ironic that those "good Japanese" who work hard, sacrifice, and create bright futures for their children are those who produce the most integrated offspring. Those Issei with the most education were best able to prepare their children for American life. This process has continued with each generation. As Levine and Rhodes (1981) assert, *"the transformation of the Japanese American community into one with fewer and fewer effective normative constraints could already have been forecast before the Issei set sail from Japan"* (p. 142).

In the remainder of this chapter we update these trends using the Public Use Microdata Samples of the 1990 census. Our data focus on married men and women.

RESULTS

Education

Consistent with past data, 1990 census data show Japanese Americans to be a highly educated group. Ninety percent of Japanese American married men and 89 percent of Japanese American married women have graduated from high school. This compares to the national averages of 77 and 80 percent. The educational achievements are more dramatic for college graduation. Forty-four percent of Japanese American husbands and 28.3 percent of Japanese American wives have at least a college degree, compared to the national averages of 24.5 and

18.6 percent. These numbers are comparable to the 1980 educational levels for Japanese Americans.

Earnings Income

Since Japanese Americans are highly educated, we would expect high levels of education to translate to professional occupations and high income levels. The PUMS data do not include a precise measure of occupation, but we can examine earnings. In 1990, the average annual earnings for husbands was $32,673. For whites, the average was $34,478, and Japanese American husbands earned $43,493. We also conducted a multiple classification analysis (see panel 1 of Table 1) to adjust income for education, age, and ability to speak English. This allows us to explore whether Japanese Americans receive less of a return in earnings from their education than other groups do. The highest amount of variance in income is explained by education. The means in the adjusted column show the earnings of Japanese Americans when the effects of the independent variables have been controlled. Even when controlling for these three variables, Japanese American husbands earn $6,023 more a year than the average American. Whites earn $924 more and blacks earn $7,238 less a year. In other words, education, age, and English proficiency explain some of the differences between earnings for Japanese Americans, but they do not explain it all. Perhaps Japanese American husbands are in occupations that pay better, or they may work more hours. But these 1990 data do not show evidence that they are getting less return for their education than whites do.

The results for the married women in the PUMS data are also interesting (see panel 2 of Table 1). The results are for all married women, and many may not work. Many likely also work only part time. The overall mean yearly earnings for married women in 1990 was $11,777 a year. White married women earned $11,913, black wives $12,848, and Japanese American wives $13,710. When these figures are adjusted for education, age, and English ability, the yearly earnings of white women actually drop $131 below the mean, black women's increase $1,428, and Japanese Americans' increase by $1,357. The earnings of white women drop due to their likelihood of being more educated, but not working.

Table 1

Total Earnings Income of Japanese American
and Black and White American
Married Men and Women, 1990

	Mean	Adjusted Mean*
Married Men		
Japanese Americans	$43,493	$38,695
White Americans	34,478	33,597
Black Americans	22,128	25,435
Married Women		
Japanese Americans	$13,710	$13,134
White Americans	11,913	11,646
Black Americans	12,848	13,205

*Based on multiple classification analysis of 1% of Public Use Micro-
data sample of the United States census. Adjusted means were adjusted
on the basis of education completed, age (in decades) and English-
speaking ability. All other ethnic groups were included in the analysis,
but data are not presented for them.

The last issue we can explore in terms of earnings is change over
time. Table 2 shows the same multiple classification analyses performed
on 1980 census data that has been adjusted for changes in the cost of
living between 1980 and 1990. These data allow us to compare earnings of married people in 1980 to those in 1990, once inflation has been
taken into account. Panel 1 of Table 2 shows the multiple classification
analysis for husbands, and panel 2 shows a similar analysis for the
married women. The 1980 patterns look much like those from 1990.
Japanese American husbands earned a mean income of $33,286 in
1980, compared to $24,489 for whites and $18,287 for blacks. All
three groups improved their incomes from 1980 to 1990, but the more
the group made in 1980, the more they improved over the 10 years.

Japanese Americans' mean earnings increased by $10,207, whites' by $6,989, and blacks' by $3,841. Additionally, the gap between Japanese American husbands and white and black husbands increased. The gap between Japanese American and white American males increased from $5,797 to $9,015 a year, and the gap between Japanese American and black American husbands increased from $14,999 to $21,365 a year. Not only did Japanese American husbands make more money than blacks or whites in both 1980 and 1990, they made the most improvement. Furthermore, when the independent variables were controlled, Japanese American husbands still earned more than their white or black counterparts.

Table 2

Total Earnings Income of Japanese American
and Black and White American
Married Men and Women, 1980 in 1990 dollars

	Mean	Adjusted Mean*
Married Men		
Japanese Americans	$33,286	$30,403
White Americans	27,489	25,778
Black Americans	18,287	18,959
Married Women		
Japanese Americans	$9,956	*8,748
White Americans	7,130	6,723
Black Americans	8,767	8,853

*Based on multiple classification analysis of 1% of Public Use Microdata sample of the United States census. Adjusted means were adjusted on the basis of education completed, age (in decades) and English-speaking ability. All other ethnic groups were included in the analysis, but data are not presented for them.

The 1980 patterns for wives are also similar to 1990. Japanese American wives earn the most ($9,956), followed by black wives ($8,767), and white wives ($7,130). Also, like 1990, the adjusted earnings reduce the mean for white wives, and increase the means for black and Japanese American wives. The unadjusted means show that all three groups of women improved their earnings, but the differences are not nearly as dramatic as those found with the husband data. Japanese American wives improved $4,962, white American women $4,783, and black American women $4,081. Unlike the pattern with the husbands, the disparity between the groups for wives actually declined from 1980 to 1990.

Overall, our analyses of earnings show that in both 1980 and 1990, Japanese American husbands had higher average earnings than white or black husbands, and they improved more than whites or blacks over the ten-year period. Finally, they showed no evidence that their returns for education are any less than those of whites. The earnings for married women of all three groups are considerably lower than their husbands'. Black and Japanese American wives have higher incomes than white wives, and these trends have remained steady over the ten-year period. These data, however, do not present a picture of women as a whole, since they are from wives only, who are less likely than other women to be employed full time.

Region of Country/Outmarriage

The last two variables we can examine are region of country and rates of outmarriage. Research suggests that Japanese Americans who live outside of California or Hawaii are more likely to marry non-Japanese. The percentage of Japanese Americans living in California increased by one percent during the 1980s, but fewer were living in Hawaii (from 36 to 30 percent) at the end of the decade. Thus, the percentage of Japanese Americans living in states other than California or Hawaii increased from 28 to 33 percent. This increase of Japanese Americans in "other" states is an indicator of more assimilation.

The outmarriage rates for Japanese Americans also show some important trends. These trends are shown in Table 3. First, Japanese American women outmarry at higher rates than do Japanese American men. Second, the higher proportion of a state's population that Japanese Americans are, the more likely they are to marry other Japanese

Americans. Hawaii has the highest rate of homogamous marriages and the "other" states have the lowest rate. The number who outmarry is much larger in California and "other" states than it is in Hawaii. A third trend is that, with the exception of women in "other" states, all groups have higher rates of outmarriage in 1990 than they did in 1980. Overall, these marriage data suggest that Japanese Americans are becoming more assimilated.

Table 3

Outmarriage Dates of Japanese Americans
by State in 1980 and 1990

| State | Japanese Americans Percentage of State | | Percent Outmarriage Rate | | | |
| | | | Men | | Women | |
	1980	1990	1980	1990	1980	1990
California	3.9	1.5	15.6	25.9	36.6	42.7
Hawaii	39.9	27.8	14.1	15.9	18.7	21.8
All other states	0.7	0.2	32.6	35.5	66.0	61.4

Source: 1% Public Use Microdata Sample, 1990 U.S. Census.

CONCLUSION

Our analysis of Japanese American husbands and wives shows that trends toward assimilation are continuing. Married Japanese Americans have remained a highly educated group, have made increases in their mean income levels compared to whites and blacks, and Japanese American husbands have remained the ethnic group with one of the highest mean earnings. Most Japanese Americans still live in California and Hawaii, but more are moving to other states, and marrying non-Japanese at greater rates than in the past. Married Japanese

Americans are a highly educated, successful group that continues to show movement toward more structural assimilation.

REFERENCES

Bonacich, Edna and John Modell. 1980. *The Economic Basis of Ethnic Solidarity: Small Businesses in the Japanese American Community.* Berkeley: University of California Press.

Fendrich, James Max. 1983. "Race and ethnic relations: The elite policy response in capitalist societies." *American Behavioral Scientist* 26:757-772.

Fugita, Stephen S. and David J. O'Brien. 1991. *Japanese American Ethnicity: The Persistence of Community.* Seattle: University of Washington Press.

Handlin, Oscar. 1951. *The Uprooted.* New York: Grosset and Dunlap.

Hechter, Michael. 1975. *Internal Colonialism: The Celtic Fringe in British National Development, 1936-1966.* Berkeley: University of California Press.

_____. 1978. "Group formation and the cultural division of labor." *American Journal of Sociology* 84:293-318.

Kitano, Harry L. 1976. *Japanese Americans: The Evolution of a Subculture.* Englewood Cliffs, NJ: Prentice-Hall.

Levine, Gene N. and Colbert Rhodes. 1981. *The Japanese American Community.* New York: Praeger Publishers.

Reitz, Jeffrey G. 1980. *The Survival of Ethnic Groups.* Toronto: McGraw-Hill Ryerson Limited.

Wong, Harold H. 1974. *The Relative Economic Status of Chinese, Japanese, Black and White Men in California.* Ph.D. dissertation, University of California, Berkeley.

Family Resemblance? How New Asian Immigrants Compare with the "Model Minority"

Carolyn G. Jew

INTRODUCTION

Although Asian immigrants date back to the nineteenth century, they have long been ignored as a logical topic of study. Their presence in America was considered temporary, insignificant, and unworthy of attention. First, immigrants in general were assumed to eventually assimilate and distinctions would eventually disappear into the "melting pot." Second, they were too "different" and minuscule to be considered a part of migration studies, once migration gained legitimacy. Not until the early 1900's were notable works on Asians published (Hune, 1977).

Since then, Asian Americans have become an important part of the study of race relations in the United States. As one of the most prominent minorities to have rapidly assimilated into mainstream American society, they are extensively studied as the leading example of ethnic group success (Jiobu, 1988). Despite severe discrimination and prejudice, including riot and mass murders as well as legal means of exclusion and oppression (Hraba, 1994; Marger, 1994), this ethnic group has achieved remarkable success in American society. Overall, Asian Americans tend to rank higher than most other ethnic groups on measures of SES. They even surpass the dominant white group in income, occupational prestige, and level of education (Jiobu, 1988; Hirschman and Wong, 1986; Marger, 1994). To some degree, this can be attributed to both corporate and entrepreneurial success (Marger, 1994). Furthermore, their rates of intermarriage, particularly for the

157

Japanese, show further integration and social acceptance than most other ethnic groups (Jiobu, 1988; Marger, 1994).

However, notwithstanding this attention, white America perceives Asians as a single, homogenous group. Such a designation represents the type of "we-they" categorizing (Ringer and Lawless, 1989) which obscures substantial variation. Until just recently, most quantitative demographic comparisons have combined Chinese, Japanese, Korean, Filipino, Cambodian, Vietnamese, Hmong, Burmese, Sri Lankan, Polynesians, Malaysians, and Asian Indians into a single group. These studies ignore that each group has significantly unique histories, legal and structural and political constraints, values, cultures, languages, immigration experiences, physical and intangible resources. All are important factors in producing distinctively different economic, political, and social consequences for each Asian ethnic group.

Table 1

1990 Asian American Populations

Filipinos	1,400,000
Chinese	1,260,000
Vietnamese	859,000
Koreans	814,000
Japanese	804,000
Asian Indians	684,000
Other: Cambodian, Laotian, and Pacific Islander	706,000
TOTAL	6,527,000

Source: Butterfield, *New York Times*, Feb. 24, 1991.

Since the 1965 Immigration Act supporting family reunification, a comparatively large influx of new Asian immigrants has arrived in America. Because of tremendous growth of the Asian population (about seven times faster than the general population), and particularly the presence of new groups, data are finally being collected on each group as distinct ethnicities. These data provide answers to such questions as: How are new Asian immigrants similar to and different from the Chinese and Japanese, who have achieved such remarkable gains? Do they follow in their footsteps of successful assimilation? Are they finding a new path? Are they struggling like many other ethnic groups?

Studies by Hirschman & Wong (1986), Hune (1977), and Model (1988) shed light on the reasons for Asian economic and educational success. Ortiz (1994) is able to introduce Filipino, Asian Indian, and Vietnamese demographics to the comparisons of female minorities. Chow (1994) examines working Asian American women in the Washington, D.C., metropolitan area. This paper is an extension of their analyses. Using the most recent data available, Asian ethnic groups are compared by variables that indicate the level of assimilation achieved. New Asian groups formerly combined under a single "East Asian" category were separated out and also examined. This provided new quantitative comparisons and insights that were previously unknown.

HISTORICAL AND SOCIO-POLITICAL REASONS FOR IMMIGRATION

Contemporary efforts toward cultural pluralism have eased some tensions. However, immigrant groups and ethnic minorities must still enter an already existing social, political, and economic structure (i.e., public schools, legal system, job market, government) and find their niche. Much of their success depends on the resources they have at their disposal. The national and world economies at the time of their immigration also help determine the context in which they enter the American scene. As a whole, Asian Americans today encounter similar difficulties of prejudice and discrimination. Beyond this basic commonality of struggle, however, there are extensive disparities. They have dissimilar historical and legal constraints, resources and backgrounds, that become visible when comparing demographic outcomes.

The new Asian immigrant groups no longer face the same legal barriers as earlier immigrants. The Exclusion Acts of 1882 and 1924 (laws preventing family formation in order to ensure Asians remain only temporary workers) have been repealed. Society no longer condones the involuntary internment of the Japanese during World War II. Laws against interracial marriage were repealed by the Supreme Court in 1967. There is generally less hostility than a century ago, although specific acts of violence against Asians have occurred as recently as five or ten years ago (Marger, 1994). Once they become citizens, Asian American immigrants receive the full right to participate in voting and in election to public office.

On the other hand, modern Asian immigrants also face a new America, with new social norms, new economic pressures, a new labor market and a new world economy, as well as new problems. Many leave their country under different circumstances. Two decades ago, Koreans left in the wake of political unrest and the threat of war. These conditions brought college graduates and classified professionals rather than unskilled or semi-skilled workers in agriculture and marginal jobs. Today, Koreans bring their families, which decreases the rates of professional and technical worker immigration. Filipinos, on the other hand, replaced the Japanese agricultural workers in the 1930s when the Japanese turned from agriculture in search of other occupations. Some Filipinos next moved into industrial positions. During the 1960s, they were able to bring over their spouses and children. Now less than 2 percent remain in agriculture; over half work in white-collar jobs. In 1975, 130,000 Vietnamese fled with the fall of Saigon. The resulting damage of the Vietnam War forced boat people refugees to flee to neighboring countries. They eventually came to U.S. reception centers (Hraba, 1994). Some have since settled here permanently. Many other Southeast Asians also leave homelands torn by political turmoil and abject poverty.

With such diversity in experiences bringing Asians to the U.S., one would expect the immigration process to result in different incomes and lifestyles. Moreover, it is unlikely that all Asian Americans would become the "model minority."

FINDINGS

Using the Public Use Microdata Sample data (PUMS), demographic variables of the white, black, Chinese, Japanese, Filipino, Asian Indian, Korean, Thai, Vietnamese, Cambodian, Hmong, Laotian, and "other Asian" (Bangladeshi, Burmese, Indonesian, Malaysian, Okinawan, Pakistani, Sri Lankan, etc.) groups were compared to determine assimilation levels as exhibited by socioeconomic status.

Income

The Chinese and Japanese have been hailed as the "model minority" and other Asian groups tend to be lumped in with them. When these groups were analyzed separately, the statistics were markedly distinct. Predictably, the Japanese, both males and females, surpassed the white income, the males by over $1,000 in 1980 and by almost $7,000 by 1990. However, Chinese males still lagged by a few thousand dollars at both time periods. Chinese women, on the other hand, surpassed the white group by a few thousand dollars. Filipino women also earned more.

Incomes varied widely among the remaining new Asian groups. Whereas Asian Indian males and females have surpassed the dominant white population, every remaining Asian group regardless of gender, earned less than whites. Many had poverty-level incomes. Although 1980 figures are not available, the 1990 data revealed that many of the Southeast Asian groups earned much less than either East Asians or the white group. The Hmong males were particularly disadvantaged, making less than one-fourth the income of Japanese males. In this instance, the new Asian immigrants generally have not yet been able to become the "model minority." The single notable success of Asian Indians may be due to their dramatically higher levels of education and technical skills that they bring when they immigrate to the United States.

Educational Attainment

The traditional measures of success include socioeconomic status as measured in level of education, occupation and income. Education is usually described as the "great equalizer," the one accessible path to social mobility, an entry into the official structure of the formal economy. For both men and women, higher education was correlated with higher incomes. The 1980 PUMS coded responses from 0 years of education to 22 years. The 1990 PUMS calculates the same category of 17 or more years as "17." Thus, averages are not comparable across decades but can still be compared in relative gains across ethnic groups.

Not surprisingly, education was the strong point for many Asian ethnicities. The Chinese, Japanese, and Asian Indian males all surpassed their white counterparts in 1980, with the Filipinos, Koreans, and Thai following suit in 1990. High Asian Indian education levels

Table 2

Income Levels of Men and Women
by Ethnic Background, 1980 and 1990

Income	Men		Women	
	1980	1990	1980	1990
White	14,409.36	26,415.46	5,329.40	12,031.33
Black	8,029.00	14,104.12	4,903.76	10,212.79
Chinese	12,486.73	23,574.57	6,013.66	12,593.90
Japanese	15,552.33	32,965.97	6,691.65	14,380.58
Filipino	11,322.38	19,749.73	7,113.19	14,534.63
Asian Indian	17,452.60	31,273.69	5,655.33	11,805.57
Korean	13,334.08	20,216.76	4,679.53	9,368.49
Thai	*	18,559.24	*	11,259.08
Other Asian	*	19,738.25	*	8,975.36
Vietnamese	*	15,087.59	*	8,944.75
Cambodian	*	10,361.85	*	6,323.77
Hmong	*	7,643.72	*	4,516.43
Laotian	*	10,264.57	*	6,693.64

Data taken from Public Use Microdata Sample, 1980 and 1990.

may be explained in part by selective immigration laws. Also, although the last three groups still earned less than the dominant group, the gap between their incomes is decreasing as their education increases. When comparing education levels with actual earnings, however, Asians are usually not able to translate their high education into correspondingly high incomes.

The remaining Southeast Asian groups fared dramatically less well: The Vietnamese, Cambodian, Hmong and Laotian educational deficiency ranged from almost a year to over four years in 1990.

The women also followed patterns similar to their male counterparts. The Chinese, Japanese, Filipino and Asian Indian females all equaled or surpassed white females in 1980 and 1990. The Southeast

Asian females, on the other hand, had one and a half to five and a half years less education. Hmong men and women had the least of all.

Table 3

Educational Comparison of Different
Ethnic Groups, 1980 and 1990

| | Years of Education* | | | |
| | Men | | Women | |
Ethnic Group	1980	1990	1980	1990
White	12.0	8.8	12.0	8.8
Black	10.1	7.4	10.7	7.8
Chinese	12.8	9.5	11.8	8.8
Japanese	13.5	10.2	13.1	9.8
Filipino	11.4	8.9	12.1	9.4
Asian Indian	13.7	10.2	12.0	9.0
Korean	11.3	9.0	10.8	8.3
Thai	*	9.1	*	8.7
Other Asian	*	8.5	*	7.6
Vietnamese	*	7.9	*	7.1
Cambodian	*	5.5	*	4.5
Hmong	*	4.4	*	3.3
Laotian	*	6.0	*	4.8

*Different scales for 1980 and 1990.

Data taken from Public Use Microdata Sample, 1980 and 1990.

Occupational Ranking

Asian males in all categories still do not fare well on measures of occupation. Education does not necessarily translate into high positions, as it is assumed to do. In a recent study of diversity and discrimination in corporations in the 1990's, Asians still expressed concern that they were being channeled into technical areas that were necessary and respected, but not upwardly mobile. They were seen as unfit for the managerial positions that would have provided them with higher income and greater power. The reason for withholding administrative promotions was their perceived submissiveness and passivity, despite similar or superior qualifications otherwise. Even positions that required an Asian language and cultural expertise were given to either "outside experts" for temporary consultation or to whites well entrenched in the old-boy networks that remain alive and well (Jew, 1995).

Conversely, some of the Asian females were able to score higher on occupation scales than their white female counterparts. This was true for the Chinese, Japanese, Filipinos, Koreans, Vietnamese, Thai, and Laotian. Many Asian women have more years of education than their white counterparts. Perhaps they were able to translate this advantage into occupational prestige because they competed against other white women, who were similarly disadvantaged by the old-boy network. Also, more Asian women worked full-time, or longer hours per week. Nevertheless, Asian women usually earned less income than their white counterparts, with the exceptions noted under the discussion for "income."

English Proficiency

Further investigation shows the reason for such disparity in education, occupation, and income attainments: unlike the Japanese and Asian Indians, most other Asian groups struggle to speak English.

Linguistic isolation significantly restricts the abilities of most Asian immigrants in education and the available jobs in the labor market. Regardless of gender, it lowered earnings. In fact, to not speak English fluently (anything more than "0" on a 0 to 4 scale) consistently produced an average income below the grand mean average of all incomes, for both men and women.

Only about 4 to 8 percent of the Japanese, Filipinos, and Asian Indian men could speak English fluently. Nearly 20 percent of the Chinese, Vietnamese, and Koreans, and around 30 percent of the Cambodian, Laotian, and Hmong men were not proficient in English. This dissimilarity is a reflection of foreign-born versus native-born Asians. Most of the Japanese have become well established, whereas most other

Asians in America are foreign born. Sixty percent of the Chinese and Filipinos, 70 percent of the Asian Indians, and 90 percent of the Vietnamese are first-generation immigrants (Marger, 1994). Most well-educated Asian Indians who immigrate, however, may have learned their English before arriving.

Table 4

Comparison of English Proficiency
among Different Ethnic Groups, 1980 and 1990

| | Percent Who Cannot Speak English Well | | | |
| | Men | | Women | |
Ethnic Group	1980	1990	1980	1990
White	1.2%	1.5%	1.5%	1.6%
Black	0.4	0.9	0.4	0.9
Chinese	19.0	20.1	26.6	26.0
Japanese	6.1	7.8	10.7	11.0
Filipino	5.5	4.8	5.9	5.2
Asian Indian	3.8	4.2	7.9	10.1
Korean	21.3	23.0	24.5	26.8
Thai	*	13.5	*	15.1
Other Asian	*	6.6	*	9.3
Vietnamese	*	21.7	*	29.0
Cambodian	*	27.6	*	38.9
Hmong	*	31.8	*	41.5
Laotian	*	28.9	*	35.7

Data taken from Public Use Microdata Sample, 1980 and 1990.

Asian women fared even worse than their male counterparts. In every group, Asian women spoke English less fluently than the men. Sometimes as many as 10 percent more were unable to speak English well. This may be due to social interaction patterns in which women are expected to care for the family, and, therefore, spend less time interacting with English speakers. Compared to other Asian women,

Hmong were eight times less likely to be fluent than Filipinos, and almost four times more likely than the Japanese. One surprising finding was that 20 percent of Chinese men and 26 percent of Chinese women were not proficient in English. These findings may indicate a greater interaction within an ethnic enclave that allows for the use of the native language and which, therefore, does not require much English proficiency. Also, there appears to be some indication of continuing immigration for some of the earlier Asian groups.

Age

Age can affect income levels in several ways. First, a very young population within an ethnic group may indicate a lower level of work experience and fewer years of seniority. This in turn affects income. It also indirectly affects promotions and access to benefits. Second, they may not face ageism. Finally, they may obtain higher levels of education, and at an earlier age, than their older counterparts, because education has become increasingly accessible over the twentieth century. This advantage may be further intensified because many technical and service jobs today require training that was not available decades ago. Also, retirement usually equates a significant decrease in income. These factors contribute to the increase in income with age, with a sharp drop after the age of 60 for men. Age affects women somewhat differently. The drop occurs ten years earlier, after the age of 50, but the drop in income is less, perhaps because women tend to earn less initially.

The Japanese had the highest means at 37.9 years, an increase of 2 1/2 years in the past decade. The Hmong had a youthful 18.3 years. Other Southeast Asians, except for the Thai, had extraordinarily young populations. Their averages ranged from 21.9 to 26.6 years. Nearly all group ages increased over the past decade, perhaps indicating a falling birth rate and increased longevity. In comparison, the average age of the white group also increased, from 34.5 in 1980 to 36.2 years in 1990. Blacks were younger than the white group and the "model minorities" but hovered above the Southeast Asians at 30.5 years. The causes of these differences are discussed under the fertility variable.

Average Hours Worked per Week

Of those who worked for pay, men showed a similar pattern across all groups. About 90 percent of all men in 1980 and 1990 worked full time (36 hours or more per week). Of the women who worked, a larger percentage of the ethnic minorities worked full time than did white females (71 percent). This is about 5 to 10 percent more women among blacks and the Asian groups. This pattern continued in the 1990 data, with *even more* ethnic minority women working full time than 10 years earlier (among 77 percent of Japanese and 88 percent of Laotian women). Those who were unemployed or working without pay were not included in these figures.

The increasing number of dual-income families may have a devastating effect on the socialization of their children. In his research on Asian gangs, Frogley (1993) found that gang participation was due, in part, to the lack of parental guidance in the home. Although Asian secret societies date back for centuries, the ranks of many of their new recruits in Asian American gangs are filled with disgruntled children of immigrants. With increasing numbers of women working away from home, and a breakdown of the traditional extended family structure that allowed grandmothers to care for and teach values to their grandchildren, Asian youth increasingly sought acceptance and meaning in "disorganized-organized crime," or street gangs (Frogley, 1993). Furthermore, these children have adopted the current American standards of middle-class wealth and materialism but are seriously disadvantaged. They lack the same resources, education and skills necessary to achieve and maintain a middle-class lifestyle. Instead, some choose to compete in the underground economy involving murder, kidnapping, extortion, drug trafficking, prostitution, gambling, weapons smuggling, smuggling of illegal aliens, insurance fraud, and money laundering. The FBI considers Asian gangs the most violent criminal perpetrators today (U.S. Senate Committee on Governmental Affairs, 1992).

Occupational Class

The type of jobs these groups held varied from corporate work to local, state, and federal governments, and self-employment. The Chinese have traditionally been called the "middle-man minority" because of their ability to carve a niche in their own community and build self-employing businesses that cater to these Chinatowns (Hraba, 1994:436). Such traditional strategies have been responses to existing legal and social barriers that made entry into the mainstream labor market much more difficult for ethnic minorities, and particularly the Asian immigrants.

Traditionally, certain immigrant characteristics become advantages for these ethnic minorities. For example, cultural values supporting the work ethic and business practices have assisted Asian groups to develop and use financial assets effectively. Asians, like other immigrants, have experienced relative satisfaction with jobs that have low money returns, job-related dangers, long hours and domestic penury because even such dire conditions are considered better than the situation they left. Solidarities have emerged as ethnic consciousness and group cohesion developed in a country with a somewhat hostile dominant group. Some sojourners have benefited from their temporary efforts to access work and business opportunities. These immigrant cultural and ethnic resources are hypothesized to help encourage eventual prosperity (Light, 1984).

However, the 1980 and 1990 census data show Chinese are no longer working for themselves in great numbers. Their statistics almost parallel the white group. The Japanese have also apparently gained such a foothold with their native-born population, that such immigrant advantages are no longer exploited (perhaps because they no longer exist for the Japanese). As Light (1984) suggested, only the foreign-born without class resources must rely on such benefits in the entrepreneur labor market. Once a strong network is established and some native-born are able to gain access to the formal economy through educational, linguistic and skill attainment, such immigrant ethnic resources are no longer necessary for survival or success.

In recent years, Koreans have become well known for their entrepreneurial success, and in fact, many more in both the 1980s and the 1990s own and work in their own business than the general population. Many fewer Koreans work in government. Asians in general either parallel or are less likely to work in government than whites and especially blacks. Although this study was not able to measure participation in the underground economy, Asian gang activity may be much greater than is currently detected, even with increasing awareness over the last decade. Less dangerous than predatory crimes but equally important may be involvement in household production, unlawfully conducted legal enterprises, and illegal enterprises. None of these activities is included in official statistics.

Fertility Rates

Another indicator of available resources is the dependency ratio. With finite funds, the choice to invest in children, or in business enterprises, savings, and material comforts is revealed in fertility rates. The greater the number of children, and/or the number of elderly, the greater portion of income must be diverted from other areas.

Fertility rates also help indicate potential "job squeeze" (Jiobu 1988:70). Different immigrant groups bring with them different resources and different backgrounds with which to bargain for positions. Some have more education and will enter the job market at technical and professional levels, while others come from such desperate circumstances that they are willing to accept jobs that no one else desires. (Technically, this would probably equate to no competition at all.) Because of this, these groups compete at different levels of the labor market. If, for some reason, the entire group competes in the same level, then age distribution helps predict whether there will be a surplus or shortage of labor at that level. It may also indirectly determine income, educational and work experience levels as well.

Chinese, Japanese, Korean, and Asian Indian groups all consistently had lower fertility rates than the white population in both 1980 and 1990. In fact, Japanese and Asian Indians had a more rapid *drop* in fertility rates as well, over the ten-year span, than the general white population. Filipinos had slightly more. Of the new groups, all but the Thai had higher rates; the Hmong had the highest of all at almost double the rate of the white group (5.06 versus 2.79).

Marital Status

One similarity across most Asian groups, both old and new, were marital patterns. Except for the Cambodian group in 1990, each group at both time periods had notably lower divorce rates than either the white or the black group. Some of these rates are less than one third of the white Americans. Of those over 20 years old, 11 percent of whites were divorced. Divorce rates among blacks fell during the past decade to 18.5 percent. Chinese, Japanese and Koreans were around 6 to 8 percent, while Asian Indians had a remarkable 4 percent, an actual drop from 1980 figures. The highest divorce rates among the Asians were found among the Cambodian and the Hmong, at over 15 percent and almost 10 percent, respectively. This is explained in part by their low incomes, education, and occupational status, which may put additional financial strain and psychological stress on marriage.

Results of Multiple Regression of Race, Education, Age, and English Proficiency

To what extent do the variables of education, English proficiency, and age affect income levels? Again, Asian American groups were separated and compared to white, black, Hispanic, and Native Americans, according to gender. In the table below, the unadjusted column shows the ranking of ethnic groups by average incomes, reflecting varying levels of education, ages, and English proficiency. The adjusted column shows the rankings of average incomes when these three variables are held constant, comparing ethnic group incomes if their education, ages, and English proficiency were equivalent. Of the three variables, education had the greatest impact, followed by age and English proficiency, respectively.

With the adjustment, Asian Indian males were the only group who fell from above average to below. Southeast Asian males had a significant increase, relative to other groups, as did Hispanic men. Considering the high levels that most Asian Indian males bring with them, this advantage is severely reduced, as reflected in their adjusted incomes. Conversely, Southeast Asian male educational levels are comparatively some of the lowest, as were the other two variables, and when adjusted, the disparity was dramatically reduced.

Asian Indian females had a similar significant drop of income, once the variables of education, age, and English proficiency were held constant. Southeast Asian females rose from below-average incomes to above-average incomes, and the Hispanic females, though still not earning above-average incomes, improved relative to other groups. The average incomes of all Chinese and Japanese fell with the adjustment, probably due to the removal of the education advantage. Both Native American males and females remained consistently at the bottom, regardless of education, age, or English proficiency adjustments.

Table 5

Ethnic Group Income Rankings
for Married Men and Women

Men		Women	
Unadjusted	Adjusted	Unadjusted	Adjusted
1. Asian Indian	1. Japanese	1. Filipino	1. Filipino
2. Japanese	2. White	2. Chinese	2. White
3. White	3. *Hispanic*	3. Asian Indian	3. Southeast Asian
4. *Chinese*	4. Asian Indian	4. Japanese	4. Black
5. *Korean*	5. *Chinese*	5. Black	5. Japanese
6. *Filipino*	6. *Southeast Asians*	6. White	6. *White*
7. *Black*	7. *Black*	7. Korean	7. *Hispanic*
8. *Hispanic*	8. *Native American*	8. *Southeast Asians*	8. *Korean*
9. *Native American*	9. *Korean*	9. *Native American*	9. *Native American*
10. *Southeast Asians*	10. *Filipino*	10. *Hispanic*	10. *Asian Indian*

*Italicized groups show those whose incomes are below the average income of all groups combined.

Data taken from Public Use Microdata Sample, 1980 and 1990.

In the table below, the unadjusted column shows the average incomes of each ethnic group, reflecting varying levels of education, ages, and English proficiency. The adjusted column shows incomes when these three variables are held constant, comparing ethnic group incomes if their education, ages, and English proficiency were equivalent.

The disparity among adjusted income averages shows that despite holding education, age, and English proficiency constant, notable variance remains. Although the difference is reduced, its continued existence is thought provoking. Why do Chinese and Filipino males earn less on average than whites, despite their higher education levels—why are they having difficulty translating their assumed advantage into reality? Why do the Japanese males continue to earn higher incomes on average, even when their education is taken into account?

What other advantages might they have, apart from those already measured in this study? Why do the rankings of the Chinese, Japanese, blacks and Native Americans remain nearly the same, regardless of the adjustment? Is the United States truly closer to a meritocracy, allocating incomes according to supposed knowledge gained through its academic institutions? How much is a result or reflection of lasting racial discrimination and misunderstood stereotypes? Or do other ethnically-influenced advantages and disadvantages not included in this research significantly influence income?

Table 6

Average 1990 Incomes (unranked)
for Married Men and Women

	Men		Women	
	unadjusted	adjusted	unadjusted	adjusted
White	34478.28	33598.38	11913.16	11644.79**
Black	22128.27	25435.15	12847.97	13205.17
Native American	21100.83	25424.04	9285.11	10554.60
Hispanic	21916.04	30630.73*	8554.32	11607.44
Chinese	32607.33	28852.78	14046.52	13583.00
Japanese	43492.86	38686.59	13710.13	13138.56
Filipino	26977.14	24286.82	17287.31	15176.76
Asian Indian	44438.75	30420.20**	3832.22	10176.80**
Korean	29991.06	24782.89	10516.96	11168.96
Southeast Asians	20547.32	26269.90*	10154.96	13530.04

*Indicates groups whose incomes rose from less than average income of all groups combined to higher than average.

**Indicates groups whose incomes fell from more than average income of all groups combined to less than average.

Data taken from Public Use Microdata Sample, 1980 and 1990.

CONCLUSION

With this influx of new Asian immigrants, many significant questions arise. How will the face of America change? Are these new immigrants similar to or different from Asian immigrants of a century ago? Can we expect all Asian immigrants today to follow in the footsteps of those who came before them? Will they all join the "model minority" who are able to attain notable levels of SES success rapidly? Why or why not? What impact will they have culturally, economically, socially, and politically? How will this affect current race relations? Part of the difficulty in assessing the progress and the reasons for progress is the diversity within this ethnic group, particularly the demographic make-up and reasons for migration of each Asian immigrant group. The similarities and differences in this study are striking, and its implications cannot be ignored.

Asian Americans as a classification cannot be studied without breaking this misleading category down further into its separate ethnicities. To the uninformed, Asians may all "look alike" and be from the "same place." However, sharing a few traits of physical appearance and a few thousand miles of geographic origin is hardly a flawless predictor of assimilation and chance of success in American society. The differences in demography reveal serious variations that would be lost if these groups were considered a homogenous entity. To accurately measure the level of assimilation into American culture, each ethnicity must be considered separately.

Most of the new Asian Americans are not following in the footsteps of the Chinese and Japanese and becoming the "model minority." Despite our assumptions that Asian Americans fare remarkably well under their own efforts, we ignore that their success is not universally distributed among all Asian Americans. Rather, because some have received great publicity for surpassing the white group in certain categories, it is assumed that *all* Asian Americans have become economically successful. They are believed to face little hardship or discrimination today.

This is not true. Violence for Asians in general continues, and is sometimes even more hostile precisely *because* of their economic gains. Furthermore, specific Asian ethnicities who are struggling in poverty are wholly ignored because they are subsumed under the blanket assumption that all Asians are doing well. On the contrary, they have tremendous needs that are not being addressed. Some Asian groups much more closely resemble some Hispanic ethnic groups than they do their Asian (i.e., Japanese or Chinese) counterparts, in amount of available resources, linguistic ability, educational attainment, fertility patterns, and income. Unlike the stereotypical successful Asian image, some Asian ethnicities earn less than blacks. Consequently, some Asians have an even greater need for financial assistance, maternal and nutritional information and aid, education support, and health care to help them fully enter the American formal job market and economy.

The price we pay for ignoring these differences can be tremendous: 1) individual alienation or survival; 2) the community ability to enhance its workforce and compete more effectively on an international market; 3) increasing socioeconomic disparity and its subsequent discontent, which may surface in the forms of 4) crime and violence, and despair; 5) the weakening of families caused by financial and consequent marital stress and strain; 6) racial and class tensions, and 7) impediment to the cultural and social progress of America.

REFERENCES

Butterfield, Fox. (24 February) 1991. "Asians spread across a land, and help change it." *New York Times* 1 (3):22.

Chow, Esther Ngan-Ling. 1994. "Asian American women at work." In M.B. Zinn and B.T. Dill (eds.), *Women of Color in U.S. Society*. Philadelphia: Temple University Press.

Frogley, Drew. 1993. *Asian Crime and Patterns of Networking: Three Case Studies: San Francisco, Las Vegas, and Salt Lake City*. Provo, UT: Brigham Young University Master's Thesis.

Hirschman, Charles and Morrison G. Wong. September 1986. "The extraordinary educational attainment of Asia-Americans." *Social Forces* 65:1.

Hraba, Joseph. 1994. *American Ethnicity*. Itasca, IL: Peacock Publishers.

Hune, Shirley. 1977. *Pacific Migration to the United States: Trends and Themes in Historical and Sociological Literature.* Washington, DC: Smithsonian.

Jew, Carolyn. 1995. *Diversity and Discrimination in Organizations: A Case Study.* Paper presented at Pacific Sociological Association 1995 Conference, San Francisco.

Jiobu, Robert M. 1988. *Ethnicity and Assimilation.* New York: State University of New York Press.

Light, Ivan. April 1984. "Immigrant and ethnic enterprise in North America." *Ethnic and Racial Studies* 7:2.

Marger, Martin. 1994. *Ethnic Relations: American and Global Perspectives.* Third Edition, Belmont CA: Wadsworth Publishing.

Model, Suzanne. 1988. "The economic progress of European and East Asian Americans." *Annual Review of Sociology* 14:363-380.

Ortiz, Vilma. 1994. "Women of color: A demographic overview." In Maxine Zinn and Bonnie Thornton Dill (eds.), *Women of Color in U.S. Society.* Philadelphia: Temple University Press.

Ringer, Benjamin B. and Elinor R. Lawless. 1989. *Race, Ethnicity and Society.* New York: Routledge, p. 26.

U.S. Senate. 1992. *The New International Criminal and Asian Organized Crime.* 102nd Congress, 2nd Session, Committee on Governmental Affairs, Permanent Subcommittee on Investigations. December.

Parenting and Socialization

in

Ethnic Families

"Make Room for Daddy": Patterns of Family Involvement among Contemporary African American Men

Vânia Penha-Lopes[1]

INTRODUCTION

Recent interest in fathers abounds. On the one hand, the Census Bureau reports a significant increase in child care by fathers in the last ten years, both among married and unmarried men (Chira, 1993:A20), and a "growing number of black fathers raise daughters and sons by themselves" (*Ebony*, 1991). The main character of a current television show, "Deep Space 9," is a black single father. Programs such as "Operation Fatherhood," in New Jersey, assist absent fathers of welfare children in not only securing steady employment but also in learning to "take responsibility for their offspring and start paying child support" (Peterson, 1992:B5).

On the other hand, there is growing concern for the "flight of the Black man": *Newsweek* dedicated a special report on "A World Without Fathers" (30 August, 1993), with alarming statistics on out-of-wedlock births in all socioeconomic strata among African Americans. This account emphasizes the age-old idea that the black family is on the verge of extinction because of the growing separation between marriage and childbirth. Yet the same *Newsweek* feature showcases black fathers who have overcome odds to partake in the raising of their children (p. 21).

Thus the question emerges: How and why do black men participate in family life? What leads some men to higher involvement in paternal and spousal activities than others? This paper is a preliminary exploration of that question.

Explanations of the variations in child care and housework among blacks are rare. The bulk of the research has either compared blacks with whites or has focused exclusively on blacks of a given socioeconomic status (cf. Cazenave, 1979; Connor, 1986; McAdoo, 1981). Existing research tends to focus on the role of black men's employment status and work opportunities in their family involvement. These studies imply that men with steady employment can afford to be effective fathers, while poverty and chronic unemployment make men—especially younger men—undesirable marriage partners and poor fathers (Staples, 1989; Wilson, 1987).

While employment stability is clearly an important determinant of stable family structure, economically deprived men are not totally incapable of being involved fathers or egalitarian partners. Other social forces also influence black men's behavior, and many are able to develop options in the face of adversity. Similarly, all good providers are not automatically highly involved fathers.

The premise of the present study is that black men's involvement in families is determined by more than their current socioeconomic status. I argue that a man's responses to structural conditions over the course of his life, i.e., what he faces and how he deals with it from childhood to adulthood, ultimately determine the extent to which he participates in family life. Early socialization is important because it provides the first context for forming familial behavior and attitudes. We need to examine the influence of all those present, be they grand-mothers, uncles, or older siblings, rather than assuming that growing up without a father *per se* leads a black man to become uninterested in family life.

However, human socialization does not end with childhood. As that process continues in adulthood, early gender attitudes interact with mate choices (including a mate's own perceptions and expectations). A partner's encouragement of (or resistance to) a man's participation in family life may affect his own paternal decisions, just as a man's role in the decision to form families and rear children may also influence his behavior.[2]

This study takes a life-course, or developmental approach, to explaining family involvement among contemporary African American men. Since exploration of men's roles in families has been largely confined to white Americans, much of what we believe about the paternal involvement of black men is based on myth rather than research. Using life history analysis, I shall examine the extent to which each major life stage—childhood, employment, and love relationships—leads to variations in paternal experiences. As Gerson (1985:38) convincingly demonstrated in her investigation of divergent adult pathways among modern American women, *"Life history analysis offers an ideal method for examining the interplay between social constraints, psychological motivation, and the developing actor."*

DATA AND METHODS

In this paper, I focus on two dependent variables: "involvement in child care," and "involvement in housework." "Involvement" refers to the self-reported degree of participation in domestic and parental activities. I separate these two spheres of household labor because of their qualitative differences: certain aspects of child care, such as play and spending time together, are often perceived as more pleasurable (and thus easier to undertake) than other household duties, such as cooking and cleaning (cf. Gerson, 1993; Hochschild, 1989).

I conducted life history interviews with eight African American men who live in New York City, randomly selected through contacts with public school officials. The interviews, which lasted an average of three hours, took place in the summer of 1993, mostly at the respondents' homes and workplaces. Interviews typically followed respondents' life course through their childhood, work history, and intimate relationships. Respondents were then asked detailed questions about child care arrangements, attitudes about fatherhood, division of housework, and social networks. The interview concluded with attitudinal questions about gender equity.

Respondents range in age from 22 to 49, with a median age of 38.5 years old. Two are working class—a doorman, and a security officer—while the remainder include two small businessmen, a senior student loans manager, a temporarily unemployed computer operator, a full-time student, and an engineer; together, they work an average of 39 hours per week.[3] The average number of children is 1.6. While most respondents live with their children full time, one father, who is separated from the mother of his sons, spends two weeks a month with them; only one respondent lives away from his daughter on a full-time basis, and he visits her twice a year. There is some variation in marital status and living arrangement: of the two working-class respondents, one is living with his fiancée, and the other is married. Of the middle-class fathers, one is divorced, three are separated from their wives, and two are married. Two of the women who live with these men are full-time workers and share expenses with them. Table 1 summarizes the major sample characteristics.

Table 1

Sample Characteristics

Occpn	Age	Marital Status	Family Composite	Number Chldrn < 18	Hours work	Partner's Occupation	Total family Income
Doorman	22	Engaged	Fiancée, son, mother, sister	1	48	Homemaker	40,000-59,999
Security officer	39	Married	Wife, children nephew	3	40	Homemaker	25,000-59,999[a]
Student	32	Married	Wife	1	20	Nurse	40,000-59,999
Pet groomer	49	Sep	Son	1	40	---	40,000-59,999
Investor	38	Sep	Sons[b]	2	20-80	---	25,000-59,999[c]
Data ent operator	29	Married	Wife, sons	2	35	Assistant supervisor	40,000-59,999
Engineer	46	Div	Son	1	40	---	80,000-99,999
Loans officer	43	Sep	Son, daughter	1	35	---	40,000-59,999

a. Income variation due to overtime.
b. Live with respondent 2 weeks per month.
c. Self-employed; income variation due to market fluctuations.

DATA ANALYSIS

Involvement in Child Care

Description of tasks. Respondents were read a list of child care tasks and asked how they divide them up on a weekly basis. Table 2 shows that, while all respondents claim at least some responsibility for

Table 2

Percentage of Participation
in Child Care Activities

Father-Child Activities	% Respondent	% Partner/ Child's Mother		% Shared		% Other	
Feeding	25 % (2)	25 %	(2)	25 % (2)		25 %	(2)
Bathing	25 (2)	25	(2)	38	(3)	13	(1)
Dressing	13 (1)	38	(3)	38	(3)	13	(1)
Toilet training	13 (1)	38	(3)	25	(2)	25	(2)
Outings	50 (4)	13	(1)	38	(3)	0	
Play/afternoon	50 (4)	13	(1)	0		38	(3)
Playing/evening	38 (3)	13	(1)	25	(2)	25	(2)
Assign chores	25 (2)	13	(1)	50	(4)		
Discipline	63 (5)	0		38	(3)	0	
How/spnd money	63 (5)	0		38	(3)	0	
Homework help	38 (3)	38	(3)	25	(2)	0	
Reading	50 (4)	25	(2)	13	(1)	13	(1)
Talk/teachers	63 (5)	0		38	(3)	0	
Pickup/school	63 (5)	25	(2)	0		13	(1)
Take/doctors	25 (2)	50	(4)	25	(2)	0	
Stay home/wknds	63 (5)	13	(1)	25	(2)	0	
Shopping/toys	75 (6)	25	(2)	0		0	
Shopping/clothes	38 (3)	63	(5)	0		0	
Buying medicines	25 (2)	50	(4)	25	(2)	0	
Babysitting	13 (1)	13	(1)	50	(4)		
Illness	50 (4)	25	(2)	25	(2)	0	

Actual numbers are in parentheses.

all tasks, their participation varies widely. Clearly, among father-child activities, the lowest paternal participation is in dressing and toilet-training their children (for which fathers rely on their partners, baby-sitters, and other sources of help), whereas fathers are primarily responsible for discipline, teaching their children how to spend their allowance, talking to their teachers, picking them up from school, and staying home with them on weekends. As for other child care tasks which do not necessarily involve face-to-face contacts between fathers and children, most respondents unquestionably are most involved in shopping for toys, and least involved in making baby-sitting decisions, a task many claim to share with their partners.

Reading

Reading and helping with homework are also child care areas in which these fathers like to participate. Among the seven men who live with their children, four are primarily responsible for reading to their children, whereas one leaves that activity to his fiancee, and another reports that his 11-year-old daughter takes it upon herself to read to her two younger brothers. Only three of the fathers do most of the homework help: the two who have raised their sons alone, and the loans manager.

The correspondence between engagement in reading and responsibility for talks with teachers suggests that these men play a very active role in their children's education. Given that African American women have had better chances for educational achievement than their male counterparts, it is significant that these fathers are so concerned with their children's education. In no other activity, aside from playing, do these men show a higher level of involvement or such a strong commitment. Even the absent father has "lately" been trying to take over this task, which is obviously difficult from such a distance.

Discipline

One aspect of child care that has been traditionally delegated to fathers is discipline. Only three of these fathers share this task with the mothers of their children; although most are solely responsible for it, they do not enjoy it necessarily—very much unlike playing, another popular father-child activity. The 39-year-old security officer, for example, expressed resentment that his wife leaves discipline to him:

> . . . *the other day she gave [my youngest son] some barbecue chicken. I mean, what is a 4-year-old eating barbecue chicken for anyway? So she gives him the chicken—no plate, no napkin, no nothing. Then he finishes and he goes to the <u>white</u> curtains to wipe his hands. My wife is sitting there, and she's not saying nothing! I says to her, "Why don't you tell him to stop?" And she goes, "I don't wanna be the bad guy. You're here—you do it."*

Primary responsibility for discipline, whether desired or not, counteracts the view that black men do not care for their children. All of these fathers rejected this view, regarding it as another form of racism, or a way to keep African American men subordinate. Thus, rather than making fathers the "bad guys" before their children, it is possible that most mothers yield discipline to fathers in solidarity with their partners.

Explanations for Child-care Involvement

What accounts for this variation in child-care involvement? One explanation may be a father's ability to perform a task well. For example, it may be more difficult for a man without prior training to be primarily responsible for traditionally female tasks, such as dressing children. As the 29-year-old father of two infant boys put it, "the main difference between raising a son and a daughter, I imagine, is to dress a little girl. I mean, grooming takes a <u>long</u> time!"

There may be other reasons as well. In the space below, I will show that the three life-course factors on which I am focusing—childhood experiences, economic stability, and love relationships—not only account for paternal involvement separately, but also interact with each other.

Childhood Experiences

When Daddy is not there. A man's perception of his own father's performance when he was growing up may explain these fathers' participation in and enjoyment of father-child activities. On the one hand, half of the men in the sample (two working-class, two middle-class) spoke of the resentment they felt toward their fathers for not having shown enough interest in their childhoods; these men make a conscious effort to be more involved with their children, from feeding to playing with them. On the other hand, the men who were satisfied with the participation of their own fathers tried to emulate their attitudes and behavior now that they are fathers themselves.

The youngest father in the sample, a 22-year-old doorman, tells of his frustration with his father:

> *Before I was 9, we were very close. After that . . . it was up and down. . . . He wasn't satisfied, never played sports with us. He was more interested in his friends; his friends were always there. . . . From 16 on, we were distant. . . . He was also physically violent. He kicked me out of the house when I finished high school.*

After having spent a couple of years in his aunt's house, he entered the military service, where he stayed for four years. At age 20, when his fiancee told him she was pregnant, he was "excited! And worried. I want him to be perfect, you know, I don't want anything to go wrong." When his son was born, he was temporarily unemployed. However, since they lived with his mother, a full-time traffic administrator, they could weather the loss of income, so that he spent most of his time taking care of his house, his baby, and his fiancée. Now that his son is 15 months old, he is still the main focus of his life:

> *I feel like he's gonna be at my side forever, you know. I mean even into the teens, I can see he and I still doing things to-gether! And like I said, I wanna take more of a role in his life than my father did in mine. I mean, even the little things, like sports. You know, I can't even remember, I think it's only been two times that my father went with us to the movies. . . . But he never did anything with us. . . . With [my son], when I see him, I see me. And I see a chance to make him happy, to show him that he doesn't have to have the same life that I had. It's like going back in time, being able to correct all your mistakes! I mean, obviously, you can't undo them all, but. . . .*

The wish to undo the feelings of a frustrated childhood can manifest itself even in men with non-biological children. It was not until I asked him whether he had attended the birth of his children that another father, a 29-year-old computer operator with two sons, finally disclosed that his older child is really his wife's son, whom he is in the process of formally adopting. Throughout the interview, this father made it clear that he was still unhappy with his own father's departure when he was only 5 years old:

> *I think if he'd stayed with it, he would have been a good father. If he were there through puberty, a lot of questions of sexuality and spirituality would have been easier, though church helped. I disagreed greatly with him leaving. . . . I feel children need a father.*

Barely in his twenties, he saw himself embarking on a serious relationship with a woman who already had a baby:

> *So how did you feel about becoming a "father" then?*

> *It was scary—he's not yours. I've always loved children, but I had to deal with being a father for someone else's child. It was a rough time.*

In the meantime, the boy's biological father seldom kept his promises to visit his son. The boy's mother, worried about the effect this might have on him, gave her former lover an ultimatum: "Either come see your son regularly or don't come at all." Eight years later, as the biological father opted for the latter, this respondent clearly enjoys the time spent with his "first boy."

Devotion to his sons is so high that taking up fatherhood has delayed his plans to go back to college and finish his degree. Asked to speak about his involvement, he said:

> *[My older son] and I do everything together. I learned to roller-skate so that I could teach him and then go skating together. I'm the one who picks him up from school. I'm one of his Sunday school teachers, so he spends Sundays with me*

at church, while my wife stays at home with [our two-month-old son].

Comparisons with Others

Another childhood experience that can have a later impact on a man's fathering is how one compares oneself to others when growing up. Many of the men interviewed disclosed an early awareness of the subordinate position of blacks in this country, and a desire to improve their social condition. The social inequality between blacks and whites, especially in educational opportunities, was most apparent to the 43-year-old father of two, a loans manager whose wife has left. Growing up in the rural South, this man was aware of its "inferior education school system. And segregated." In the eighth grade, he "went through one of the most traumatic experiences": the revelation that he couldn't read, which was clear to all of his classmates. As his teacher threatened not to let him go on to high school, he spent the summer teaching himself how to read. From that time on, ". . . *it's something I said, I'll just determine my kids will never, you know, experience it.*" In his late teens, living in the North and attending college, he again felt inadequate vis-à-vis "the academic preparation of the students here," most of whom were white:

> When I came here, it was something I had to adjust to, you know. I never interacted socially with a lot of white kids, white people, till I got here. Experience to overcome. The years to undiminish myself. Be comfortable in conversation, you know, social atmosphere. But that's what I want my kids to never have problems with. Maybe I overdid it, but it's just something I just said I will be committed to and I will want anywhere. I put time on it, so I spent a little time reading to them, you know, they said if you read to your kids 15 minutes a day, when they're very young, it will be marvelous, so, I did those things and, it worked! [Both my children] could read way before they went to kindergarten.

His diligence has shown results. At interview time, his 13-year-old daughter had just received a full scholarship to a prestigious prep school in Manhattan; his 19-year-old son, a college sophomore, is intent on following the career his father never had a chance to pursue, and has already planned to go to Law School. It is not surprising that this father has also taken the responsibility of talking to his children's teachers, an activity for which 63 percent of the sample claim to be primarily responsible.

Economic Stability

A man's economic stability allows him to take on more child-care responsibilities or even, if necessary, be a single father. This is the case of the 49-year-old pet groomer, the father of a 9-year-old boy. Even though he wasn't living with the mother of his child when she told him she was pregnant, they have maintained a friendly relationship, and, by "mutual decision," he has been his son's "primary parent" since he was a toddler: *"His mother knew I had a steady job, and besides, she has another child; it was common judgment."* To this deeply religious man, raising his son comes naturally, and it gives him a chance *"to expand [his] conscience spiritually."*

That economic stability can play a significant part in a father's involvement is illustrated by the experiences of the only father in the sample who lives away from his daughter. Confronted with unexpected fatherhood at the age of 18, he at first accused his pregnant girlfriend of trying to entrap him. Nonetheless, he returned to his hometown to spend the first two weeks of his daughter's life with them and has since maintained a friendly relationship with both of them. Meanwhile, this 32-year-old man faced many bouts of unemployment and even homelessness; a high-school dropout, his lack of skills would only land him minimum-wage jobs that quickly bored him. He admits that he *"got into the bottle and drugs, lost the reason for living and my self-esteem."* Then, at age 29, he *"faced reality,"* enrolled in college (*"so that I can get better jobs in the future"*), where he met and fell in love with his wife of two years. He credits her for his turnaround, and sees her as *"my friend, my daughter, mother, brother, sister, enemy at times—she's very interesting."* As a registered nurse, she is the main breadwinner in their household, which allows him to devote himself full time to getting a degree in social work.

Love Relationships

These factors are not mutually exclusive: clearly, his economic stability is a result of his relationship with his wife. His relationship with his daughter also seems to have improved since he met his wife. When his daughter was about 10 years old (she is now 14), she lived six months with him, for her mother wanted the girl to grow up knowing her father. However, he is painfully aware of his limited participation in his teenage daughter's upbringing: besides shopping for toys, he takes over only discipline, helping her decide how to spend money—which he does by telephone or letter—and for the past two years, talking to her teachers about her progress in school. Perhaps because he wants to make up for lost time, he considers what he does "always a pleasure," and classifies himself as a "distant caretaker." But it is clear that he could only take a more active role in his daughter's life after he was able to "put [his] life in order" economically, which he could not have done without his wife's significant help.

Another illustration of how the interaction between a man's economic stability and the women in his life may explain his paternal involvement comes from another full-time single father in the sample. An engineer with a prosperous employment history, he separated from his second wife when their son (now a college-bound 17-year-old) was about a year old. In an unusual move, she asked that he keep their son. About five months later, she filed for alimony and child support (even though he was the one with the child), which prompted him to counter-file for sole custody of their son. When he won custody, he asked his first ex-wife, with whom he had three children, to take care of his baby son on weekdays for about a year:

For that period of time, she took care of him.

And was she the main caretaker at the time?

She was working, and she had a baby-sitter during the day. But she was the main person...during the week; on the weekend, he stayed with me.

And when he was with you, did you have baby-sitters, or. . .?

No, I didn't. I did <u>everything</u>.

His steady income allowed this father to pay a baby-sitter on weekdays and even maintain a talking home computer, which he programmed to wake his son up, and remind him to brush his teeth. Today, this 46-year-old man admits that *"[The computer]. . . sort of made things easy for me."* On the other hand, one can see that, was it not for his supportive ex-wife, being a full-time single father might have been much more difficult for this man.

How do these men think of themselves as fathers? Almost all of them feel they are good fathers, that they are doing the best that they can, and that the advantages of fatherhood far outweigh any disadvantages. The youngest father put it most poignantly:

Well, . . . I'd just like to say I'm doing the best I can, hopefully it's enough to guide [my son] in the right direction . . . I guess . . . 20 years from now, I'll be asking [him] that question, "How was I as a father?" And hopefully, I hope to hear, with a hug, you know. . . that I was a good father. . . . You know, there wasn't a lot of hugging between my dad and I. . .

While many acknowledged their wish to give more to their children materially, all but the father who lives away from his daughter still feel proud of their parenting, because "it takes a good father to deny himself," to give their children a solid foundation, and to "hope that they turn out for the best, the best they can be."

The fathers in this sample display considerable involvement in their childrens' lives in a variety of ways, both in tasks that are regarded as traditionally male and otherwise. Their involvement also transcends social-class barriers, which gives credit to the argument that, although very important, economic stability is not the sole determinant of a man's participation in child care. The next section describes my findings regarding men's participation in the household division of labor.

Involvement in Housework

Ever since the separation between household and job site in the nineteenth century, housework has been associated with women and assigned very low status (Gerstel and Gross, 1987:13). Housework is also referred to as "invisible work" (DeVault, 1991) and "work that is never finished." Now, as more Americans rely on two paychecks, the division of household labor has begun to change. If American men and women are spending more time at the workplace, "who is doing the housework?"

Comparing national data from 1965, 1975, and 1985, Robinson (1988) reported a decrease in the amount of time women allot to housework per week—seven hours less—and an increase in men's housework time—five hours more. While the two-hour-per-week increase in men's housework time between 1965 and 1975 has been attributed to more time spent on traditionally male tasks, in the 1975-85 period the increase was due to men's greater performance of female tasks (Robinson, 1988). In all, men's share of the housework has increased from 15 percent in 1965 to 33 percent in 1985. Robinson explains this trend by the decline in the number of households with children, the decline in the proportion of married couples, and by the overall increase in housework time by fathers.

Tasks performed. How much do these fathers participate in housework? Table 3 shows how these fathers divided various household tasks.

Fathers without partners. Obviously, fathers who are currently living without partners (n=4) have no choice but to do the tasks themselves or hire paid help. No single father counts on paid help, however; either they do housework by themselves or they allocate some chores to their children. The fathers see this arrangement as a necessary part of their children's socialization. For instance, as I commented on the neatness of his apartment, the engineer indicated that his son was responsible for vacuuming, and cleaning the bathtub. Then, when I assumed that the father did everything else, including the laundry, the engineer corrected me:

Table 3

Percentage of Participation in Household Chores[a]

	Respondent	Partner	Shared	Other
Grocery shopping	0%	25%(1)	75%(3)	0%
Meal planning	25 (1)	50 (2)	0	0
Cooking	25 (1)	50 (2)	25 (1)	0
Meal cleanup	50 (2)	25 (1)	0	25 (1)
Laundry	25 (1)	50 (2)	25 (1)	0
Ironing	50 (2)	25 (1)	25 (1)	0
Vacuuming	50 (2)	25 (1)	25 (1)	0
Dusting	33 (1)	33 (1)	0	0
Wash/wax floors	100(3)	0	0	0
Repairs	75 (3)	0	0	25 (1)
Paying bills	75 (3)	25 (1)	0	0
Take out garbage	50 (2)	0	0	50 (2)
Pet care	50 (1)	0	0	50 (1)

a. Includes only those who have live-in partners (n=4).
Actual numbers are in parentheses.

Oh, he does that too. Oh no, he has to cooperate! I used to do it all, but now he's old enough he can pitch in and do laundry or dishes, or whatever has to be done. Oh no, I'm not gonna raise no sissy. You gotta do everything that has to be done. You know, he's gotta do his part, when he gets old though, he has to. . . chip in. That's part of the values, give them values, and things.

This father includes competence in housework in his definition of masculinity, despite knowing that a man well-versed in household chores can be called a "sissy." Among African Americans, however, this father's approach may be closer to the norm. For example, Peters

(1988:234) suggests that African American subculture stresses the importance of finishing a task over the sex of the child who performs it. These respondents support this argument: as boys, most men were assigned not only "masculine" chores such as taking out the garbage, but also more "feminine" ones, such as laundry, dishes, and cooking (even when they had sisters). Only the future loans manager, now also a single father, grew up in a household that followed a division of labor based on "natural lines": the boys helped their father pump water and start the fire, while the girl and the mother took care of the laundry, ironing, shopping and cooking. But even this man indicated that his father shared shopping and cooking with his mother.

Fathers with partners. The fathers who live with wives or fiancée can and do share the housework with them. Indeed, all are active participants. Although two out of the four fathers in this group live with full-time homemakers, each is primarily responsible for at least one traditionally female task, including ironing clothes, vacuuming, washing/waxing floors, cooking, laundry, and planning meals. When asked about how they got to their current division of labor, men tend to attribute it to "nature" and "physical characteristics"; only the computer operator actually admitted "sitting down and discussing it," despite being ". . . taught to shop, to keep house, to cook, to sew, and to clean" by his single mother, who said, "Anything can happen, so be prepared."

Under closer scrutiny, all couples have clearly arrived at their current situations by trial, error, and need. After all, washing floors does not require any more physical strength than laundry, yet in the households where this takes place, it is always done by the men. Similarly, two of the men regularly iron clothes because their partners "can't do it well." The youngest father admits that he prefers to take care of both tasks because his time in the armed forces has taught him how to do them better than his fiancée would ever care to. The absentee father, who is married to a full-time nurse, is responsible for vacuuming, meal cleanup (the task he enjoys least of all), laundry and, again, ironing, for he believes that his wife ". . . is a terrible ironer."

For some, control over certain household tasks is a matter of necessity. The security officer explains that it is necessary to accompany his wife to the grocery store or she would never buy him the foods he likes to eat. He also cooks when he "get[s] tired of her slop":

> *She put the food on the table, my kids look at me and ask, "Daddy, do we have to eat this?" I says to them, "No, you don't, 'cause I ain't eatin' it either! Go ahead and make yourselfs some sandwiches." Then [growing exasperated], my wife complains that that's why she never cook, 'cause nobody ever likes her food. I tell her people gonna start appreciating her food when she puts some love into it.*

In sum, while it may be true that, nationally, married black women are still more likely than their husbands to do most of the traditionally female tasks (Broman, 1988), the fathers in this sample display a relatively egalitarian participation in housework. And their attitudes toward it are not far behind: asked to evaluate the statement, "If his wife works, a man should share equally in household chores such as cooking, cleaning, and washing," all the fathers with partners agreed, stating that "it is better for the both of them" or "Everything should be shared! Besides, men are the best cooks anyway," or "Yes. We [his previous girlfriend] did it before, it was fun" and "I always agree; it's a big job."[4]

Childhood experiences emerge as a potentially significant explanation of housework involvement. The fact that most of these men, when they were growing up, were assigned household chores that did not necessarily follow traditional gender roles seems to play a role in their current participation. Additionally, all but three respondents had working mothers who counted on their sons to help them with housework.

CONCLUSION

How can we explain the variations in the family involvement of these African American men? At this stage, the factors that seem most influential are: a) childhood experiences, including perceptions of their own father's performance when they were growing up; b) economic stability in adult life; and c) love relationships.

Perception of father's performance can be very influential. Those men who were disappointed with their father's involvement tended to fashion their own parenting as a reaction against their dissatisfying childhoods, either because they were unhappy with the amount of time their fathers had devoted to them, such as the doorman and the investor, or because they had longed for an absentee father, as was the case of the computer operator and the security officer. While these men credit their mothers, grandparents, and fellow church members for their emotional stability today, they still compare their own experiences as children, decide what went wrong, and try not to repeat it with their own children.

Economic circumstances and love relationships can lead a man to reevaluate his own life. Thus, we see the only father who does not live with his teenage daughter trying to make up for lost time even if long distance. He had faced fatherhood at a very young age; now, over ten years later, happy with his marriage and a renewed religious faith, he recants his opinion of his daughter's mother as having tried to "trap" him. We also see that so far, he has only been able to be involved in the areas least favored by the fathers in the sample: discipline, which potentially puts them in the position of the "bad guy," and money management.

The other fathers also experienced events in the course of their lives that prepared them for future household activities. For example, the youngest father credits his time in the military service for his attention to detail and more patience for certain traditional household tasks, such as ironing and washing floors. Even though his fiancée is a homemaker, he prefers to take over these tasks.

Finally, the absentee father is also the only father who has experienced an unstable employment history. At 32, he has had over 20 jobs and was unemployed many times. In the meantime, the prospect of fatherhood at age 18 made him feel angry and irresponsible. It has taken him over ten years, a decision to improve his life, and a supportive spouse to turn his concern for his daughter into a realistic endeavor. Majoring in social work and tutoring at his college part-time, he now agrees that having a child did change his career plans, *"because one-third of what I'm doing is for her."*

This research has shown that paternal involvement is a multicausal phenomenon. We must look both at its three causes and at the connections between them. This paper started by observing the recent interest in American fatherhood. It ends by posing that that interest is bound to increase as we learn more about the varieties of fatherhood experience among African American men.

NOTES

[1] An earlier version of this paper was presented at the 20th Annual Center for Studies of the Family Conference: Race/Ethnic Families in the United States, Brigham Young University, Provo, Utah, October 13-14, 1993. The author wishes to thank Mary Bernstein, Daniel J. Fisher, Kathleen Gerson, Cynthia Gordon, Edith Grauer, Cardell K. Jacobson, Margaret Ketley, Jane Poulsen, Yvonne Zylan, and especially Claudia Kowalchyk for helpful comments on earlier versions of this paper. Also many thanks to the fathers in the sample, without whom this study would not be possible.

[2] In his study of black street-corner men, Liebow (1967:86) found that *"differences in father-child relationships do not depend so much on whether the man is in continuous as against intermittent or occasional contact with the child but on whether the man voluntarily assumes the role of father or has it thrust upon him."*

[3] Social class is operationalized as occupational status, so that "working class" refers to blue-collar occupations, and "middle class" refers to white-collar occupations (Landry, 1987).

[4] These attitudes are similar to those of national samples: Research shows that, compared to whites, blacks are significantly more flexible about gender roles in the family (Huber and Spitze, 1981; Penha-Lopes, 1993; Taylor et al., 1990:995)

REFERENCES

Broman, Clifford L. 1988. "Household work and family life satisfaction of blacks." *Journal of Marriage and the Family* 50 (August): 743-748.

Cazenave, Noel A. 1979. "Middle-income black fathers: An analysis of the provider role." *The Family Coordinator* 28:583-593.

Chira, Susan. 1993. "Census data show rise in child care by fathers." *New York Times* (September 22):A20.

Connor, Michael E. 1986. "Some parenting attitudes of young black fathers." Pp. 159-168 in *Men in Families*, edited by Robert A. Lewis and Robert E. Salt. Beverly Hills, CA: Sage.

DeVault, Marjorie L. 1991. *Feeding the Family: The Social Organization of Caring as Gendered Work*. Chicago: The University of Chicago Press.

Ebony. 1991. "They call them 'Mr. Mom.'" (June):54, 56-57.

Gerson, Kathleen. 1993. *No Man's Land: Men's Changing Commitment to Family and Work*. New York: Basic Books.

_____. 1985. *Hard Choices: How Women Decide about Work, Career, and Motherhood*. Berkeley and Los Angeles: University of California Press.

Gerstel, Naomi and Harriet E. Gross, eds. 1987. *Families and Work*. Philadelphia: Temple University Press.

Hochschild, Arlie. R. 1989. *The Second Shift: Working Parents and the Revolution at Home*. New York: Viking Penguin.

Huber, Joan and Glenna Spitze. 1981. "Wives' employment, household behaviors, and sex-role attitudes." *Social Forces* 68:797-812.

Landry, Bart. 1987. *The New Black Middle Class*. Berkeley and Los Angeles: University of California Press.

Liebow, Elliot. 1967. *Tally's Corner: A Study of Negro Streetcorner Men*. Boston: Little, Brown & Company.

McAdoo, John L. 1981. "Involvement of fathers in the socialization of black children." Pp. 257-269 in *Black Families*, edited by Harriette P. McAdoo. Beverly Hills, CA: Sage.

Penha-Lopes, Vânia. 1993. "Roots that don't die: Explaining gender-role attitudes of black and white men." Paper presented at the 88th Annual Meeting of the American Sociological Association (August), Miami.

Peters, Marie F. 1988. "Parenting in black families with young children." Pp. 228-241 in *Black Families*, edited by Harriette P. McAdoo. Beverly Hills, CA: Sage.

Peterson, Iver. 1992. "For absent fathers, a ray of hope." *New York Times* (September 29):B5.

Robinson, John P. 1988. "Who's doing the housework?" *American Demographics* (December):24-28, 63.

Special Report. 1993. "A world without fathers: The struggle to save the black family." *Newsweek* (August 30):18-28.

Staples, Robert. 1989[1978]. "Masculinity and race: The dual dilemma of black men." Pp. 73-83 in *Men's Lives*. Second edition, edited by Michael S. Kimmel and Michael A. Messner. New York: Macmillan.

Taylor, Robert Joseph, Linda M. Chatters, M. Belinda Tucker, and Edith Lewis. 1990. "Developments in research on black families: A decade review." *Journal of Marriage and the Family* 52 (November):993-1014.

Wilson, William J. 1987. *The Truly Disadvantaged: The Inner City, the Underclass, the Public Policy*. Chicago: The University of Chicago Press.

The Intersection of Ethnic and Gender Identities: Northern Cheyenne Women's Roles in Cultural Recovery

Carol Ward, Gregory Hinckley, and Kae Sawyer

Recent research on Native Americans has begun to focus more on the changing roles and contributions of women to family, educational, economic and religious life (e.g., Allen, 1986; Medicine, 1988; La Fromboise et al., 1990). These studies have been an important remedy to the earlier neglect of women's roles and experiences in Native American communities. Work in this area has emphasized the diversity among tribal groups as well as the effects of the dominant society's efforts to assimilate Indian populations. Still, it has not ignored the continuity of tribal cultural practices in the face of efforts to change Indian families, communities and institutions. As a contribution to this emerging literature, in this paper we examine the shifting roles of Northern Cheyenne women in the areas of family, work, education, and religion. Our discussion is intended to reveal the effects of assimilationist practices for this population as well as how changes in women's roles are contributing to a kind of reversal of assimilation.

A case study of Northern Cheyenne women is relevant for both theoretical and empirical reasons. First, the study of a culturally distinct community helps to bring specific cultural dimensions of community life into focus. Additionally, because this reservation population has many of the same types of social, political and economic conditions experienced by other Native American communities and minority populations, this study should help us to understand the role of a variety of factors in the development of contemporary women's roles. Moreover, in this study we will be able to see specifically how these minority women have asserted their cultural preferences in the formation of their identities and the performance of current roles.

The formation of gender and ethnic identities and associated roles is a complex process that has been the object of recent study by both Indian and non-Indian social scientists. Among these efforts, the approach of Nancy Bonvillain is useful for its attention to the changing circumstances of Native American women. Specifically, Bonvillain (1988) suggests that ". . . *sex role plans [or models of gender behavior and related ideologies (Sanday, 1981)] express differences in men's and women's autonomy, prestige, power and authority*" (p. 3). She contends that understanding Native American gender roles must take into account the ecological, social and historical factors which shape subsistence activities. Important features of Native American communities include post-marital residence patterns and descent rules, household dynamics and relations, rights of participation in public decision-making as well as religious rituals, and the degree of disruption from policies of European colonization. Bonvillain suggests that knowledge of these aspects of community life will provide the basis for a more thorough analysis of gender roles, identities and how they change.

Since the Cheyennes, like other Native Americans, have been subject to severe assimilationist policies, the persistence of traditional cultural practices, especially those concerning gender roles and relations, is an important issue. In her analysis of contemporary Native American literature, Rebecca Tsosie (1988) notes a recent interest among Indian women writers to "recover the feminine in American Indian traditions [Allen, 1986]." As explored in literature, this process has involved recognition of oppression, letting go of self-directed anger, and identifying self-worth through connections to traditions and kin (p. 29). The results for Indian women have included, first, a rejection of Western cultural polarities which have victimized women and minority ethnic groups, and, second, the restoration of a voice consistent with traditions ". . . *which emphasizes their bond to the female life-forces of the universe.* . ." (p. 32).

Teresa LaFromboise and her associates (1990) also have strongly urged that those studying Native American gender roles identify each specific tribe's traditional structures, the varying effects of Euro-American culture on the tribe, the factors which mediate the amount and direction of Euro-American influence, and the personal responses and adaptations of Indian women to cultural and social changes (p.

456). In this paper, we will trace some of the important changes to traditional Cheyenne gender roles, and then discuss recent efforts by women to retrieve or "recover" some traditional cultural practices of the Cheyennes. Interestingly, this "cultural recovery" is occurring, in part, in relation to the recent expansion of women's roles in their families and communities. Thus, we will show how the experiences of Cheyenne women, as mediated by their contact with both the dominant society and their Cheyenne culture, affect their current roles.

HISTORY AND BACKGROUND

The Cheyenne family has remained central to Cheyenne culture despite the many changes in Cheyenne society which have come with the advent of the reservation system. These changes have had profound effects on the roles of both men and women. However, as our ethnographic data reveal, family continues to be a dominant force in the lives of women in particular. This continuity in the context of forced assimilation raises an interesting question regarding current feminist explanations of women's roles. Specifically, how do changes in Cheyenne women's roles relate to essentialist and structural explanations of women's roles? In other words, can the roles of Cheyenne women be understood in terms of essentialist notions concerning biological imperatives for women, or are they better explained as adaptations to the dramatic structural changes imposed on Cheyenne families and communities? The answer to this question will take shape as we present a brief review of the historical and social forces affecting ethnic and gender assimilation in Cheyenne culture and society.

Historical and anthropological information is useful for understanding developments in Cheyenne social life. Cheyenne families have been largely matrilocal and bilineal although these patterns have varied by time period (Moore, 1987). As in many other tribes, in traditional society Cheyenne women had a primary and dominant role in the domestic sphere within a patriarchal system. However, unlike other plains tribes, the residence of women near their parents and siblings often resulted in the protection of their rights and authority (Llewellyn and Hoebel, 1978). In Cheyenne culture, at least during nomadic and pre-reservation periods, women had the authority and power to make decisions regarding the socialization of children as well as other activities central to the family. Men's decisions, on the other hand, more often concerned larger issues of family and community life such as band movement, warfare, religious rituals and political-juridical issues. They also pursued central productive activities such as hunting while women engaged in subsistence horticulture.

The Northern Cheyenne reservation was established in southeastern Montana in 1884. It now includes 447,000 acres spanning across two counties located 100 miles southeast of Billings, MT. The reservation has a population of about 4,000. Although it has never been developed, 5 billion tons of low-sulphur coal lie just beneath the surface of the reservation (Chestnut, 1979). However, development of coal deposits by energy companies has occurred to the north and south of the reservation and has provided the basis for boom and bust periods in the local economy. Today, similar to many other reservations, the Northern Cheyenne reservation economy is tightly tied to public sector activities. In fact, the majority of jobs on the reservation are located in federal agencies, such as the Bureau of Indian Affairs (BIA) and Indian Health Service (IHS), tribal government programs and services and public and tribal schools. According to the 1989 Educational Census of the Northern Cheyenne Reservation, among the 50-60 percent of adults on the reservation who work, only about 12 percent work in private businesses. A larger percentage of employed adults are women (53 percent) than men (47 percent), and among young adults (ages 18-24), young men are much more likely to be unemployed (70 percent) than women (52 percent) (Ward and Wilson, 1989).

The Northern Cheyenne Tribe is similar to other tribes in Montana in that this population is very young and poor—the percentage of Northern Cheyennes under the age of 18 was 50 percent in 1980, and 46 percent of the reservation households had incomes below the poverty level (State of Montana, 1985). Again, similar to other reservation populations, the Northern Cheyennes have a high dropout rate (46 percent) (Ward, 1992; Snipp, 1989). Additionally, young women have a higher dropout rate than males—among recent high school students, young women dropped out at a rate of 48 percent compared to 44 percent for males (Ward, 1993). Finally, Northern Cheyennes have a high rate of substance abuse. A study conducted by the National Institute on Drug Abuse (NIDA) in 1987 found that a much higher proportion of Indian students than white students abuse substances often enough to impair their physical and emotional health.

Recent social and cultural information for Northern Cheyenne tribal members reveals that many continue to have a strong sense of tribal identity based on shared language, culture, history, political organization and social structure (U.S. Bureau of Land Management, 1989). An important factor for the maintenance of this identity is the physical isolation of the reservation. Additionally, Northern Cheyennes make up the majority of the reservation population. The result is that Northern Cheyennes have more opportunities for interaction with members of their own tribe than do most other tribes (Ward and Wilson, 1989).

On the other hand, several changes in reservation life have contributed to the increasing diversity of the population. These changes include improved roads, increasing availability of television via satellite and cable, and increases in the regional population. Additionally, Northern Cheyenne tribal members often leave the reservation for military service, work and education opportunities. Most people also leave for short trips for recreation and shopping. Finally, another source of diversity is the increased participation in new institutions such as tribal government, formal schools and the labor market (U.S. Bureau of Land Management, 1989).

Kinship, however, is a fundamental element in the social relationships and culture of the Northern Cheyennes. Many members of extended families still choose to live close to each other although they are increasingly more scattered (U.S. Bureau of Land Management, 1989). In fact, the location of family groups on the reservation today still follows, to some extent, the location of the bands which settled on the reservation in the 1880s. Social status within the tribal population also is still related to the membership of individuals in family groups, or bands, that comprise the five geographic districts of the reservation— Ashland, Birney, Busby, Lame Deer and Muddy. These communities differ in size, character and history.

SOCIAL AND CULTURAL CONTEXTS OF THREE GENERATIONS OF WOMEN

Changes in the sex role plans for women on the reservation today can be traced from the early reservation period. In this period, women's roles still reflected, to a large extent, the types of activities that characterized the earlier nomadic and horticultural periods in which women's responsibilities and authority in the family were primary.

While men had been the primary providers in these periods and had assumed central roles in religious and governance activities, women contributed to both production and cultural activities by gathering, growing, storing, preparing and distributing food and by participating in religious and social activities (Llewellyn and Hoebel, 1978).

Despite some continuities, both men's and women's roles began to change as a result of confinement to the reservation and assimilationist policies. For example, men were required to take on farming and ranching as new types of production, and they had to give up many of the traditional religious and governance roles they had held. Although women continued to provide for the sustenance of the family by gardening and working with their husbands in the fields (Weist, 1977), other family roles changed. In particular, women lost their central role in the socialization of children as federal Indian education policies required Indian children to leave their homes at an early age to attend boarding schools. These children spent long periods of time away from family members, were forced to learn English and give up traditions including dress, language, religion and social activities while they were at school.

Subsequently, as subsistence activities continued to respond to federal agency policies and economic conditions, gender roles underwent further changes. Specifically, men's roles in production shifted again as BIA decisions brought about the termination of tribal ranching activities while, at the same time, wheat growing declined with changes in the regional economy. These changes dramatically affected the oldest generation of women living on the reservation today who were born in the late 1920s and early 1930s. A profile of the oldest generation focusing on the social, cultural and economic circumstances affecting their lives will be reviewed below, followed by profiles of the second and third generations of Cheyenne women. Although some the social conditions affecting the oldest generation have persisted, each of the three generations have faced some distinctive circumstances which have shaped their roles.

First Generation Reservation Women

An important element of the economic environment for the oldest generation was recovery from the depression of the 1930s. Federal programs created the Indian Civilian Conservation Corp (CCC) (Weist, 1977) which provided reservation-based jobs for men primarily in construction of roads and housing, a wage-earning alternative to growing wheat and ranching. Women continued to work at whatever jobs they could find, such as cooking, cleaning and laundering, in non-Indian households. Most women expected to either help their husbands in the fields or to have wage jobs in order to support their families. When the CCC jobs ended, however, many families were left with no livelihood and, thus, became dependent on welfare.

Schooling was available at three schools—the BIA boarding school, the Catholic Mission boarding school, and the off-reservation public school established in the 1940s. Most Cheyennes went to the BIA and Catholic boarding schools, two Indian schools whose programs focused on assimilation of their students. Most Cheyenne women in this generation went to boarding schools and dropped out to marry and start their families (Sawyer, 1993). The Cheyenne language was commonly spoken at home although English was required at all three schools. Cheyenne cultural activities were still central to everyday life.

Women in the oldest generation had direct personal contact with family members who had lived the old ways and practiced traditional religion, although during their childhood these practices were outlawed. Many of the oldest generation women were taught by their mothers and grandmothers about the traditional Cheyenne ways of life, spoke the language and knew about the traditional religious practices (Hinckley, 1994).

Second Generation Reservation Women

For the second generation of Cheyenne women born in the early 1950s, conditions also shifted in some new and important ways. Economic opportunities for this generation included many more jobs compared to the earlier period. This was directly related to the growth of federal programs, particularly the Office for Economic Opportunity (OEO), a key element of the War on Poverty. The programs which resulted from this effort produced a large number of service-oriented jobs which many young women of the second generation (as well as some of their mothers) held. For example, the Community Action Program provided for a range of social services and community development activities. Although Indian and non-Indian men were more likely to be the administrators of these programs, women filled the many lower-level administrative and clerical positions needed to operate the programs. Some new opportunities for men also became available from expansion of energy (coal) development activities in the area (Weist, 1977).

Schooling opportunities expanded for this generation as more funding became available for Indian education nationally. The Catholic Mission school and public schools expanded to meet the needs of the increasing population that settled there during the boom periods of coal mining and construction of power plants, and the BIA school became one of the first tribally-controlled schools in the nation (Weist, 1977; Bryan and Yellowtail, 1985). Larger numbers of the second generation women attended the non-Indian public school although the majority attended the two Indian schools serving reservation students. The emphasis of schooling was still assimilation of Indian students. This group has the highest rate of high school graduation, an achievement for which many postponed marriage (Sawyer, 1993).

Cultural change continued for the second generation as fewer of these women grew up speaking Cheyenne. Their parents often did not insist that they learn Cheyenne since they would not be able to speak it at school. Many of the second generation women understand Cheyenne, although they generally say that they do not speak it well. Because the American Indian Religious Freedom Act of 1978 restored the rights to participate in traditional spiritual practices, Cheyenne ceremonies became more available and public. Many of these women grew up attending traditional ceremonies and social activities but to a lesser extent than their mothers. Most second generation women joined churches that had been established on the reservation (Hinckley, 1994).

Third Generation Reservation Women

The third generation of Cheyenne women, born in the early 1970s, grew up in still different social, economic and cultural conditions. Economic opportunities declined for this generation with the decrease in federal programs in the 1980s. Funding cuts which resulted in the loss of jobs contributed to an increase in unemployment to over 50 percent through the 1980s. Women, however, continued to have a larger proportion of the clerical and service jobs in agencies, schools and programs on the reservation. As mentioned earlier, women in this age group also have a higher rate of employment than men (Ward and Wilson, 1989).

Schooling opportunities changed for the third generation as BIA funding for the Tribal School declined. However, the Catholic school still operated as a boarding school and expanded its facilities and programs. The largest proportion of Indian students attended the public and Catholic schools. Among this generation, more women dropped out of high school than their mothers, and more women dropped out than men (Sawyer, 1993). However, more women in this generation have obtained General Education Diplomas (GEDs) and attend college than men (Northern Cheyenne Adult Education Evaluation Report, 1992).

This group of women has the smallest proportion of Cheyenne speakers. Few say they know much about the cultural practices, religious or social ceremonies of their tribe. Although they attend tribal events, these young women have been more engaged than other generations with the dominant white culture which they experience when they leave the reservation to shop, through television and through their schooling in the off-reservation public school. Many were baptized into Christian churches but do not participate in them today.

In sum, up to the first half of this century, Northern Cheyenne women had prominent roles in social, economic and cultural activities of the tribe although their participation was influenced by both the patriarchal system and matrilocal residence patterns. These patterns have shifted and changed across time and are still fluid today. Early changes in Cheyenne women's sex role plans reduced their roles in central institutions, such as the family, as cultural and religious activities were outlawed and children were sent away to school. However, later changes resulted in the expansion of women's roles to include greater financial responsibility for their family as work opportunities declined for men. Although schools now contribute to the socialization of all Cheyenne children, fewer attend boarding school. Thus, women have once again become primary figures in their children's socialization while their responsibilities for financial support of the family continue to be important as well. Men have been able to resume key roles in government and traditional culture as the availability of Cheyenne social and religious practices has increased across the generations. However, the youngest generation of men and women has the least knowledge of Cheyenne traditions.

ETHNOGRAPHIC RESEARCH FINDINGS

Given this background, we now turn to the findings of our on-going ethnographic research which illustrate role changes among Northern Cheyenne women. From twenty intensive interviews with women of three generations and key informants representing eight family groups, and extensive participant observation from 1987 to the present, we have identified changes in women's roles which reveal some contradictory trends in both ethnic and gender assimilation. In the remainder of the paper, detailed findings concerning women's education, work, family and religious roles will be presented.

Educational Attainment

Despite little direct encouragement for educational attainment, the women in this study saw themselves as good students, and many had been quite active in extracurricular activities, most prominently basketball and cheerleading. Respondents felt that there was no difference in the educational expectations among parents for boys and girls. Although the members of the youngest generation were more likely to define "success" as including achievement in education and the work place, more generally personal success for women on the reservation is **not** measured in terms of school achievement, career status or accumulation of wealth. In fact, individuals who drop out of school rarely receive serious negative sanctions, although they do receive encouragement to pursue alternative routes to graduation, such as obtaining a GED. Several interviews illustrate common patterns:

> *When I think back to grade school there was a lot of parents who didn't see the importance of having a productive home for their kids. A lot of the kids had to babysit instead of coming to school or they kept them home mostly to babysit because they needed them. They didn't really need them that bad but they were drinking or something. So a lot of the girls in the eighth grade quit, they didn't go on to high school. A lot of boys quit just because of no encouragement* (second generation).
> *Some of them stuck through it through high school, but I'd say about fifteen percent of them just went to school, transferred to different schools, got kicked out and had problems*

> *with drinking and at home and they were like two grades short from graduating* (third generation).
>
> *I think I was expected to go to college, but I don't feel like I was prepared, and I think they expected me to go, but it was never a big issue. They expected it of me but it just wasn't really talked about, or they didn't really explain why I needed an education or anything like that* (second generation).

The lack of direct guidance or involvement with children's schooling by parental and other adult authority figures is related to several facets of Cheyenne community life. Three particularly important features of Cheyenne culture suggest why adolescents may not feel a great deal of pressure regarding educational attainment. First, traditional Cheyenne parents often use a parenting style which includes noninterference in the decisions children make although they do provide general expectations and guidance about living. Second, some parents have little experience with schooling and how to help their children in school. A third factor concerns the effects of substance abuse which may make parents less available to assist their children. As a result, many adolescents do not receive the practical assistance they may need with decisions about schooling or help with schoolwork. Thus, they have a great deal of independence in their schooling. While such factors may help to explain the high dropout rate, however, they don't really clarify why young women drop out more often than young men. As shown elsewhere (Ward, 1993), the gender gap in school completion is better explained by key features of social life such as the expectations for women concerning family roles as well as the types of peer, family and community support they receive for school achievement compared to other activities. For many young women, schooling is secondary to family and financial concerns.

Work and Occupational Patterns

The current social climate on the reservation is one that accepts the fact that many women have to work for pay outside the home due to financial necessity. Data collected in this case study show that economic survival is the reason women most often articulate for pursuing employment. In other words, working women are less motivated by career aspirations and fulfillment or vocational ambition than by financial need;

for each generation of women, working is directly related to the need to provide for their families. A first generation, divorced woman reported her need to work while her children were still at home and she was still married:

> *I started working when (my third child) was about . . . he wasn't even a year old when I started working. I had to get out and go to work.*

A second generation, married mother of five children stated:

> *The only reason I went back is because I had to start working to get some more income.*

A young divorced mother of two from the third generation explained why she is working now:

> *Right now I'm working because I want to get my financial situation in order and then I'd like to go back to school for a while.*

Women feel strongly that part of their responsibilities as a mother is providing financial resources for their children to make a better life for them, and they do not (or cannot) always rely on male partners. For a variety of reasons, males are often not expected to fulfill obligations as the sole breadwinner for the family. The high unemployment rate for men is reflected in the strong push women feel to enter the labor force.

Another divorced woman from the third generation defined her role in the household in these terms:

> *I would see my role as working and supporting my family financially and taking care of my kids and the house.*

Often, working in the jobs they choose is not seen as a planned strategy, but rather the only recourse they have, given their marital and economic circumstances, to maintain an acceptable standard of living:

I see it as not being a real choice, it's something that if you are going to survive, it's just got to be done. I know I see myself in that position. I don't have a choice in the matter anymore, it's just something that has to be done (second generation).

Working women also reported the need to continue their training or education in connection with their jobs. However, pursuing educational interests and career was secondary to making the household's financial ends meet. In fact, continuing education often got put on the back burner as the economic situation combined with the family circumstances and limited social opportunities often precluded active and consistent pursuit of individual goals once women married and started families. However, gaining further education is perceived as a way women can increase earning power and better provide for their children. A divorced mother in her late thirties stated it this way:

Women . . . have said, "I realize that I needed to have my schooling and if my husband's not working or my partner's not working then I'd better get out there and do it, because we've got to provide for these kids, we've got to support this family" (key informant).

While aspirations for individually fulfilling careers were often articulated by these women as part of their expectation upon completion of their high school education, most of these aspirations remain unfulfilled. Women have all held jobs that were available in order to be financially secure. For these women working outside the home does not merely provide supplemental income. Their families are financially dependent on their working to provide the main source of support.

Variation exists between generations in the kinds of jobs that have been available to women. The oldest women started out doing cleaning and washing and babysitting for reservation institutions or local families. Second generation women are more likely to have worked in clerical and service/care-giving jobs which developed with the expansion of federal programs. Some factory work has also been available from time to time. However, clerical and service work continue to be the main job opportunities for women. One first generation woman had hopes of becoming a nurse, but has now moved into an administrative position at the tribal college. Even if they completed training in another area, women have been drawn by the job market on the reservation into these clerical positions. An example of this is a second generation woman who completed training as a dental assistant at a program in another state, but after returning to the reservation could not find positions available in this field.

Some women have found their opportunities to have expanded recently, while others feel there is no change.

> *Most of the jobs [for women] I think are more secretarial positions, clerical positions, you see a lot of that. I know with my own experience, whatever is available is what you apply for, and if you get it you're lucky. That's kind of the way it's been for me. I've seen myself gain a lot of experience that way, though. A lot of the other positions that are more like care-giving jobs, like day care, matrons, kind of like that role that women play, I think* (third generation).

As opportunities have expanded in some areas on the reservation, some women have advanced from clerical jobs into areas of specific expertise. They have assumed such positions as program directors and other administrative positions in the tribal court and tribal council, the Northern Cheyenne Chamber of Commerce, and Native Action, a local advocacy organization.

In spite of the recent changes in opportunity, all of the women in this study have chosen to remain on the reservation and, therefore, have had to adapt their career/job aspirations to match the essentially limited opportunity structure in their communities. Many prefer jobs or careers which currently do not exist in the reservation job market.

Women in the youngest generation especially expect to receive college degrees and pursue careers in an area of interest to them. Programs at the high schools have assisted these students to pursue education related to specific career choices. Whether or not there will be opportunities for these young women on the reservation when they complete their degrees remains to be seen. However, regardless of the increased expectations and accessibility of attending college, many of these young women are choosing to start families early, beginning in pathways much like their mothers.

The Relationship between Family and Work Roles

As Northern Cheyenne women have made choices concerning schooling and work, they are informed and influenced by their social and family networks which form a central part of community life on the reservation. Specifically, since many women with children who work outside the home do not have husbands, help with child care and community support are necessities. However, women who do not work outside the home also look for support from their friends, family and community for their choice not to work. Although perceptions of the support women receive varies with their network of family members and peers in the community, the importance of support for their choices is clearly present among all Northern Cheyenne women. One key informant commented on the support available for women's decisions to work:

> *I kind of think there always was a certain acceptance for women to work over the last 50 years because there are a number of older women that I have talked to that wanted to work and did work. There was someone I was talking to yesterday. Her grandmother had been in the Army in WWII and there was one of the people that I interviewed, the older lady last time, she said she wanted to work, wanted to graduate from high school and work. So I think there are some feelings like it was okay. It may have varied from family to family.*

The availability of more practical types of support to women also contributes to their decisions to work. A key informant indicated, for example, that one of the main reasons women leave their jobs is inadequate child care. In many cases grandparents and other relatives provide care-giving services for women with children who work. Several women indicated that this is consistent with traditional Cheyenne practices in which grandparents assume responsibility for helping to raise their children's children. Some of the women in the study are also child care providers for other family members or friends. However, this type of child care is not always a reliable source of support. One informant explained:

There's not a lot of basic support like child care, good child care, and some of the things where their minds can rest easy while they're actually working and so sometimes they've actually pulled off the job because they don't have a baby-sitter, the babysitter's sick or day cares open and close again, they don't seem to function on a regular schedule.

Some women initially feel guilt about not being home with their children. They, nevertheless, must participate in the work force, adjusting their family life and priorities accordingly. A young, third generation, divorced mother expressed her feelings about working while there were still children at home:

Oh, I feel so guilty. I wanted to be like Betty Crocker and June Cleaver and Ghandi and Mother Theresa all rolled up into one and just can't, oh and Wonder Woman, too. But it has affected my child rearing. I think I've gotten closer to my kids since I started working. The time is so precious that I have to spend with them that we do talk on a deeper level, on a real feeling level to try to get at what's bothering us and deal with it. More so than what we did before. It was like we have all the time in the world, we can deal with this later. But now that I am working it is a little different story.

In this case, the respondent had to negotiate between the financial needs of her family and the strong inclination she felt to remain at home while she was still raising children. In such a situation, both her family needs and her access to support were determining factors in the choice she made.

Women also indicate that sometimes men feel threatened by working women, both spouses and co-workers. One second generation woman told about an occasion when her husband appeared to be supportive of her as she prepared to go on a business trip. The morning she was to leave, however, her husband stayed home from work to keep her from going on the trip. This was repeated on other occasions. Other women commented that male co-workers are threatened by women in authority or power in the organizations in which they work.

Interestingly, women were less likely to mention work roles in relation to their personal achievements but focused instead on their roles in the family. Although women in the older two generations most clearly emphasized the roles of women as wife and mother, all have been employed outside the home. Regardless of the generation, women indicated that caring for the family is a central role. However, this role typically involves a range of activities including work outside the home. Income-producing work is, in fact, one of the most important ways that women care for their families. The variety of activities associated with caring for family and the strength required of women for performing their roles are expressed in the following comments:

> *I would see my role as working and supporting my family financially and taking care of my kids and the house* (third generation).

> *I think if you take a good look at my mother and my grand-mother, we were all like the dominant spouse, we were the ones that made all the major decisions. My sisters are the same way . . . they do take the responsibility, the total responsibility* (second generation).

Women in each generation have expected to support their families although each generation has done this in its own ways.

Summary: Critical Changes in Women's Roles Across Generations

Differences in the experience of women across generations coincide with historical, social and cultural changes. One of the most important differences concerns schooling. The oldest generation women were forced to go to school and most dropped out before graduating, while the second generation typically finished high school, and some have college experience although few have college degrees. In contrast, the third generation has a higher dropout rate than their mothers. The oldest generation saw little advantage to gaining an education. Although schooling was generally perceived positively, it often meant the loss of their native language and did not necessarily lead to better jobs. Obligations to family and desire to marry were much more important. These women generally withdrew from school by the time they were fifteen or sixteen to marry or to work to help support the family. The second generation received more encouragement to complete their high school education. Their parents wanted something more for them than they had for themselves. It was for this group that increased schooling and work opportunities became available on the reservation. The second generation women used their school credentials to gain access to new opportunities to work, although they have been concentrated in service and clerical jobs. Because of the limitations they see for job advancement, however, these women have begun to question the relevance of their educational credentials to obtaining good jobs in the reservation context. As one second generation respondent states:

> *My best friend went to college and finished. And I always wondered where it got her because she's sort of in the same position I am in the BIA up at Billings* (second generation).

Ambiguity about educational goals seems to have increased for the youngest generation of women who attended high school in the late 1980s. This generation has had the most exposure to white culture and society. In their high schools, special programs identified the best and brightest among the reservation students and encouraged them to pursue higher education goals. These responses from a third generation woman convey her experiences with support for pursuing higher education.

> *Q. Was there support in the community for education?*
> *A. There was some, but not really a whole lot.*
>
> *Q. In Lame Deer?*
> *A. Yeah, in Lame Deer community.*
>
> *Q. When you say some, who would that be from?*
> *A. Just like the career development and when they come down and work with you to decide what sort of jobs you want to go into and talk to you about college. That was probably the most support for going to college.*

Such programs provide alternative signals about schooling expectations which conflict with what students see on the reservation and in their own families. At the same time they receive increased demands for assimilation to white society, the youngest generation of women reports more negative personal experiences (e.g., prejudice) associated with being Native American than previous generations. This is due largely to their greater interaction with non-Indians and non-Indian culture. For many young adults and adolescents, such conflicts have resulted in serious problems with self-esteem (Ward, 1992).

While there is a great deal of continuity across generations about marriage and family, an important difference is the age at which women marry and start families. While the oldest generation typically married before age eighteen, the second generation married within a year after finishing high school, and among the youngest who are in their twenties, many have not married. However, they all expect to marry and have families.

Another important generational difference concerns participation in and knowledge of Cheyenne cultural practices. Ethnographic data on women's roles in Cheyenne cultural activities reveal a recent increase in women's participation in this area. It is to these new roles for women that the discussion now turns.

Women and Cultural Recovery

Many of the women in the second and third generations take part in traditional ceremonies today. Interestingly, this participation has taken on new and important meanings for these women. Unlike schooling and work roles which require greater participation in non-Indian culture, where religion is concerned, many women are becoming more traditional. A growing number of the younger generations of women who have more education and who have not grown up speaking Cheyenne are now returning to their Cheyenne cultural heritage. However, only women in the oldest generation had direct personal contact with family members who at one time lived a traditional life, although even during their childhood it was outlawed and not publicly practiced. The second and third generations women have had few living examples of traditional life-styles. Consequently, the younger generations have had to rely on the oldest generation for this information. Many have not been successful in learning about Cheyenne culture and religion. When asked about the sources of their knowledge about the traditional ways, some women of the youngest generation answered:

*I really don't know my culture, as the Indian religion, I don't
really know how that goes or I never practiced it or nobody's
ever taught me how to.*

 *No one ever taught me about the Cheyenne ways. My
parents were not really traditional.*

In contrast, another young woman's response shows the effects of
recent changes:

*Growing up I did not know very much. . . when I was older
my dad gave me articles to read. . . Now my [family] is really
into the Indian way of life, the Cheyennes. And we go around
to Sun Dances and all kinds of Cheyenne ceremonies and
we're always exposed to something, so it's pretty normal going
to ceremonies and things like that now.*

Although women in the second generation were more likely to have
heard about some features of the traditional life-style during their
childhoods, many are learning the traditional ways as adults. Some
examples are:

*My grandmother told me a lot of the superstitions maybe, but
she wasn't into like Indian dancing or anything like that. Her
mother, her father was a medicine man, a fairly well-known
medicine man in his tribe, and her mother was a real strong
Christian, so she had those two views, and I was raised in the
Mennonite Church, because that's where she went to church
and that's where I grew up.*

 *Yeah, she [her grandmother] told us about some of the
stuff, but she never had really taken part. . . but now it is [her
husband] who tells me all the meaning behind like the Sun
Dance, the renewal of life, everything, and the sweats.*

 *Yeah, and what I, like I said, you know, what I know
about the Cheyenne ways I learned from my present husband.
I know there must have been a reason for the Creator to bring
us two together, you know, otherwise I probably would have
never learned because my ex-husband wasn't that interested.
He didn't really care to go to powwows or anything like that
and my family, when I was growing up, they weren't that*

> *interested in traditions, we never went. . . I don't know, it's like it took that long and then, you know, meeting [her husband] for me to come back to my, to our ways, to Cheyenne ways.*

Women in the oldest generation recount being taught by their mothers and grandmothers about the traditional ways. One woman even told of receiving instruction with her brother about religious traditions:

> *Yes. I go to sit with my brother when they instruct him and he put on a Sun Dance so I go to sit in on it and listen in. . . they selected four women [for the Elk society] and they were the last ones.*

All of the women interviewed said that they felt it was important to pass these traditional ways on to their children. One second generation woman commented on how she has learned about traditional religion over the last ten years and her feelings about it today:

> *I started learning how to sing at Sun Dances and then I started sweating and I learned about the sweats and the meaning of the sweats. I . . . feel, like out right now, the way my present husband's grandmother believed, you know, she was the Sacred Hat Keeper for a long time and that's how [he] was raised, that way, you know.*

Such women are "rediscovering" traditional practices that have been lost or not available to them through the families they were raised in. One third generation woman relates her feelings about the process of returning to more traditional ways.

> *I'm 33 and I'm just now starting to learn what it's like to be who I am as a Cheyenne, you know, to appreciate the earth, to appreciate the water, to appreciate family.*

When asked how she had learned about traditional religion and how it had become a part of her everyday life, a second generation woman answered:

*I think losing members of my family made me realize just how
precious life truly is and how I dealt with some of my grief
was going to like sweats and fasting and sitting around and
listening to the old women. I don't know, it was just time. It
was time for me to learn and it was there. It just happened.*

For many of these women the impetus for a return to or discovery
of Cheyenne cultural traditions comes from their participation in recovery from substance abuse or chemical dependency. Women are
more frequently involved in recovery than men; generally women have
outnumbered men in treatment programs as well as in support groups
like Alcoholics Anonymous on the reservation. This has implications
for families affected by addiction and substance abuse as women have
become better able to care for their children, continue their education
and move into the labor force. For these women, recovery activities
have also included efforts to establish new understandings of personal
identity which are healthier and more closely tied to their Cheyenne
heritage.

For other women, current interest in Cheyenne spirituality and
traditions is a result of their maturation within a context in which
learning about and practicing Cheyenne traditional ways is more available and accepted. Regardless of the reasons for or the factors which
have produced it, this renewed interest in Cheyenne spirituality and
culture is seen as an important way in which women (and men) can find
support for their roles in Cheyenne family and community life.

CONCLUSION

The information presented from a case study involving Northern
Cheyenne women's experiences suggests some interesting patterns regarding both gender and ethnic assimilation. Bonvillain, Tsosie, and
LaFromboise suggested that to understand Native American women's
roles today requires careful consideration of features of traditional
native societies, such as their complexity, residence patterns, subsistence and cultural activities and how women and men participated.
Additionally, sources of changes must be identified, such as assimilation practices and federal policies that affect subsistence and political
activities, as well as the direction and impact of these forces. In
response to these recommendations, we have indicated that Northern

Cheyenne social life has become considerably more complex than in earlier periods. Cheyenne society now includes all the specialized institutions established by the dominant society for meeting the needs of communities. However, these institutions have not met the needs of Cheyenne community members both in terms of their quantity and quality. That is, they typically have resolved the problems or tasks they were designed for in ways that do not represent the material or cultural interests of the Cheyennes. For example, because of the dominance of non-Indian political economy and culture, work roles have reflected the hierarchical sex role plans that have typified American society—men have held the higher-paying (often administrative) jobs while women assumed lower-paying clerical jobs. However, the smaller number of jobs in the reservation economy overall, which are still located primarily in the public sector, has never adequately provided for the employment needs of Cheyennes, particularly men. Consequently, men now have a higher unemployment rate than women. Similarly, while schooling opportunities have increased with each generation, men have generally graduated at higher rates but have been less able to use their schooling for obtaining work. Women, on the other hand, have dropped out more often, but typically have been able to access jobs needed to support their families. In these ways, assimilation efforts have affected not only the social organization of Cheyenne life but have resulted in increasing the gender gap between men and women, particularly in the areas of education and work.

In contrast, family and kinship groups persist as focal points in the lives of Cheyennes despite the assaults they have taken from efforts to transform Indian families. However, even within the family which remains the source of cultural and spiritual life, changes have occurred. While women and men have continued to engage some aspects of their cultural and religious heritage within the family, these roles have adapted in response to financial need, the exclusion of men from important productive activities, and cultural assimilation of the community in which families are located. Thus, while men have resumed some public roles in traditional ceremonies and government, they have moved away from important family responsibilities. On the other hand, while women have continued many of their roles in the home, they have now moved into more public roles as well. Our data suggest that these changes among women can be understood as an expansion of the cultural principles associated with care for the family and kin to include working outside the home in community organizations. This adaptation has occurred among all three generations of women living on the reservation today. However, it has been the most pronounced among members of the second generation. By virtue of their increased work experience in a number of areas, women of the second generation are now beginning to move up within the hierarchies of the organizations for which they work, taking on such new jobs as administrators of programs, teachers, tribal court judges, tribal council members, lawyers, social workers, counselors and company executives. Importantly, however, none of these work roles are seen as being either superior to or in conflict with women's central roles in the family.

Despite less practical knowledge of their traditions generally, members of the two younger generations of women are looking to their cultural heritage to meet identity and spiritual needs. Thus, they have been at the forefront of a process of "cultural recovery" which often extends beyond their own personal quests for identity and spirituality to include the participation of their partners, children or other family members and friends. While men held key roles in public areas in all three generations, women have recently become more involved in community, educational and traditional religious activities. Importantly, these new efforts do not represent a return to the past but rather involve forging a link with traditions that are perceived as relevant to contemporary society and culture. Thus, women's shifting and expanding roles within the family and community have emerged as being particularly important in helping Cheyenne families to reconcile their cultural past with their current realities. Moreover, Cheyenne cultural recovery does not mean that Cheyenne women necessarily give up their church memberships or participation in such non-Indian institutions. Rather, the increasing awareness and revitalization of the Cheyenne culture among women is helping to bring these practices into other, often non-Indian, institutional settings.

In answer to the question posed at the beginning of this paper, our research shows that Cheyenne women, like other American Indian women, typically pursue family goals often associated with essentialist views of women. However, Cheyenne women have had to combat the specific structural forms of ethnic and gender oppression directed at all Native Americans. They have done this by expanding their critical family roles to include both public and private spheres in which they can pursue activities essential for personal, family and community survival. Thus, Cheyenne women are working toward a kind of gender equity which is consonant with their cultural worldview. That is, recent efforts at cultural recovery do not attempt to re-establish the Cheyenne patriarchal roles of the past but instead are intended to create a new voice and identity for Indian women (and men) within the Cheyenne culture of today. While such efforts may appear similar to or overlap with those of women in other contexts, they also differ considerably in their attention to the spiritual and cultural goals that are meaningful to Cheyenne women.

REFERENCES

Allen, P.G. 1986. *The Sacred Hoop.* Boston, Massachusetts: Beacon Press.

Bonvillain, N. 1988. "Gender relations in native North America." *American Indian Culture and Research Journal* 13 (2):1-28.

Bryan, W.L. and W.P. Yellowtail. 1985. *Future High School Education Options for the Northern Cheyenne Tribe: An Education Planning and Strategy Study.* Bozeman, MT: Silvertip Consultants.

Chestnut, S. 1979. *Coal Development on the Northern Cheyenne Reservation.* Pp. 159-183 in U.S. Commission on Civil Rights, Energy Resource Development, A Selection of Papers presented at a Consultation sponsored by the Colorado, Montana, North Dakota, South Dakota, Utah and Wyoming Advisory Committee.

Hinckley, G.S. 1994. *Coming Full Circle: Changes in Northern Cheyenne Women's Sex Roles.* Master's Thesis. Provo, UT: Brigham Young University.

LaFromboise, T., A. Heyle, and E. Ozer. 1990. "Changing and diverse roles of women in American Indian cultures." *Sex Roles* 22 (7/8):455-476.

Llewellyn, K.N. and E.A. Hoebel. 1978. *The Cheyenne Way.* Norman, Oklahoma: University of Oklahoma Press.

Medicine, B. 1988. "Native American (Indian) women: A call for research." *Anthropolgy and Education Quarterly* 19 (2):86-92.

Montana, State of. 1985. *1980 Profile of the Montana Native American.* Helena, Montana: State Department of Statistics.

Moore, J.H. 1987. *The Cheyenne Nation.* Lincoln, Nebraska: University of Nebraska Press.

National Institute of Drug Abuse. 1987. *Drug Use Among Indian Students on the Northern Cheyenne Reservation.* Western Behavioral Studies, Fort Collins: Colorado State University.

Northern Cheyenne Adult Education Program: Annual Evaluation Report. 1992. Prepared for Dull Knife Memorial College, Northern Cheyenne Tribe, Lame Deer, Montana.

Sanday, P.R. 1981. *Male Dominance and Female Autonomy.* New York: Cambridge University Press.

Sawyer, K. 1993. *Women's Choices About Family and Work: Three Generations of Northern Cheyenne Women.* Master's Thesis. Provo, UT: Brigham Young University.

Snipp, C.M. 1989. *American Indians: The First of This Land.* New York: Russell Sage Foundation.

Tsosie, R. 1988. "Changing women: The cross-currents of Ameri-can Indian feminine identity." *American Indian Culture and Research Journal* 12:1-37.

Ward, C. 1992. *Social and Cultural Influences on the Schooling of Northern Cheyenne Youth.* Unpublished dissertation. Chicago: Sociology Department, University of Chicago.

_____. 1993. "Explaining gender differences in Native American high school dropout rates: A case study of Northern Cheyenne schooling patterns." *Family Perspective* 27 (4):415-444.

_____ and D. Wilson. 1989. *1989 Educational Census of the Northern Cheyenne Reservation.* Report for the Northern Cheyenne Tribe, Lame Deer, Montana.

Weist, T. 1977. *A History of the Cheyenne People.* Billings, Montana: Montana Council for Indian Education.

U.S. Bureau of Land Management. 1989. *Economic, Social and Cultural Supplement: Powder River I Regional Environmental Impact Statement.* Miles City, MT: U.S. Department of the Interior, Miles City District Office.

Autonomy, Community, and the Mediation of Value: Comments on Apachean Grandmothering, Cultural Change, and the Media[1]

Kathleen S. Bahr and Howard M. Bahr

It is a truism that American families are "in crisis," or at least, "in transition." Sometimes the nation's family problems are seen as an aspect of a corresponding crisis in community, or responsibility, or morality. From a family point of view, one recent overview of the research evidence concludes that the "family change" of the past three decades represents "*a stunning example of social regress*" (Whitehead, 1993:80). From the standpoint of community, a contemporary essayist cites evidence of widespread community disintegration in America, and argues that external economic aggression—the subjecting (not dependence) of a local economy to a larger "*aggressive monetarily powerful outside economy*" subverts and destroys community (Berry, 1993:125-127). The author of a history on the rise of selfishness in America tries to explain how in this century the U.S. has changed from a country where self-restraint was a prime virtue to one where self-gratification has become a central ideal, where "*self-seeking is not merely condoned but actually urged upon us by philosophers, schools, television pundits, even recent governments*" (Collier, 1991:4). And a chronicler of America's dominant civil religion, "obeisance to wealth," identifies a widespread absence of meaningfulness in life, an absence of what we shall later refer to as *experiencing value*, in a memorable comment that "*never in the history of the world have so many people been so rich; never in the history of the world have so many of those same people felt themselves so poor*" (Lapham, 1988:7).

Searching for solutions, some people look to an earlier time in our history when people had stronger commitments to family and community. But close investigation reveals that what many define as an excess of individualism can be seen as an outgrowth of an ongoing tension between individual and community, between commitment and utilitarian/expressive individualism that has characterized most of American history (Bellah, et al., 1985).

Indian American cultures have managed the problem of individual in community (or individual *and* community) differently, and perhaps more successfully. More than two decades ago Vine Deloria (1970:179-80, 197) warned his white readers that they would have to adopt aspects of Indian tribalism to survive. Highwater (1981:207) spoke glowingly of the positive possibilites for a receding West of the widespread adoption of the *"perspective of primal mentality"* and of ecological and other crises that will force *"the Native American vision upon the mind and consciousness of the non-Indian."*

Much research on the American Indian's encounter with Euro-American culture and the processes of modernization, urbanization, and assimilation/acculturation focuses on Indian family disruption and social pathologies (Unger, 1977; Levy and Kunitz, 1971). Contemporary writing on Indian American families continues the emphasis on problems, but recently there has been a significant affirmation of the *strengths* of Indian families (e.g., Niethammer, 1977; Hoffman, 1981; Allen, 1986; Stockel, 1991), and some writers have contrasted them favorably to the problem-ridden families of middle Americans.

To focus on Indian family strengths, or aspects of Indian society that emphasize community as opposed to individualism, is not to say that *all* Indian cultures have these characteristics, or even that these cultural ideals were fully exhibited by any individual. Neither position—Native American families as bastions of strength or as weak shadows of their traditional selves—has been systematically documented from the standpoint of the interactional context in which family tasks and family values are transmitted. The present essay is a small step in that direction.

We shall draw upon interview and observational data collected 1989-1991 in an exploratory study of the role of shared household work in the transmission of family values between Apachean (Navajo and Apache) grandmothers and grandchildren.[2] The interviews in that project included questions about family change since the early 1900s, including changes in grandmothers' responsibility for the education of their grandchildren, changes in contact time and the activities formerly shared between grandparents and grandchildren, and perceived changes in filial responsibility and commitment between parents, grandparents, and grandchildren.

The Apachean grandparents proved to be astute observers of what has happened to their culture. They had strong opinions about what had caused problems for their children and how their traditional ways of life had been challenged. Many of their comments supported our initial theoretical notions about the importance of shared family work in creating strong families. However, the easily documentable changes, such as children spending less time in traditional work activities, and less time working in the company of parents or grandparents, are only a fairly obvious part of the story. Also important are more subtle changes associated with the meaning or value of shared family work activities for the participants and for Apache society as a whole.

Although our initial focus was the relation between family work and the transmission of cultural values in the home, it soon became apparent that family-centered education could not be considered independently of education in other contexts. An extensive literature on ethnic differences in "styles of learning" is relevant to the study of value transmission in families. Some of that literature is cited below.

We will begin with a discussion of value mediation and learning styles in which we introduce Dorothy Lee's conceptual distinction between cultural and cognitive mediation of values. Her typology may be extended to Anglo-Indian differences in learning styles that have been reported by many observers of Indian America. The basic dichotomy may also be applied to meaning systems, personality types, or entire societies or aggregates of societies, as when Indian peoples are characterized as community- or tribally-oriented in contrast to individualistic, capitalistic Anglos. In fact, Lee's dichotomy is useful because it expresses a universal polarity: all cultures may be seen as occupying some temporary balance point on the cultural value—cognitive value continuum. Managing the tension between autonomy and community is an ongoing part of social life.

Having introduced Lee's cultural/cognitive or autonomy/community distinction, and noted comparable concepts in other writings on Indian America, we consider traditional parenting and grandparenting as recalled by Apache and Navajo grandmothers. Their childhood experiences are contrasted with their reports about relationships with their own children and grandchildren today. The grandmothers' accounts of their own childhoods are congruent with the "cultural mediation" model. Their descriptions of the lives of their children and grand-children reveal some continuity of cultural mediation, along with a larger role for cognitive mediation. The grandmothers' reports also reveal the addition of a third process, which we tentatively label "media mediation."

Finally, we speculate about the long-term impact of "media mediation" upon American Indian cultures, and its power relative to the "cultural mediation" that has played such an important part in the survival of tribalism and Native values despite long-term Anglo efforts to detribalize and assimilate Indian Americans.

VALUE MEDIATION AND LEARNING STYLES

Coherent community life requires the transmission of culture between generations. It depends upon processes of child socialization whereby a rising generation learns language, behavior patterns, and the structures of meaning or value that accompany the ways of living and thinking that constitute a community's "culture." In human history, the social group most responsible for passing along the accepted ways of living and interpreting life has been the family. We can consider contexts where families have done this successfully as representing cultural continuity, and situations where they have been unable or unwilling to transmit to their children the community's distinctive ways of thinking and living as representing a form of "cultural crisis."

Sidestepping the enormous technical literature on values, we will repeat Rokeach's (1969, 1973) definition that values are fundamental beliefs, partly intellectual constructs but also involving emotions, beliefs about abstract, general, and diffused ideas, that form the basis of attitudes, behaviors, and choices. They are learned and shared, but much of that learning is implicit or tacit. Jamieson (1991:40) captures both of these aspects in his comment that

> *Sometimes values are named and associated with rules or programs for behavior, but for the most part values are implicit. They are learned and shared biases for making choices that are so taken for granted that people are largely unaware of them and do not talk about them or even consciously think about them. Certain ways of acting just*

> *"naturally" (i.e., culturally) feel "right" (i.e., coherent) to
> people raised within a certain culture . . . while other ways
> are so alien, so unfamiliar, they would normally not even
> occur to people as alternatives . . . .*

So values may be reflected in the ways people choose among possible behaviors, or ways that they organize their behavior "meaningfully." Anthony Giddens' (1991:42-43) discussion of cultural meaningfulness, that it involves " *'what cannot be put into words'— interchanges with persons and objects on the level of daily practice"* and that it grows out of *"the routine enactment of day-to-day life"* applies equally to cultural values. They are the *"avenues through which relatedness is channeled"* (Lee, 1976:6), and they are partly conscious and partly implicit.

Now let us distinguish between the ways we *experience value* and the ways we learn *about values.* The process of experiencing value has to do with how much meaning we find or feel in life, with our sense of purpose. The experience of value has to do with the interplay of individual activity, cultural values or meanings, and relationships with others. According to Dorothy Lee (1976:5-6):

> *We experience value when our activity is permeated with satisfaction, when we find meaning in our life, when we feel good, when we act not out of calculating choice and not for extraneous purpose, but rather because this is the only way that we, as ourselves, deeply want to act. . . . Further, to experience value in the situation, the relation between self and other, self and surround, must be immediate. Labeling previous to experience, categorizing, analysis, assessment, calculation, measurement, evaluation, all erect barriers diminishing or even destroying true relatedness.*

She is referring to "culturally mediated value," or what today's writers might label as "moral" or "ethical" value.

Cultural values are an aspect of the process of experiencing value. They are manifested and take on meaning in a process that involves the whole of a person—heart and soul, mind and body. They are not separate from being or interaction but an integral part of both, and reflect a conception of human beings as interrelated and interdependent.

In contrast to experiencing value, the process of learning *about values* is primarily cognitive—what Dorothy Lee refers to as "cognitively mediated value." This way of looking at values is the product of a way of thinking that separates thinking and living, that divides the action of the mind and the heart. It builds from a conception of the "self" that exists separate and apart from, independent of other "selves." In this view of the self, an essential aspect of personal mental health is the ability to be "autonomous" and "independent," to be able to get along without others, or at least without any particular other (cf. Bellah, et al., 1985). What is more, this "self" is conceptualized as not only separate from other persons, but also somehow separate from the person to whom it belongs, such that this self, or more correctly, image of a self, is subject to cognitive manipulation. It may be clothed in "freely selected" values that are chosen, supermarket fashion, in much the same way that the physical image is draped in fashionable clothing.[3]

In contrast, culturally mediated value is not chosen. It "resides in the reality which is mediated by culture," and is experienced where there is "*true relatedness*," where an experience is infused with "*social value*" (Lee, 1976:5). To experience value or find meaning in a situation "*the relation between self and other, self and surround, must be immediate*," not labeled, analyzed and assessed previous to experience as is the case for cognitively mediated values. In order to experience social value, the self must be to some degree open and continuous, and the relatedness have some of the attributes of unconditional love. It is in the sharing of culturally mediated values that life has meaning (Lee, 1976:6, 12).

Culturally mediated values reflect the situations and interpersonal networks in which one lives. The values (and we do violence to them to separate them from each other and from their context in living) grow out of day-to-day life with family and community members. In contrast, cognitively mediated values are learned explicitly in "teaching situations," and are activated and prioritized according to cultural patterns of cognitive choice. When values are conceived as "freely chosen" from some cultural pool, as a result of individual cognitive assessment, there is little need for family members or "family values," except as contributors to the pool of potential values available for rational assessment.

Return briefly to Lee's description of "experiencing value" quoted above. Her statement that "*labeling previous to experience, categoriz-*

ing, analysis, assessment, calculation, measurement, evaluation, all erect barriers diminishing or even destroying true relatedness" captures the essential distinction between cognitive mediation, which emphasizes and prizes such self-conscious intellectual activities, and cultural mediation, to which they are irrelevant, superfluous, or positively destructive.

The differences between culturally mediated and cognitively mediated learning go beyond the contextual difference of holistic, active participation versus attention to specialized information. What is here labeled "cognitive mediation" includes the mental activities associated with acquiring cultural information, such as listening to stories and watching others. Cognitive learning often is facilitated by specialized teachers, but storytelling by tribal elders also qualifies as cognitive instruction. Not only the process, but also the ends of the process, must be considered in classifying an experience as one or the other. The emphasis in cognitive learning is accumulating images and information, on learning *about* things, on knowing rather than being or doing.

Another way cognitive (bureaucratic, institutional, Anglo) learning differs from cultural learning is in the mediating agents involved. Cultural mediation involves the people closest to one—parents, grandparents, other relatives, people who participate with the one being instructed, who are linked to him or her by bonds of kinship, clan, or tribe. Cognitive mediation is more apt to be dominated by experts, specialists more skilled than one's family members at storytelling, doctoring, or whatever is being taught. However, the cognitive leaders may belong to the same community as those being taught, as in, for example, schoolteachers, college professors, or expert professionals who are also neighbors, or at least residents of the same community or city.

Research on ethnic differences in learning style among students in classroom contexts has documented a consistent set of differences that frequently, though not always, distinguish Indian from non-Indian students both in Canada and the United States. More (1987:17) concludes that while *"the differences are not consistent enough to suggest a uniquely Indian learning style . . . they occur often enough to warrant careful attention."* He contrasts traditional learning styles with the typical modern approach to classroom instruction, and attributes differences in learning styles to different child-rearing practices. According to More, the primary vehicle in traditional Indian society for transmitting attitudes and values is story-telling, and the acquisition of skills is based on a global watch-then-do or listen-then-do or think-then-do. He stresses the importance of *doing*, of participating in family process, as the essential mode of teaching life skills:

> *Watch-then-do . . . was a primary method whereby the child acquired skills within the family group. Explanations and questions in verbal form were minimized. Supervised participation was a major characteristic of skill learning* (p. 23).

In traditional Indian communities,

> *children were allowed to explore and be independent as soon as they were able. They were allowed to learn from their mistakes. A policy of non-interference existed unless there was real danger. Often misbehaviour was ignored so that the child would learn the natural consequences of misbehaviour and learn to be in charge of his or her own behavior. Another major factor was that grandparents and other elders in the extended family were responsible for much of the teaching of the child* (More, 1987:23-24).

Contemporary Indians educated in public schools combine elements of traditional child rearing with more modern practices, but today's Indians still draw extensively from tradition. Indian students raised on reservations are said to differ from their non-reservation peers both in thinking and observational processes. Reservation Indians are more holistic in approach, seeing "*everything [as] . . . a part of everything,*" while Anglos and less traditional Indians are more apt to compartmentalize and categorize. Among Navajos, in particular, aspects of traditional learning styles persist. Navajo child-rearing practices foster the holistic learning style and the sequence of learning for Navajo students has four stages: observe, think, understand/feel, and act. Anglo students reverse the process: they act, observe/think/clarify, and finally understand (Rhodes, 1988:23-24; Becktell, 1986).

There are many other versions of the oft-observed distinction between Indian "cultural mediation" (community-oriented, holistic learning) and the Anglo "cognitive mediation" (individualistic-oriented, specialized learning).

Echoing Lee's depiction of community-orientation among the Sioux is Little Soldier's (1992:147) statement that *"the Navajo emphasize giving, sharing and cooperating rather than saving and competing."*

Other relevant examples includes Fiordo's (1988:24-25, 29-31) comparison of learning that produces feeling and that which *"merely intellectualizes."* He identifies the latter with the "hidden curriculum" of the typical Anglo school, a curriculum that reiterates that *"what is worth knowing is that which is taught in academic institutions,"* as opposed to *"the rediscovery of traditional Native cultural values that preserve and enhance life"* such as holistic standards incorporated in the metaphor of the medicine wheel.

Deloria (1973:200, 204) taps a parallel dimension in a comparison of tribal and Anglo religions. The former are communal religions where *"there is no salvation . . . apart from the continuance of the tribe itself."* Indian religion represents *"a covenant between a particular god and a particular community,"* whereas Christian religion emphasizes the personal relationship between deity and an individual. Tribal religions, the basis of tribal community, *"made a place for every tribal individual,"* whereas Western Christianity *"created the solitary individual,"* abstracted from community context.

Also paralleling Lee's cultural/cognitive distinction is Dreyfus's (1981) distinction between two kinds of knowledge, "knowing-that" and "knowing-how." Knowing-that, a product of cognitive mediation, refers to knowledge compatible with the scientific, "rational" tradition. It is knowledge that can be accumulated or possessed as objects are possessed, knowledge conceptualized as existing in disciplines, separate and apart from each other, and from potential knowers. In contrast, knowing-how is commonsensical, yet also reflective of *"a deeper understanding of what knowing is"* than is available to philosophers who by disciplinary fiat are limited to the cognitive. Knowing-how is

> *an ability to cope with things—an ability that resides in our bodies more than in our minds. . . . At the deepest level such knowing is embodied in our cultural skills and practices, rather than in our concepts, our beliefs, and our values* (Dreyfus, 1981:512).

Much of the process is implicit. Meaning is conveyed through social practices and embedded in them in ways that cannot be made fully explicit (Dreyfus, 1981:513).

AUTONOMY, COMMUNITY, AND THE SELF

To its long history of self-reliance and rugged individualism, Anglo-America in recent decades has added the ideal of the free, untrammeled "self," including *"pure, undetermined choice, free of tradition, obligation, or commitment"* (Bellah et al., 1985:152). Contemporary middle-class individualism, full of ambiguities and contradictions, is itself a type of the cultural mediation—cognitive mediation dialectic. It insists upon the importance of *"finding our true selves independent of any cultural or social influence, being responsible to that self alone, and making its fulfillment the very meaning of our lives."* Yet it also expresses in many ways the conviction that *"life has no meaning unless shared with others in the context of community."* Today, when some observers conclude that *"separation and individuation have reached a kind of culmination,"* there is much concern for renewal of community and commitment lest American society self-destruct (Bellah, et al., 1985:150-152, 276-277).

Indian America has long offered an alternative approach, in which both autonomy and community are prized, and conceived not as precariously balanced opposites, but rather as different manifestations of a unitary social life. Among the Plains Indians autonomy and community are alternate faces of a central unity. Each is the necessary precondition of the other, *"each presupposes the presence of the other for its very definition"* (Lee, 1976:29). In many tribal cultures, the self is open, *"there is uninterrupted relatedness. . . the self is open to the experience of the other, of the surround . . . [and] value resides in the reality which is mediated by culture"* (Lee, 1976:5). But in Anglo society, there tends to be *"a conception of the self as completely bounded, and where the values strengthen the barriers which separate the self from the surround, . . . only [cognitively] mediated experience is encouraged, valued, and recognized as valid"* (Lee, 1976:13).

In Sioux society, the necessity for both autonomy and community was taken for granted. There was no need to talk about or defend it; the necessity of both was simply self-evident. *"Of course an infant [has] dignity and worth, to be recognized and valued,"* Lee wrote, and *"just as individual dignity is taken for granted so is communal responsibility and concern; they are there, given. . . . For these unimaginably autonomous, self-dependent, strong individuals, community was an ever-present reality"* (pp. 31-32).

Some readers may react to these accounts of sharing and cooperation with doubt or disbelief, given current rates of violence, suicide, crime, drug and alcohol abuse on many Indian reservations. If cooperation and caring is so pervasive, then why all of the poverty, illness, and family conflict? First, it should be remembered that most tribes have now endured at least a century, and typically several centuries, of political and social domination, exploitation, disease, modernization, assimilationist social programs, poverty and general assaults on Indian culture. In many instances, the tribal land base, essential to the people's identity and spirituality, has been forcibly taken away. In others, the children have been taken away, educated in alien ways, thereby disrupting the passing of the traditional culture to the rising generations. Some tribes have ceased to exist; others are scattered, barely viable as tribes. In view of the scale of the assault on Indian cultures, for *any* traditional customs to have survived represents a victory. In fact, it is noteworthy that so much of the heritage, and so many of the traditional values, have survived.

Lee's autonomous, community-oriented Sioux may sound like nostalgic idealizations of the noble savage. They are not. Here, in the words of Indian writers from different tribes, are other accounts of the community-oriented autonomy born of the cultural mediation that so starkly separates Indian Americans from the Anglo mainstream. Note the frequent reference to family work, to the day-to-day tasks of ordinary life.

> *Certainly the modern American Indian woman bears slight resemblance to her forebears . . . but she is still a tribal woman in her deepest being. Her tribal sense of relationship to all that is continues to flourish. . . .*
>
> *Through all the centuries of war and death and cultural and psychic destruction have endured the women who raise the children and tend the fires, who pass along the tales and the traditions, who weep and bury the dead, who are the dead, and who never forget. There are always the women, who make pots and weave baskets, who fashion clothes and cheer their*

*children on at powwow, who make fry bread and piki bread,
and corn soup and chili stew, who dance and sing and
remember and hold within their hearts the dream of their
ancient peoples. . . . We watch and we wait* (Allen, 1986:45,
50).

*It is through relationships that Native Americans comprehend
themselves. Such relationships are richly orchestrated . . . by
elaborations of languages and ritual activities. Underlying the
identity of the tribe and the experience of personality in the
individual is the sacred sense of place that provides the whole
group with its centeredness. The Indian individual is spiritually
interdependent upon the language, folk history, ritualism, and
geographical sacredness of his or her whole people. Relationships between members of families, bands, clans, and other
tribal groups are defined and intensified through relational and
generational language rather than through personal names,
which are considered to be sacred and private to the individual. The relatedness of the individual and the tribe extends
outward beyond the family, band, or clan to include all things
of the world. Thus nothing exists in isolation. Individualism
does not presuppose autonomy, alienation, or isolation. And
freedom is not the right to express yourself but the far more
fundamental right to be yourself* (Highwater, 1981:172).

*In synchronous time, Indians shear sheep and drive the sick to
Public Health Service hospitals, plant corn and collaborate on
native language curricula, attend powwows and go to college,
make native art and learn modern planning techniques for
economic growth necessary to survival. These present-day
people believe in themselves as Indians and act on that belief,
within their own definitions. They realize themselves within a
sense of Indian community. Their Indianness is not individually
seized, but tribally granted and personally carried out, as the
old ones carried time down to where it is on their backs. In
the older traditions, time is not passing around the people; we
are time* (Lincoln, 1983:188).

Navajo Blessing Way prayer:

I will walk in his shoes.
I will walk with his legs.
The words that he speaks I will speak.
What he thinks with I will think with.
With the words that he speaks and that things happen
    accordingly will I speak.
I am his grandchild (Benally, 1987:138).

APACHE PARENTING:
FAMILY WORK AND CULTURAL MEDIATION

How were these autonomous representatives of cohesive community socialized? Lee (1976) wrote that "*much in the life of these people bewildered and confounded me, until I gave up my original definition of autonomy.*" What she eventually identified was an attempt to provide "unfiltered experience," to allow the child to see for herself, combined with deliberate parental effort to guide the child's thinking with clear instruction, observation, and example as the child's capacity to learn increased.

In our Apache fieldwork, when the grandmothers were asked what they had learned from *their* grandmothers, they answered with stories of work experiences. They told of shared activities, expeditions with grandmothers to gather firewood, food, or wild herbs. On such forays, the grandmothers would teach the uses of various wild plants, and back home, under the scrutiny of the grandmothers, children learned the intricacies of food preparation and many other life-supporting skills. These accounts of childhood activities with grandparents were not the kinds of responses we expected. Our questions were intended to reveal principles that the women had "learned" about how to live and relate to others. Instead, we had been given expeditionary tales. Only later, reading Dorothy Lee, did we understand why the grandmothers had not articulated the answers we sought. What they learned had been mediated by cultural process, and they had tried to describe the process for us. We, seeking answers mediated by cognitive analysis and introspective evaluation, had not understood valid responses when they were given.

Thus we glimpse the disorientation and miscommunication that may occur when culturally mediated experience collides with cognitively mediated experience. The grandmothers recalled family work experiences that were steeped in meaning, not cognitive, analytical meaning, but meaning embedded in the contexts, connections and relationships in which the experiences occurred.

In Anglo-American culture, at least in our scientific conceptualizations of it, work and life often are separated. We like the idea of getting "housework" out of the way so we can get on with the real business of living. In traditional Apachean cultures, work and life were fused, and one could not separate the work needed to sustain life from the social dimensions that gave life meaning. Housework, or rather family work, *was* the real business of living. Religious, educational, and social values were intermixed, intertwined, embedded in these ordinary, everyday activities.

Among the Apache and Navajo, and in many other tribes, an extended kinship circle helped to educate the children, and grandmothers typically played a dominant role. Often "*children were raised by their grandmothers while their mothers were busy with jobs that required youth and strength*" (Niethammer, 1977:24). Among the Navajo, the grandparent often adopted the grandchild, and the alliance between the grandparent and grandchild was considered "*the strongest bond in the Navajo culture . . . a warm association in which perpetuation of traditional teaching could be effected*" (Shomaker, 1989:3).

Incorporating children into the world of adult work taught them the shared meanings of their culture and at the same time infused the experience with social value. Judging from our interviews, traditional education among Apache and Navajo grandmothers centered about the processes of observation, imitation, and participation. Children were taught to observe carefully the lives of their parents and grandparents. At every step of the way they were invited to participate in the life-sustaining activities of their families. Through shared work, the grandchildren not only learned work skills but also learned ways of teaching and learning, and the worth of shared work experience. In this process the parents and grandparents were the exemplars. Their lives were worthy of imitation, and the young could safely pattern their own lives after them.

The work experiences shared by grandmothers and grandchildren were an essential means of educating children in "knowing-how."

"Knowing-how" embodied more than technical skills, it included the example of a person one could hope to become like, a life worth imitating as well as an art or skill useful in everyday life. Verbal communication was part of the education process, but more important than words were careful observation and imitation. Nisa,[4] a young Apache grandmother, remembered walking with her grandmother to gather herbs:

She was quiet. She was real quiet. She just told me about different herbs and what was good for what and how she hoped I would turn out—maybe something like her.

Marie, the oldest of the grandmothers we interviewed, had been reared by a grandmother. She remembered how her grandmother taught her to cook:

She cut me a little dough and tell me to make it like this and I try my best to make it. And there was a hot coal under it, and when it bubbled up I turned it over and I just do that and that is how I learned how to cook.

Marie explained how her grandfather had taught her to be a lady: "*After I grew up, he told me, 'you do this and help your grandma, and what your grandma does, you do.'*"

Motivating children to learn and to work was not much of a problem in traditional Indian culture. Social responsibility was valued, as was participation in the life of the group. Lee's (1976:34) comments about Sioux children apply equally to the Apache:

And the growing child saw the socially responsible valued and honored, truly and consistently. Even the opportunity to take on responsibility for others was offered as an honor.

Children were eager to share in the activities of the group, and parents built on this *natural interest* of children in the work of adults.

James, an Apache grandfather, remembers:

*Our mothers were sewing and we liked to help our mothers
sew, and then [I watched] my Dad doing the hammering,
going to make a table or chairs. [Dad would say] "Son, give
me the saw, the pliers, the nail . . . ." So we got to learn to
help each other. It seemed like I could do anything.*

And here James points to the fruit of great love and high expectations:
the child learns he can do *anything*. With cultural mediation, one
doesn't learn "about values" but rather learns to "experience value" in
shared meanings and shared effort in behalf of the group. As a result,
Indian children felt useful, needed, and important.

Among the cultural values passed on to the children were
generosity and sharing. Very early in life, Navajo and Apache children
learned to share whatever they had. The norms about sharing included
the expectation that children would share their time and energy and
help with family tasks. Generosity was not equated with sacrifice, but
with maturity and togetherness. In Indian America to be generous, to
share with family and friends, was an affirmation of being, belonging
and loving.

The Navajo artist Mary Morez (1977:164) has aptly summarized
the place of sharing and generosity in Navajo life. She writes,

*We Navajo cry with joy and sorrow together. We help each
other. We feel close even when we are far apart in distance.*

   *We know love because we feel it. Some people talk of love
all their lives but never get or give it and therefore really
don't know it.*

   *But love learned at the feet of the old people and from the
innocence of little children—that day-by-day lesson in feeling
love, not just talking about it—is one of the things that makes
a hogan more than a physical home.*

   *When I grow old, I want to know I've left something
behind. Not as an artist, but as a human being who loves and
cares and tends and helps other human beings. To do that is
to walk in beauty.*

This norm has also been expressed in the saying that the Navajo life cycle consists of three stages: "being cared for," "preparing to care for," and "assuming care of." An essential part of the "care of" phase as lived by elder family members has always been the sharing of the past, the passing on to a new generation of the most valuable relics and memories of the old days.

Primarily because of the influence of grandmothers, many Apache and Navajo children still get a good start, learning who they are through cultural mediation of value. Many grandmothers still do traditional tasks, gathering herbs and pollen, making tortillas, chopping wood, and doing native crafts. In all this they welcome the participation of their grandchildren. Grandmothers today also teach their grandchildren by their example and their words. Estelle, now a great-grandmother, reflects the expectation that the grandmother's life will be worthy of imitation, and that her words of advice will be timely and useful:

I want to be a grandmother. When [my grandchildren] grow up they are going to be like me and be strong and tough. And talk to their own grandchildren. Right now they take time [to listen] when I talk to them, so they can remember. Like [my great granddaughter] wrote about me and said that she was going to be like grandma.

The grandmothers seem to welcome the opportunity to give their grandchildren "good words," and they take pride in the grandmotherly roles of exemplar and teacher. Typically they are encouraged and supported in this responsibility by their adult children, the parents of the grandchildren.

Grandmother Mary, an Apache, had this to say about "helping out" in teaching her grandchildren:

It is a hundred percent okay for a grandparent to help out. That is how I feel as a grandmother and that is why I say every white hair that I have up here, every silver lining, I earned it.

Sometimes my daughters bring my grandchildren over. If they want me to talk to them I will do it. My daughter will say to her children, "Well grandma wants to talk to you about something; you listen." I like to be there and talk with all of them.

Exhibiting traditional grandmotherly generosity, Mary says that helping to teach her grandchildren is renewing for her. She said that after the births of her first three grandchildren, people would ask her if it made her feel old to be a grandmother:

I said, "No, I am starting my life all over again, my life goes on with them. I was born today [when my grandchild was born]." And when they tell me that I am seventy years old today, I say, "I might look old but I am [only] a year old."

Not everyone interprets grandmothers' generosity as positively as they might have in former times. As one grandmother was telling us of the satisfaction she gets from caring for her grandchildren, her grown daughter interrupted, *"My Mom doesn't know how to say no."* From the daughter's perspective, her mother's caring for the grandchildren was an added burden, an imposition on her mother's busy schedule. She felt it was not in the grandmother's best interest to do so much for her grandchildren. Also, it may be worth noting that the grandchildren at issue here were those of another sibling and not this daughter's children. From the cognitively oriented perspective of the Anglo interviewer, there was some merit to the daughter's point of view; the grandmother did seem overworked. But she did not define herself that way. She was a grandmother, her critics were not. Only by the imposition of an external, artificial calculus were her time and energy scarce resources.

CONTEMPORARY PARENTING
AND COGNITIVE MEDIATION

Now let us consider some of the changes that have taken place as the traditional ways of learning—observation, imitation, and participation—have had to compete with modern institutions and technology. Today, as in the past, mothers and grandmothers continue to play an important role in the cultural education of the grandchildren, and the grandmothers often bear the ultimate responsibility for the wellbeing of their grandchildren (Bahr, 1994). Some observers who characterize the Apachean family as fractured and disintegrating point to high rates of teenage pregnancy and a pattern of young mothers going outside the household for paid work or education, leaving their young children with the grandmother, who essentially raises them. It is sometimes argued that modernization has forced, or at least encouraged, the mothers to leave the home, and that the pathologies of contemporary Navajos and Apaches arise at least in part from a situation where grandmothers are forced to rear their daughters' children. It should be remembered that, to the contrary, the pattern of the grandmother, and to a lesser extent, the grandfather, functioning as key socializers of the young is very traditional among the Navajo and Apache.

Our own observations during field trips to the Navajo and Apache reservations suggest that some grandparents still do the traditional activities, and some are still accompanied by their grandchildren, while the parents are away in town working for pay. For many households, however, it appears that the traditional activities have been replaced by more modern substitutes. In these families, the children are less likely to work in essential family production. Much of their socialization takes place in school or in front of the television, and they are more likely to play than to work with members of their own households.

Formerly, there were many work activities in which grandparents and grandchildren participated. Grandparents used to take children with them to care for the sheep, children helped in carding the wool, children participated in gathering and drying of herbs and berries. During these shared activities, grandparents told the children the lore of the tribe and passed on tribal culture and values. The mutual activity devoted to real, essential activities built love, trust, and family solidarity.

Now the public schools and television compete for the children's time and attention, and these two modern means of education have greatly changed the contexts in which today's grandparents must try to communicate the traditional balance of autonomy and community-orientation to their grandchildren.

Traditionally, Indian children internalized the values of their communities as mediated in the day-to-day processes of working, living and loving. Anglo-administered schooling introduced Indian children to new ideas about values and, at the same time, introduced the modern version of autonomy wherein "self interest" is in competition with "other interest," and the individual is in competition with other members of the community.

In contemporary public education, values are conceived in the mind, prioritized, and chosen in cognitive processes that are separated from the processes whereby community life is sustained. The student goes to school and learns about values by talking of them, discussing the options, and then picking and choosing for herself from the explicit options presented. Along with these modern ideas about values goes the ultimate modern criterion of choice, self-interest.

Interview data from our Apachean grandmothers and other informants suggest that while the pattern of grandmother and grandchild working together is still common, it is not as large a component of life as it used to be. Grandchildren may help their grandmothers gather cattails to harvest yellow pollen, "pick worms" to sell to fishermen, catch fish to help supplement the family diet, or make tortillas. The grandmothers encourage the children in their schoolwork, and many of the grandchildren help with household chores, chopping wood, sweeping floors and washing dishes.

Even so, the grandmothers lament that they cannot spend as much time working with their grandchildren as their grandparents spent with them, and as a result, they are not able to teach as much. School accounts for part of that difference in time allocation, but none of the grandmothers seem to begrudge the time children spend in school. There is, however, a sense of frustration in trying to communicate family and cultural values in the hours that remain. An often-mentioned reason for the shortage of time with children and grandchildren is that when the children are home from school, they watch television. Many of the grandmothers seem unable to compete successfully with this technological wonder for the attention of a child.

CONTEMPORARY PARENTING, MEDIA MEDIATION, AND CULTURAL SURVIVAL

The electronic media, and especially television, have introduced yet another way of acquiring values, which we will call "media mediated." Thus we have three categories: culturally mediated value, cognitively mediated value, and media mediated value. Media mediated value, or learning one's values from the media, involves neither heart nor mind to any great extent, and even less, the body. Yet it represents a major, if not the dominant Anglo-American form of values education, and it has vast influence in Indian America.

The grandmothers we interviewed seemed to have made their peace, or learned to coexist with, cognitive mediation as represented in the schools. They are among the strongest proponents of formal education and higher education for their grandchildren. But they expressed great concern and frustration over having to compete with the television, VCRs, and videogames for the attention of their grandchildren. It seems that for many the "natural interest" that once motivated children to observe, imitate and participate in family work or other activity with their grandparents has been displaced by a "natural interest" in television. Furthermore, the application to television viewing of the traditional cultural learning processes of observation and imitation portends trouble for grandparents and grandchildren alike.

Ruby is an Apache grandmother whose large household sometimes includes several grandchildren. At the time of our interview her household also included an adult son and his live-in girlfriend. Ruby expressed some irritation at the arrangement, yet she had allowed them to stay: "*I tell him 'we don't do that, that's not our way,' and he says, 'But they do it on these TV shows.'*"

Denise, a "modern" Navajo grandmother, reflected about television versus traditional ways in her family's experience:

> *I think there's a lot of learning from those VCRs and TVs. I think kids are learning a lot. What I've heard from my aunt—she's in her 90s, she's the only survivor on my mother's side . . . she has grandkids, again they're in the [her] home. She was telling me that they are not doing the work that they used to do. What I mean, they used to bring the wood in—they still burn wood and coal—they used to bring wood and they used to bring water. They used to become concerned about the sheep out there, they had to be fed and watered. They used to be concerned about patching up the home and staying home. "There's a lot of work to be done," she said. "But when we got a TV into our home," she said, "The kids don't do that anymore."*

When the same processes of learning that served well for absorbing culturally mediated value—observation, participation, and imitation—are applied to television, the results are sobering. Thus, a modern grandmother laments,

> *When I was young my dad and mom used to sit down with us in the evening after supper and they'd tell us what's wrong and what's right. And I taught that to my children. But the younger ones have a mind of their own now. I'll talk to my grandson I'm raising and he'll just sit there, and then I yell again, then he finally turns around and says, 'Oh, are you saying something to me?' He's too involved with the TV instead of listening to what's being said to him.*

An Apache tribal historian expressed some of the same concerns:

> *The school—they have the kids all day long. When school is out, where do you see the kids? Right in front of the television. Where do you see the mother and the dad? In front of the television. The grandmother is left in the corner. Every night the children see different programs. Grandmother is left out now.*

Asked if he knew families who watched little or no television, and where grandparents, parents and children worked together, he laughed: "*They are really rare.*"

While the invasion of "media mediated values" poses a challenge to all ethnic groups and subcultures, its potential for cultural destruction seems especially great for Apache, Navajo, and other American Indian populations who had barely accommodated to print media before they were immersed in the electronic media.

What happens when a people whose meaning in life has been tied to culturally mediated value, and where "*relatedness [has had] the character of unconditional love*" (Lee, 1976:6), are absorbed and indoctrinated into a cognitive system of valuing? Apparently the grandmothers, for the most part, continue to be what they "*deeply want to be*"—the purveyors of their culture and the caretakers of last resort for their grandchildren. But it becomes increasingly difficult for them to play these roles, for now the days and hours of their grandchildrens' lives are occupied by school and by the media.

Compulsory public schooling administered by Anglo America presented Indian children with a new view of autonomy and community, but could not destroy their native view entirely. Television, on the other hand, may do just that, and without generating a fraction of the resistance the tribes initially mounted to compulsory mainstream education. In fact, media mediated value has great potential to attenuate both autonomy and community.

Consider a modest example of tribal radio, presumably media "tamed" in service of tribal goals. Tribally administered radio was introduced on the Ramah Navajo reservation in 1975. Tribal members who had worked to get a radio station operating on the reservation anticipated it would help strengthen the community.

> *For example, it was the hope of the Chapter House officers [that the use of] radio [would] generate increased interest and attendance in Chapter meetings. With this in mind, the Chapter Secretary would broadcast an agenda of the next meeting several days prior to that meeting. Following the meeting, she would broadcast a synopsis of what had transpired. Rather than generate new interest, the opposite occurred. . . .* [A Chapter House Secretary reported that] *"People stay home because they know they can hear a report of the meeting over the radio. This makes for less participation in the Chapter Meetings"* (Rada, 1978:365-366).

Radio has had many unanticipated effects, and on balance may have weakened rather than strengthened tribal solidarity. Television promises much more dramatic changes. No one is yet sure about the ultimate effects of television upon a society, but there are some tentative answers which suggest that television and all forms of traditional society are at odds. More importantly, there are indications that television as used in the U.S. is hostile to both autonomy and community.

The dominant American society has "grown up" with television. Advances in media technology, technique, and programming have seemed to occur in an additive, linear fashion, and there has been a sense that society and television were "growing up" together. If some of the changes have been rapid, they have not been entirely unexpected. Innovations have been accompanied by a public sense of modernizing progress, of the future unfolding in anticipated directions and not suddenly appearing full grown.

In contrast, television and home viewing of videos have taken the Apache and Navajo reservations, and presumably other Indian communities, by media storm. Places that a few years ago lacked electricity and running water now have television sets and access to the latest video releases. Grandparents who once taught Navajo culture to their grandchildren by working with them now watch as their grandchildren are mesmerized by televised sports, soaps, and the Simpsons.

Like their mainstream American counterparts, Apache and Navajo families, if they are aware of the menace television poses to their culture, have not known what to do about it. To these outside observers, it appears that television and videos may, in a very brief time, do what more than a century of efforts at forced assimilation by Anglo missionaries, educators, and government agents could not do, namely trivialize and displace traditional Apache and Navajo culture.

Cultures are lived, not watched. Both Anglo America and ethnic America may find that they have watched away many of the life-affirming, essential elements of their communal life, replacing them not with other cohesive patterns for living, but rather with a superficial set of shared images dominated by commercial messages and suitable more for light conversation and "trivial pursuit" than for assigning meaning to life and guiding people in the essential tasks of living.

CONCLUSIONS, CAVEATS, AND CONJECTURES

To reflect upon the apparent impacts of modern electronic media on traditional ways of living, and to speculate about their future impacts, is not to argue for a single "cause" of a decline of community, an attenuation of culture, or whatever other impact is being discussed. It should also be remembered that the original focus of the present investigation was patterns of grandparenting and family work, and that many of the comments about the role of television were unsolicited.

Presumably cultural mediation and cognitive mediation of value are as old as history. Values mediated by electronic media are, historically speaking, something new. These types differ as essentially in the "players" involved as in the nature of learning that they foster, and it is important to note the change in the "significance" of the significant others who participate in the learning process. Culturally mediated value tends to be taught in a process of social participation with or under the tutelage of one's family and close relatives. The people who make the decisions about when and how to transmit culturally mediated value, to the extent that such values are explicitly taught, are usually one's kindred, people who share one's interests and one's blood.

Cognitively mediated values may be taught by family members or acquaintances but generally are the bailiwick of "experts." Sometimes these experts are members of one's community, and sometimes not. Decisions about cognitively mediated value often are made "objectively," perhaps at considerable administrative or bureaucratic distance from the learning context, but the context where the cognitive mediation occurs is typically a group context where some two-way communication is possible and where there is, theoretically at least, an opportunity for genuine interaction.

Lastly, we come to media mediation, which generally does not involve personal participation, is not directed by members of one's own community, and is not tailored to one's unique circumstances. The "stories" to be told derive from elsewhere, they are told (enacted) by strangers who are employed by other strangers who control the corporate media, and decisions about the pace and nature of the mediation are made primarily for the benefit of the controlling strangers. Generally, the intent is neither that the viewers learn to care about each other nor that they learn to think, but merely that they buy, and that they continue to watch.

That the electronic media pose a threat to local cultures, even national cultures, is apparent from the efforts of powerful European nations to limit and control their citizens' exposure to media messages from other nations. In Europe, the potential impacts of foreign broadcasting and new communications technologies on national cultural values and traditions continue to generate controversy (Hoffmann-Riem, 1987), and there are concerns that a "lowest common denominator" level of underregulated commercial broadcasting will weaken national ethnic and regional cultures (Humphreys, 1990). However, it is not clear that even if governments and ethnic interest groups have the power to enact culture-protective media policy, they have the information and foresight to do so in ways that will achieve their objectives. After summarizing the history of new French and German media policies, Le Duc (1987:443) concludes that there, as in the U.S., government has been forced "*either to suppress what it has been unable to guide, or to authorize what it has been unable to restrain.*" If the advanced, modern nations, perceiving a threat to the uniqueness of their cultures, have been unable to deal with it successfully, might there be cause for concern in the presumably more fragile, and certainly smaller and weaker, contemporary American Indian cultures?

In the book *Technopoly*, Neil Postman (1992:165-66, 170-71) writes that "*the adoration of technology pre-empts the adoration of anything else,*" and claims that the contemporary media offer a worldview "*that sees tradition [any form of tradition] as an obstacle to its claims.*" He characterizes the symbol overload, trivialization and cannibalization of formerly meaningful symbols and words, all in the service of commercial messages, as "*a form of cultural rape, sanctioned by an ideology that gives boundless supremacy to technological progress and is indifferent to the unraveling of tradition.*"

Postman may be an alarmist, his pessimism unwarranted, but a quick overview of research on effects of electronic media on tribal and national societies is not reassuring. As early as 1970, there was concern among South Dakota Sioux that their children were "*surrounded by the TV,*" and that viewing was eroding Native values such as the norm of marrying within the tribe (deMontigny, 1970:235). An evaluation of local radio on the Ramah Navajo reservation concluded that despite some benefits, "*the culture of electronic communication—in this case, radio and the cassette tape recorder—and in a broader sense, the culture of technology, is contributing to the decay of the Ramah Navajo culture.*" Navajo children preferred listening to rock and country music to listening to their grandparents tell the old stories, and it seemed that the younger generation were "*losing their memories*" to the radio and the tape recorder (Rada,1978:367-369). A rare participant observation study on the Navajo reservation found that if Navajo families had television, viewing was the dominant evening and night activity. There was a continuing potential for the dilution of traditional culture both because of conflicts between Navajo beliefs and what was seen on television, and because viewing was associated with a marked reduction in the diversity of family activities. It simply did not leave time for many traditional practices (Kent, 1985).

After demonstrating that heavy television viewing seemed to have reduced regional diversity in the U.S., Morgan (1986:136) speculated that the massive exporting of American programs to other nations and cultures would make *"distinct pluralistic identities and characteristics increasingly difficult to sustain."* Among Brazilian villagers television had a mainstreaming effect, and the extent of people's viewing was a key predictor of what they thought and did. Viewing also minimized local community activity, for *"the medium keeps people indoors, with their immediate families, off the streets, and . . . detracts from activity in the central square"* (Kottak, 1991:86). An evaluation of the probable impacts of Aboriginal broadcasting in Australia finds that while English language broadcasting will maximize the size of the tribal audiences, it will also erode tribal culture. Also, the presence of Aboriginal broadcasting will create new elites and new forms of leadership among the Aboriginal peoples, while at the same time increasing the power of the Western media in the region (Browne, 1990).

In the early 1980s Canadian studies of television and national culture showed that *"the electronic media, and television in particular"* had contributed to the loss of regional and national identities and that the new technologies provided *"threatening avenues for the complete annihilation of what remains of a distinct Canadian culture, [and] of its regional and other unique components"* (Siegel, 1983:249).

Confronting a modern airliner, a Navajo elder once affirmed the dominance of his own culture by asking, *"How many sheep will it hold?"* (Toelken, 1976). What might he now say, confronting grandchildren whose sheepherding is vicarious, whose lives are dominated by modern viewing. Cultural mediation *depends* on action, on doing, on participating. What is now to become of autonomy and community?

We are haunted by a vision of Indian families, still geographically isolated in the deserts which for so long buffered their culture against Anglo America, their family members huddled together around the never-tiring electronic story-teller, learning their new culture. They are physically close to each other, but there is little meaningful interaction as they absorb the images and ideas beamed their way by the corporate heads of Anglo-American media networks. After all, *"what does it mean for a parent to sit close to a child when both are more aware of the car chase on the screen than they are of each other?"* (Collier, 1991:245).

NOTES

[1] This paper draws on field research supported by a grant from Brigham Young University's College of Family, Home, and Social Sciences to the senior author, who personally conducted all of the interviews with Apache respondents. Navajo respondents were interviewed jointly.

[2] In the summers of 1989, 1990, and 1991 in-depth interviews were conducted with five Navajo grandmothers, a Navajo grandfather, 13 Apache grandmothers, and an Apache grandfather. Observational and less intensive interview data were obtained from other informants who lived, or formerly had lived, among the White Mountain Apache. The interviews were conducted on the Fort Apache Reservation and in the Shiprock area of the Navajo Reservation.

[3] Cognitively mediated values are values freely chosen from among alternatives, and logic and reason are the idealized criteria for choice. However, as Bellah et al. (1985:75) have observed, in practice "there is simply no objectifiable criterion for choosing one value or course of action over another. One's own idiosyncratic preferences are their own justification." In a mind-self tautological relation, the "individual" is said to be the ultimate arbitrator of what is right or wrong for the self, and "the self is defined by its ability to choose its own values." Dorothy Lee says that cognitive mediation of values is characteristic of cultures, like the dominant Anglo-American one, where the self is viewed as "bounded," and the ideal self is one freed from, or not constrained by the demands of family and culture. The bounded self is closed from deep connections to others that might come through deeply held, culturally shared meanings (Lee, 1976).

[4] All names of respondents are pseudonyms.

REFERENCES

Allen, P.G. 1986. *The Sacred Hoop: Recovering the Feminine in American Indian Traditions*. Boston: Beacon Press.

Bahr, K.S. 1994. "The strengths of Apache grandmothers: Commitment, culture, and caretaking." *Journal of Comparative Family Studies* 25:233-248.

Becktell, M. 1986. *The Adult Navajo Learner: Learning Styles and Corresponding Teaching Strategies*. Bachelor's research paper. Plainfield, VT: Goddard College.

Bellah, R.N., Madsen, R., Sullivan, W.M., Swidler, A., and Tipton, S.M. 1985. *Habits of the Heart: Individualism and Commitment in American Life*. New York: Harper & Row.

Benally, H.J. 1987. "'Diné Bo'óhoo'aah Bindii'a': Navajo philosophy of learning." *Diné Be'iina': A Journal of Navajo Life* 1:133-148.

Berry, W. 1993. *Sex, Economy, Freedom & Community*. New York: Pantheon.

Browne, D. R. 1990. "Aboriginal radio in Australia: From dreamtime to prime time?" *Journal of Communication* 40:111-120.

Collier, J.L. 1991. *The Rise of Selfishness in America*. New York: Oxford University Press.

Deloria, V., Jr. 1970. *We Talk, You Listen: New Tribes, New Turf*. New York: Delta.

_____. 1973. *God Is Red*. New York: Delta.

deMontigny, L. 1970. "Modern psychology and child development: The American Indian case." Pp. 219-246 in American Indian Historical Society (eds.), *Indian Voices: The First Convocation of American Indian Scholars*. San Francisco: Indian Historian Press.

Dreyfus, H.L. 1981. "Knowledge and human values: A genealogy of nihilism." *Teachers College Record* 82:507-520.

Fiordo, R. 1988. "The great learning enterprise of the Four Worlds Development Project." *Journal of American Indian Education* 27 (3):24-34.

Giddens, A. 1991. *Modernity and Self-Identity: Self and Society in the Late Modern Age.* Stanford: Stanford University Press.

Highwater, J. 1981. *The Primal Mind: Vision and Reality in Indian America.* New York: Meridian Books.

Hoffman, F. (ed.). 1981. *American Indian Family: Strengths and Stresses.* American Indian Social Research and Development Associates.

Hoffmann-Riem, W. 1987. "National identity and cultural values: Broadcasting safeguards." *Journal of Broadcasting & Electronic Media* 31:57-72.

Humphreys, P.J. 1990. *Media and Media Policy in West Germany: The Press and Broadcasting since 1945.* New York: Berg.

Jamieson, N.L. 1991. "Communication and the new paradigm for development." Pp. 27-50 in F.L. Casmir (Ed.), Communication in Development. Norwood, NJ: Ablex Publishing.

Kent, S. 1985. "The effects of television viewing: A cross-cultural perspective." *Current Anthropology* 26 (1):121-126.

Kottak, C. P. 1991. "Television's impact on values and local life in Brazil." *Journal of Communication* 41:70-87.

Lapham, L.H. 1988. *Money and Class in America: Notes and Observations on the Civil Religion.* New York: Ballantine.

Le Duc, D.R. 1987. "French and German new media policies: Variations on a familiar theme." *Journal of Broadcasting & Electronic Media* 31:427-447.

Lee, D. 1976. *Valuing the Self: What We Can Learn from Other Cultures*. Prospect Heights, IL: Waveland.

Levy, J.E., and Kunitz, S.J. 1971. "Indian reservations, anomie, and social pathologies." *Southwestern Journal of Anthropology* 27:97-128.

Lincoln, K. 1983. *Native American Renaissance*. Berkeley: University of California Press.

Little Soldier, L. 1992. "Building optimum learning environments for Navajo students." *Childhood Education* 68:145-148.

More, A.J. 1987. "Native Indian learning styles: A review for researchers and teachers." *Journal of American Indian Education* 27 (1):17-29.

Morez, M. 1977. "Walk in beauty." P. 164 in Jane B. Katz (ed.), *I Am the Fire of Time: The Voices of Native American Women*. New York: E. P. Dutton.

Morgan, M. 1986. "Television and the erosion of regional diversity." *Journal of Broadcasting & Electronic Media* 30:123-139.

Niethammer, C. 1977. *Daughters of the Earth: The Lives and Legends of American Indian Women*. New York: Macmillan.

Postman, N. 1992. *Technopoly: The Surrender of Culture to Technology*. New York: Knopf.

Rada, S.E. 1978. "Ramah Navajo radio and cultural preservation." *Journal of Broadcasting* 22:361-371.

Rhodes, R.W. 1988. "Holistic teaching/learning for Native American students." *Journal of American Indian Education* 27 (2):21-29.

Rokeach, M. 1969. *Beliefs, Attitudes, and Values*. San Francisco: Jossey-Bass.

_____. 1973. *The Nature of Human Values*. New York: Free Press.

Shomaker, D.M. 1989. "Transfer of children and the importance of grandmothers among the Navajo Indians." *Journal of Cross-Cultural Gerontology* 4:1-18.

Siegel, A. 1983. *Politics and the Media in Canada*. Toronto: McGraw-Hill Ryerson.

Stockel, H.H. 1991. *Women of the Apache Nation: Voices of Truth*. Reno: University of Nevada Press.

Toelken, B. 1976. "Seeing with a native eye: How many sheep will it hold?" Pp. 9-24 in W. H. Capps (Ed.), *Seeing with a Native Eye: Essays on Native American Religion*. New York: Harper & Row.

Unger, S. (ed.) 1977. *The Destruction of American Indian Families*. New York: Association on American Indian Affairs.

Whitehead, B.D. 1993. "Dan Quayle was right." *Atlantic Monthly* 271 (4):47-84.

Choice of Child Care and Mother-Child Interaction: Racial/Ethnic Distinctions in the Maternal Experience[1]

Marilou C. Legazpi Blair and Sampson Lee Blair

Dual-earner and single-parent families in the United States face a common dilemma: the provision of adequate childcare. Such care is particularly problematic for mothers of young children. As of 1991, 59.9 percent of married mothers with children under the age of 6 were employed outside the home, as were 48.8 percent of their single counterparts (U.S. Bureau of the Census, 1992). The acquisition of adequate childcare, then, is a major factor in freeing mothers, both physically and emotionally, for paid employment. This study will examine the relationship between childcare choice and employed mothers' experiences within parenthood.

Employed mothers typically must arrange for the best care which they are able to locate, yet the various forms of childcare arrangements (e.g., in-home care, daycare centers, babysitters) may differ considerably in both their quality (e.g., educational content, teacher/child ratio) and cost (Christensen, 1988). As the usage of outside-the-home care has increased, so too has the amount of research on childcare, with the vast majority of studies focusing on the impact of childcare arrangements on the children themselves (King and MacKinnon, 1988). Childcare (outside the home) has been shown to have both positive and negative effects on children, depending upon the trait or characteristic in question. For example, studies have found that nonfamilial care is associated with increased aggressiveness and noncompliance in preschool children (Haskins, 1985) and insecure parent-child attachments (Belsky and Rovine, 1988), yet such studies have also found that exposure to the daycare environment may enhance language development (McCartney, 1984) and social competence (Phillips et al., 1987).

While considerable research has examined the effects of non-parental childcare, the potential effects of childcare choice on the mothers themselves has seemingly been overlooked. Although several researchers have acknowledged the emotional and scheduling quagmires in which employed mothers often find themselves (e.g., Maume, 1991; Willie, 1992), as well as the dyadic nature of the mother-child relationship (e.g., Bretherton et al., 1991; Schuster, 1993), the linkage between childcare choice and the "maternal experiences" of employed mothers needs to be considered. The present study will examine the association between childcare choice and maternal behaviors and attitudes and will specifically focus on differences by race.

Previous research has failed to address the racial/ethnic distinctions within the association of childcare choice and the maternal experience. Such distinctions are readily apparent. For example, in 1991, 59.0 percent of white mothers with children under the age of 6 were in the paid labor force, while 73.4 percent of comparable black mothers were employed outside the home (U.S. Bureau of the Census, 1992). As such, black mothers and white mothers, as groups, will necessarily cope with the work/family interface in different manners. Given differences in age at marriage, percentage of mother-only families, rates of divorce, and family living arrangements (Farley and Bianchi, 1991), black and white mothers are likely to have distinctly different experiences of motherhood (see also Collins, 1991). Black mothers have also been reported to have better access to kin and to be more likely to receive unpaid kin-provided child care, as compared to white mothers (Hogan et al., 1990). Hence, this study will also examine racial/ethnic distinctions in the maternal experience, specifically as they pertain to childcare choice.

MATERNAL EMPLOYMENT

Over the past few decades, the employment rate of women with young, dependent children has been steadily increasing. In 1975, 32.7 percent of mothers with children under the age of 3 were in the paid labor force. By 1985, this figure had increased to 50.5 percent, and had reached 55.5 percent in 1990 (U.S. Bureau of the Census, 1992). Clearly, the roles of mother and provider have become more corresponding than separate. Indeed, even the majority of mothers with children under 12 months of age (55.8%) are currently in the paid labor force (U.S. Bureau of the Census, 1992). Such increases in maternal employment have brought about a sizeable amount of research on the effects of employment on maternal behavior (Willie, 1992).

Several studies have suggested that maternal employment may influence mothers' levels of anxiety and concern for the development of their children (e.g., Hock et al., 1988). The effects of employment may, however, be partially due to the mothers' reasons or rationale for being employed (Volling and Belsky, 1993). Although numerous women return to work following the birth of a child, primarily because of economic concerns (i.e., need for additional family income) (e.g., Gerson, 1985), they may do so for a variety of reasons, including gender-role attitudes (Morgan and Hock, 1984), marital quality (Gerson, 1985; Hoffman, 1989), and the temperament of the children themselves (Galambos and Lerner, 1987). In fact, most research on maternal employment suggests that, despite the problems associated with childcare arrangements, mothers who prefer to work and do so report higher levels of satisfaction than mothers who wish to work but remain at home (King and MacKinnon, 1988).

One general conclusion of this research is that nonfamilial childcare which is initiated during the child's first year may increase the likelihood of insecure child-parent attachments (Belsky and Rovine, 1988). Since use of nonfamilial childcare necessarily prohibits mother-child contact, the sense of attachment between mother and child should logically be less. More importantly, though, mothers' sense of general effectiveness as a mother may be affected by the use of nonfamilial childcare. As Lamb and Easterbrooks state: "the greater the amount of interaction, the greater [are] the opportunities to learn how to read the infant's signals, interpret them correctly, and respond appropriately" (1981:140).

Theoretically, then, the use of nonfamilial childcare may limit not only mother-child interaction, but may also affect mothers' perceptions of how well they have fulfilled their maternal role. Indeed, Shea and Tronick (1988) posit that mothers' perceptions of being effective in mother-child interactions is vital to their sense of self-esteem in the parental role. The linkage between women's employment and the maternal experience seems readily apparent. For example, Crnic and Greenberg (1990) conclude that mothers' perceptions of the "daily hassles" with their children were predictive of mothers' satisfaction with their parental role, their mental well-being, and several aspects of mother-child interaction. Furthermore, the stressors and challenges associated with managing the schedules of work and childcare arrangements will likely affect maternal behaviors. Characteristics and qualities associated with the various forms of childcare (e.g., cost, availability, ease of access) should have varied effects on mothers' attitudes and behaviors within the maternal experience.

RACIAL/ETHNIC DIFFERENCES IN FAMILY DYNAMICS

As previously mentioned, black mothers and white mothers will, on average, have different levels of participation in the paid labor force, and may subsequently be affected by their employment experiences. Yet the differences between the maternal experiences of black and white mothers may also arise from differences in their respective family structures and family dynamics. For example, black mothers are slightly less likely than white mothers to be married (with their spouse present), and also tend to marry at a later age than do comparable white females (Taylor, 1994). As of 1991, female-headed households represented approximately 46 percent of all black families, whereas female-headed households represented about 13 percent of all white families (U.S. Bureau of the Census, 1992). Given that single mothers have been shown to have greater difficulty in rearing children (e.g., role overload)(Sanik and Mauldin, 1986), such difficulties may be more common among black mothers than white mothers.

The larger familial networks of black and white mothers may also affect their maternal attitudes and behaviors. Previous studies have posited that black single-parent families may be more likely to avail of assistance from other relatives within their family (Cherlin, 1981). Such support from mothers' kin network has been shown to have a positive effect on parenting skills and economic achievement (Taylor, 1994).

Additionally, the median annual income of white families in 1991 was $36,140, while black families earned an annual average of $25,168 (U.S. Bureau of the Census, 1991). While the size of the family or its annual income do not necessarily lead to differences in the relationship between childcare choice and maternal behaviors, some of the basic differences between black mothers and white mothers (e.g., income, marital status) must be considered. Differences in absolute income may influence the actual choice of childcare.

CHILDCARE CHOICES

Much of the previous research in this area has treated childcare as a relatively uniform set of measures. Most studies classify childcare into either "homecare" or "daycare" categories (see Scarr, Phillips, and McCartney, 1989). As the demand for nonfamilial childcare has grown, however, so too has the variety of childcare arrangements. Families may rely upon a relative or opt to use a "homecare" provider, who takes care of several different children in her (i.e., the provider) home. Parents may also utilize the services of a licensed daycare center. The quality, cost, and availability of these different forms of childcare will vary considerably from one family to the next.

A broad variety of family characteristics may influence the choice of childcare arrangements. The income level of families, in particular, will affect their subsequent choice of childcare. Most studies have posited that higher levels of mothers' income and educational attainment increase the probability of choosing paid versus unpaid forms of childcare (Hofferth and Wissoker, 1992). Hence, racial/ethnic group differences in income should also affect families' choice of childcare.

A sex-bias may also exist in regard to childcare choice. Howes and Stewart (1987) conclude that mothers who have more nurturant childrearing practices are likely to choose stable, high-quality care for sons, whereas less nurturant mothers (who also have lower marital quality) are likely to choose unstable, low-quality care for daughters.

The quality of childcare has also been shown to vary by the types of childcare arrangements. In-home sitters, for example, are typically untrained, unskilled providers who are often related to the child (King and MacKinnon, 1987). The use of nonemployed relatives, such as retired grandparents, is a typical childcare arrangement for mothers who opt for in-home sitters. Such providers are likely to provide more adult-child interaction with the child, yet these children are likely to have comparatively little interaction with same-age peers. Additionally, since the care is provided in-home, children are likely to spend more time watching television (Clarke-Stewart, 1987).

Licensed daycare homes provide a quality of care somewhere between the traditional "babysitter" and that of daycare centers. Daycare homes are still likely to be operated by untrained and unskilled providers, yet they will typically have greater knowledge of childcare and children's needs (e.g., play activities) than will babysitters (King and MacKinnon, 1988). Since such providers are usually caring for more than one child, they may also be likely to have more formalized schedules of daily activities for the children, and the children in daycare homes will probably watch less television, as compared to children at home with babysitters (Clarke-Stewart, 1987).

Formal daycare centers are still likely to offer the "best" quality of childcare. Children in daycare centers will obviously have greater opportunity for same-age peer interactions, which may positively influence the development of their social skills. And though the child-to-provider ratio is higher in daycare centers, the providers are more likely to be trained and to have appropriate educational backgrounds.

The choice of childcare arrangement will not only affect the children (e.g., their intellectual development), but should also affect the parents themselves. Parents, and particularly mothers, first have to choose a suitable form of childcare and then, subsequently, will have to deal with the consequences of that choice (e.g., cost, scheduling). Secondly, once children are placed in some form of childcare, the socialization of the child is no longer limited to the familial sphere. The behaviors, attitudes, and personality of the child are at least partially influenced by his or her experiences in the childcare arrangement he or she happens to be in. Hence, mothers may have to cope with changes in their child (e.g., undesirable behaviors) which have come about due to the child's experiences in the childcare environment.

In this study, we therefore propose that childcare choice should have a significant effect on the maternal experience. Such effects may be mediated by parental characteristics (e.g., income, stress, family and kin support). Furthermore, since racial/ethnic differences exist in paid employment, entry into motherhood, and family living arrangements, we also expect to find racial/ethnic differences in the choice of childcare arrangements, as well as in the effects of childcare choice on the maternal experience.

Data and Variables

Data for this study are taken from the 1988 National Survey of Families and Households (Sweet et al., 1988). The NSFH provides a primary cross-sectional national sample of 9,643 respondents aged 19 and older. The sample used here is limited to 349 employed mothers whose oldest child is less than 5 years of age. Only mothers who provided complete responses to each of the variables required herein are included in the analyses.

Childcare choice was assessed with the construction of three separate dummy variables. *Daycare* (1=yes, 0=no) indicates that the mother responded that one of her children attends a daycare center, nursery school, preschool, or kindergarten. The second measure, *babysitter* (1=yes, 0=no), indicates that the mother uses either a neighbor or babysitter (specifically, a non-relative) for the care of a child while she is employed. The third childcare choice measure, *relatives* (1=yes, 0=no), indicates that the mother uses either the child's grandparent or some other relative (aside from her husband or older children) for the care of a child.

Given that approximately 15 percent of the employed mothers in this sample had more than one child under the age of 5, and were likely to utilize more than one form of childcare (either different types of care for each child, or different types of care for the same child), a measure which indicates the use of more than one type of childcare, *multiple caregivers* (1=yes, 0=no), is included. If the choice of childcare is associated with parenting, it seems appropriate to assume that the use of multiple forms of childcare would also affect parenting (e.g., parental stress associated with the scheduling of different childcare arrangements). Finally, the time spent by children in the various forms of childcare per week, *time in childcare*, and the *cost of care* (dollars per week) are included.

Parenting factors were measured in several ways. First, a series of variables assessing the importance which parents place upon three **qualities of children** are included. The first, *independence*, is an indexed variable created from mothers' responses to the following questions: "How important is it to you that your children be independent?" Scores ranged from 1 to 7, with a low score indicating "not at all important" and a high score indicating "extremely important." The second, *obedience*, is created from responses to the same question, but dealing with how important it is that children "always do what you ask." Scores ranged from 1 to 7, again indicating low to high importance on the part of the mother. The third characteristic, *school performance*, is taken from a single question, "How important is it to you that your children do well in school?" These three qualities are conceptualized as traits which parents desire in their children. Hence, these measures may also encompass mothers' perceptions of the end results of their own parenting experience.

The second set of parenting factors address the more direct sources of parent-child interaction. Specifically, the levels of parent-child interaction and parental control over their children are assessed. Two basic measures are utilized. *Reading to child* is a variable based upon responses to the question: "How often do you spend time with your children: reading to child?" Responses ranged from a low of never or rarely (1) to a high of almost everyday (6). *Spanking/slapping* is a variable based upon responses to how often mothers: "spank or slap child." Here, responses ranged from a low of never (1) to a high of very often (4). These measures are intended to assess the behavioral aspects of parenting or, simply, the overall quality of parental treatment of children.

A variety of control variables were included in the analyses, most of which address traits of the mothers. *Parental stress* is taken from responses to the statement: "I often wish I could be free from the responsibility of being a parent." Possible responses ranged from strongly disagree (1) to strongly agree (5). Mothers' *weekly labor force hours*, *educational attainment* (years of formal schooling), *race* (black=1), and marital status are included (single=1, married=0). Finally, measures of the *number of sons* and *number of daughters* under the age of 5 were included.

RESULTS

Table 1 presents the means and standard deviations for the childcare variables by the racial/ethnic category of the mothers. Substantial and significant differences appear in the forms of childcare utilized by black and white mothers. For example, 20.4 percent of black mothers report using a daycare center, whereas fully 30.0 percent of white mothers use a daycare center. Babysitters (i.e., in-home childcare) were used by 22.2 percent of black mothers, but were used by 40.0 percent of white mothers. As expected, black mothers were considerably more

Table 1

Means and Standard Deviations of Childcare
Variables among Working Mothers, by Race

	Black (54)	White (295)
Daycare	20.4%	30.0%
	(.407)	(.458)
Babysitter	22.2%*	40.0%
	(.420)	(.490)
Relatives	51.9%*	34.9%
	(.504)	(.478)
Multiple Caregivers	20.4%*	40.3%
	(.407)	(.491)
Time in Childcare	34.7*	28.2
(hours per week)	(24.3)	(21.5)
Cost of Care	$37.71*	$50.05
(per week)	(21.53)	(39.95)

* p < .05 (difference between means)

likely to use relatives as a childcare choice (51.9%) than were white mothers (34.9%).

White mothers appear to utilize a greater number of childcare arrangements. Among white mothers, 40.3 percent utilized more than one form of childcare, while only 20.4 percent of black mothers did so. Interestingly, the children of black mothers spent more time per week in childcare than did the children of white mothers (34.7 hours versus 28.2 hours, respectively). Finally, white mothers spent considerably more on childcare, with an average of about 50 dollars per week, compared to approximately 38 dollars per week for black mothers.

As discussed earlier, previous research had suggested that black and white mothers' maternal experiences should be substantially different. Table 2 presents the mean levels for the various parenting variables. While black and white mothers' reports of parenting do indeed vary, only two statistically significant differences appear between black and white mothers. Black mothers report a significantly higher concern for obedience in their children. Given the greater propensity for black mothers to be single, this difference is somewhat expected. Single parents may have a greater need for control over their children, at least as compared to parents who can look to their spouse for assistance in the supervision of their children.

Table 2

Means and Standard Deviations
of Parenting Variables
among Working Mothers, by Race

	Black (54)	White (295)
Concern for child Qualities:		
School Performance	6.04	5.74
	(1.50)	(1.12)
Obedience	5.87*	5.30
	(1.45)	(1.15)
Independence	5.93	5.95
	(1.61)	(1.02)
Parenting:		
Reading to child	4.59*	5.05
	(1.69)	(1.29)
Spanking/Slapping	2.33	2.30
	(0.89)	(0.80)

* $p < .05$ (difference between means)

In terms of the direct measures of parent-child interaction, white mothers are significantly more likely to read to their children (5.05 versus 4.59). Again, this difference may result not from cultural/ethnic differences, but rather, from the differences in the family structures of black and white families. In this sample, 20.7 percent (61) of the white mothers were single parents, as compared to 50.0 percent (27) of the black mothers. Hence, the family structure (i.e., availability of spousal assistance) may be the factor underlying the differences shown in parenting between black and white mothers.

One of the central issues of this study, however, is that of the potential effects of childcare choice on the maternal experience. Table 3 presents the mean levels of parenting measures across the three basic forms of childcare choice. As shown, several differences are evident across the different forms of childcare. For example, mothers' concern for their children's school performance is greater among mothers who use daycare centers (5.92) as compared to those who use either a babysitter (5.79) or relatives (5.61). As previously suggested, this may be indicative of mothers' concern for their child's development (i.e., they placed their child in a daycare with the assumption that it would enhance the child's intellectual development).

In seeming contrast to the concern for children's school performance development, mothers who use daycare centers also report higher levels of concern for obedience in their children, compared to mothers who use the other two forms of childcare. Interestingly, maternal concern for a sense of independence in their children is greatest among mothers who use a babysitter (although the differences are rather small). Conceivably, children who are cared for by a babysitter are left to their own accord more than children in daycare centers. This may subsequently lead mothers to expect their children to be more independent.

Moreover, although mothers who use formal daycare centers are more concerned about the school performance of their children, such mothers also report the lowest levels of reading to their children. These findings seem rather contradictory, and actually raise further questions concerning the quality of the various forms of care.

Table 3

Means and Standard Deviations
of Parenting Variables among Working Mothers,
by Choice of Childcare

	Daycare (99)	Babysitter (129)	Relatives (131)
Concern for child Qualities:			
School performance	5.92	5.79	5.61
	(1.31)	(1.11)	(1.14)
Obedience	5.56	5.25	5.31
	(1.25)	(1.24)	(1.13)
Independence	5.93	6.16	5.89
	(1.17)	(0.98)	(1.11)
Parenting:			
Reading to child	4.86	5.20	5.07
	(1.41)	(1.13)	(1.25)
Spanking/slapping	2.43	2.41	2.29
	(0.79)	(0.74)	(0.84)

Of central concern, however, is the association between the various measures of childcare choice and the experience of motherhood. Table 4 presents the multivariate regression results (standardized regression coefficients) for the models of the five measures of the maternal experience. For the most part, these models support the results drawn from the previous cross-tabulations.

The model of maternal concern for children's school performance yields only one significant effect, that of parental stress. As shown, an increase in parental stress substantially reduces mothers' concern for children's school performance ($\beta = -.11$). Hence, when employed mothers feel stressed in their maternal role, their concern for children's

Table 4

Multivariate Regression Coefficients for Models
of Parenting Variables among Working Mothers (N = 349)

| | Concern for Child Qualities | | | Parenting | |
	School performance	Obed-ience	Indepen-dence	Reading to child	Spanking/slapping
Daycare	-.02	-.07	.07	.09	.20***
	(-.06)	(-.18)	(.19)	(.28)	(.35)
Babysitter	-.10	-.03	-.03	.04	.09
	(-.23)	(-.06)	(-.07)	(.12)	(.15)
Relatives	.05	.01	-.02	-.01	.07
	(.13)	(.02)	(-.05)	(-.03)	(.13)
Multiple caregivers	.03	.12**	.01	-.11**	-.02
	(.07)	(.31)	(.00)	(-.32)	(-.03)
Time in childcare	.02	-.03	.01	.01	.05
	(.00)	(-.00)	(.00)	(.01)	(.00)
Cost of care	-.01	-.04	-.04	-.03	-.15**
	(-.00)	(-.00)	(-.00)	(-.00)	(-.00)
Parental stress	-.11*	.04	.01	-.09*	.09 *
	(-.13)	(.05)	(.01)	(-.12)	(.07)
Weekly labor force hrs		.09	.08	.14*	-.08-.03
	(.01)	(.01)	(.01)	(-.01)	(-.00)
Ed attainment	-.06	-.13**	.02	.21***	-.26***
	(-.03)	(-.07)	(.01)	(.12)	(-.09)
Race (Black=1)	-.07	-.14**	.02	.14***	.04
	(-.22)	(-.47)	(.05)	(.55)	(.09)
Single mother	.01	.06	.05	.14**	.05
	(.03)	(.17)	(.12)	(.44)	(.10)
Number of sons	-.00	.03	-.16*	.05	.24 ***
	(-.00)	(.05)	(-.30)	(.12)	(.32)
Number of daughters	-.09	-.02	-.16*	.14**	.18 ***
	(-.16)	(-.03)	(-.28)	(.30)	(.23)
R^2	.06	.09	.06	.12	.18
F	1.58*	2.61***	1.74*	3.35***	5.68***

Note: unstandardized coefficients are shown in parentheses
*** $p < .01$; ** $p < .05$; * $p < .10$

school performance diminishes. This finding is somewhat disconcerting, as it suggests that parents under stress may disregard their child's school performance.

The model of maternal concern for children's obedience provides several significant results. Here, the use of multiple caregivers is positively associated with a concern for obedience ($\beta = .12$). This may imply that the scheduling difficulties and general hassles associated with the use of more than one childcare provider decreases mothers' tolerance of disobedient children. As well, the children may be less obedient because they have multiple caregivers (who may have different styles of discipline). A racial/ethnic difference appears within this model, in that black mothers are shown to be less concerned with children's obedience ($\beta = -.14$), even after controlling for the effects of childcare choice. Additionally, increased educational attainment of mothers is associated with decreased concern for children's obedience.

The effects of maternal employment are shown in the model of mothers' concern for independence in their children. As shown, an increase in the number of hours mothers spend in paid employment is positively associated with concern for children's independence ($\beta = .14$). This seems appropriate, given that mothers who are not in the home environment may expect their children to fend for their own needs more than mothers who are not employed. This conclusion may be partially supported by the effects for number of sons and number of daughters. As the number of children increases, parental concern for children's independence decreases. This finding suggests that single children will attract more maternal concern for independence.

The models of direct parent-child interaction explain a greater proportion of the variance and are also more robust than the models of maternal concern for child qualities. In the model of reading to children, the use of multiple childcare providers is again a significant determinant. Mothers who use multiple childcare providers appear to read less to their children ($\beta = -.11$). Predictably, an increase in mothers' educational attainment is positively associated with reading to children. In contrast to the mean levels of reading to children shown in Table 2, black mothers are actually shown to read to their children more ($\beta = .14$), after controlling for the effects of childcare choice. Additionally, single mothers are significantly more likely to read to their children than are married mothers ($\beta = .14$). Finally, a sex-bias in maternal treatment of children does appear, in that mothers are shown to be more likely to read to daughters than to sons.

The model of spanking/slapping children also yields several interesting findings. Most notably, mothers who utilize formal daycare centers are substantially more likely to slap or spank their children (β = .20). This is rather surprising, given that previous studies had suggested that parents who use daycare are, on average, more concerned with their child's development. There are several possible explanations for this finding. It may be that children who are in the daycare setting have difficulty coping with the different "parenting" styles of their caregivers at the daycare and their actual parent in the home environment. Another possible linkage is that of the effect of the cost of childcare. As shown, a decreased cost of childcare is associated with a decreased tendency to slap or spank children (β = -.15). Hence, while the factors associated with childcare had little effect on maternal attitudes (i.e., concern for child qualities), they do appear to be substantially associated with maternal behaviors.

Mothers' stress with the parental role is also positively associated with spanking or slapping children. On the other hand, increased educational attainment by mothers significantly reduces the incidence of spanking or slapping children (β = -.26). Finally, there again appears to be a sex bias in regard to maternal treatment of children. While the overall number of children appears to increase mothers' likelihood to spank or slap their children, the effect is stronger for the number of sons (β = .24) as compared to the number of daughters (β = .18). Hence, after controlling for the effects of childcare choice, mothers are more likely to spank or slap sons than daughters.

CONCLUSIONS AND DISCUSSION

This study was initiated with two primary goals: 1) to examine racial/ethnic differences in childcare choice, and 2) to examine the associations between childcare choice and the maternal experience. While each goal was achieved and answers were provided, several questions were also raised by the analyses.

Black and white mothers were shown to differ substantially in regard to their choices of childcare. White mothers were more likely to use formal daycare centers, in-home babysitters, and to use multiple forms of childcare at the same time. On the other hand, black mothers were more likely to use relatives (e.g., grandparents) as a choice for childcare. Additionally, although white mothers spent more on weekly childcare, the children of black mothers spent more time per week in some form of nonmaternal care. Black mothers also reported higher concern for obedience as a quality in their children, and, at least in the bivariate comparisons, were slightly less likely to read to their young children.

As suggested earlier, many of these differences between the maternal experiences of black and white mothers may be attributable to their respective family structures. That is, since black mothers are more likely to be single and also more likely to be employed outside the home, the demands placed upon them as both parent and provider are clearly distinct from those of white mothers. Previous research has suggested that single mothers, particularly low-income single mothers, will experience more stress than married mothers (Campbell and Moen, 1992). The finding that black mothers are more concerned about obedience should be taken in its proper context, and not necessarily assumed to be a true cultural or ethnic difference.

An examination of the maternal experience measures across the three basic forms of childcare also revealed the effect of childcare choice. In particular, mothers using daycare appeared more concerned about the intellectual development of their children, yet were somewhat less likely to read to their children (as compared to mothers who used either a relative or babysitter as their childcare choice).

After controlling for the multivariate relationships in the regression analyses, childcare factors revealed several interesting associations. In particular, the use of multiple caregivers was associated with increased concern for children's obedience and a decrease in mothers' reading to children. In this regard, the use of multiple caregivers may limit both mothers' time to spend with their children and their tolerance of misbehavior.

Oddly, the use of formal daycare was associated with an increased propensity to spank or slap children. As previously mentioned, this finding seems to provide more questions than answers. One possible interpretation of this finding is that children who attend daycare centers are exposed to a broader variety of same-age peers behaviors, some of which may be deemed as undesirable by the mothers (e.g., a child may learn how to throw a temper tantrum by watching another child do so at the daycare). It is also possible that the children who attend daycare centers have difficulty in adjusting between the behavioral requirements of their daycare caregivers and the expectations of their mothers in the home setting. Mothers' reported stress in the parental role was also associated with the likelihood to spank or slap children. These findings clearly require further investigation in future research.

Finally, aside from the effects of childcare choice, the employed mothers in this sample appeared to display a sex bias in their parent-child interactions. Controlling for all other variables, mothers were more likely to read to daughters than to sons and were more likely to slap or spank their children when those children were sons rather than daughters. The significance of same-sex relationships between parents and children seems apparent in these findings. However, direct comparisons with paternal behaviors and attitudes would be necessary to definitively state that such sex-biases exist.

Overall, childcare choice and the related factors (i.e., cost and time) account for some of the variation in the maternal experience. Though childcare factors are significant, factors related to family structure (e.g., number of children, single parenthood) and also mothers' individual traits (e.g., race, educational attainment) account for a larger portion of the explained variance. Of course, other characteristics of childcare choice not included in these data (e.g., distance traveled to childcare, number of available providers) may more substantially affect mother-child relationships. Future research should focus more squarely on the impact of variations in family structures on the maternal experience.

NOTE

[1] Paper presented at the Center for Studies of the Family's 20th Annual Conference, Brigham Young University, Provo, Utah (October 14, 1993).

REFERENCES

Belsky, Jay and Rovine, Michael. 1988. "Nonmaternal care in the first year of life and security of infant-parent attachment." *Child Development* 59:157-167.

Bretherton, Inge, Zeynep Biringen, and D. Ridgeway. 1991. "The parental side of attachment." Pp. 1-25 in Karl Pillemer and Kathleen McCartney (eds.), *Parent-Child Relations Throughout Life*. Hillsdale, NJ: Lawrence Erlbaum Associates.

Campbell, Marian L. and Phyllis Moen. 1992. "Job-family role strain among employed single mothers of preschoolers." *Family Relations* 41:205-211.

Cherlin, Andrew. 1981. *Marriage, Divorce, Remarriage*. Cambridge, MA: Harvard University Press.

Christensen, Kathleen E. 1988. *Women and Home-Based Work*. New York: Henry Holt.

Clarke-Stewart, K. Allison. 1987. "Predicting child development from care forms and features: The Chicago study." Pp. 21-41 in D.A. Phillips (ed.), *Quality in Child Care: What Does Research Tell Us?* Washington, DC: National Association for the Education of Young Children.

Collins, Patricia Hill. 1991. "The meaning of motherhood in black culture." Pp. 169-178 in Robert Staples (ed.), *The Black Family: Essays and Studies*. Belmont, CA: Wadsworth.

Crnic, Keith A. and Mark T. Greenberg. 1990. "Minor parenting stresses with young children." *Child Development* 61:1628-1637.

Farley, Reynolds and Suzanne M. Bianchi. 1991. "The growing racial differences in marriage and family patterns." Pp. 5-22 in Robert Staples (ed.), *The Black Family: Essays and Studies*. Belmont, CA: Wadsworth.

Galambos, Nancy L. and Jacqueline V. Lerner. 1987. "Child characteristics and the employment of mothers with young children: A longitudinal study." *Journal of Child Psychology and Psychiatry* 28:87-98.

Gerson, Kathleen. 1985. *Hard Choices: How Women Decide about Work, Career, and Motherhood*. Berkeley, CA: University of California Press.

Haskins, Ron. 1985. "Public school aggression among children with varying day-care experience." *Child Development* 56:689-703.

Hock, Ellen, Debra DeMeis, and Susan L. McBride. 1988. "Maternal separation anxiety: Its role in the balance of employment and motherhood in mothers of infants." Pp. 191-229 in Adele E. Gottfried and Allen Gottfried (eds.), *Maternal Employment and Children's Development*. New York: Plenum.

Hofferth, Sandra L. and Douglas A. Wissoker. 1992. "Price, quality, and income in child care choice." *Journal of Human Resources* 27:72-111.

Hoffman, Lois W. 1989. "Effects of maternal employment in the two-parent family." *American Psychologist* 44:283-292.

Hogan, Dennis, Ling-Xin Hao, and L. Parish. 1990. "Race, kin networks, and assistance to mother only families." *Social Forces* 68:797-812.

Howes, Carollee and Phyllis Stewart. 1987. "Child's play with adults, toys, and peers: An examination of family and child care influences." *Developmental Psychology* 23:423-430.

King, Donna and Carol E. MacKinnon. 1988. "Making difficult choices easier: A review of research on day care and children's development." *Family Relations* 37:392-398.

Lamb, Michael and M. Ann Easterbrooks. 1981. "Individual differences in parental sensitivity: Origins, components, and consequences." In Michael Lamb and Lonnie R. Sherrod (eds.), *Infant Social Cognition: Empirical and Theoretical Considerations*. New York: Basic Books.

Maume, Jr., David J. 1991. "Child-care expenditures and women's employment turnover." *Social Forces* 70 (2):495-508.

McCartney, Kathleen. 1984. "Effect of day care environment on children's language development." *Developmental Psychology* 20:244-260.

Morgan, Karen Christman and Ellen Hock. 1984. "A longitudinal study of the psychosocial variables affecting the career patterns of women with young children." *Journal of Marriage and the Family* 46:383-490.

Phillips, Deborah, Kathleen McCartney, and Sandra Scarr. 1987. "Child care quality and children's social development." *Developmental Psychology* 23:537-543.

Sanik, Margaret M. and Teresa Mauldin. 1986. "Single versus two-parent families: A Comparison of mothers' time." *Family Relations* 35:53-56.

Scarr, Sandra, Deborah Phillips, and Kathleen McCartney. 1989. "Working mothers and their families." *American Psychologist* 44 (11):1402-1409.

Schuster, Claudia. 1993. "Employed first-time mothers: A typology of maternal responses to integrating parenting and employment." *Family Relations* 42:13-20.

Shea, E. and Edward Z. Tronick. 1988. "The maternal self-report inventory: A research and clinical instrument for assessing maternal self-esteem." In Hiram Fitzgerald, Barry Lester, and Michael Yogman (eds.), *Theory and Research in Behavioral Pediatrics* (Vol. 4). New York: Plenum.

Sweet, J.A., L.L. Bumpass, and V. Call. 1988. *The Design and Content of the National Survey of Families and Households* (NSFH Working Paper No. 1). Madison: University of Wisconsin, Center for Demography and Ecology.

Taylor, Ronald. 1994. "African American families in the United States." Pp. 17-46 in Ronald L. Taylor (ed.), *Minority Families in the United States: A Multicultural Perspective*. Englewood Cliffs, NJ: Prentice-Hall.

U.S. Bureau of the Census. 1992. *Statistical Abstract of the United States* (112th edition). Washington, DC: U.S. Government Printing Office.

_____. 1991. *Statistical Abstract of the United States* (111th edition). Washington, DC: U. S. Government Printing Office.

Volling, Brenda L. and Jay Belsky. 1993. "Maternal employment: Parent, infant, and contextual characteristics related to maternal employment decisions in the first year of infancy." *Family Relations* 42:4-12.

Willie, Diane E. 1992. "Maternal employment: Impact on maternal behavior." *Family Relations* 41:273-277.

How We Parent:
Race and Ethnic Differences

Katherine McDade

Family theorists and family practitioners are becoming increasingly aware of the importance of ethnicity in understanding the attitudes and behaviors of parents toward their children (Gray and Cosgrove, 1985; Garcia Coll, 1990; Harrison et al., 1990). In addition to parent-child relationships, the ethnicity of families has implications for understanding child socialization and development and for understanding and preventing child maltreatment. Anderson (1992) suggests that families operate within a cultural reality that is heavily influenced by both ethnicity and social class position. This cultural reality determines family members' value and norm dispositions, and includes rules for appropriate childrearing practices. While stressing that the similarities in parenting among ethnic groups in the United States are striking, Hamner and Turner (1985) maintain that important cultural differences exist that cannot be attributed to social class alone. Because "each subculture has unique language patterns, each has traditional rituals, and each has its own perception of family structure, roles and functioning," differences in parent-child interaction are inevitable (p. 156)

In reviewing research on the development of parental beliefs, Okagaki and Johnson-Divecha (1993) concluded that ethnicity is an important determinant of the way that parents think about children, their child-rearing goals and their behavior toward their children. They discuss, as particularly relevant, the difference between ethnic groups in the United States that emphasize familism and group identity, e.g. Hispanics and Asian Americans, versus those that emphasize independence and individual autonomy, e.g. Anglo-Americans. In an attempt to link these different cultural values with parental beliefs and behaviors, Okagaki and her associates ranked parents' responses to a series of questions related to child rearing on the dimensions of conformity versus autonomy and found significant differences related to both ethnicity and immigrant status.

Unfortunately, much of the literature on minority families has been distorted by a failure to distinguish between factors related to ethnicity versus factors related to social class, resulting in an overemphasis on the dysfunctional aspects of minority family life (Staples and Mirande, 1980; Garbarino and Ebata, 1983; McLoyd, 1990). Garcia Coll (1990) recommends that future research on family dynamics and child development consider the effects of culture, social class, family structure, health, and biological factors as separate yet interacting forces and that we recognize and affirm different yet normal developmental pathways for children from minority families.

Many researchers have noted the influence of extended family networks, which are more common and more pronounced among ethnic minority families in the United States, on parent-child relationships and interaction. In extended families, grandparents and other real and fictive kin often play important roles in child socialization and discipline (London and Devore, 1988; Garcia Coll, 1990; Harrison et al., 1990). Other researchers have noted that raising children in a climate of cultural racism is also an important factor that must be taken into account when examining parenting beliefs and practices in minority families (London and Devore, 1988; Holton, 1992).

In addition to extended family structures and the reality of racism that all minority families share, researchers and theorists have identified specific values and practices in ethnic minority families that seem to transcend social class position. Since the research data are limited and often do not rule out the confounding effects of socio-economic and/or immigrant status, these differences must be viewed as generalizations that require additional empirical verification.

Although Native Americans cannot be considered a monolithic group because of the extreme diversity among tribes, common structures such as reservation life and the resulting strong community ties have resulted in an emphasis on cooperation as a socialization goal and the devaluing of private ownership (Staples and Mirande, 1980; Harrison et al., 1990). Loyalty, humility, respect for elders, reticence, and the avoidance of personal gain are values that seem to transcend tribal groups. Children are valued by all adults in the community, are included in social events, and disciplined gently. For example, hitting a child or talking loudly while correcting a child are not normative among Native American parents (London and Devore, 1988).

In contrast, African American parents are reported to be more severe, punitive, and power assertive in disciplining children, although this may be a consequence of socio-economic status rather than ethnicity (McLoyd, 1990). African American families are characterized as highly adaptable with high achievement expectations and a strong work ethic. The church remains a dominant force in African American families and communities (London and Devore, 1988). Male-female relationships tend to be egalitarian and socialization goals for male and female children are similar (Staples and Mirande, 1980). The development of coping skills and mental toughness are encouraged in children, who must function in often hostile social environments (London and Devore, 1988).

Hispanic families are characterized by the ideal of familism whereby the individual self is considered less important than the family. Within the Hispanic community the family is regarded as the primary social unit and familial self-reliance is emphasized. This often leads to ambivalent attitudes about accessing support systems and seeking help from professional sources (Vega et al., 1983). Solidarity and interdependence among parents and their children is actively fostered. (Harrison et al., 1990; Wagner and Haug, 1971). Consequently, parents tend to be less authoritative and more protective and to emphasize conformity and the development of social skills among their children (Okagaki and Johnson-Divecha, 1993). Individual responsibility and achievement are not emphasized (Garcia Coll, 1990).

Asian American families stress interdependence and respect for authority, and children are expected to obey their parents without question (London and Devore, 1988; Harrison et al., 1990). Traditional Asian cultures stress filial piety, whereby children are expected to make sacrifices for the well-being of their parents and children are socialized to conform to family and societal expectations rather than pursuing individual interests (Staples and Mirande, 1980; Hong and Hong, 1991). Self-discipline, emotional control and logical thinking are emphasized as socialization goals (London and Devore, 1988). Compared especially to Hispanic parents, Asian American parents grant more autonomy and latitude to their children (Hong and Hong, 1991).

Ethnicity is also important in understanding the dynamics of child maltreatment and in formulating effective strategies to prevent it.

Culturally specific childrearing practices that differ from Anglo-American norms are sometimes (erroneously) interpreted as detrimental to children simply because they are different (Giovannoni and Becerra, 1979). These include the use of folk remedies, methods of discipline and control, degrees of warmth and affection, and achievement expectations, among others (Gray and Cosgrove, 1985). Further research and evaluation is needed in order to determine the consequences of these practices for children. Research also indicates that parents from different ethnic groups perceive maltreatment differently and recommend different responses to allegations of child maltreatment (Gray and Cosgrove, 1985; Hong and Hong, 1991). For example, Asian Americans judge parental conduct less harshly than parents from other ethnic groups and are less likely to welcome outside intervention in families (Hong and Hong, 1991).

Efforts to prevent the maltreatment of children have centered on the development of parent education programs. The goal of parent education is to help parents understand the variability in parent-child relationships, to help them evaluate their current parenting practices and, if necessary, learn new and more effective ones and to understand the developmental needs of children (Heath, 1987). Parent education programs however, have been less successful among ethnic minority groups, possibly because they are based on and reflect Anglo-American middle-class values. Service providers have demonstrated that parents from ethnic minority groups and from low socio-economic groups will attend and complete parent education programs if the setting and the content are compatible with their values and their lifestyles. For example, Hispanic parents may be more likely to attend parent education programs that are informal rather than structured learning experiences, if extended family are included and if child care is provided (Leon et al., 1984; Martinez, 1988). African American parents may respond to programs that incorporate the church, that include extended family members and use community elders as key resources, that utilize music, dance and visual arts as vehicles for outreach and retention and that place equal emphasis on male and female roles (Peterman, 1981; Glanville and Tiller, 1991; Holton, 1992). Native American parents would likely benefit from programs that blend child development information with the spirituality and traditions of their tribe and that are designed and implemented by providers who are sensitive to historical events that have shaped Native Americans' attitudes toward social workers and other professionals (Horejsi et al., 1992).

The available research confirms that race/ethnicity is an important factor to consider when investigating the dynamics of parent-child relationships. It is clear that adults parent differently and some of these differences may be rooted in a cultural heritage. These differences have important implications for strengthening families, for assuring the optimal care for children, and for designing and implementing services and programs for parents.

Probability Sample

The probability sample was chosen from a list of randomly selected households purchased from telephone companies serving all parts of King County, Washington. Parents who were part of this sample responded to surveys administered over the phone. The surveys took from 20 to 30 minutes to complete and were conducted at various times throughout the day and evening, including weekends. Four hundred and thirty-one parents, with children aged 18 or younger living at home, were included in this sample and were interviewed in March of 1993. The racial/ethnic background of the parents was determined by self-report. Responses were coded into 8 categories: Native American, Asian/Pacific Islander, Black/African American, White/Caucasian, Hispanic/Latino, Alaskan Native, Other, and Refused. Eighty-four percent of the parents identified themselves as Caucasian, 2.1 percent as Native American, 3.5 percent as Asian/Pacific Islander, 4.2 percent as African American and 2.1 percent as Hispanic/Latino. One percent of the respondents were coded as "other" and 1.4 percent refused to respond to the question.

Sixty-five percent of the respondents were women, 35 percent were men, and 29 percent were single parents. Ninety-six percent of the respondents had completed high school, and 43.9 percent had completed college. Average household income was just under $35,000, and 69 percent of the respondents reported household incomes above $35,000. The age of respondents ranged from 19 to 61 and their children's ages ranged from newborns to 22-year-olds. The number of children in each family ranged from one to eight, with an average of two children per family. Approximately 52 percent of the children represented in this sample were age 5 or under.

Comparing these figures to the 1990 census data indicates that the sample is quite close to population demographics in King County, with the exception of education levels and the proportion of Asian/Pacific Islanders in the sample (see Table 1). Our sample is slightly more educated than the King County population. This is not unusual for a telephone survey. People with higher levels of education are more likely to have a telephone and to choose to participate in research. The race/ethnic distribution of the sample was very close to King County population distributions with the exception of Asian/Pacific Islanders, who are underrepresented by approximately 4 percent. This could be due to a relatively large population of recent immigrants from South East Asia who are unable to speak English well enough to participate in a telephone survey.

THE SURVEY

The survey was part of an effort to evaluate the effectiveness of a media campaign sponsored by the Council for the Prevention of Child Abuse and Neglect. The focus of the campaign was to send a strong message to the community that parenting is difficult and that most people need information and support in order to parent effectively. Parents were encouraged to seek help from a variety of sources, including an anonymous telephone helpline, and to refrain from "losing their cool" and/or becoming violent with their children. Questions on the survey addressed four constructs related to attitudes about parenting in general, and help seeking behavior in particular. These included: 1) attitudes about seeking help as a parent; (2) the sources of help most likely to be used by parents; 3) beliefs about parental autonomy versus community involvement in childrearing; and 4) the acceptability of various methods of disciplining children.

ATTITUDES ABOUT SEEKING HELP
AS A PARENT

We were interested in our respondents' attitudes about the difficulty of parenting, whether they thought parenting is learned or instinctive, and under what conditions they thought it was okay for parents to seek

Table 1

Comparisons of King County Demographics and
the Sample:
Income, Education, and Race/Ethnicity

Characteristic	King County	Sample
Income:		
Less than $15,000	8.8%	6.5%
$15,000 - $24,999	11.4	9.5
$25,000 - $34,999	14.6	15.1
$35,000 - $49,999	23.2	23.4
$50,000 - $74,999	24.6	25.1
$75,000 or more	17.4	12.3
Missing data		8.1
Education:		
No high school	3.7%	1.6%
Some high school	8.0	2.1
High school diploma	22.8	19.3
Tech/AA degree	7.7	3.2
Some college	25.0	29.9
College degree	22.8	30.4
Graduate degree	10.0	13.5
Race/ethnicity:		
Caucasian	82.6%	84.0%
African American	4.8	4.2
Asian/Pacific Islander	7.7	3.5
Hispanic/Latino	2.7	2.1
Native American	1.1	2.1
Other	1.0	2.8
Refused		1.4

help. Six statements on the survey reflected attitudes that are receptive to seeking help with parenting while seven statements on the survey reflected attitudes that are resistant to seeking help with parenting. These are listed below but ordered differently than on the actual survey.

Receptive Statements

1) Once in awhile even good parents need help or advice with their kids.
2) Parents should not be embarrassed to ask for help.
3) It's important for parents to have someone to talk to when they need help or advice.
4) Because it's more difficult nowadays to be a parent, it's okay to ask for help.
5) Some of the tips other people offer on raising kids can be pretty helpful.
6) Most parents need help or advice about parenting.

Resistent Statements

1) Being an effective parent is mostly just following your instincts.
2) Most parents do a fine job of raising their children without help or advice.
3) Unfortunately, there just aren't many good resources for parents who want help.
4) Most people would think there's something wrong with a parent who needs help with their children.
5) Parenting is a lonely job. There is no one to turn to for help.
6) Most of the advice parents get from others is impractical or useless.
7) Parents who have to ask for help are probably not very good parents.

SOURCES OF HELP
MOST LIKELY TO BE USED BY PARENTS

In addition to a general question about the likelihood that they would seek help with parenting, we asked our respondents to assess the likelihood that they would seek help from a variety of specific sources, including family members and friends, health care providers, social service agencies and counselors, school personnel, and clergy and child protective services. We also asked them the likelihood that they would participate in a parenting class, attend a parent support group, call a telephone helpline and/or use print or video materials.

BELIEFS ABOUT PARENTAL AUTONOMY VERSUS COMMUNITY INVOLVEMENT IN CHILD RAISING

Related to the campaign goal of encouraging parents to seek help when they need it, are beliefs about parental autonomy and family privacy. Consequently, we were interested in how parents perceived these issues. To what extent do parents feel accountable to the community for their behavior as parents? Do parents think that family matters should be kept private? We asked our respondents the extent to which they agreed or disagreed with four statements related to parental autonomy. These included statements read as follows:

1) Parents should be able to discipline their children any way they want.
2) How people treat their kids is nobody's business but their own.
3) Family problems should be kept inside the family.
4) Other people should not interfere when parents appear to be having a hard time with their children.

ACCEPTABILITY OF VARIOUS METHODS OF DISCIPLINING CHILDREN

In addition to the general issue of parents' rights to discipline their children, we were interested in the extent to which parents used and felt justified in using various methods of discipline. These included: taking away privileges, sending a child to his or her room, slapping the child's hand, using your hand to spank the child, raising your voice or yelling, threatening the child with physical punishment, spanking with an object such as a switch or a belt, shaking the child, hitting in anger, and making fun of the child or calling the child names.

ANALYSIS

Data analysis for the probability samples consisted of frequency and percentage distributions plus cross-tabulations of selected independent and dependent variables. Parent characteristics, (such as age, sex, race/ethnicity, income and education), number and sex of children, and geographical location were correlated with selected items from the survey. Chi square tests of significance were conducted to test the statistical significance of relationships between independent and dependent variables. In this paper, relationships between the race and ethnicity of parents and their responses to questions about parenting attitudes are reported.

FINDINGS

Attitudes About Seeking Help as a Parent

Six statements on the survey reflected receptive attitudes about help-seeking behavior and elicited strong agreement from the parents in our sample. For example, 98 percent agreed that even good parents need help with their kids sometimes. Statistically significant differences related to the race/ethnicity of parents occurred in response to the statement "Parents should not be embarrassed to ask for help." Only 44 percent of the Native American parents strongly agreed with this statement, compared to 80 percent of the Asian/Pacific Islander, 83.3 percent of the African American, 83.7 percent of the Caucasian and 88.9 percent of the Hispanic/Latino parents.

Seven statements on the survey reflected resistant attitudes about help-seeking behavior. The majority of our respondents disagreed with these statements, but not so strongly as they agreed with the receptive statements. Statistically significant differences related to the race/ethnicity of parents appeared in response to the statement "Unfortunately, there just aren't enough resources available for parents who want help with their kids." Thirty-three percent of Hispanic/Latino respondents strongly agreed with this statement, compared to 8.3 percent of all of the parents in the probability sample. Forty-five percent of

African American parents agreed with the statement, either "strongly" or "somewhat," compared to 22 percent of the parents in the sample. These differences may reflect a lack of materials available in Spanish as well as a lack of culturally relevant parenting materials for both Hispanic/Latinos and African Americans.

The Sources of Help Most Likely to be Used by Parents

Eighty-seven percent of the respondents said they were either very likely or somewhat likely to seek advice or help with parenting from some source. Only 12 percent of the respondents said they were unlikely to seek help. The most likely sources of help for these respondents were print and video material (94%), followed by family members (88%), and parenting classes (84%). The sources of help mentioned by the fewest respondents were child protective services (17%), and a telephone helpline (26%). Statistically significant differences related to race/ethnicity occurred in responses to the use of print and video material and to seeking help from friends. African American parents were less likely than other groups to use print and video materials while Hispanic/Latino parents were less likely than other groups to seek help from friends. Hispanic/Latino parents' preference for print and video materials is expecially noteworthy given their agreement with the statement about the lack of good resources for parents who want them.

Beliefs About Parental Autonomy Versus Community Involvement in Child Raising

Four statements on the survey reflected attitudes about parental autonomy and family privacy. Statistically significant differences related to race/ethnicity occurred in two of the items. Only 6 percent of the parents in the probability sample strongly agreed with the statement, "Parents should be able to discipline their children any way they want." An additional 16 percent agreed somewhat with the statement. Parents from different race/ethnic groups responded quite differently to the statement and these differences were statistically significant. Twenty percent of Asian/Pacific Islander parents strongly agreed with the statement compared to 5.6 percent of African American parents, 4.8 percent of Caucasian parents and none of the Native American and

Hispanic/Latino parents. If we combine the number of parents who agreed somewhat to the statement with those who agreed strongly, dramatic differences remain. Forty-seven percent of Asian/Pacific Islander parents agreed with the statement, which was more than double the percentage of any other race/ethnic group.

Only 2.6 percent of the parents strongly agreed with the statement, "How people treat their kids is nobody's business but their own" and an additional 6.3 percent agreed somewhat. Apparently, and somewhat surprisingly, the majority of our respondents believe that the community has a stake in how they raise their children. Statistically significant differences occurred in how parents from different race/ethnic groups responded to this statement. Twenty-seven percent of Asian/Pacific Islander parents strongly agreed with the statement and an additional 13 percent agreed somewhat, while not one Hispanic/Latino parent agreed with the statement at all. Native American, Caucasian and African American parents fell in between these two extremes with percentages of 11.1, 7.5 and 5.6 respectively.

Acceptability of Various Methods of Disciplining Children

In addition to the general issue of parents' rights to discipline their children, we were interested in the extent to which parents used, and felt justified in using various methods of discipline, particularly physical punishment. We asked parents to tell us whether eleven commonly used methods of discipline were acceptable or unacceptable to them.

The majority of parents in the probability sample felt that talking things over with children, sending them to their room, and/or taking away privileges were acceptable methods of discipline. Approximately half of our respondents felt that yelling, slapping a child's hand, and/or spanking were acceptable. Fewer parents (22%) felt that threats of physical punishment and spanking with an object (10%) were acceptable. Very few parents agreed that name calling, shaking and hitting in anger were acceptable. Parents from different race/ethnic groups felt differently about some forms of discipline, and these differences reached statistical significance on four items: taking away privileges, sending a child to his or her room, threatening the child with physical punishment and spanking with an object, such as a switch or a belt. Seventy-eight percent of Native American and Hispanic/Latino parents agreed that taking away privileges was an acceptable method of discipline, compared to 85.7 percent of the Asian/Pacific Islander parents, 96.6 percent of the Caucasian parents and 100 percent of the African American parents. Sixty-seven percent of the Hispanic/Latino parents felt that sending children to their room was acceptable, compared to 85.7 percent of the Native American parents, 94.4 percent of the Africian American parents, 96.6 percent of the Caucasian parents and 100 percent of the Asian/Pacific Islander parents. Forty-seven percent of the Asian/Pacific Islander parents and 41.2 percent of the African American parents agreed that threatening children with physical punishment was acceptable, compared to 21.1 percent of the Caucasian parents and none of the Native American and Hispanic/Latino parents. Fifty percent of the African American parents thought that spanking with an object was acceptable, compared to 9.6 percent of the Caucasian parents, 7.1 percent of the Asian/Pacific Islander parents, and none of the Native American or Hispanic/Latino parents.

SUMMARY OF FINDINGS

The race or ethnicity of parents in our study was a significant factor in parents' attitudes about seeking help, the sources of help they would most likely use, their attitudes about parental autonomy and the types of child discipline they felt were acceptable.

Attitudes About Seeking Help

Most parents in our survey reported positive attitudes about seeking help with parenting, with some exceptions. Native American parents were less likely than other parents to agree that parents should not be embarrassed to ask for help and many Hispanic/Latino and African American parents felt that resources currently available for parents are not very helpful.

Preferred Sources of Help

Most parents in our study mentioned family, friends, and print and video materials as the most likely sources of help. However, parents from different race/ethnic groups preferred to seek help from different sources. African American parents were less likely than any other group to utilize print and video material, and African American and

Hispanic/Latino parents were less likely than other groups to consult with friends. All of the parents in our study were less willing to consult professional or semi-professional sources for help. Parenting classes and support groups were important sources of help for some parents but not others. These differences were related to levels of education and gender but not to race/ethnicity.

Parental Autonomy

There was surprisingly little agreement with our statements about parental autonomy. The majority of our respondents felt that parents are accountable to their communities for how they raise and discipline their children, that family problems should not be kept inside the family, and perhaps most surprisingly, that it's okay for people to "interfere" when parents are having a hard time with their children. There was considerable variation in how parents responded to these statements however, with consistent differences correlated with race/ethnicity.

Asian/Pacific Islander parents were more likely to agree with the statements, indicating, perhaps, a stronger cultural value about family privacy and parental authority than exists among other parents. African American parents were less tolerant of interference from others when they were having a hard time with their children, although they did not score high on other measures of parental autonomy. Native American and Hispanic/Latino parents scored lower on measures of autonomy than other race/ethnic groups.

Child Discipline

Parents from different race/ethnic groups disagreed on the acceptability of four methods of child discipline. Spanking with an object was acceptable to many African American parents but to none of the Native American or the Hispanic/Latino parents. Threatening a child with physical punishment was acceptable to many African American and Asian/Pacific Islander parents but, again, to none of the Native American or the Hispanic/Latino parents. Taking away privileges or sending a child to his or her room, while acceptable to a majority of all parents, was less acceptable to Hispanic/Latino and Native American parents.

CONCLUSION

This paper begins to explore the issue of multi-cultural perspectives on parenting. Given the increasingly diverse society we are living in and the increasing acceptance of difference, this issue is ripe for exploration. Parenting materials and services abound; however, few of them attend seriously to differences in parenting beliefs and behaviors that are embedded in the culture of a family or community. In this paper the race and ethnicity of families is examined as a possible source of difference in attitudes about parenting. The data indicate that similarities far outweigh differences; however, some differences exist. These include differences in how comfortable parents feel in asking for help and advice with parenting, differences in the sources of help and advice parents are likely to turn to, differences in attitudes about family privacy and parental autonomy, and differences in how children are disciplined.

Most parents in this study expressed attitudes receptive to seeking help with parenting. There seems to be a growing social consensus that parenting is becoming more difficult, and that, in order to be effective, parents need advice and education. The parents in our study reflected this attitude, and they were willing to seek help from a variety of sources. However, most parents sought help informally from family and friends or from written or video materials. Fewer parents were willing or likely to seek advice in face-to-face encounters with teachers, doctors, clergy, counselors or social service providers. This is ironic in that professionals are likely to be more informed sources of information. Many of the barriers to accessing help with parenting that were mentioned by our respondents are rooted in cultural differences. Many of the parents who represented racial and/or ethnic minority groups understood that their beliefs and values about families differed from that of the dominant culture. In discussing their reluctance to seek help with parenting, they expressed concern that they would be misunderstood, that professionals would be unable to understand the reality of their lives, that their beliefs and values about family life would be ignored or challenged, and that the values of the dominant culture would be imposed upon them. Clearly, people who provide materials and services to parents need to be informed about the nuances of cultural difference.

Another important issue related to race/ethnicity that was not addressed in this paper is the effect of racism on the internal dynamics of family life, including the attitudes parents hold about how best to raise children. Parents who believe that their children are likely to be targets of racism and discrimination will no doubt develop parenting strategies and goals that take this into account. This is one possible explanation for the significant differences in methods of discipline, particularly the acceptance of physical punishment, that we found in this study. The effect of racism on family relationships is an issue that needs more attention and research.

In this paper, I focus on the race and/or ethnicity of families as an important source of cultural difference, but other factors need to be considered in developing a comprehensive multi-cultural perspective on family life. Some of these other factors are social class, family structure, geographic location, neighborhood/community, and immigrant status. Those of us who do research on families and those who provide materials and services to families need to move beyond the monocultural approach that has dominated this field and recognize that families differ and that these differences are often a source of family strength and cohesion.

REFERENCES

Anderson, Joseph D. 1992. "Family-centered practice in the 1990s: A multicultural perspective." *Journal of Multicultural Social Work* 1 (4):17-29.

Garbarino, James and Aaron Ebata. 1983. "The significance of ethnic and cultural differences in child maltreatment." *Journal of Marriage and the Family* 45 (4):773-783.

Garcia Coll, Cynthia T. 1990. "Developmental outcome of minority infants: A process-oriented look into our beginnings." *Child Development* 61:270-289.

Giovannoni, Jeanne M. and Rosina M. Becerra. 1979. *Defining Child Abuse*. New York: The Free Press.

Glanville, Cathryn L. and Cynthia M. Tiller. 1991. "Implementing and evaluating a parent education program for minority mothers." *Evaluation and Program Planning* 14:241-245.

Gray, Ellen and John Cosgrove. 1985. "Ethnocentric perception of childrearing practices in protective services." *Child Abuse and Neglect* 9:389-396.

Hamner, Tommie J. and Pauline H. Turner. 1985. *Parenting in Contemporary Society*. New Jersey: Prentice-Hall.

Harrison, Algea O., Melvin N. Wilson, Charles J. Pine, Samuel Q. Chan, and Raymond Buriel. 1990. "Family ecologies of ethnic minority children." *Child Development* 61:347-362.

Heath, Phyliss A. 1987. "Developing parent education courses: A review of resources." *Family Relations* 36:209-214.

Holton, John. 1992. "African America's needs and participation in child maltreatment prevention services: Toward a community response to child abuse and neglect." *Urban Research Review* 14 (1):1-5.

Hong, George K. and Lawrence K. Hong. 1991. "Comparative perspectives on child abuse and neglect: Chinese versus Hispanics and whites." *Child Welfare* LXX (4):463-475.

Horejsi, Charles, Bonnie Heavy Runner Craig, and Joe Pablo. 1992. "Reactions by Native American parents to child protection agencies: Cultural and community factors." *Child Welfare* LXXI (4):329-342.

Leon, Ana M., Rosaleen Mazur, Elba Montalvo, and Mairiam Rodrieguez. 1984. "Self-help support groups for Hispanic mothers," *Child Welfare* LXIII (3):261-268.

London, Harlan and Wynetta Devore. 1988. "Layers of understanding: Counseling ethnic minority families." *Family Relations* 37:310-314.

Martinez, Estella A. 1988. "Child behavior in Mexican American/ Chicano families: Maternal teaching and childrearing practices." *Family Relations* 37:275-280.

McLoyd, Vonnie C. 1990. "The impact of economic hardship on black families and children: Psychological distress, parenting, and socio-emotional development." *Child Development* 61:311-346.

Okagaki, Lynn and Diana Johnson-Divecha. 1993. "Development of parental beliefs." Pp. 35-67 in Tom Luster and Lynn Okagaki (eds.), *Parenting: An Ecological Perspective*. Hillsdale, New Jersey: Lawrence Erlbaum Associates.

Peterman, Phyllis J. 1981. "Parenting and environmental consid-erations." *American Journal of Orthopsychiatry* 51 (2):351-355.

Staples, Robert and Alfredo Mirande. 1980. "Racial and cultural variations among American families: A decennial review of the literature on minority families." *Journal of Marriage and the Family* 42 (4):887-903.

Vega, William A., Richard L. Hough, and Annelisa Romero. 1983. "Family life patterns of Mexican Americans." Pp. 194-251 in G. J. Powell (ed.), *The Psychosocial Development of Minority Group Children*. New York: Brunner/Mazel.

Wagner, Nathaniel N. and Marsha J. Haug. 1971. *Chicanos: Social and Psychological Perspectives*. St. Louis: The C. V. Mosby Company.

African American Households and Community Effects on Economic Deprivation[1]

Monica D. Griffin

INTRODUCTION: ECONOMIC DEPRIVATION

General Hypothesis

According to E.E. LeMasters (1970), "poverty in single-parent families merely proves that our economic, political, and social welfare systems are not properly organized to provide adequate standards of living" (in Staples, 1986:167). This study on poverty contributes to a sociological understanding of an "adequate standard of living" according to an economic dimension of poverty experienced by single-parent families. I will argue that levels of economic deprivation vary by household structure, in addition to community characteristics. I will also assert that the statistical interaction between measurements of household structure and community characteristics is a significant one which may provide explanations beyond the focus on deviation from mainstream family structure as a cause of poverty. In short, I hope to demonstrate that the role household structure plays in affecting economic deprivation is contingent on elements of community.

Wilson (1991) argues that "poor individuals with similar educational and occupational skills confront different risks of persistent poverty depending on the neighborhood they reside in, as embodied in the *formal and informal networks to which they have access*, their prospects of marriage or remarriage to a stably employed mate, and *the families or households to which they belong*" (10; italics added). According to Wilson's model, areas with a higher concentration of poverty are "plagued by massive joblessness, flagrant and open lawlessness, and low-achieving schools" (Wilson, 1987:58). He uses the term "concentration effects" to describe those elements which differentiate the residential experiences of lower-income families from higher-income families.

Morrill and Wohlenberg (1971) argue that the spatial segregation of the poor and the ghettoization of minorities help maintain poverty by isolating them from jobs (Morrill and Wohlenberg, 1971:85). However, these authors ultimately present a culture of poverty explanation for the perpetuation of deprivation which fails to account for structural constraints and influences. An alternative explanation offered by Wilson (1987) is the social isolation of inner city minorities. Social isolation is the "lack of contact or sustained interaction with individuals and institutions that represent mainstream society" (p. 60).

McLanahan and Garfinkel (1989) also discuss the social isolation of members of impoverished communities in terms of concentration effects. They argue:

> . . . *social isolation may occur because the community no longer functions as a resource base for its members, as when a neighborhood has no jobs, no networks for helping to locate jobs, poor schools, and a youth culture that is subject to minimal social control* (McLanahan and Garfinkel, 1989:99).

This paper considers all these aspects of poverty—lack of sustained contact with mainstream society, isolation from jobs, as well as a youth culture and inadequate socializing institutions—in its use of the concept of deprivation. Deprivation refers to all of the above dimensions which in some way affect individuals who experience persistent poverty. My thesis maintains that individuals exist in changing contexts of household and community structures. Economic deprivation refers to the ever-changing strains on monetary resources which individuals encounter at both levels.

Valentine (1968) asserts that poverty subcultural behavior patterns reflect "creative adaptation to conditions of deprivation" (Valentine, 1968:143). The "creative adaptations" individuals use to cope within given contexts or communities of deprivation are the key interest of this paper. Hogan and Kitagawa's (1985) qualitative index of neighborhood characteristics commonly used in ethnographic literature includes:

proportion of families below poverty, sex ratios, number of children, and incidence of juvenile crime (Hogan and Kitagawa, 1985:837). As the example of juvenile crime suggests, the concept of deprivation might be measured both economically and socio-culturally; however, for this project I will focus primarily on economic consequences of household and community structure. Specific hypotheses regarding the effects of household and community variables on economic deprivation follow.

Specific Hypotheses

A common thesis asserts that family structure affects one's income, and therefore one's likelihood of surviving the snares of poverty. The obvious argument is that families with higher numbers of income earners present in the household are more likely to fall into higher categories of economic well-being. However, individuals and families do not exist apart from one another in unchanging structures of interaction. Some members die or get divorced, while some are born. Some are related by blood, some by marriage, friendships, or adoption, and some by relationships understood only between the members themselves. As members progress through the life course, the structure of the household itself sometimes changes. Members are employed, lose jobs, gain other sources of income. The family has access to changing resources, and likewise, the penalty of alternating strains. The household is not a static entity to be observed as a structure preserved against the inevitably changing circumstances in human lives. Differences in household composition and organization will result in varying levels of economic deprivation.

Another part of the dynamic occurs in larger communities of interaction such as neighborhoods, the workforce, and districts of residence. Resources for mobility (or sustenance) tend to vary across geographical regions, as well as community distinctions such as neighborhood type (urban, suburban, etc.). The demographic composition of any of these communities is likely to accommodate or deny an individual's changing needs in maintaining a life of well-being.

Several other variables emerge in the literature as general factors influencing poverty. In addition to household and community effects, these variables are especially relevant to the present study: race, gender, education, and employment. I will address these variables before continuing with specific hypotheses about household and community variables.

Race. Race is a significant characteristic in most discussions of poverty. Race is controlled by focusing exclusively on African American households. While whites make up 69 percent of the poor, a disproportionate amount are represented by nonwhites. *Twenty-eight percent of the poor are black, yet blacks only make up 11.9 percent of the entire population* (Ropers, 1991:48). Also, Hogan and Kitagawa (1985) note that an emerging concern in stratification studies is the increasing "internal stratification of the black population and the development of a black underclass that will be excluded from socio-economic advancement" (Hogan and Kitagawa, 1985:826). It is likely that there is considerable variation in poverty even across different types of African American households.

Sex. Gender plays an important role in elaborating the circumstances of the poor. Pearce (1984) elaborates the female causes of poverty according to the tendency for women to bear the economic and emotional burdens of raising children alone, and by virtue of the fact that women are "handicapped" by their gender in the labor force, in terms of the earnings they receive compared to men (in Ropers, 1991: 46). Duncan and colleagues (1984) found that less than 2 percent of the population remained poor for more than eight to ten years (Duncan, 1984:4). Garfinkel and McLanahan (1986) argue that among female-headed families poverty lasts much longer (twelve years on average) and is more severe (Garfinkel and McLanahan, 1986:15). Female-headed families are not only likely to be in poverty, but also they are likely to be persistently poor.

Education. Wilber's (1975) analysis of poverty alludes to Blau and Duncan's (1968) findings that intergenerational mobility occurs based primarily on achievement rather than ascriptive characteristics (Wilber, 1975:7-8). Education was found to be the most important determinant of occupational success (Blau and Duncan, 1968:201). Although the availability of educational and training resources to individuals or within the community is not easily measured (or included within the dataset used in this study), the individual's level of educational attainment is likely to have a strong, independent influence on levels of social and economic deprivation.

Employment. Another resource, which is most obviously an economic resource within the household, remains for discussion—employment.

Staples (1986) argues that economic trends in industrialization and changes in workforce composition are basic causes of black male unemployment and have further isolated blacks physically and socially from mainstream society (Staples, 1986:5-6). While macro-structural data for employment composition are unavailable for this study, a household's investment in legitimate employment activities arguably influences measures of deprivation. Stable and regular employment not only implies gainful investment in the workforce for the household, but also it suggests a cultural norm of legitimate self-reliance in the community as well.

Marital status. Wilson argues that sex and marital status are the most important determinants of poverty in urban areas (Wilson, 1987: 71). Without delving into the psychological and moral ramifications for children who do not grow up in two-parent families, the social and economic implication is that two providers (of income *or* child care) are better than one. Although the data in this study do not allow for the measurement of sex ratios within populations, marital status is available.

Wilson (1987) supports Hogan and Kitagawa's (1985) hypothesis that while many whites are delaying marriage and parenthood because of educational or career aspirations, blacks are doing so because of the poor "marriage market" which black women face (Wilson, 1987:74). Similarly, Staples' (1985) explanation for low marriage rates among black women is black male joblessness, with incarceration and high rates of homicide as additional contributing factors to the low marriageable pool of men (Staples, 1986:22).

Yet, the focus on the mismatch of black males to females as potential marriage partners denies further insight to the real question of subsistence and survival from poverty, particularly for those who disproportionately experience poverty—female-headed families. The issue of whether or not individuals should or can marry, and furthermore its influence on poverty, is one which is debated endlessly. The conspicuous impact of low marriage rates among blacks appears to be in the growing prevalence of black single *mothers*, which then involves the influence of fertility and patterns of teenage pregnancy on deprivation.

Fertility. Hogan and Kitagawa (1985) determined that teenage girls in "high risk social environments (lower class, poor inner city neighborhood residence, female-headed family, [etc.]) are more likely to become pregnant by age eighteen than are teenage girls from low-risk backgrounds" (Hogan and Kitagawa, 1985:852). The authors note, however, that the influence of social environment (measured as neighborhood quality) is indirect and mediated through the extent of parental supervision in the household (Hogan and Kitagawa, 1985:846, 851). Garfinkel and McLanahan (1986) also note that never-married mothers represent a greater proportion of single-parent families for blacks than they do for whites (Garfinkel and McLanahan, 1986:83).

Ellwood (1988) points out that while teen births have increased only slightly and appear relatively stable for blacks, black men and women are simply less compelled to get married (Ellwood, 1988:72). Also, the increased proportion of teenage pregnancy among blacks is related to the decrease in marital fertility among blacks (Hogan and Kitagawa, 1985:828). Wilson (1987) explains the greater proportion of out-of-wedlock births for blacks in particular, not as a result of a substantial increase in extramarital births, but due to the "percentage of women married and the rate of marital fertility [which] have both significantly declined" (Wilson, 1987:67). Yet, the issue of the black female-headed household as a structure vulnerable to deprivation remains. A further examination of household structure dynamics provides insight to this living arrangement.

Living Arrangements and Extended Kin

According to Wilson (1987), the general decline in marriage and marital fertility explains the propensity of black women to form their own households. Two of the main reasons that Mayfield (1986) offers for low-income, adolescent black mothers being less likely to marry early are that (1) the presence of single-headed households is likely and familiar to them, thus reducing the urgency for marriage as a step toward adulthood, and (2) they receive greater family support through uses of extended kin for child care, and through residence with their parents (Mayfield, 1986:216). Hogan and colleagues (1990) make similar claims:

> *[H]igh rates of single parenthood among blacks are less prob-
> lematic than among whites because intergenerational ties in
> black families are strong, and because kin and friend networks
> are ready sources of social and economic support, particularly
> for ethnic minorities* (Hogan et al., 1990:798).

Hogan and colleagues did find that black mothers are more likely to be
involved in support networks than whites, because black mothers more
often live with an adult relative or more often get free child care
assistance from kin; whereas, white families are more likely to provide
and receive financial assistance (Hogan et al., 1990:805; Madigan and
Hogan, 1991:615). Hill and Shackleford (1975) elaborate various types
of African American families, pointing to the predominant use of extended family members as resources for child care and supervision (in
Staples, 1986:195).

In addition to being potential resources for child care, extended kin
are financial strains on the household, especially if they are not employed. Depending on the stability of relations in the household, the
regularity and effectiveness of child care and supervision are question-
able. Therefore, household structure must be examined with regard to
marital status, fertility, and the dynamics of living arrangements for
implicit variations in child care and supervision. These variations are
likely to affect economic deprivation. Hypotheses regarding community
variables' influence on deprivation follow.

Child care resources. The effect of child care resources on deprivation deserves further comment. While child care can be specific to
the individual household as yet another strain on resources, the variable
may also be considered a community-level resource in the case of child
care from a neighbor or relative residing in close proximity. Peters and
deFord (1974) explain that child care arrangements for the poor are not
usually with daycare facilities or community services; the members of
the household—the mothers, grandmothers, relatives, or even other
neighbors—are child care providers (in Staples, 1986:169). Jackson
(1971) asserts that "grandparents [in urban communities] take on the
responsibilities of and function as independent departments of welfare"
(in Staples, 1986:194; see also Hogan, Hao, and Parish, 1990:806).
Hill and Shackleford (1975) agree that most of the financial support for
"informally adopted children" (children who reside in households headed by relatives) comes from those adopting relatives. In 1975, 45

percent of black children resided in such homes (in Staples, 1986:195). Levels of contact with networks of child care, *whether it is within the household (as extended kin, for example) or from the community*, are likely determinants of levels of both economic and social well-being.

Race composition. The singular effect of race on the likelihood of experiencing deprivation is evidenced by the disproportionate representation of blacks and other minorities in poverty. Recent advances toward social and economic equality in American history are overshadowed by the consequences of racial residential segregation which remain pervasive (Farley and Allen, 1987:136-145). The percentage of a community that is black is a likely indicator of both social and economic deprivation.

Age. The black population is essentially young. Blackwell (1991) reports the median age for blacks as 27.3 years, compared to 33.1 for whites. More than one-third of the black population is under the age of 18. 8.9 percent were 65 and older in 1980 and that dropped to 8.4 percent in 1988. For whites, 11.7 percent were 65 and older, while in 1988 that figure *increased* to 12.8 percent (Blackwell, 1991:30). These figures are congruent with the growing proportion of teenage mothers in the black population. I expect that in communities with high percentages of a younger population, members are more likely to experience poverty.

Population change. Particularly relevant to this study, population change in a community might indicate a change in the structural resources of the community as suggested by Wilson (1991). He argues that the economic marginality of the ghetto poor develops primarily as a result of the outmigration of higher-income residents. Willie (1988) effectively challenges Wilson's claim that outmigration exacerbated the underclass condition by noting an overall decrease in poverty for blacks and all families, which further suggests a macro-level explanation based on general economic conditions (Willie, 1988:40-1). In this study, population change measures the possibility of lower job opportunities or fewer support networks for the remaining residents in the area.

Geographical region. Obviously, the standard of living and the means for living vary across geographical boundaries of the United States. In the '40s and then in the '70s, black outmigration from the southern states was highest. Reasons for migration to the northern and western areas include escaping the residue of a quasi-caste system (Jim Crow laws and custom), the mechanization of agriculture, and the promise of a "better life" in the North and West (Blackwell, 1991:28). We would expect that the greater likelihood of discrimination in the South or lower job opportunities due to changes in agricultural economy would translate to greater likelihood of poverty for blacks, and therefore outmigration. But over time, even up to the late 1980s, the South has accounted for about 53 percent of the black population (Blackwell, 1991:27). By isolating the southern geographical region of the United States, this study measures the cultural as well as employment influences of region on economic life for blacks.

Urbanicity. "Urban life is a highly complex one that requires adjustments, adaptations, resilience, and both formal and informal support structures," (Blackwell, 1991:153-4). While this study is not constrained to inner city analysis, it accepts the conditions of the inner city as valid and influential predictors of deprivation. Blackwell (1991) describes conditions which are prevalent in urban areas: restricted access to a legitimate opportunity structure; divergent family structures (deviant male-female relationships); shift of maintenance and survival functions from the family to other institutions, such as the church or welfare agencies; breakdown of patriarchal family structure (alternative systems of authority); and social isolation (lack of organization for child care and supervision of teens, for example) (Blackwell, 1991:152-3). In urban areas, where life requires more "adjustment" and "resil-ience" than other areas, the relationship between deprivation and house-hold structure and organization is likely to be pronounced in the family type most vulnerable to change.

RESEARCH DESIGN

Data

Data for this study are taken from the National Survey of Families and Households (NSFH), funded by the Center for Population Research of the National Institute of Child Health and Human Development, and conducted in 1987. The NSFH includes a main sample of 9,643 respondents who represent the non-institutional United States population age 19 and older. For this study, black respondents were selected out of the original sample (for reasons previously detailed), yielding a study sample of 2,391 black respondents.

Dependent variable. As mentioned earlier, the concept of economic deprivation combines the dimensions of social isolation, joblessness, and cultural as well as structural constraints addressed earlier by scholars of poverty. Those dimensions cite isolation from mainstream resources (such as networks, contacts, etc.) and institutions, the mismatch of job opportunities with the skills and residential location of those who experience poverty, and the cultural norms which accompany poverty such as delinquency and crime. The economic measure of deprivation, as it is used in this study, refers to a household's total income, including income of the respondent and spouse from interest, dividends, and other investments, earned in the last year. For cohabiting partners, income from both partners are included in the total; and for single households, as for all other types, additional sources of income such as child support and welfare are included. Income values for this variable ranged from no income to extreme six-digit figures which were difficult to determine as authentic. Since the regression equation is a statistical model based on the deviation of values from the mean, it was necessary to eliminate extraneous, and possibly false (keypunch error), values which skew results. In the final analysis, values in the upper fifth percentile are recoded to equal the minimum of that range, $70,500. The mean income for the study sample, then, is $19,108 per year, with a median income of $14,100 per year. See Table 1 for a summary of mean incomes for all household types.

Control variables. Control variables for this study include gender, education, and workforce participation. Education, as provided by the NSFH, ranges from zero to twenty years of education completed. The mean and median level of education completed for the sample is approximately twelve years. As argued earlier, an individual's investment in the workforce is likely to influence his or her economic well-being. The NSFH variable which measures the number of weeks the respondent has worked in the previous year (1986) is used; however, since the mapping scheme of the questionnaire did not ask this question of unemployed respondents, "inapplicable" responses were coded as zero weeks worked, assumed to be representative of those unemployed respondents. The number of weeks worked in the last year therefore ranges from zero to fifty-two weeks worked in the past year (sample mean=31 weeks; median=51 weeks).

Table 1

Mean Income According to Household Type

| Household Type | Parents | | Non-parents | |
	Mean	N	Mean	N
Married	$31,406	392	$27,871	191
Cohabiting	20,324	49	27,160	30
Single	10,882	419	13,171	564
Total Mean:	$19,108		N = 1645	

Source: National Survey of Families and Households.

Independent variables. Household structure is measured on two levels: marital status and number of children. From the NSFH, a variable (MARCOHAB) measures a respondent's living arrangements basically according to married, cohabiting, and single categories. Another variable from the NSFH asks the number of children in the household. This study combines the two to create six dummy variables representing the following categories: married without children (12.3 percent), cohabiting without children (2 percent), single without children (39.1 percent), married parents (20.5 percent), cohabiting parents (3.1 percent), and single parents (23 percent). All dichotomous variables were constructed for compatibility with regression statistical procedures, a score of one on each representing association with that category of household structure and a zero referring to non-association with the category. Therefore, three of the six dummy variables (those representing parental households) appear in the statistical equation and analysis. Respondents without children are theoretically irrelevant to its analysis and are therefore excluded. Fifty-three percent of the sample have no children; 17.3 percent have one child; 15.7 percent have two; and 13.5 percent have at least three. Also, the number of children in the household taps into the social and economic strain experienced by larger households of children. The sample mean is one child per household and a median of no children per household.

The extended kin variable in this study ranges from zero to four extended members in the household, including grandparents, brothers or sisters, step- or half-brothers or sisters, grandchildren, or other relatives. Roommates, friends, or other non-relatives are not counted in the number of extended kin residing in the household. This sample yields a mean of one and a median of no extended kin in the household.

Although the theoretical model posed by this study assumes that extended kin members of the household are likely resources for child care, the NSFH does provide a measure of actual sources of child care. To summarize the survey question, parents of children under age 4 are asked how the child(ren) were cared for in the past week, with a list of sources as possible responses. For parents of children, ages 5 to 11, the question asks who is with the child(ren) before (and assumably after) school when the respondent leaves for work, with a list of sources as possible responses. Five dummy variables are constructed as dichotomous representations of those possible responses for both age groups and the variable categories are: relative (or not) as a resource, spouse (or not) as a resource, neighbor (or not) as a resource, organized center (or not) as a resource of child care for the household, or in the fifth possible case, the child stays home alone. Categories representing "other" resources are not very useful for analysis and were therefore omitted.

Community variables in this study measure demographic composition as well as geographical region. They include a) the percent of the county population that is black, b) the percent of the county population that is over age 65, and c) the percent of the county population that is urban. The range for each of these variables is possibly from 0 to 100 percent. Also included is d) the percent change in county population between 1970 and 1980. Since this measures in- and out-migration, percentages range from negative values to positive. Lastly, a dichotomous variable is used to measure e) the geographical location of the respondent according to residence in the U.S. South, coded as one. Otherwise Northeast, North Central, and West are all coded as zero.

For the community-level variables, 75 percent of the respondents reside in areas with less than 38 percent composition of blacks in the county, while less than 10 percent live in areas with more than 50 percent composition of blacks. Most of the respondents (70 percent) live in areas with less than 12 percent composition of persons 65 years and older. Thirty-two percent of the respondents live in an area that has experienced a decrease in county population between 1970 and 1980, and 4 percent of the respondents live in areas where the county population has increased by 50 percent. Similar to Blackwell's (1991) figure for blacks in the South, 54 percent of the respondents reside in southern counties. Yet, 70 percent of the respondents reside in areas that are described as at least 75 percent urban in 1980.

Interaction effects. As stated earlier, this study examines the independent effects of both household and community variables on deprivation. I expect to find statistically significant interactions between household variables and community-level variables which improve the explanatory capabilities of the linear regression model in predicting poverty. Several combinations for interaction effects are possible. Since child care can be measured at both levels of analysis, according to the presence of extended kin (as potential child care providers) or child care resources within various community contexts, the model will examine child care as a community resource which interacts with household structure to influence deprivation.

Therefore, the analysis focuses on interactions between household structure and both community and child care variables. The idea is simple: which combinations of parental household structure and community variables (including child care resources) have substantially positive or negative effects on social and/or economic deprivation? To statistically model this question, it is necessary to create interaction terms for each living arrangement dummy variable with each child care dummy variable and each community variable.

RESULTS AND DISCUSSION

Household structure, child care resources, and community variables explain 56 percent of the variance on income in this model (significant at the .05 level; see Table 2 for a summary of both independent and interaction effects). When interaction effects are added the equation explains 58 percent of the variance in income (R^2 is significant at the .05 level). R^2 increases by only 2 percent, yet this small change achieves statistical significance at the .05 level. A discussion of the results for income follows.

Table 2

Regression of Income on Family, Community,
and Interaction Effects

INDEPENDENT VARIABLES	b*(beta)		b*(beta)	
Family Structure:				
Single parents	-17554.84*	(-.53)	-38344.06*	(-1.15)
Cohabiting	-9588.19*	(-.13)	-31665.28*	(-.44)
Married	------Reference Category-----			
# of extended kin	-48.67	(-.00)	52.80	(.00)
# of children	107.10	(.01)	187.73	(.01)
Community Composition & Geography:				
% change in county population	-15.33	(.02)	-92.69*	(-.14)
% over age 65 in county population	-491.45*	(-.09)	-1139.75*	(-.21)
% urban in county population	18.47	(.03)	-9.68	(-.02)
% black in county population	12.56	(.01)	-29.22	(-.03)
Resides in the South	-4086.66*	(-.12)	-5695.10*	(-.17)
Child Care:				
Child is alone	-6731.01	(-.03)	-21178.88	(-.11)
Spouse daycare	564.47	(.01)	2755.92	(.03)
Organized center	1414.90	(.02)	9156.37*	(.10)
Neighbor daycare	-2633.24	(-.04)	-3067.36	(-.04)
Relative daycare	-1682.86	(-.03)	1257.85	(.03)
CONTROL VARIABLES				
Sex	1009.06	(.03)	451.34	(.01)
Education	1676.23*	(.23)	1645.90*	(.23)
# of weeks worked	228.03*	(.31)	228.02*	(.31)
INDEPENDENT VARIABLES				
Interaction Effects for Cohabiting Parents:				
Cohabiting parents * % Change			48.58	(.01)
Cohabiting parents * % Elderly			1117.38	(.19)
Cohabiting parents * % Black			-20.25	(-.01)
Cohabiting parents * % Urban			111.14	(.13)
Cohabiting parents * Residence in South			1440.10	(.01)

Table 2 (continued)

	b*(beta)		b*(beta)	
INDEPENDENT VARIABLES				
Cohabiting Parents * Child stays alone	--missing/constant--			
Cohabiting Parents * Spouse as daycare			-6339.00	(-.02)
Cohabiting Parents * Organized center			-3062.41	(-.01)
Cohabiting Parents * Neighbor daycare			880.75	(.00)
Cohabiting Parents * Relative daycare			-4228.29	(-.02)
Interaction Effects for Single Parents:				
Single Parents * % Change			129.39*	(.14)
Single Parents * % Elderly			1138.54*	(.41)
Single Parents * % Urban			50.98	(.13)
Single Parents * % Black			76.13	(.08)
Single Parents * Residence in South			3382.36	(.09)
Single Parents * Child stays alone			17051.84	(.08)
Single Parents * Spouse as daycare	-2059.22	(-.01)		
Single Parents * Organized center	-9341.98*	(-.09)		
Single Parents * Neighbor daycare	287.50	(.00)		
Single Parents * Relative daycare	-3578.20	(-.06)		
Summary of Equations:				
(Constant)	6410.325862		18666.26*	
	$R^2 = .56*$		$R^2 = .58*$	
	N = 835		N = 816	
	R^2 - change = .21*		R^2 - change = .02*	

*Regression coefficients, R^2's, and R^2 -change are statistically significant at the .05 level.

Source: National Survey of Families and Households.

Again, this analysis focuses on parental families only, and married parent households represent the reference category. Excluding control variables, other household categories, and the interaction terms, all independent variables (such as community characteristics and child care resources) are the effects for married parent households on income. The interaction terms are the estimated *differences* from the married household effect for the particular family type used to construct the term.

Control variables estimate the effects on income for all respondents. In the final regression equation, each week increase of the number of weeks worked increases income by $228 on average per year. Each year increase in the level of education increases income by $1,646 on average per year. Being female, for African Americans, increases income by approximately $451 on average per year; however this increase does not achieve statistical significance ($p < .05$) in the final equation.

Married Parents

For married African American parents, the average income in the last year is $31,405. Community and daycare factors which achieve statistical significance are percent change in county population, the percent of county population over 65 years of age, residence in the South (as opposed to the Northeast, North Central, or Western parts of the United States), and the use of an organized center as a daycare resource. For married parents, each percent increase in population change results in about $93 less income on average, a slight effect per year. Each percentage increase in the elderly population results in a $1,140 decrease in income on average for married African American parents. Residence in the South is associated with $5,695 less income on average.

Cohabiting Parents

For cohabiting African American parents, income is $31,665 *less* on average than married parents. However, no interaction factors (community and daycare effects for cohabiting parents) achieve statistical significance. The effect from cohabiting households poses an interesting dilemma for interpretation. The interactive dynamics of such households are difficult to measure and its effect on income near impossible to predict. Cohabiting households possibly consist of transient partners whose income is rather unreliable. This probably includes cohabiting singles (such as students or roommates), single parents with cohabiting girlfriends or boyfriends, and divorced partners who do not opt for remarriage. These are just a few of the possibilities which suggest that the cohabiting household's influence on income will vary greatly according to the range of social dynamics which might characterize this household structure.

Single Parents

For African American single parents, the effects are pronounced. Single parenthood stands out as the strongest (statistically significant) predictor of income. For African American single parents, income is $38,344 *less* on average than married parents. Community and daycare factors which achieve statistical significance for single parents are percent change in a population, percent elderly, and the use of an organized center as a daycare resource (see Table 2).

The main effect on income for married parent households was a decrease of $93 on average per year (b=-93, Table 2). The interaction effect for single parents (b=129, Table 2) represents the difference from the main effect for married parent households; therefore, each percentage increase in change in the county population results in a small $36 increase in income on average for African American single parents. This is a seemingly minute difference between household types, but the substantive dynamics are apparent. While a community's change for married household structures is associated with a decrease in income, for single parent households this community variable translates into a slightly increasing effect on income.

The main effect of the percent elderly county population for married parents is $1,140 less on average per year. The interaction effect of percent elderly with single parent households (b=1,138, Table 2) represents the difference from the main effect on married households; therefore, each percentage increase in the county's elderly population results in a mere $2 decrease in income on average for single parents. The difference of community effects for single parent households and married parent households is striking here. The effect of a percent increase in elderly population for married parents results in a much larger decrease in income than for single parents. The implication here is that married parents residing in neighborhoods with a large elderly population are likely to live in *poor* neighborhoods, thereby explaining their lower income. For single parents however, the implication is that an increase in the elderly population of a neighborhood is also a likely increase in resources for child care, minimizing decreasing income effects.

For married parents, the main effect of using an organized daycare center as child care is an $8,156 increase on average per year. The interaction effect of this variable for single parents (b=-9,342, Table 2) is the difference from the main effect for married parent households; therefore, for single parents, the use of an organized daycare center as child care results in $1,186 less per year on average. This finding clearly illustrates that child care effects on income are mediated differently for varied household structures. The use of organized daycare, the most expensive child care resource measured, is in all likelihood associated with patrons earning higher-level incomes, so the variables might plausibly explain each other. However, for *single* parents, the costly use of organized daycare is a likely *strain* on income, and therefore it is associated with a decrease in income in this model. (See Table 2 below for a summary of statistics on income.)

In sum, community distinctions, such as percent change in a county population and percent elderly, do affect the relationship of family structure on income. More interestingly, these effects differ for married and single parents. While the percent change in county population has the effect of decreasing income for married parents, it increases income (slightly) for single parents. Each percent increase in the elderly population means less income on average for both married and single parents, but the decrease is greater for married parents. The use of organized daycare indicates an increase in income for married parents, whereas for single parents use of this resource involves a decrease in income. Community and child care distinctions did not achieve statistical significance for cohabiting parent households, possibly for reasons discussed above. Additionally, the small sample of cohabiting parents (N=73) is unlikely to yield significant results.

However, as posed by the theoretical model of this paper, the dynamics for survival and adaptation differ for various family structures, as evidenced by distinctions in the effects of community composition, geography, and the use of various child care resources, particularly between married and single parents. The interaction terms add 2 percentage points of explanatory power to the equation, for an R^2 total of 58 percent.

CONCLUSIONS

It is asserted that levels of economic deprivation vary across household structures. For economic deprivation, statistical analysis has yielded married, cohabiting and single parent living arrangements as important independent indicators. Also, it is asserted that deprivation varies across communities. Statistical analysis yields percent change in the county population, percent elderly, and the use of an organized day-care center as significant indicators for all three household types. Southern residence matters only for married parents, exacerbating their economic position. Finally, it is asserted that the statistical interactions between household structure and community characteristics, and household structure and child care resources, may provide explanations beyond deviation from mainstream family structure as a cause of poverty. Several combinations maintain significance and have been discussed at length above. They do suggest that certain combinations fare better than others. That is, household structure, community characteristics, and child care resources independently influence deprivation; but as posed in the theoretical model, for certain households, the combinations of those characteristics have differing effects.

These differing effects should inform sociological research about the network dynamics between households and communities, as well as the social articulation between households and child care resources in the upbringing of America's children. For example, social policy which seeks effective alleviation of impoverished conditions for single families should consider the positive effects of an elderly population on income for these families. I would propose that the mutual exchange of social interaction (child care for parents, stimulating company for the elderly) is one worth economic support and compensation. These findings suggest that adopted grandparent programs should be further encouraged. This is by no means an argument which places the responsibility of raising children solely on the shoulders of grandparents with limited access to amenable resources. I forward these findings as an indication that community programs should expand beyond the protection of property. Perhaps Neighborhood Watch programs should extend to the responsible care of America's children.

NOTE

[1] Paper presented at the 1993 Annual Conference for the Center for Studies of the Family at Brigham Young University, Provo, UT 84602.

REFERENCES

Blackwell, James E. 1991. *The Black Community: Diversity and Unity.* Third Edition. New York: Harper Collins.

Blau, Peter M. and Otis D. Duncan. 1968. *The American Occupational Structure.* New York: John Wiley and Sons, Inc.

Duncan, Greg J. 1984. *Years of Poverty, Years of Plenty.* Ann Arbor: University of Michigan, Survey Research Center.

Ellwood, David T. 1988. *Poor Support: Poverty in the American Family.* New York: Basic Books.

Farley, Reynolds and Walter R. Allen. 1987. *The Color Line and the Quality of Life in America.* New York: Russell Sage Foundation.

Garfinkel, Irwin and Sara McLanahan. 1986. *Single Mothers and their Children.* Washington, DC: The Urban Institute Press.

Hill, Robert P. and Lawrence Shackleford. 1975. "The Black extended family revisited." *The Urban League Review* 1 (75):18-24.

Hogan, Dennis P., Ling-Xin Hao, and William L. Parish. 1990. "Race, kin networks, and assistance to mother-headed families." *Social Forces* 68(3):797-812.

_____ and Evelyn Kitagawa. 1985. "The impact of social status, family structure, and neighborhood on the fertility of black adolescents." *American Journal of Sociology* 90(4):825-854.

Jackson, Jacquelyne. 1971. "Black grandparents: Who needs them?" In Robert Staples (ed.), *The Black Family: Essays and Studies*. Third Edition. California: Wadsworth Publishing Company.

LeMasters, E.E. 1970. "Parents without partners." In Robert Staples (ed.), *The Black Family: Essays and Studies*. Third Edition. California: Wadsworth Publishing Company.

Madigan, Timothy J. and Dennis P. Hogan. 1991. "Kin access and residential mobility among young mothers." *Social Science Quarterly* 7(3):615-616.

Mayfield, Lorraine. 1986. "Early parenthood among low-income adolescent girls." In Robert Staples (ed.), *The Black Family: Essays and Studies*. Third Edition. California: Wadsworth Publishing Company.

McLanahan, Sara and Irwin Garfinkel. 1989. "Single mothers, the underclass, and social policy." *The Annals of the American Academy of Political and Social Science* 501:93-104.

Morrill, Richard L. and Ernest H. Wohlenberg. 1971. *The Geography of Poverty in the United States*. New York: McGraw-Hill Book Company.

Pearce, Diana. 1984. "Farewell to alms: Women's fare under welfare." Pp. 121-130 in Terry Reuther (ed.), *Sociology: Empowerment in a Troubled Age*. Boston: Copley Publishing Group.

Peters, Marie and Cecile deFord. 1974. "The solo mother." In Robert Staples (ed.), *The Black Family: Essays and Studies*. Third Edition. California: Wadsworth Publishing Company.

Ropers, Richard. 1991. *Persistent Poverty: The American Dream Turned Nightmare*. New York and London: Plenum Press.

Staples, Robert. 1985. "Changes in Black family structure: The conflict between family ideology and structural conditions." In Robert Staples (ed.), *The Black Family: Essays and Studies*. Third Edition. California: Wadsworth Publishing Company.

_____. 1986. *The Black Family: Essays and Studies*. Third Edition. California: Wadsworth Publishing Company.

Valentine, Charles A. 1968. *Culture and Poverty*. Chicago: University of Chicago Press.

Wilber, George L. 1975. *Poverty: A New Perspective*. Kentucky: The University Press of Kentucky.

Willie, Charles V. 1988. *A New Look at Black Families*. Third Edition. New York: General Hall, Inc.

Wilson, William J. 1991. "Studying inner-city dislocation: The challenge of public agenda research." 1990 ASA Presidential Address. *American Sociological Review* 56 (February):1-14.

_____. 1987. *The Truly Disadvantaged*. Chicago: University of Chicago Press.

Interracial Dating,

Mate Selection,

and

Marriage

The Impact of Racial Climate on Selected Social Behaviors: Who's Dating and Who's Not

Larry E. Williams, Kenneth L. Clinton, Jr., and Lisa Wyatt

A recent article on declining segregation among college students in the 1990s trumpeted the reality of ethnic diversity achieved at some of the larger universities in the United States (Duster, 1991). Many others refer to the subtle and not so subtle manifestations of racism that still persist (Leo, 1990; Mabry, 1991; Skelly, 1990; Tuch, 1991). The image that emerges is both confusing and confounding. Perhaps additional clarity might be generated if researchers shift their attention to include non-academic dimensions of college life. That is, behaviors that might well be considered as purely social in nature (i.e. dating) might also be a reflection of racial attitudes and, thus, provide insight into the true level of social and ethnic interaction. In this project we examined a small, liberal arts university because it provided the ideal setting for interaction between various racial and ethnic groups in a somewhat controlled setting.

Certainly the manifest functions of any university include the formal acquisition of knowledge in a variety of subject areas. But it would be naive to conclude that the responsibilities of the various institutions end with class lectures and final examinations. The millions of dollars spent on athletics, fraternity and sorority houses, or other extracurricular activities attest to the importance attributed to the social development of university students. While the average university budget might well include funds for library expansion, the lure of Saturday nights spent on the favorite "drag" cannot be dismissed as an even more powerful magnet drawing the average undergraduate to the campus in the first place. As any alumni director or office of student services can attest, the campus without a social life is a campus without students. While the university is concerned with presenting a favorable academic image of itself to current as well as prospective students, it remains a constant challenge to provide enough interesting activities to fill their free time. It is not enough to recruit students; their social and cultural maturing process must necessarily complement the academic curriculum if a total education is to be achieved. It is also a social fact that these activities are usually more enjoyable if we have someone to share them with. The question is: "Is there someone for everyone?"

BACKGROUND

The university setting for this analysis is a relatively small, liberal arts institution of approximately 6,000 students in the Southwestern United States. Because of its regional isolation, the administration has committed its recruitment office to vigorously encourage ethnic minority students to attend. It is worth noting that several of the nearby communities actually boast of their lack of minority population. Although the university is located in a community that did not desegregate its public schools until almost 1970, the campus has publicly voiced its support of policies welcoming all students who choose to attend.

By the fall of 1991 the total minority enrollment within the university was just over 8 percent, or approximately 475 students. The vast majority of these students were either black (285) or Hispanic (175). There were, during the time of this study, two dormitories located on a rather compact 167-acre tract of land. On this particular campus the student center is the traditional meeting place for students before and between classes during the peak hours between 8 a.m. and 1 p.m. each week day. Recently, the center was renovated at a total cost of over 23 million dollars. Much of this cost was borne by students in the form of activity fees levied by the university. Although the process of renovation for the student center was completed in stages lasting nine years, the final price tag was viewed as essential to the continued growth and development of the overall physical plant. It contains various meeting rooms, a snack bar, the school's only cafeteria, ballroom, and theatre. Its central focal point is its atrium. During the morning and early afternoon hours this large, well-appointed room is filled with students.

Classes are, in most cases, relatively small with an average of fewer than 50 students. Because it is primarily a teaching institution (most professors teach a twelve-hour load) the level of interaction between student and teacher is closer than at many large institutions. It follows that a certain camaraderie develops among many of the undergraduates. Whether it is due to sharing more than one class over their college career, living in the same dorm, or simply seeing them on a fairly routine basis, the fact remains that many of the students feel a sense of "community" during the time of their stay.

Besides the liberal arts curriculum, the university has formally recognized over 90 separate clubs, Greek letter fraternities and sororities, and various social/service organizations to meet non-academic needs of its students. It also provides a full range of social, cultural, athletic, and spiritual programs that all students are encouraged to attend. In short, the total educational and social needs have been addressed at least on the surface.

THEORETICAL CONSIDERATIONS

Sociologists are, as other social scientists, constrained to develop some specific theoretical framework to guide their data gathering and eventual analysis. This particular study was framed in a rather conventional conflict perspective. That is, we assumed that a certain degree of inequality in the form of institutional racism would provide the clearest background for an accurate analysis of interracial contact on college campuses in the 1990s. To be sure, a certain degree of racism must be recognized as part of the "baggage" that students and faculty bring with them to the campus each day. It can also be argued that the resulting interplay generates some degree of "victim" mentality among minority students. Unlike many of the victimization studies that have focused on an educational setting, however, we set out to explore the possibility that both majority and minority participants might be victims.

In the initial studies of victimization in the 1960s researchers were intent on establishing a link between an individual's experiences and his/her subsequent fear of crime, fear for his/her personal safety, or fear of future victimization. Populations "at risk" such as women, the elderly, or those living in high crime areas were studied in an attempt to establish the relationship between a victim's status and the level of his/her fear (Balkin, 1979; Toseland, 1982; Shotland et al., 1979; Taylor et al., 1984; Kennedy and Silverman, 1985; Gomme, 1986).

Unfortunately, these efforts were less than successful. Subsequent studies employing demographic variables, psychosocial factors, or crime victimization variables were also less than satisfactory in clarifying the relationship between crime, victimization, and the fear of crime (Toseland, 1982; Baker et al., 1983; Stafford and Galle, 1984).

These same issues were examined by Litt and Turk (1985) in an educational context when it was suggested that the environment that existed in many desegregated schools was one where crime, violence, or the threat of either created a climate of fear that was felt by many students as well as teachers. The concept of "socially defiant" representing nonphysical yet disruptive attitudes on the part of some students came to symbolize one of the harsher realities of desegregation (Algozzine, 1977a; 1977b). This is a crucial shift in that research was expanded to include not only traditional measures of victimization experienced through assault or theft but also the "soft" or more subtle, psychological attacks on an individual's sense of self. It was this tack which we followed in the present study. If social isolation, or the inability to pursue anything beyond academic advancement, is the direct or indirect result of racial prejudice, then it is very conceivable that a victim mentality might emerge among minority students. If, in turn, they react in an isolationist manner or demand additional activities or organizations that cater to them, then majority students might feel that they have been victimized.

METHODOLOGY

This study is unique because it represents a combination of three separate data gathering procedures over a period of almost three years. It is also different because it combines what school officials, campus leaders, professors, and students perceive as their world. We have gathered, through a variety of basic research techniques, both a quantitative and qualitative assessment of everyday living on a college campus that is over 90 percent white but which is in the process of changing. Unlike the larger campuses that have witnessed a large influx of ethnic minorities or those which have had to deal with explosive outbursts of racial hatred, to the casual observer, this campus has experienced relative harmony and accommodation.

Beginning in the late spring of 1989 and continuing through 1991, the Office of Institutional Research provided a master list of all students attending the university on a part-time or full-time basis. Selected sub-sets of minority students were also obtained. At various times random samples of these groups were drawn to provide the necessary data generated through some of the more common research techniques. Telephone, face-to-face, and taped interviews provided the qualitative data while survey questionnaires supplied the more quantitative information. Various members of the administration and key faculty were also included in our data gathering in an effort to provide as complete as possible an account of the total university environment.

STUDENT PERCEPTIONS

Blacks

As previously mentioned, the University Student Center has traditionally served as the focal point for informal socializing among undergraduates. Located in the geographical heart of the campus, it is an easy walk from all points on campus and contains several entrances on all sides. Although it is continually filled with students, race has become the deciding factor in predicting location within the building itself. Generally during the morning hours there are easily over 100 students visiting, waiting for friends, or having something to drink between classes. Virtually all of these students are white. For black students this area is generally considered "off limits." Many blacks who were interviewed said that they felt extremely uncomfortable even passing through what some referred to as "no man's land." Although the overt types of reactions were not present, the expressions of what might best be termed as indifference was clearly felt by the black student who might venture into the area. They argue that they are made to feel as though they are trespassing or intruding upon occupied space. One student's reaction seemed to illustrate most black students' concern about this special area of the university's social hub:

> *I feel uncomfortable in the Student Center, but I think whites and blacks feel uncomfortable because they are separated. One side [of] the atrium is for the whites and the other side [of] the T.V. room is for the blacks and that's just the way it is. When the whites come on the T.V. room side they feel uncomfortable and when the blacks go on their side they feel uncomfortable.*

Another place is the dorms. I've noticed that if the blacks are in the lobby there are hardly any whites and if the whites are in there the blacks stay out of the lobby. I don't think that we should have this type of separation in the school because it makes everyone feel uneasy.

This feeling of social isolation extends into the classroom as well. Although the university claims that it actively recruits minority faculty and administrators, there is only one black administrator (Dean of Students) and one black professor. Both were hired after 1985. This glaring lack of role models has not been lost on the black students interviewed for this study. When asked why they did not participate in school activities and organizations, one responded:

[We] don't feel the enthusiasm to attempt to make a difference at the university because the lack of positive role models in the faculty and administration contributes to the lack of involvement.

Other black students accused the university of failing to implement new programs or actively support the few existing ones designed for blacks. The result for many blacks on campus is to "serve their time and escape." Another respondent echoed this sentiment by saying:

The university does not encourage the act of growth by the black student population. I'm not saying that the university physically holds the students back, but the school does not make an attempt to connect with the [black] students.

Other black students that were interviewed pointed to the low levels of interaction with white students in any area other than the classroom. Even here, the social nature of the contact was de-emphasized as racial differences became the focal point of most discussions. One student summed up this attitude by saying that he was tired of giving the "black experience" to his fellow white classmates and that his "blackness" was constricted by such encounters. Other respondents argued that "*the relationships with white students vanish after class; there is not much interaction between black and white students unless the event is organized.*"

Many of the blacks interviewed expressed a similar concern for the faculty. The lack of genuine concern was missing due, in part, to the blacks believing that faculty members generally "ignored and taught over them." One student expressed her concern by saying:

> *[There is] a subtle, condescending attitude on the part of the faculty; I'm sick of being treated as if I'm stupid. Every time I turn around I have to prove I'm smart enough to be here.*

These interviews also yielded some additional insight about some of the more subtle aspects of being racially isolated on a college campus. When we inquired about how they spent their leisure time we were surprised to discover that almost thirty-five percent of the black students did not date.

Although these students began dating before they were seventeen, their college dating experiences left much to be desired. Fewer than 20 percent of the black respondents reported any exclusivity in their dating pattern. As a matter of fact, nearly 60 percent of those black students who reported that they were currently dating said that they had not dated anyone on campus. The general feeling among both black males and females seemed to center around availability. That is, most indicated that were virtually no "acceptable" dating partners for them. They also argued that even if there were, there was nothing for them to do. Most blacks said that the social activities were really intended for the white students.

Hispanics

The Hispanic students proved to be another story. Their dating experience began, on average, at fifteen, almost two years earlier than for the blacks that we interviewed. Another interesting point we discovered through our interviews was that even though their numbers were lower than blacks, they seemed to have little or no trouble finding suitable social activities. That is, all of our Hispanic respondents indicated that they were currently dating. Although half of them reported that they looked for acceptable dating partners away from campus (i.e. clubs, church, work) they unanimously agreed that there were a number of suitable dating partners on campus. That is significant in that the thirty Hispanic students interviewed seemed to define the social environment as one which they could readily tolerate. As a matter of fact, the modal number of "acceptable dating partners" (according to the survey format) was between four and seven persons. Thus, the reality for most Hispanic students is the clear realization that most campus-related activities are controlled by the fraternities and sororities. This realization does not seem to disturb them even though very few Hispanics are members. While we did not get specific information concerning their perception of racism (let alone their potential reactions), we sense that the status quo is one in which they can exist. This conclusion is based on the large number of Anglo relationships reported by the majority of this group and their acceptance of the level and type of activities that exist on campus. Their major concern was any and all uses of stereotypical terms that might be used to describe them as a group. They seemed to be more conscious of the stereotypes of their culture than just the labels assigned to them personally. For instance, over two-thirds preferred the term Hispanic to Mexican-American or Mexican. They resent the connection between the image of the lazy, uneducated Mexican driving a "low-rider" that is all too often applied with broad strokes to anyone of Mexican decent.

Whites

The white students who attend this university obviously enjoy more than just numerical superiority. Virtually all campus leaders and social groups are comprised by their fellow whites. This doesn't seem to be a conscious realization as much as a simple matter of fact. At least for Greek-affiliated students, this fact does not seem to seriously impact the general level of social interaction with ethnic minorities on campus. As on many campuses, the Greek-affiliated students are the most involved in day-to-day activities. Their organization lends itself to close ties to any university-sponsored activity. These activities also bring them into closer contact with the black fraternity and sorority, as well as any other campus-related activity. However, since Greeks are only 4 percent of the total student body, it is safe to assume that levels of interaction between other whites and blacks are largely reserved for class- (i.e., academic) related areas. Apart from isolated exchanges, overt friction is minimal. Many of the Greeks complained that the black fraternities and sororities make little real effort to participate in the full range of campus activities. In any event, confrontations—social, emotional, or physical—between the white and black students, Greeks or independent, remain relatively rare.

This supposition is supported by information obtained from the office of Vice President for Student and Administrative Services. There have been only two major interracial incidents handled by this office during the three-year period of this study. While this does not preclude the possibility of unreported cases, the virtual absence of interracial conflicts necessitating official action strongly suggests support for this position. Further investigation revealed that most racial incidents involving black students that are reported to the administration are, in fact, intraracial. The confrontations (some involving firearms) have resulted in increased security for social events sponsored by the black fraternity, dismissal or suspension of students for fighting with local black youth, and, ultimately, the suspension of many black-sponsored activities on campus.

The prevailing social attitude seems to be one of selective, benign neglect. Overall, most white students we interviewed expressed little or no concern for racial matters. That is, they saw no real problems between themselves and the minority students on campus. This seems rather ironic in that while none of the respondents admitted to harboring prejudice, they did compartmentalize this attitude with numerous qualifiers. One white student said, "*I'm not prejudiced toward groups, just individuals if they act like the stereotype.*" Another claimed that he did not hold a "*supreme amount [of prejudice] because I was raised in Pennsylvania, you see.*" This seemingly inconsistent pronouncement is little more than a reflection of the attitudes of most Americans when the issue is race. That is, situation-specific behavior may or may not be a valid reflection of our attitudes.

Interestingly enough, behavioral measures of white student attitudes yielded some of these same inconsistencies. We were able to obtain various measures of social distance, the real or psychological distance that we maintain between ourselves and others. While the trend over time has reflected declining R.D.Q.s between white and non-white (Bogardus, 1958; Owen, Eisner, & McFaul, 1981; Taylor et al., 1979; Schaefer, 1987; and Tuch, 1988), the results have failed to provide any real insight into the actual processes involved in the acquisition of an egalitarian perspective on race.

Those students with the lowest Racial Distance Quotients, or those students who exhibited the least degree of social distance were those who claimed a Greek affiliation. With the exception of black, Greek-affiliated females, those persons who belonged to a campus fraternity or sorority were the students who interacted most closely with members of a different ethnic group. A saturation sample of over 90 percent of the 255 Greek-letter organization members indicated that they would (and did) maintain rather close interactional ties with other students Greek or non-Greek, regardless of ethnic identity. A sample of white and black independents (non-Greeks) who were given the same social distance scale generated greater levels of desired distance between themselves and any ethnic group other than their own. Thus, close ties with the university and its everyday activities seems to help create more of a climate of tolerance. Perhaps the university would be best served by encouraging its students to become more involved in extracurricular activities that provide opportunities to interact with a large number of students.

ADMINISTRATION

While all administrators voiced an official concern for the plight of minority (especially black) students on this campus, a rather disturbing theme seemed to contradict this stance. They, along with several faculty who were interviewed, placed the major responsibility for racial harmony upon the minority students themselves. Said one:

> *We would suggest that the black population [on campus] is very unmotivated but we [administrators] feel thwarted in our efforts to bring about a change for the students if the students can't make a concerted effort to cooperate with the administration.*

Another top-level administrator echoed these sentiments when he said:

> *The need of the university is to help people get farther up, but we can't do it for them. The atmosphere is better this year than in previous years but what the university needs now is a person (minority student advisor) who can take time to make a change.*

The one black professor on the campus agreed with the need for a minority advisor but was concerned that the addition of one minority representative, in any capacity, could only do so much good. He stated:

There is an absence of real support from faculty. I am forced into the role of becoming advisor to every black student on campus, something that my white colleagues don't do. While I don't mind it, I feel that I was pushed into this position because of my race instead of my credits. Like these students, I feel isolated instead of alienated.

SUMMARY AND CONCLUSION

It is difficult to paint the completed portrait of a campus and its students without using the broad descriptive strokes which may obscure the fine lines between truth and the painter's definition of the situation. However, some conclusions must be reached based on what has been reported. As with most social interaction in which the key participants come to view the same situation differently, the failures are probably located with the principals themselves; that is, there's usually enough blame to go around. It would seem to be the case here.

This is a campus that is, like most college campuses, run by an administration that sees its job in rather analytical terms. They are responsible for providing a physical plant staffed with the requisite faculty teaching a prescribed curriculum. Additional (i.e. extra-curricular) activities are also part of the menu but they are rarely elevated to "full academic proportion" as evidenced by the status and power of the administrators who are in charge of these aspects. It is also conceded that there should be relatively little hostility in the day-to-day interaction of those students who participate in such activities. In any event, if there are little or no outward signs of conflict, it is generally assumed that "things are O.K." However, if an administration is committed to the recruitment of minority students, it has the additional responsibility to fully attend to the social and cultural needs of all of its students. Just because there is little or even no outward signs of distress does not absolve the school's administration of its responsibility; in the same way, a physician is charged with the total care of his/her patient even though he/she appears healthy. To wait until serious symptoms manifest themselves might doom the patient to serious consequences.

To their credit, university officials have responded, at least in part, and have given their Vice-President for Student and Administrative Services increased authority to hire a black, highly qualified Dean of Students as well as a black dormitory resident advisor. Unfortunately, the single, black faculty member has not been joined by any additional blacks although additional Hispanic faculty (teaching Spanish) have been added. It would also be unfair to suggest that just because an administrator or faculty member is white that he or she is incapable of sensitivity to any student who is not white.

It should also be recognized that the students must also share in the responsibility of creating a favorable climate while they pursue their academic careers. For instance, the social concerns of many of the black students centered around the lack of activities and the unavailability of anyone of their own race to date. The reality is that, proportionately, there are just as many blacks to date as for whites or Hispanics. When we utilized black female interviewers to investigate the social atmosphere on the campus they found that the major stumbling block was the black students themselves. This impression was supported by the data generated through sixty interviews with black students. Almost 60 percent (57%) of these respondents reported that they had dated three or fewer other students during their tenure on campus. Over 40 percent reported that they did not date. The lack of socializing seemed to center around their perception that there was no one to date and nothing to attend if one did have a date. Further investigation of the interview data suggested other possible reasons. Black females rated most black males as unacceptable as dates let alone as potential marital partners. They found them to be socially immature and primarily interested in themselves or sexual conquest. Black males viewed the black females as having an "attitude," that is, too dominant or demanding in their expectations.

So, in the final analysis, where does the truth lie? We contend that, as in the larger society, all involved parties are the victims. Without engaging in finger pointing and the pitfalls of political correctness, we conclude that there is enough blame to go around. This campus is like much of America in the 1990s, unsure of its true nature and of its future direction. While there is no panacea, it would seem that people of good will should complement and support those programs which help people to discover the best in others or at least accept the reality of their presence.

This rather unique attempt to assess the social climate in the context of an educational setting represented a number of separate studies over a period of three years. It is also unique in that we spoke to and listened to hundreds of students and numerous faculty and administrators. Although minority status, by itself, is not predictive of a student's perception of social climate, variation among ethnic group experiences must be considered. That is, while Hispanic students who attend a virtually all-white campus seem to have little difficulty in obtaining dates, the same is not true for black students on the same campus. Although they might think themselves fully integrated into the campus lifestyle and its activities, many of the white students are also isolated. That is, they are racially isolated from most ethnic minorities on campus. Most of the whites we interviewed seemed to believe that the distance between the races (especially blacks) was due to the impact of self-segregation among black students. Ultimately, we believe that college life, like the larger society, must be viewed in its proper context. And if the participants are going to reasonably accept their position in that world, they must also accept and respect the presence of others. Perhaps that is the key element—genuine conversation—that represents an honest attempt to accurately determine just what is going on.

REFERENCES

Algozzine, B. 1977a. "The emotionally disturbed child: Disturbed or disturbing?" *Journal of Abnormal Child Psychology* 5:205-211.

_____. 1977b. "Perceived attractiveness and classroom interactions." *Journal of Experimental Education* 46:63-66.

Baker, M.H., B. C. Nienstedt, R. S. Everett, and R. McCleary. 1983. "The impact of a crime wave: Perceptions, fears and confidence in the police." *Law and Society* 2: 319-35.

Balkin, S. 1979. "Victimization rates, safety, and fear of crime." *Social Problems* 26:343-58.

Bogardus, E.S. 1958. "Racial distance changes in the United States during the past thirty years." *Sociology and Social Research* 43 (2):127-135.

Duster, T. 1991. "Understanding self-segregation on the campus." *The Chronicle of Higher Education* 8 (5):11-14.

Gomme, I.M. 1986. "The role of experience in the production of fear of crime: A test of a causal model." *Canadian Journal of Criminology* 30 (1):67-76.

Kennedy, L.W., and R.A. Silverman. 1985. "Perception of social diversity and fear of crime." *Environment and Behavior* 17:275-95.

Leo, J. 1990. "Racism on American college campuses." *U.S. News and World Report* 108 (1):53-54.

Litt, M., and D. Turk. 1985. "Sources of stress and dissatisfaction in experienced high school teachers." *Journal of Educational Research* 78:178-85.

Mabry, M. 1991. "Racism on American college campus." *The Black Collegian* 22:73-78.

Owen, C.A., H.C. Eisner, and T.R. McFaul. 1981. "A half century of social distance research: National replication of the Bogardus studies." *Sociology and Social Research* 66 (1):80-98.

Schaefer, R.T. 1987. "Social distance of Black college students at a predominantly white university." *Sociology and Social Research* 72 (1):30-33.

Shotland, R.L., M.J. Rovine, E.F. Danowits, C.S. Hayward, C. Young, M.L. Signorella, K. Mindinghall, and J.K. Kennedy. 1979. "Fear of crime in residential communities." *Criminology* 17:34-45.

Skelly, M.E. 1990. "The reality of racism on college campuses." *School and College* 29 (8):11-15.

Stafford, M.C., and O.R. Galle. 1984. "Victimization rates, exposure to risk, and fear of crime." *Criminology* 22:173-85.

Taylor, D.G, P.B. Sheatsly, and A.M. Greeley. 1979. "Attitudes toward racial integration." *Scientific American* 238 (6):42-49.

Taylor, R.B., S.D. Gottfreson, and S. Brower. 1984. "Block crime and fear: Defensible space, local social ties and territorial functioning." *Journal of Research in Crime and Delinquency* 21 (4):303-331.

Toseland, R.W. 1982. "Fear of crime: Who is most vulnerable?" *Journal of Criminal Justice* 10:199-209.

Tuch, S.A. 1988. "Race differences in the antecedents of social distance attitudes." *Sociology and Social Research* 72 (3): 181-183.

———— 1991. "The derisory tower." *The New Republic* 204 (7):5-7.

Disapproval of Interracial Unions:
The Case of Black Females[1]

Yanick St. Jean and Robert E. Parker

Studies of the reactions of blacks towards intermarriage are rare and episodic, making it difficult to either fully understand or to accurately predict the responses. Despite their infrequent nature, however, available studies do show a tendency towards marginal acceptance with variations by gender (Spickard, 1989:341). Black men are tolerant of the unions; black women more likely condemn them (Staples, 1973; Spickard, 1989).

Given the imbalanced sex ratio of the black population, the attitudes of black females towards marriages uniting a black male and white female are not surprising. The 1990 Census reports a total of 15,816,000 black females, but only 14,170,000 black males; by contrast, the census reports 102,210,000 white females and 97,476,000 white males (U.S. Bureau of Census, 1992). The sex ratios of 89.5 percent black males for every 100 females contrast with 95.3 sex ratio for whites, yielding male deficits of -0.5 percent and -.02 percent, respectively.[2] The deficit is greater for blacks.

When the 25 to 64 age category of working segment of the population is isolated, it produces a white male deficit of -.0095, whereas the black male deficit for that segment is greater: -.07889. As Wilson (1987) has pointed out the high proportion of unemployed black males further reduces the number that are marriageable. And as Lichter and colleagues (1992:797) have stated,

for a large share of young unmarried black women, access to
economically advantaged potential males is clearly limited.
For every three black unmarried women in their 20s, there is
roughly only one unmarried man with earnings above the pov-
erty threshold.

Since employment is a predictor of marital eligibility (Wilson, 1987),
black females are faced with a significant dilemma. If, as often reported, interracial marriages are indeed a middle-class phenomenon
(Cox, 1976; Monahan, 1976; Davis, 1991),[3] a significant number
would drastically reduce the small segment of middle-class black males,
leaving black women with an even more limited choice of black mates
(Lewin, 1991).

White females in such unions may thus be viewed by black counterparts as extractors of scarce resource and threats to their happiness
and well-being. Black females may also presume that black males engaged in such unions have adopted the dominant standards of beauty
and that their selection of a white mate is a statement about the ultimate
benefits of assimilation and, consequently, the lack of desirability of
women of color. This line of thinking would reinforce black women's
negative reactions, particularly toward unions which join a black male
and white female.

For less obvious reasons, however, black females apparently also
disapprove of marriages uniting a black female and a white male. This
is counterintuitive and unexpected. A male deficit, it seems, would encourage rather than discourage the crossing of racial borders. One good
example is Brazil where, according to Telles (1993:146), "the shortage
of white women during the colonial (slavery) era prompted a high rate
of miscegenation between Portuguese men and (at first) Indian women
and (later) black and mulatto women."

In addition to the apparent inconsistency with demographic circumstances, black women's attitudes towards intermarriage also contrast
with popular beliefs regarding the meaning of assimilation for blacks.
These beliefs were well expressed by Gunnar Myrdal (1944:56):

It seems frankly incredible that the Negro people in America
should feel inclined to develop any particular race pride at all
or have any dislike for amalgamation, were it not for the com-

mon white opinion of the racial inferiority of the Negro people
and the whites' intense dislike for miscegenation.

Myrdal's perception that it is whites—not blacks—who control the
degree of color mixing in American society is shared by a number of
respected social scientists (Morton, 1991). Many of the same scholars
believe blacks "wish to marry white." In fact, psychologist John
Dollard went so far as to suggest that "a very common delusion of
black women [is] that they [are] white" (Dollard, cited in Morton
1991:74). Thus, given their dream for *whitening*, black women's approval of interracial unions would make a great deal of sense. This,
however, is hardly the case.

Finally, the negative reactions of black women also conflict with
middle-class aspirations for social mobility. Assuming that union with
a white male serves as a buffer to obstacles created by *double jeopardy*[4]
—the interaction of race and gender—it might ultimately open the way
for greater socioeconomic and personal freedom. Yet, as indicated
earlier, black female/white male marriages are rare phenomenon, representing only an insignificant proportion of interracial marriages.[5]

If data for this analysis confirm that black women indeed disapprove of intermarriage despite significant shortages of eligible black
males, evidence of potential socioeconomic benefits, and popular beliefs
about wishes of blacks for *whitening*, probing into cultural representations may yield important insights. Historically black women have been
subjected to cultural domination through fictitious portrayals. It is
likely, therefore, that their interactions with members of the dominant
group are influenced by these characterizations and by the guiding
norms they create.

As black females conform to cultural requirements that intermarriage—one of the most severe racial code violations—be avoided,[6] the
characterizations are maintained and their exclusionary purpose served.
Because intermarriage places black women on an equal footing with
white males in the most intimate of circumstances, it nullifies the
expected modes of black/white interactions and, from the point of view
of society, elevates the status of black women to a level inappropriate
to her racial and gender categories. Thus, exclusion through powerful
cultural controls may be one of the most effective mechanisms to avoid
the formation of a *forbidden* unit, and to keep black women "in their
place," thereby preserving the social order.

We suggested earlier that potential candidates for interracial unions often hold middle-class status. Presumably, most have been trained in American educational institutions and have developed familiarity with the culture. It seems, therefore, that the familiar images would deter black women from developing relationships with white males at any level. As Essed (1991:31) proposes,

> *the construction of black sexuality causes many black women*
> *to restrict the goal they pursue and the choices they make for*
> *reasons of self-protection . . . Issues of interracial dating. . .*
> *[are] integrated in the socialization of black children.*

In sum, in order to safeguard their reputation, women of color might overconform to expected rules of behavior and avoid engaging even in casual friendships with white males.

However, disapproval of interracial marriages by black women can also be a form of resistance. The development of racial consciousness and racial identity may shape the countercurrent. As black women become increasingly aware of their group's circumstances, they may challenge the cultural representations by behaving in ways that run counter to societal expectations. The disapproval may be a response to dominant characterizations and a form of social protest, rather than pure conformity to societal rules.

Thus, identifying the separate contributions of conformity and resistance to the disapproval of black/white marriages by black women is difficult and obviously beyond the scope of this analysis. One way to detect their separate effects would be to conduct a qualitative study of black women using in-depth interviews concerning their reasons for disapproval.

White males may also not want to engage in relationships with black females (Staples, 1973). Interviews with white males about their attitudes towards intermarriage with black females will be necessary in order to shed light on this important issue.

The present analysis will be limited to a reassessment of black women's reaction to intermarriage using data from the General Social Survey (Davis and Smith, 1988). Subsequently, an attempt will be made to determine if the results support our assumption that negative cultural characterizations influence the women's attitudes towards interracial unions.

METHODS AND RESULTS

Intermarriage between blacks and white has been a neglected issue in the social scientific literature, so it should be no surprise that available data are grossly inadequate. Only two questions in the General Social Survey deal with intermarriage.

1. "How about having a close relative or family member marry a black person?" Responses were: strongly favor, favor, neither favor nor oppose.

2. "Do you think there should be laws against marriages between (Negroes/Blacks) and whites?" Responses were: yes, no, don't know.

The first question was asked only in 1990, making the number of black female responses inadequate for any extensive analysis. Although in 1982 and 1987 the General Social Survey oversampled the black population, for all other years, data are either lacking or non-representative.

The second question also suffers from weaknesses. Even if the respondents strongly disapprove of laws banning interracial marriages between blacks and whites, this would not necessarily indicate they approve of intermarriage. They could still oppose intermarriage for themselves and their close relatives. While advocating freedom of choice in the abstract and disagreeing with restrictive laws, the same individuals may want to enjoy their own rights of freedom and to preserve the private sphere from color contamination. The interpretation of responses becomes a complex task.

Neither of the two questions accurately measures the attitudes of black females towards intermarriage—the goal of this analysis. Despite its weaknesses, the law question from 1987 to 1991 is used in this analysis to assess the attitudes of black females towards intermarriage. The question is a better tool than the first because it was asked over a number of years, including 1987 when the oversampling occurred. Another reason for using the law question is that it forces respondents to think of intermarriage in the abstract rather than purely on the basis of emotions.

Table 1

Attitudes of Black Women Towards Laws
Prohibiting Interracial Marriage,
by Selected Variables, 1987 to 1991

Variables Probability	% Favoring	% Against	
Age: (n=598)			
≤35	2.74	97.26	0.000
>35	10.03	89.97	X^2=10.81 df/1
Income: (n=343)			
≤15,000	6.25	93.75	0.012
>15,000	0.74	99.26	X^2=6.35 df/1
Education: (n=603)			
<high school	16.58	83.42	0.000
≥high school	3.41	96.59	X^2=32.28 df/1
Place Size: (n=606)			
<10,000	18.48	81.52	0.000
≥10,000	5.64	94.36	X^2=18.33 df/1
Region: (n=568)			
North East	9.09	90.01	0.002
North Central	3.61	96.39	X^2=14.50
South East	6.29	93.71	df/3
South Central	15.57	84.43	
Religiosity: (n=555)			
Strong	10.26	89.74	0.012
Not strong	4.53	95.47	X^2=6.27 df/1

Note: Probability on X^2 of individual variables.

Independent variables used in this analysis are sex/race (black male and black female), age (35 and below, above 35), income (under $15,000, $15,000 and above), education (no high school, high school, high school and beyond), place size (under 10,000, over 10,000), region (North East, North Central, South East, and South Central), religiosity (strong, not strong). We reasoned that each one of these variables would be related to familiarity with mainstream culture. The findings are as follows:

1. Black females who are over the age of 35 favor laws banning intermarriage more than their younger counterparts (10.3 percent versus 2.74 percent; Prob. = 0.000).

2. Black females who earn less than $15,000 favor laws banning intermarriage more than their wealthier counterparts (6.25 percent versus 0.74 percent; Prob. = 0.012).

3. Black females without a high school degree favor laws banning intermarriage more than their counterparts with a high school or higher degree (16.58 percent versus 3.41 percent; Prob. = 0.000).

4. Black females who live in cities of less than 10,000 favor laws banning intermarriage more than their counterparts in larger cities (18.48 percent versus 5.64 percent; Prob. = 0.000).

5. Black females who live in the South Central area favor laws banning intermarriage more than their counterparts from other regions (15.57 percent versus 9.09 percent, 3.61 percent, and 6.23 percent; Prob. = 0.000).

6. Black females who are strongly religious favor laws banning intermarriage more than their counterparts who are less religious (10.26 percent versus 4.53 percent; Prob. = 0.012).

No significant differences were found in the attitudes of black males and black females towards the restrictive laws.

To summarize, age, education, place size and region appear strongly correlated with black women's attitudes towards laws banning intermarriage. These variables were found significant at the .01 level. Income and strength of religious conviction also appear related with the women's attitudes towards restrictive laws at the .05 significance level.

CONCLUSION

The main purpose of this analysis was to assess the attitudes of black females towards interracial marriages using the General Social Survey. A second purpose was to determine if negative cultural representations, as evidenced in the social scientific literature, have consequences for black women's attitudes towards intermarriage. The results indicate:

1. A majority of black females disapprove of laws banning intermarriage.
2. Black females who favor laws seem to have fewer contacts with whites, and less familiarity with mainstream American culture as indicated by age, income, education, place size, region and religiosity. Each variable yielded significant chi-squares.

But disapproval of restrictive laws does not necessarily mean approval of intermarriage. Consequently the data neither prove nor disprove that black females condemn intermarriage. Nor do the data indicate that familiarity with American culture would tend to increase the women's awareness of detrimental characterizations as depicted in the literature, and lead them to promote laws banning intermarriage. This was not supported by the evidence. Black women overwhelmingly reject laws prohibiting interracial marriage.

Given the many limitations of the data, further conclusions cannot be made. Rather, the study needs to be replicated to test for the accuracy of results and interpretation.

More data on the attitudes of black females towards intermarriage, as well as better measuring tools, are needed. At present such data are scarce and, as clearly demonstrated, tools for measurement are either nonexistent or grossly inadequate. In addition, given the sensitive nature of the issue, qualitative analyses will need to be conducted to sharpen understanding.

NOTES

[1] Direct all correspondence to Yanick St. Jean, Department of Sociology, University of Nevada, Box 455033, 4505 Maryland

Parkway, Las Vegas, Nevada 89154-5033, e-mail:stjean@ nevada.edu. Thanks to Donald Carns, Nancy Wingfield, Esther Langston, James Frey, Nikitah Inami, Clara Cunningham and anonymous reviewers for providing helpful suggestions on earlier drafts of this paper. We would also like to thank Veona Hunsinger for assistance with the presentation of tables on a previous draft, Donald Carns and Nick Byrnes with the data. A portion of this project is being supported by a grant from the University of Nevada, Las Vegas.

[2] a) The sex ratio (the number of males per 100 females) or P_{male}/P_{female} x 100. b) The male deficit is $P_{male}-P_{female}/P_{total}$ x 100. For details, see Henry S. Shryock and Jacob S. Siegel, 1976: 108.

[3] Spickard (1989:349) suggested otherwise. "The exact relationship of class to intermarriage is still unclear [. . .]. However [i]intermarriers from all groups tended to marry people with social standing similar to their own."

[4] See Joe R. Feagin and Clairece Booher Feagin, 1990, page 164.

[5] Approximately 1 percent of all marriages. *Vital Statistics of the United States* show that in 1987 there were approximately 134,720 black brides and 10,010,126 white grooms yielding a percentage of 0.0134315. It is, however, important to mention that many large states, such as California and New York, where such marriages are likely to be common, keep no statistics on the racial characteristics of brides and grooms. (U.S. Department of Health and Human Services. *Vital Statistics of the United States, 1987*, 1991. Table 1-21 pages 1-26, footnote #1.)

[6] It has been suggested that segregation and other forms of exclusion are ultimately for the purpose of minimizing biological intermixture and preventing societal chaos.

REFERENCES

Cox, Oliver C. 1976. *Race Relations.* Detroit: Wayne State.

Davis, James Allan and Tom W. Smith. *General Social Survey, 1987-1991.* Chicago: National Opinion Research Center.

Davis, F. James. 1991. *Who Is Black: One Nation's Definition.* University Park: Pennsylvania State.

Essed, Philomena. 1991. *Understanding Everyday Racism.* Newbury Park, CA: Sage.

Feagin, Joe R. and Clairece Booher Feagin. 1990. *Social Problems: A Critical Power-Conflict Perspective.* New Jersey: Prentice-Hall.

Lewin, Arthur. 1991. "A tale of two classes: The black poor and the black middle-class." *The Black Scholar* 21:7-13.

Lichter, Daniel T., Diane K. McLaughlin, George Kephart, David J. Landry. 1992. "Race and the retreat from marriage: A shortage of marriageable men?" *American Sociological Review* 57:781-799.

Monahan, Thomas P. 1976. "The occupational class of couples entering into interracial marriages." *Journal of Comparative Family Studies* 7:175-92.

Morton, Patricia. 1991. *Disfigured Images: The Historical Assault on Afro-American Women.* New York: Praeger.

Myrdal, Gunnar. 1944. *An American Dilemma: The Negro Problem and Modern Democracy.* New York: Harper.

Shryock, Henry S., Jacob Siegel, and Associates. 1976. *The Methods and Materials of Demography.* San Diego: Academic Press, Inc.

Spickard, Paul R. 1989. *Mixed Blood.* Madison: Wisconsin.

Staples, Robert. 1973. *The Black Woman in America.* Chicago: Nelson Hall.

_____. 1990. "Social inequality and the black sexual pathology." *The Black Scholar* 21:29.

Telles, Edward E. 1993. "Racial distance and region in Brazil: Intermarriage in Brazilian urban areas." *Latin American Research Review* 28:149-162.

U.S. Bureau of Census. 1992. *Statistical Abstract of the United States, 1992.* (112th edition). Washington, DC.

U.S. Department of Health and Human Services. 1991. *Vital Statistics of the United States, 1987.* Vol III. Washington, DC: U.S. Government Printing Office.

Wilson, William Julius. 1987. *The Truly Disadvantaged.* Chicago: Chicago University Press.

White Attitudes Towards Black and White Interracial Marriage

*Deborah S. Wilson and
Cardell K. Jacobson*

This study first documents, through the use of the General Social Survey, the recent historical trend in attitudes toward interracial marriage. Historical trends are important and need to be documented in order to identify and understand recent patterns of interracial marriage. Longitudinal data allow this to be done. Second, the study examines specific predictors of attitudes toward intermarriage: religion, sex, age, social class, occupation, and education. Subsequently, Multiple Classification Analysis is used to examine which characteristics best predict attitudes toward black and white interracial marriage when all the others are controlled statistically.

ATTITUDES TOWARD INTERRACIAL MARRIAGE

Interracial marriage in the U.S. has a long history. During slavery, the white master often engaged in sex with black house slaves and blacks and whites sometimes cohabitated. The case of Hugh Davis, a white servant in Virginia, is the earliest record available of such cohabitation. On September 17, 1630, he was publicly beaten before whites and blacks for "defiling himself with a negro" (Washington, 1970:42). The first slavery law was proposed in 1661 in Maryland; in 1662, Virginia proposed a similar law to prevent interracial affairs and marriages. Nevertheless, black-white marriages still took place, and at times some white masters even encouraged the relationship in order to gain more slaves (Washington, 1970).

In the 1700s, many famous Americans purportedly married or had mistresses across racial lines, including Benjamin Franklin, George

Washington, Thomas Jefferson, Patrick Henry, and Alexander Hamilton (Porterfield, 1978). Even though many of these well-to-do people did not marry their mates, these relationships between blacks and whites were widely accepted and practiced during the slave period (Porterfield, 1978).

Through time, laws continued to restrict intermarriage. During the nineteenth century, thirty-eight states prohibited interracial marriages. As recently as 1930, thirty states had laws against intermarriage. Sometimes those who intermarried were disowned by their family and friends, and were punished by the court system as well (Beigel, 1966). In Florida and North Carolina, the penalty for interracial marriage was ten years' imprisonment (Zabel, 1965). Who was considered a Negro under these laws? The most common definition classifying a Negro was "any person of one-eighth or more of Negro blood." For instance, in Missouri as recently as 1965, a jury could decide if a person were a Negro from his or her appearance (Zabel, 1965). As a result of the interracial unions, Zabel (1965:118) suggests that one-third to three-fourths of U.S. Negroes have some Caucasian ancestry.

On June 12, 1967, the United States Supreme Court struck down the laws banning interracial marriages. The court argued that the 14th amendment guarantees freedom of choice to marry without restrictions of racial discrimination. In declaring the laws against interracial marriage unconstitutional, this United States Supreme Court decision opened the way for an increase in mixed marriages.

Attitudes towards interracial marriage have gradually changed, however, especially since the 1960s. An example of the attitude in the 1960s was Albert I. Gordon (1964), who argued against interracial marriage. He believed that intermarriage actually threatened ultimate happiness because of major differences in religion and race. He talked about intermarriage as a threat also to the children and the religious way of life. Intermarriage, he said, "holds no promise for a bright and happy future for individuals or for mankind" (Gordon, 1964:370).

As negative attitudes toward black-white marriages have decreased, the rate of intermarriage is increasing (Jeter, 1982; Alba and Golden, 1986; and Labov and Jacobs, 1986). According to the current population surveys, the number of interracial married couples increased from 310,000 (.007 percent) in 1970 to 956,000 (.018 percent) in 1988, two-and-a-half times more interracial marriages than in 1970. The number of black husbands and white wives is almost double that of black wives and white husbands. This ratio of black husbands and white wives continued to be about the same in 1970, 1980, and 1988 (U.S. Bureau of the Census, 1990). Many other research reports indicate that more marriages consist of black males and white females than of white males and black females (Rice, 1990:186-187; Schoen and Wooldredge, 1989; Heer, 1966; and Pavela, 1964). Not only has the overall number of interracial marriages increased, but the percentage of all marriages that are black and white has increased also.

Even though the number of these interracial marriages is increasing, those who enter into these marriages still experience many social pressures. Mixed marriages have been and still are somewhat taboo. Some communities have not treated those in interracial marriages very well. Not only do some couples lose jobs because of their marriages, they often do not achieve high-status jobs. Society's treatment of interracial couples also depends on the social status and social mobility of the couples. Heer (1966), for example, believes that black-white marriages reduce this status gap if the white individual is well connected.

Monahan (1976) discusses society's treatment of interracial couples. He argues that from the beginning, intermarriage has taken place in the lower class. Previous research had found that black men who intermarried were higher placed occupationally than the average black worker, but white men who intermarried were placed in a lower occupation than the average white worker. However, Monahan discovered in his Philadelphia study, "On the whole there was no distinguishable degree of 'marrying up' or 'marrying down' by the whites and the Negroes with one another" (1976:188).

Other countries view interracial marriages differently. The attitudes of the international countries who approved and disapproved of interracial marriages in 1968 are displayed in Table 1. People in the United States disapproved of interracial marriages more than people in any other country listed. Only 20 percent of the United States approved of interracial marriage, compared to 72 percent who disapproved. Swedes approved more than any other country. Since there are no up-to-date international comparisons, changes cannot be noted.

Table 1

Attitudes Toward Interracial Marriage
in Various Countries

	Approve	Disapprove	No Opinion
Sweden	67	21	12
France	62	25	13
Finland	58	34	8
Netherlands	51	23	26
Greece	50	36	14
Switzerland	50	35	15
Austria	39	53	8
Canada	36	53	11
Norway	35	44	21
West Germany	35	47	18
Uruguay	30	44	26
Great Britain	29	57	14
United States	20	72	8

Source: The Gallup Poll, 1968.

ATTITUDE CHANGE

Attitudes have changed among young Americans, however, and barriers of race and religion have lessened. These changes in attitudes affect people who intermarry. Students who attend colleges and universities seem to have more liberal attitudes, attitudes which increase the opportunity for intermarriage. The gradual integration of minority groups into mainstream American life has increased contact between groups, and social and economic obstacles separating them are deteriorating. As Porterfield has said, "*If complete acceptance comes to pass, it is likely that discrimination in the United States based on race or skin color will cease to exist*" (Porterfield, 1982:31).

Demographic Characteristics

Using data from the General Social Survey the remainder of this paper will examine attitudes toward interracial marriage. Several factors that predict attitudes toward these marriages will be examined.

Religion. Religion is thought to explain some of the variance in prejudice. Cygnar, Jacobson, and Noel (1977) found that fanaticism and importance of religion were related to prejudice, while dimensions of ritual, knowledge, and orthodoxy were not related. Consequential religiosity was positively related. More recently Roof and McKinney (1987) found 66 percent of members of national religious churches were opposed to laws prohibiting interracial marriage. Unitarian Universalists were most opposed to laws against interracial marriage (93%); Southern Baptists were the least opposed to such laws (37%). Most (84%) of those with no religious preference and liberal Protestants (73%) were opposed to such laws while the percentage of conservative Protestants was rela-tively low (42%). Those classified as "other" religions were also gen-erally opposed to such laws: Christian Scientists (87% opposed), Jehovah's Witnesses (76% opposed) and Mormons (74% opposed).

In the data analysis section which follows we shall examine two measures of religiosity. We will examine the data for Catholics and Protestants. And we expect the more religious people (how strongly they feel about their religion) to be more intolerant towards interracial marriage.

Age. Increasing rates of intermarriage have produced recent cohorts with higher proportions of mixed ancestry. Alba and Golden (1986) found that among those who trace their ancestors to Europe, ethnic boundaries have diminished, and ethnicity carries much less weight in choosing a spouse. Yetman (1985:234) also finds that rates of inter-marriage are mostly among the third generation and the youngest adult members of each ethnic group. Thus, younger people are expected to be more tolerant toward interracial marriage than older people.

Gender. Male and female attitudes towards interracial marriage, vary although not as much as the other variables mentioned. Males are generally expected to be more tolerant than females of interracial marriage for two reasons. First, a myth or stereotype exists that all black men want to rape or beat or have sex with white women (Brown, 1987:25). Second, parents influence their daughters and sons when the children consider whom they will marry. The parents may provide less support to daughters than sons in interracial marriages.

Social class. People's attitudes are likely to vary according to their social status. A very early study of interracial marriage (Davis, 1941) examined interracial marriage from an exchange theory perspective. Davis believed that marriages involve an exchange of black males' high social status and low racial status for white womens' high racial status but low social status. Many different factors determine social class status. Family of origin is an important determinant; to enter into elite positions, one must be born into a family of relatively high status (Heer, 1966). More recently, Porterfield (1978) argued that an inter-racial couple would feel more comfortable in a ghetto than in a white setting. Thus, self-described social class is expected to be associated with the tolerance of interracial marriages.

Occupational prestige. Likewise, a person's occupation may influ-ence his or her attitude toward interracial marriage. Tucker and Mitchell-Kernan (1990) discuss the concept of "connectedness," meaning that people with connections help their friends find jobs. The higher the occupational prestige of one's friends, the higher the chance to procure a high-prestige job. Blacks are often excluded from higher-prestige jobs because they lack connections and therefore are rarely able to make later connections. Those who have high-prestige occupa-tions are usually more tolerant of interracial marriage. Finally, Crain and Mahard (1978) have shown that blacks who attend desegregated high schools are more likely to get higher-status jobs because of their white contacts who have job information. Thus we expect those with higher-prestige occupations to be more tolerant of interracial marriage than those in lower-prestige occupational levels.

Education. Finally, education is expected to be associated with reception of interracial marriage. As Glick (1988:865) comments, "Mixed marriages are increasingly being considered acceptable, es-pecially by persons with average or above average education." We shall examine the bivariate relationships between each of these variables and attitudes toward interracial marriage. Subsequently, we shall examine all the variables together to determine which are the most closely related when all others are controlled statistically. For example, once age and education are controlled, several of the other independent variables may become non-significant.

DATA

The data for this analysis were taken from the General Social Survey (GSS), conducted by the National Opinion Research Center at the University of Chicago (Davis and Smith, 1988:1). The data are better than most researchers have used in the past because they cover a greater period of time, are nationwide, cover a broad spectrum, and cover recent trends.

MEASURES OF VARIABLES

The religion variable was measured by asking respondents two questions: their religious affiliation and the strength of their affiliation. The religious groupings are 1 = Protestant, 2 = Catholic, 3 = Jewish, and 4 = None. The number of those whose religion was listed as "Other" was so small that they were dropped from this analysis. Protestants constituted 64.2 percent of the respondents; 25 percent were Catholic; 2.2 percent were Jews; 7 percent had no religion.

The respondents were asked their age, which was grouped into the following categories: 1 = 18-29, 2 = 30-39, 3 = 40-49, 4 = 50-59, and 5 = 60-89. There were 24.9 percent who were 18-29 years old, 21.2 percent in the age group of 30-39 years old, 15.6 percent 40-49 years old, 14.3 percent 50-59 years old, and 23.9 percent 60-89 years old. The respondents' mean age was 45 years, with a standard deviation of 17.7.

Forty-four percent were male; 56 percent female. The Social Class variable was measured by asking what class respondents belonged to: 1 = lower class, 2 = working class, 3 = middle class, or 4 = upper class. There were 5.1 percent who were lower class, 46.4 percent working class, 45.3 percent middle class, and 3.1 percent upper class.

The GSS codes occupation prestige using the Hodge-Siegel-Rossi Prestige scores. There were eight prestige groupings: 9.6 percent in group 1, 15.3 percent in group 2, 26.6 percent in group 3, 24.5

percent in group 4, 12.9 percent in group 5, and 10.7 percent in group 6. The respondents' mean was 39 on the prestige score.

Finally, education was measured by asking how much schooling the respondent had. Six categories for education range from 1=0-8 years to 6=17-20 years of education: 14.2 percent in category 1, 17.2 percent in category 2, 33.2 percent in category 3, 19.2 percent in category 4, 9.3 percent in category 5, and 6.9 percent in category 6. The mean for education level of the respondents was 12th grade, with a standard deviation of three years.

Attitudes toward interracial marriage were measured by asking three questions. The first question was "Do you think there should be laws against marriages between (Negroes/Blacks) and Whites?" The response categories were "yes" and "no." This was asked in all years (1972-1989). The second question was "How would it make you feel if a close relative of yours were planning to marry a (Negro/Black) /White?" The response categories were "very uneasy," "somewhat uneasy," and "not uneasy." The third question was "You can expect social problems with marriages between (Black/White)?" The response categories were "agree" and "disagree." These last two questions were asked only in 1977. Thirty-nine percent favored laws against interracial marriage, while 45.6 percent said they would feel very uneasy if a relative married a person of another race, and almost 92.7 percent expected problems in an interracial marriage.

RESULTS

As we indicated earlier, racial prejudice has declined over the past several decades (Schuman, Steeh, Bobo, 1985; Firebaugh and Davis, 1988). Likewise, Americans are becoming more tolerant of interracial marriage. Examination of the GSS also reveals increased approval of interracial marriage.

Those who approved of interracial marriage tended to be the young (age 21-29), those with professional or business occupations, those in the upper classes, the college educated, and those without strong religious convictions (see Table 2). No significant gender differences were found.

The analysis of variance showed that age, prestige, education, and strength of religion remain significant at the .001 level. Once all the

Table 2

Multiple Classification Analysis of Those Who Do Not Favor
Laws Against Racial Intermarriage

Adjusted Variable & Category	Unadjusted Means	Eta	Means	Beta
GENDER				
Male	67%		66%	
Female	67%		67%	
		.01		.01
AGE				
18-29	84%		79%	
30-39	78%		74%	
40-49	70%		68%	
50-59	59%		61%	
60-89	46%		54%	
		.31		.21*
SELF-DESCRIBED SOCIAL CLASS				
Lower class	63%		71%	
Working class	65%		67%	
Middle class	69%		67%	
Upper class	72%		66%	
		.04		.02
OCCUPATIONAL PRESTIGE				
10-19	55%		63%	
20-39	62%		65%	
40-49	71%		69%	
50-89	81%		72%	
		.16		.07*

Table 2 (continued)

| Adjusted Variable | | Unadjusted | | |
& Category	Means	Eta	Means	Beta
YEARS OF EDUCATION COMPLETED				
0-8	37%		47%	
9-11	51%		54%	
12	70%		68%	
13-15	83%		79%	
16	91%		86%	
17-20	93%		88%	
		.36		.26*
STRENGTH OF RELIGIOUS CONVICTION				
Strong	62%		63%	
Somewhat strong	67%		67%	
Not very strong	71%		70%	
		.10		.06*

$R^2 = .172$ (explained 17% of variance)

*Statistically significant at .05 level.

independent variables were entered together, the best predictors of those who favor laws against racial intermarriage are education (eta = .26) and age (eta = .21), these two variables show strong effects. Gender and class are no longer significant. Strength of religion and prestige are still significant when other variables are controlled, but the effect is not as strong as in the simple bivariate relationship.

The explained variance was 17 percent. Other factors involved that might increase the R^2 significantly were not examined, such as personality and economic factors. These variables were not in included in the GSS dataset.

CONCLUSION AND DISCUSSION

The number of black and white marriages is increasing, and society is becoming more aware of interracial marriage. This study indicates that people's attitudes toward black and white interracial marriage have changed dramatically over time, becoming more tolerant.

Several factors appear to account for the increased acceptance. Age and education are strong predictors of those who are tolerant toward interracial marriage. The age variable can mean two things: First, the older people are, the less accepting they are of interracial marriage; second, age can also be a cohort effect; the older groups have lived during times of a harsher race problem. As young people attend college and meet people of all different races, cultures, and backgrounds, they become more aware of and better educated about racial problems. As exposure increases, tolerance does also. Both age and education remained strong predictors of attitudes toward interracial marriage when other variables were introduced into the analysis. Strength of religious conviction also remains significantly related to attitudes about interracial marriages even when age and education were controlled.

Social class, whether measured by occupational prestige, educational level, income, or self-described social class, was consistently related to attitudes about interracial marriages. Income, however, showed the weakest relationship, and education level no doubt accounts for some of the effects of occupation prestige and income in a multivariate analysis.

A final factor may also contribute to the changing attitudes towards interracial marriage. As interracial marriages themselves increase, acceptance increases. Some authors have suggested that the "contact hypothesis" may reduce prejudice under the following favorable conditions: 1) interracial contact, 2) absence of interracial competition for scarce resources, 3) equal status for members of both races, and 4) firm support from the relevant authorities (see for example, Pettigrew, 1971; Cook, 1978, 1988). As the number of interracial marriages continues to increase and as people increasingly know individuals involved in such marriages, the attitudes towards interracial marriages may change considerably.

Cognitive Consistency theories also argue that people mold their behavior and attitudes to their previous dispositions. As Sears, Peplau, and Taylor (1988) state:

Interracial contact is probably the most effective technique for reducing prejudice. But by itself, it is not extremely effective; it is more likely to be successful if it involves sustained close contact, cooperative interdependence, and equal status, and is supported by local norms. Our society is not organized very well to provide the kinds of interracial contact that best break down racial prejudices. For that reason, special efforts need to be made if prejudice is to be reduced substantially (Sears, Peplau, and Taylor, 1988:427).

Though the rate of interracial marriage may reflect extant racial attitudes, they may also provide the "special efforts" needed to bring about changes in racial acceptance.

REFERENCES

Alba, Richard D. and Reid M. Golden. 1986. "Patterns of ethnic marriage in the United States." *Social Forces* 65:202-219.

Beigel, Hugo. 1966. "Problems and motives in interracial relationships." *Journal of Sex Research* 2:185-205.

Brown, John A. 1987. "Casework contacts with black-white couples." *Social Casework: The Journal of Contemporary Social Work*. Pp. 24-29.

Cook, S.W. 1978. "Interpersonal and attitudinal outcomes in cooperating interracial groups." *Journal of Research and Development in Education* 12:97-113.

Cook, S.W. 1988. "The 1954 social science statement and school desegregation: A reply to Gerard." Pp. 237-256 in P.A. Katz and D.A. Taylor (eds.), *Eliminating Racism: Profiles in Controversy*. New York: Plenum.

Crain, Robert L. and Rita E. Mahard. 1978. "Desegregation and black achievement: A review of the research." *Law and Contemporary Problems* 42:17-56.

Cygnar, Thomas E., Cardell K. Jacobson, and Donald L. Noel. 1977. "Religiosity and prejudice: An interdimensional analysis." *Journal for the Scientific Study of Religion* 16:183-191.

Davis, James A. and Tom W. Smith. 1988. *General Social Surveys, 1972-1988.* Cumulative Codebook. Chicago: NORC.

Davis, Kingsley. 1941. "Intermarriage in caste society." *American Anthropologist* 43:338-395.

Firebaugh, Glenn and Kenneth E. Davis. 1988. "Trends in antiblack prejudice, 1972-1984: Region and cohort effects." *American Journal of Sociology* 94:251-272.

Glick, Paul C. 1988. "Fifty years of family demography: A record of social change." *Journal of Marriage and the Family* 50:861-873.

Gordon, Albert I. 1964. *Intermarriage.* Westport, Connecticut: Greenwood Press.

Heer, David M. 1966. "Negro-White marriage in the United States." *Journal of Marriage and the Family* 28:262-273.

Jeter, Kris. 1982. *Analytic Essay: Intercultural and Interracial Marriage.* Binghamton, NY: The Haworth Press.

Labov, Teresa and Jerry A. Jacobs. 1986. "Intermarriage in Hawaii, 1950-1983." *Journal of Marriage and the Family* 48:79-88.

Monahan, Thomas P. 1976. "The occupational class of couples entering into interracial marriages." *Journal of Comparative Family Studies* 7:175-189.

Pavela, Todd H. 1964. "An exploratory study of Negro-White intermarriage in Indiana." *Journal of Marriage and the Family* 26:209-211.

Pettigrew, Thomas F. 1971. *Racially Separate or Together?* New York: McGraw-Hill.

Porterfield, Ernest. 1978. *Black and White Mixed Marriages*. Chicago, IL: Nelson-Hall, Inc.

_____. 1982. "Black-American intermarriage in the United States." *Marriage and Family Review* 5:17-34.

Rice, F. Philip. 1990. *Intimate Relationships, Marriage, and Families*. London-Toronto: Mayfield Publishing Co.

Roof, Wade Clark and William McKinney. 1987. *American Mainline Religion: Its Changing Shape and Future*. New Brunswick, New Jersey: Rutgers University Press, XIV:279.

Schoen, Robert and John Wooldredge. 1989. "Marriage and choices in North Carolina and Virginia, 1969-71 and 1979-81." *Journal of Marriage and the Family* 51:465-481.

Schuman, Howard, Charlotte Steeh, and Lawrence Bobo. 1985. *Racial Attitudes in America: Trends and Interpretations*. Cambridge, MA: Harvard University Press.

Sears, David O., Letitia Anne Peplau, and Shelley E. Taylor. 1988. *Social Psychology*. Seventh Edition. Englewood Cliffs, NJ: Prentice-Hall.

Tucker, M. Belinda and Claudia Mitchell-Kernan. 1990. "New trends in Black American interracial marriage: The social structural context." *Journal of Marriage and the Family* 52:209-218.

U.S. Bureau of the Census. 1990. *Statistical Abstract of the United States: 1990*. (110th edition). Washington, DC: Government Printing Office.

Washington, Joseph R., Jr. 1970. *Marriage in Black and White*. Boston: Beacon Press.

Yetman, Norman R. 1985. *Majority and Minority: The Dynamics of Race and Ethnicity in American Life*. Boston: Allyn and Bacon, Inc.

Zabel, William D. 1965. "Interracial marriage and the law." *Atlantic Monthly* 216:114-125.

Perceptions of Marital Stability of Black-White Intermarriages

Anna Y. Chan and Ken R. Smith

INTRODUCTION

Limited empirical work has been done on the marital consequences of interracial marriages. Speculation on the well-being and marital stability of such marriages is mostly negative although that view has never been tested rigorously. This question warrants more research since the prevalance of interracial marriages is increasing. From 1970 to 1992, the numbers of such marriages have increased fourfold, from 310,000 to almost 1.2 million, a rise from 0.6 percent to 2.2 percent of all intact marriages in the United States (U.S. Bureau of the Census, 1992).

PREVIOUS RESEARCH

The few empirical studies that have examined the marital stability of interracial couples are inconclusive even when only one mixed-race combination is being considered (e.g., black-white marriages or Asian-white marriages). For instance, Monahan (1970) found that black husband-white wife marriages have a lower divorce rate than do white marriages. Conversely, Rankin and Maneker (1987) found that black husband-white wife marriages had higher rates of divorce compared to white marriages as well as couples comprised of black or white husbands married to black wives. At the same time, white husband-black wife marriages have a lower divorce rate compared to white marriages. Similar to research on black-white marriages, the overall findings on the stability of Asian-white marriages are mixed. Ho and Johnson (1990) and Sung (1990) found that interracial marriages between Asian

Americans and Caucasians do not have higher divorce rates than white and Asian couples. Schwertfeger (1982), however, found that the overall divorce rate is higher for intermarriages than intramarriages among Asian Americans.

Despite the inconsistent results regarding the marital stability of interracial marriages, findings on the characteristics of interracially married individuals are consistent. Higher educational level, older age at marriage, greater age differences between spouses, greater number of prior marriages, and fewer children were characteristics found more among interracial couples than among same-race couples (Kitano and Yeung, 1982; Rankin and Maneker, 1987; Sung, 1990; Tinker, 1982; Tucker and Mitchell-Kernan, 1990). These personal characteristics may confound the relation between rates of marital instability and the racial composition of the couple. For example, the absence of children and the relatively higher economic status among intermarried couples may have enhanced the prospects of divorce among interracial marriages rather than the racial makeup of the spouses *per se*. Therefore, one may expect the effect of the race of spouses on marital stability to disappear if these factors were controlled for. This study will examine this possibility.

The inconsistent findings of prior research on the marital stability of interracial marriages may be attributed to weaknesses of the data collected in these studies. Since the majority of these studies are geographically limited, the generalizability of their findings is a concern. The national random sample used in this study may provide a better picture of the marital stability of interracial marriages. Moreover, these studies have examined the marital stability of such unions based on the divorce rate of intermarriages. Although divorce is an obvious indicator that a marriage was unstable, there are other factors that may have kept an unsatisfactory marriage intact. Hence, in this study, self-reported measures among intermarried and intramarried couples who are still married will be used to measure marital stability.

Given the paucity of research on the marital stability of interracial couples, theory on closely related topics is adapted to formulate hypotheses that may describe the mechanisms underlying differences in perceived marital stability between inter- and intramarried couples. Status inconsistency theory may help to explain these differences. Status inconsistency theory is grounded on the idea that societies are based on numerous social hierarchies. For example, persons with both higher levels of income and education have more power and prestige than those who have lower levels of these resources. This theory relies on the fact that certain status categories are closely associated such that those with higher income should also be those with more education. In any hierarchical society, rankings may not be consistent such that others' expectations about a person's behavior are unclear. Again, other people may not know what to expect of someone who is highly educated but in a menial occupation. The person himself may be unsure what to do because different social norms would dictate different behaviors for both rankings, but these expectations would likely be in conflict. Being unable to resolve this conflict, a status-inconsistent individual is more likely to experience role conflict leading to undesirable social outcomes.

Originally, status inconsistency theory stated that when an individual simultaneously occupied positions of unequal rank across multiple status hierarchies such as occupation, income, education, and ethnicity, harmful consequences would result (Stryker and Macke, 1978; Vernon and Buffler, 1988). An extension of this theory to racial/ethnic issues may be appropriate for explaining attitudes and behavior among intermarried couples. From this perspective, the United States may be seen as a racially stratified country, with racial minorities historically ranked lower in status than (non-Hispanic) whites. Because social disapproval may be higher for interracial couples, status inconsistency theory would predict more negative outcomes among interracial couples. The status inconsistency between husbands and wives in interracial marriages, particularly marriages between minorities and non-Hispanic whites, may increase the social stressors on the marriages resulting in harmful consequences, including a higher chance of marital dissolution. If this theory is correct, we may expect to find lower levels of marital stability among interracial marriages. The argument is that others are simply unsure what to expect of black-white unions, partly because most persons in the United States have little first-hand experience in interacting with such couples. Moreover, prevailing social mores seldom support such unions, and both positive and negative feelings may be quite strong among in-laws. At the same time, interracial couples themselves may be unsure about what they see as appropriate expectations for themselves. In any case, the interracial marriage may encounter more role conflict and stress than otherwise comparable intramarried couples.

Research Hypotheses

Based on the literature and the types of data that are available for analysis from the 1988 National Survey of Families and Households (NSFH), two hypotheses are drawn. First, we expect interracial marriages to be less stable than same-race marriages. Second, the effect should persist even after controlling for their educational level, ages at marriage, ages at the time of the interview, age differences of couples, number of children, number of prior marriages, region of residence, and religious homogamy/heterogamy of couples. In our analyses, we specifically examine white-black intermarriages. Other racial combinations observed in the NSFH were too few in number to make their analysis meaningful.

Data

This study is based on data from NSFH, a national probability sample of noninstitutional adults in the United States in 1988. The full survey consists of interviews with an adult in 13,017 households. The survey data were collected between March 1987 and May 1988. One adult from each household was randomly selected to be the primary respondent. The spouse or cohabiting partner of the primary respondent was given a shorter self-administered questionnaire.

For the purposes of this study, only married respondents were selected from the total sample. The sample was further delimited to interracial couples and same-race couples (black and white couples only). The number of white couples (4,378) in the full NSFH sample was too large to use as a comparison group, thus 25 percent of the original white couple subsample was randomly selected. If the size of the comparison group (all white couples) is large relative to the size of other racial groups, it would generally lead to statistically significant results, even if the effect of interest is relatively small. A total of 2,101 couples were selected for the analysis (see Table 1 for the racial breakdown and frequency of the final sample).

Weights have been used for the final sample so that estimated statistics can be generalized to all couples in the United States in 1988. However, each racial group is weighted separately so that the number of couples in each racial group is the same before and after weighting.

Table 1

Frequency Distribution of Inter/Intraracial Married Couples
in the Final Weighted Sample

Couples' Race Husband's/Wife's	Frequency	%	Cum %
Black/white	27	1.3	1.3
White/black	12	.6	1.8
Asian/white	13	.6	6.6
White/Asian	14	.7	7.2
Mexican/white	48	2.3	4.2
White/Mexican	37	1.7	5.9
Native American/white	21	1.0	8.2
White/Native American	21	1.0	9.2
Black/black	534	25.4	34.6
Asian/Asian	39	1.9	46.5
Mexican/Mexican	211	10.1	44.6
White/white	1124	53.5	100.0
Total	2101	100.0	

This means that the relative influences of cases within the group will mirror the national population of all couples of that group in the U.S. in 1988. The weighted percentage of interracial couples estimated from these data is between 1.4 and 1.7 percent (not shown in Table 1). This percentage is very close to the estimation by the 1980 U.S. Census, which reported 1.5 percent for interracial marriages.

The primary independent variable in this study is the racial composition of the couple. Black men-white women marriages are coded as BW, whereas white men-black women marriages are coded as WB. Black couples are coded as BB and white couples are coded as WW. These variables are coded as dummy variables in the analysis. The control variables are respondents' educational level, ages at marriage, ages at the time of the interview, age differences of couples, number of prior marriages, number of children, region of residence, and religious homogamy/heterogamy of couples. The religion of each couple was coded into four dummy variables: 1) both husband and wife have no religion (Norel) (omitted group), 2) husband and wife have different religions (Difrel), 3) only one spouse is religious (Onerel), and 4) the couple has same religion (Samrel). Because little is known about the religion of interracial couples, it is important to examine the religion of such couples. In this study, religion homogamy/heterogamy will be controlled to test whether it may account for the variation in marital stability among interracial couples.

The dependent variable in this analysis is perceived marital stability. Spouses' attitudes towards the likelihood that their marriages will remain intact and the perception of their marriages being in trouble are based on self-reported measures. Four different questions were asked:

1. "It is always difficult to predict what will happen in a marriage, but realistically, what do you think the chances are that you and your husband/wife will eventually separate or divorce?" (CHANCESEP).

2. "During the past year, have you ever thought that your marriage might be in trouble?" (TROUBLY).

3. "Do you feel that way now?" (TROUNOW).

4. "During the past year, have you and your husband/wife discussed the idea of separating?" (SEPLY).

The TROUNOW and the SEPLY questions were asked only if the respondent had answered "yes" to the TROUBLY question.

Responses for the CHANCESEP question ranged from very low (5) to very high (1). Responses for questions TROUNOW and SEPLY were recoded as (0) "no" and (1) "yes." A no response for question TROUNOW occurs when a respondent replied no to question TROUBLY or no to question TROUNOW. Similarly, a no response for question SEPLY occurs if a respondent said no to question TROUBLY or no to question SEPLY. In general, higher values of any of the dependent variables suggest that couples are in marriages that are less stable.

The marital well-being of black-white couples will be compared to those of white couples and black couples. Because race has a potentially important interaction effect with the gender of respective spouses, the well-being of black men-white women marriages will also be compared to those of white men-black women marriages.

Method

Multiple ordinary least squares regression and logistic regression methods are used for the statistical analysis. Although the first question on marital stability (CHANCESEP) is an ordinal variable, it approximates an interval level variable. Accordingly, ordinary least squares (OLS) regression methods are used. The remaining three questions (TROULY, TROUNOW, and SEPLY) are dichotomous variables and are analyzed using logistic regression methods.

Equation 1 illustrates the specification for one of the logistic regressions, the TROULY equation. We report odds ratios estimated from this equation. Exp (b) represents the odds ratio based on a comparison between any of the intermarried groups with the white-white group (WW). For example, if exp (b13) equals 1.85, it means that black men with white wives are 1.85 times more likely to report that they were experiencing trouble with their marriages the year before the interview than husbands of white unions. If exp (b13) equals .25, it means that the marriages of black men with white wives are one-fourth as likely to be in trouble during the year before the interview than husbands of white unions. For illustrative purposes, Equation 1 treats WW as the comparison group:

(1) $\underline{\text{Probability (TROULY=1)}}$ =
Probability (TROULY=0)

exp (a + bl*Education + b2*Age + b3*(Age Difference) + b4*(Age at marriage) + b5*(Number of prior marriages) + b6*(Number of kids) + b7*Samrel + b8*Onerel + b9*Difrel + b10*South = b11*North Central + b12*West + b13*BW = b14*WB + b15*BB)

Weighted regression analyses were conducted with the couples' religious affiliation first excluded but then included. This was done so that it was possible to see more clearly how the effects of religious homogamy/heterogamy might confound the effects of racial homogamy/heterogamy.

RESULTS

Descriptive statistics of the personal characteristics for husbands and wives of different racial combination are presented in Table 2. These are descriptive statistics without any statistical adjustment except weighting. On average, both intermarried men and women were younger at the time of the interview than those who were not. Intermarried couples tended to be older at the time of marriage and appear to have greater age differences between husbands and wives in either direction compared to same-race couples. Black and white individuals who intermarried have higher educational levels and fewer children than their same-race counterparts. Their higher educational level means that they have stayed in school longer than same-race couples and hence may have delayed their marriages as well as their childbearing. Intermarried couples were also less likely to have the same religion or more likely to have only one spouse who was religious than same-race couples. High percentages of black-white couples resided in the West and Northeastern part of the country, while black couples resided predominately in the South. Lastly, couples of black men-white women unions were more likely to have married more than once compared to same-race couples. In sum, the findings coincide with many previous studies on the correlates of intermarried persons.

Almost all of the independent variables (except age differences between husband and wife) have statistically significant effects on at least two or more models (results not shown). Even though these variables have been controlled for in the models, a couple's racial status continued to affect the marital stability for black men-white women combinations.

Regression Results

This section presents weighted statistical results based on regressions that control for education, age at the time of the interview, age at marriage, age differences of couples, number of prior marriages, number of children, region of residence, and religious homogamy/ heterogamy. Results of weighted regressions before the control of religious heterogamy and results of unweighted regressions are now shown. Notable effects of weighting the data and controlling for religious heterogamy/homogamy are described where appropriate. Results

Table 2

Descriptive Statistics *(Means/Proportions and Standard Deviations)
for Dependent and Independent Variables

Racial Combinations	Husbands				Wives			
	BW	WB	BB	WW	BW	WB	BB	WW
Variables:								
Education (years)	13.45	13.52	11.28	13.17	12.12	14.32	12.19	12.99
	(2.41)	(2.17)	(3.71)	(3.15)	(2.36)	(2.42)	(2.91)	(2.60)
Age (years)	39.58	39.29	46.46	47.79	35.40	39.29	45.53	45.06
	(9.51)	(13.85)	(15.16)	(15.71)	(9.69)	(13.85)	(14.45)	(15.30)
Age at marriage (years)	30.01	30.82	27.82	27.12	25.83	25.78	24.90	24.38
	(6.88)	(10.88)	(9.13)	(8.98)	(7.04)	(3.99)	(7.67)	(8.14)
Age difference (H-W0	4.18	5.04	2.92	2.73	1.35	1.09	1.20	1.23
	(.78)	(1.44)	(.57)	(.52)	(.55)	(.30)	(.45)	(.50)
Number of prior marriages	1.49	1.84	1.28	1.24				
Number of kids	1.09	1.36	1.58	1.15	1.35	1.03	1.36	1.20
Proportion/same religion	.43	.44	.62	.62	.50	.52	.49	.48
Proportion/one spouse religious	.07	.22	.06	.09	.26	.43	.23	.28

table continues

Table 2 (continued)

Racial Combinations	Husbands				Wives			
	BW	WB	BB	WW	BW	WB	BB	WW
Variables:								
Proportion/different religions	.46	.34	.29	.25	(.51)	(.50)	(.45)	(.43)
Proportion of no religion	.05	.00	.01	.03	(.22)	(.00)	(.07)	(.16)
South	.15	.14	.60	.35	(.36)	(.36)	(.49)	(.48)
West	.42	.17	.08	.17	(.50)	(.39)	(.27)	(.40)
North Central	.26	.38	.15	.28	(.45)	(.51)	(.36)	(.45)
North East	.17	.31	.17	.20	(.38)	(.48)	(.38)	(.40)
Chance of separating**	4.37	4.53	4.51	4.70	4.09	4.57	4.41	4.71
	(.90)	(.78)	(.87)	(.61)	(1.19)	(.83)	(.93)	(.60)
Marriage/trouble in last yr	.40	.29	.20	.21	.47	.40	.26	.23
	(.50)	(.47)	(.40)	(.40)	(.51)	(.51)	(.44)	(.42)
Marriage in trouble now	.13	.04	.09	.05	.29	.12	.11	.08
	(.34)	(.20)	(.29)	(.22)	(.46)	(.34)	(.31)	(.27)
Discussed sep in last year	.23	.13	.13	.10	.20	.04	.17	.11
	(.13)	(.35)	(.33)	(.30)	(.41)	(.21)	(.38)	(.32)

*no statistical adjustment except weighting
**(5) equals very low and (1) equals very high

of the regression analyses are presented separately for husbands and wives.

Regression coefficients (b) or odds ratios (exp b) are reported in Table 3. For models estimated using OLS regressions, the coefficients indicate the estimated differences between marital stability of husbands/wives of interracial marriages and husbands/wives of the comparison group after other variables are controlled for. The entries in Table 3 for CHANCESEP represent the difference in points on this 5-point scale.

To read Table 3, one first selects a row which is labeled white couples, black couples, or black men-white women for each model. To compare one of these three groups to one of the other three, one then selects the appropriate column (labeled black couples, black men-white women, or white men-black women). After selecting a comparison, one can see how the "row" group differs from the "column" group. For example, in Table 3, husbands from black men-white women marriages are -.20 points lower on the 5-point marital stability scale than husbands from white couples. For dichotomous dependent variables that were analyzed with logistic regressions, the entries are odds ratios based on comparisons between a "row" group versus a "column" group.

Because the sample size of intermarried groups is small, it is more difficult to detect significant effects of interest. Hence, whenever the results revealed that the husbands'/wives' marital stability of a particular racial union is always either generally better off or worse off than the comparison groups, they will be described as having a tendency to be better off or having a tendency to be worse off than the comparison group.

Husbands. Overall, there were no significant differences between husbands of intermarriages from husbands of same-race marriages in any of the measures (except for CHANCESEP which was significant only before weighting). All these results remained nonsignificant when religion was controlled for the weighted sample. However, there appears to be a tendency for husbands of white men-black women to perceive their marriages to be more stable than all other groups across the four dependent variables. They were less likely to think that their marriages might have been in trouble both the year before and at the time of the interview compared to the other three groups. They also

Table 3

Differences in Perceived Marital Stability
by Four Black-White Inter/Intraracial Categories
Based on OLS and Logistic Regression

	Husbands			Wives		
Variables	White couples	Black couples	Black men-white women	White couples	Black couples	Black men-white women
Model 1 (CHANCESEP)						
Black couples	-.17****			-.26**		
Black men-white women	-.20	-.03		-.53****	-.27*	
White men-black women	-.14	.03	.07	-.02	.25	.52**
Model 2 (TROULY)						
Black couples	1.07			1.20		
Black men-white women	1.85	1.72		2.25*	1.88	
White men-black women	0.98	0.92	0.53	1.25	1.05	0.56

table continues

Table 3 (continued)

Variables	Husbands			Wives		
	White couples	Black couples	Black men-white women	White couples	Black couples	Black men-white women
Model 3 (TROUNOW)						
Black couples	1.98**			1.55**	2.80**	
Black men–white women	2.05	1.03		4.35***	0.75	
White men–black women	0.48	0.24	0.24	1.16		0.27
Model 4 (SEPLY)						
Black couples	1.37*			1.75***	0.74	
Black men–white women	2.05	1.50		1.29	0.12	
White men–black women	0.71	0.52	0.35	0.21		0.16

****p < .001
***p < .01
**p < .05
*p < .1

have a tendency to be less likely to have discussed separation with their wives.

In general, husbands of black unions viewed their marriages as less stable than husbands of white unions. The former group throught that they have higher chances of separating from their spouses compared to husbands of white unions (p < .001). They were also more likely to think that their marriages might have been in trouble at the time of interview compared to husbands of white unions (p < .01). Husbands of black unions were 1.37 times more likely to have discussed separation with their spouse than husbands of white unions (p < .1). This difference was not significant before religion was controlled for.

Wives. Overall, wives of black men-white women unions are significantly more likely to report that their marriage is less stable than any other racial combination. They thought that they have higher chances of separating from their spouse than all other groups (they do not differ from wives of black couples before weighting). This difference is significant at the p < .001 level compared to wives of white unions, at the p < .1 level compared to wives of black unions, and at the p < .05 level compared to wives of white men-black women unions.

White women married to black men were 2.25 times more likely to think that their marriages might have been in trouble the year before the interview than white women with same-race husbands (p < .1). This significant effect remained when religion was controlled for. They were also three to four times more likely to think that their marriages might have been in trouble at the time of the interview compared to white women (p < .01 level) as well as black women with same-race husbands (p < .05). Both of these two measures were nonsignificant before weighting.

Among wives of same-race marriages, wives of black unions were significantly more likely to think that their marriage might have been in trouble at the time of the interview compared to wives of white unions (p < .05). They were also 1.75 times more likely to have discussed separation with their spouses than wives of white unions (p < .01). These differences were significant both before and after religion was controlled for.

Like their husbands, wives of white men-black women marriages appear to view their marriage as being better off than wives of same-race couples, although results are not statistically significant. Furthermore, they have a tendency to report less trouble both the year before and at the time of the interview. They were also less likely to have discussed separation the year before the interview. In sum, there is a tendency for spouses in white men-black women marriages to report their marriages as being very stable, if not more stable than same-race couples.

DISCUSSION

This study does not support the general notion that black-white marriages are perceived as less stable. Although the overall perceived marital stability is significantly lower for wives of black men-white women marriages than all other groups, both husbands and wives of white men-black women appear to perceive their marriages as more stable than husbands and wives of same-race unions.

The discrepancy between husbands and wives of black men-white women unions on the stability of their marriages suggests an important race by gender effect. Although the wives significantly reported lower marital stability, the husbands do not differ significantly from any other group. Moreover, in the United States, the socioeconomic status of couples is traditionally based on the husband's status rather than the wife's. The potentially lower socioeconomic standing of racial/ethnic minorities may have lowered the social status of white women with black husbands. Thus, the marital quality of white women may have been adversely affected if they married minority men. However, some of these socioeconomic effects have been controlled for in these analyses through the inclusion of education as one of the control variables.

Another reason why black men-white women couples seem to be worse off than other groups may be that they are more concerned about the well-being of their biracial children. Intermarried couples may worry more than same-race couples about their children's social and psychological health because of the children's mixed parentage. Especially in the case of white women married to black men; their children are likely to "look" more black than white. This may create more stress for the mother who is most likely to be the primary child caretaker and have to deal with the prejudice others might have about her children. Thus, such concerns may have lowered the perceived marital quality of these couples.

This finding supports the status inconsistency theory that formal and informal social institutions serve to cause more stress and problems for status-inconsistent couples (intermarried) than status-consistent couples (intramarried) partly because of conflicting expectations that others as well as interracial couples themselves have about mixed marriages. Unfortunately, this study was unable to control directly for the actual social mechanisms that may be operating to create the negative social sanctions suggested by status inconsistency theory. Although religious homogamy/heterogamy was being controlled for in the analysis, black men-white women marriages were still found to be less stable than same-race couples.

White men-black women marriages appeared to be better off than same-race couples for both husbands and wives: Since contemporary Afro-American society tends to be a matriarchal society where social networks are maintained by women, black women who married white men are likely to have strong family ties that will in turn provide support for their marriages and their children, thus these factors may outweigh the hypothesized adverse effects of racial/social status inconsistency.

This study suggests that the stress brought on by attitudes concerning racial/ethnic minorities for both husbands and wives, and the potentially conflictual relationships with in-laws, may lower the perceived marital satisfaction and stability of intermarried couples rather than their race/ethnicity *per se*. Moreover, the dramatic sex-specific variation in perceived marital stability of black and white individuals who intermarry depending on their gender confirms earlier studies that there is a race by gender interaction effect. Future study should focus on how these factors may serve to explain the marital stability effects reported here and how they may interact with the racial combinations of the couples to produce negative effects on the marriages.

The findings from this study suggest several important future studies:

1. Examine differences in sex role expectations and their interaction with the race/ethnicity of husbands and wives and their effects on the marital stability of intermarried and intramarried couples.

2. Examine how family support and relationships with in-laws affect the marital stability of interracial couples.

3. Examine the presence and well-being of biracial/biethnic children and how these factors may affect the marital stability of intermarried couples.

As with any study there are some limitations to our analysis. First, the sample size of intermarried couples is relatively small. Some key variables were unavailable in this study including total household income and information on in-laws and social support. Also, the estimation of interactive effects between the racial/ethnic combinations with some variables was not feasible due to the small sample size of the intermarried groups.

Despite these limitations, the strengths of this study outweigh these weaknesses. This study is based on a national sample of married couples. This study examined marital quality in intact families rather than divorced couples so that potential marital problems of these intermarriages, while still intact, could be revealed. The measures for the dependent variables also explored different dimensions of marital stability, i.e., attitudes on whether one thinks there was trouble in the marriages and whether the individuals actually discussed separation with their spouses. Lastly, both the husbands' and wives' perspectives on their marital quality were obtained and, in fact, did show discrepancies in black men-white women unions.

REFERENCES

Ho, F.C., and Johnson, R. 1990. "Intraethnic and interethnic marriage and divorce in Hawaii." *Social Biology* 37 (1-2):44-51.

Kitano, H., and Yeung, W.T. 1982. "Chinese interracial marriage." *Marriage and Family Review* 5 (1):35-48.

Monahan, T. 1970. "Are intermarriages less stable?" *Social Forces* 48: 461-473.

National Survey of Families and Households, 1988. 1988. [Machine-readable data file] James Sweet and Larry Bumpass, principal investigators. Distributed by the Center for Demography and Ecology, University of Wisconsin-Madison, Madison, WI. For a description of this study see James Sweet, Larry Bumpass, and Vaughn Call. *The Design and Content of the National Survey of Families and Households.* Working Paper NSFH-1, Center for Demography and Ecology, University of Wisconsin-Madison.

Rankin, R., and Maneker, J. 1987. "Correlates of marital duration and black-white intermarriage in California." *Journal of Divorce* 11 (2):51-67.

Schwertfeger, M. 1982. "Interethnic marriages and divorce in Hawaii: A panel study of 1968 first marriages." *Marriage and Family Review* 5:49-60.

Stryker, S., and Macke, A. 1978. "Status inconsistency and role conflict." *Annual Review Sociology* 4:57-90.

Sung, B. 1990. "Chinese American intermarriage." *Journal of Comparative Family Studies* 21 (3):337-352.

Tinker, J. 1982. "Intermarriage and assimilation in a plural society: Japanese Americans in the United States." Pp. 61-74 in G. Cretser, and J. Leon (ed.), *Intermarriage in the United States.* New York: Haworth Press.

Tucker, M. B., and Mitchell-Kernan, C. 1990. "New trends in black American interracial marriage: The social structural context." *Journal of Marriage and the Family* 52:209-218.

U.S. Bureau of the Census. 1992. *Statistical Abstract of the United States: 1992* (112th edition). Washington, DC: U.S. Government Printing Office.

Vernon, S., and Buffler, P. 1988. "The status of status inconsistency." *Epidemiologic Review* 10:65-86.

Education and Family Structure

Issues

The Chicano Family and Educational Outcomes: An Interpretative Review of the Sociological and Psychological Literature

Adalberto Aguirre, Jr. and Anthony C.R. Hernandez

There is growing concern that the Chicano population will enter the 21st century relatively undereducated. While the Chicano population has made relative gains in its educational outcomes over the last four decades, it has yet to attain comparable educational outcomes with other ethnic and racial groups in the U.S. population. In 1990, for example, less than half (44.1 percent) of 25-year-old and older persons in the Chicano population had completed four years or more of high school (U.S. Bureau of the Census, 1991a, 1991b, 1992; Paisano, 1992). In comparison, the completion of four years or more of high school for other ethnic and racial groups in the U.S. population was as follows: Asian (80.6 percent), white (79.1 percent), black (65.5 percent), American Indian (65.5 percent), Cuban (63.5 percent), Puerto Rican (55.5 percent). Similarly, the completion of four years or more of college for 25-year-old and older persons in 1990 by ethnic and racial group were as follows: Asian (44.4 percent), white (28.5 percent), Cuban (20.2 percent), black (11.4 percent), Puerto Rican (9.7 percent), American Indian (9.3 percent), Chicano (5.4 percent). The educational outcomes of the Chicano population clearly lag behind those of other ethnic and racial groups in the U.S. population.

POPULATION CHANGE

Between 1980 and 1990, the Chicano population added 4.6 million persons to its number: from 8.7 million in 1980 to 13.3 million in 1990 (U.S. Bureau of the Census, 1991a, 1982). The Chicano population's share of the U.S. population increased from 3.8 percent in 1980 to 5.4 percent in 1990. The numerical increase of the Chicano population between 1980 and 1990 earned it the title of "fastest growing" minority population in the United States. In California, where the Chicano population almost doubled between 1980 and 1990, the title of "fastest-growing" is ominous. In addition to its numerical growth, the Chicano population has become more "youthful." In 1990, one-third of the Chicano population was under 15 years of age, compared to 21 percent of the U.S. population. In contrast, 32 percent of the U.S. population was 45 years old and older, compared to 16 percent of the Chicano population. In a sense, the "youthfulness" of the Chicano population became noticeable between 1980 and 1990 when the largest proportional increase in the population occurred in the number of persons under the age of 15.

A DILEMMA

Continued growth and youthfulness in the Chicano population may create a dilemma for its educational outcomes. The "youthfulness" of the population will result in Chicano students comprising a visible, and possibly significant, proportion of the school-age population in the 21st century (Chapa, 1990). If one assumes that the Chicano population will not attain a 50 percent or higher completion outcome for 4 years or more of high school by the end of the 1990s, then the Chicano population will enter the 21st century with a large proportion of undereducated persons. As a result, the Chicano population will face a dilemma in the 21st century because the proportion of undereducated persons will, in the aggregate, increase the population's social, political, and economic inequality.

A full examination of Chicano education is beyond the scope of this paper. Our purpose in this paper is more limited. We will examine one dimension of Chicano education: the Chicano family and educational outcomes. Some of the questions we use as guides for our discussion in this paper are: What does the research literature say about the Chicano family and educational socialization? What socio-cultural dimensions of the Chicano family are associated with educational aspirations? What contextual features of the Chicano family are associated with members' educational outcomes? We stress that these questions have a simple purpose—they are our guides through the research literature. As such, they are instrumental in facilitating the creation of a conceptual framework for examining both questions and answers regarding the Chicano family and educational outcomes.

UNIT OF ANALYSIS

We focus on the Chicano family in this paper for the following reasons. First, an extensive body of sociological and psychological literature exists that identifies *family socialization* as a crucial variable in shaping a child's cognitive orientation for school (Laosa, 1989; Bronfenbrenner, 1979; Coleman, 1987; Stryker and Serpe, 1983; Mehan, 1992). Second, as a challenge to popular beliefs that the Chicano family's socialization practices are detrimental to the formation of cognitive orientations in Chicano children, researchers have identified dimensions in the Chicano family that provide children with cognitive skills necessary to successful school performance (Delgado-Gaitan, 1992; Laosa, 1980a, 1980b; Delgado-Gaitan and Segura, 1989; Velez-Ibanez and Greenberg, 1992b; Martinez, 1986). As such, the family in general, and the Chicano family in particular, is identified in the sociological and psychological literature as a primary socializing agent in the acquisition and development of a child's cognitive orientations.

SCOPE OF ANALYSIS

We review primarily the sociological and psychological literature since 1980. The parameters of the literature review are limited to the Chicano family and educational outcomes. To limit the number of interpretive issues, such as ethnic designation, that often arise in a literature review, we focus our literature review on published material that utilizes "Chicano" as the principal descriptor. As a result, we excluded from our review published material that utilized competing descriptors, such as "Hispanic" or "Latino." In doing so, we hope to reinforce the observation made by researchers that the Chicano family is meaningful and deserves research attention (Williams, 1990; Velez-Ibanez and Greenberg, 1992a; Zinn, 1979). We also hope to identify "markers" in the sociological and psychological research literature that describe the association between the Chicano family and educational outcomes.

LITERATURE REVIEW

We have summarized our review of the sociological and psychological literature in Table 1. We use the term *structural factor* in Table 1 to identify factors that serve as pathways for a person's entry into and participation in formal organizations outside of the family. For example, "poverty status" not only defines a person's position in the social class structure, but it also serves as a "signal" utilized by a formal organization to determine a person's entry point and participation path. In the school sorting process, children from poor families are often tracked into contexts with limited educational opportunity. In turn, the pathways poor children travel in school result in constrained educational outcomes. In contrast, children from middle-class families are more likely to be tracked into contexts with a diverse set of educational opportunities and educational outcomes.

We use the term *contextual factor* in Table 1 to identify factors that form social meaning and construct the transmission of social experiences outside of the family. For example, as a contextual factor, "acculturation" provides a person with the ability to construct interpretative frameworks for social experiences outside of the family. These interpretative frameworks are vital to the depiction of everyday life as co-terminus with family life. As a result, an "acculturated" person is more likely to see himself or herself as a "member of the system" rather than as a limited participant. In contrast, a less acculturated person is more likely to see his or her social identity as a reflection of his or her limited appearance in everyday life.

STRUCTURAL FACTORS

Sociological Literature

In Table 1 we identify the following structural factors in the sociological literature: poverty status, householder education, family size. Based on the literature research, we make the following general observations regarding the association between the Chicano family and educational outcomes.

Table 1

Sociological and Psychological
Dimensions
by Structural and Contextual Factors

Dimensions

Sociological

Structural Factors: (1) Poverty Status (family), (2) Householder (head of) Education, (3) Family Size.

Sources: Velez-Ibanez and Greenberg, 1992a; Fligstein and Fernandez, 1982; Buriel and Saenz, 1980; McKee, 1989.

Contextual Factors: (1) Parental Acculturation, (2) Parental Teaching Style, (3) Mother's Role.

Sources: Manaster et al., 1992; Martinez, 1988; Delgado-Gaitan, 1992, 1988; Laosa, 1984; Gandara, 1982; Velez-Ibanez and Greenberg, 1992b.

Psychological

Structural Factors: (1) Home Language Background, (2) Family Generational Status, (3) Teacher Expectations.

Sources: Aguirre, 1979; Chapa and Valencia, 1993; Macias, 1993; Delgado-Gaitan and Trueba, 1991; Buriel and Cardoza, 1988; Garcia, 1985; Laosa, 1984; Wiley, 1989-1990.

Contextual Factors: (1) Achievement Motivation, (2) Self-Concept, (3) Prosocial Behavior.

Sources: Trueba, 1991; Laosa and Henderson, 1991; Valencia et al., 1985; Delgado-Gaitan and Allexsaht-Snider, 1992; Laosa, 1982, 1983; Achor and Morales, 1989; Cromwell and Ruiz, 1982; Romo, 1984.

Poverty status. As a social force in everyday life, poverty con-
strains a family's ability to promote the institutional participation of its
members. Regarding educational outcomes, poverty alters the life experience of a family such that children are not able to establish a continuous relationship and presence in the school. Poor Chicano families
are more likely than non-poor Chicano families to have children not
attending school and youth who have dropped out of high school.

Householder education. As a socializing agent in the family, the
head of the household's level of education is closely associated with the
educational outcomes of children in the home. One result is that children replicate their own household's educational characteristics. The
relatively low educational outcomes that characterize householders in
Chicano families are replicated by Chicano children in their educational
outcomes. In the aggregate then, the educational outcomes of Chicano
families have remained relatively undifferentiated across generations.

Family size. For Chicano families, family size is negatively associated with Chicano children's educational outcomes. On the one hand,
as Chicano family size increases beyond the traditional U.S. family unit
(two parents and two children), the chances that Chicano children will
not stay in school increase. On the other hand, the chances of Chicano
children staying in school increase as Chicano family size approximates
the traditional U.S. family unit.

The Chicano Family

Are the preceding general observations reflective of Chicano family
features? In Table 2 one can observe the following contrasting features
of Chicano and white families. One, almost three times as many Chicano families as white families were poor in 1990. In particular, almost
half of female householder Chicano families were poor in 1990. Two,
the majority of Chicano householders in 1990 were not high school
graduates. Three, Chicano families were larger in size than white
families in 1990. One-third of Chicano families in 1990 had five or
more persons compared to 12.6 percent of white families.

Though we are limited in our ability to speculate how the Chicano
family featured in Table 2 shapes educational outcomes, we can observe that the structural factors we identified in Table 1—poverty status,
householder education, family size—are conspicuous characteristics of
the Chicano family in 1990. Given the limitation these structural factors

Table 2

Select Features of White and
Chicano Families: 1990

Descriptor	Population	
	White	Chicano
Family Poverty		
Total Families	9.2%	25.7%
Householder not a high school graduate	20.4%	34.0%
Female householder, no husband present	30.4%	49.1%
Head of household education	20.3%	56.8%
Family Size		
1-2 persons	43.2%	22.0%
3-4 persons	4.2%	44.8%
5 or more persons	12.6%	33.2%
Mean Number of Persons	3.12	4.14

Source: U.S. Bureau of the Census, 1991a.

impose upon educational outcomes, one can speculate that educational outcomes in the Chicano population will remain relatively limited. That is, these structural factors will continue to have restraining effects on the population's educational outcomes.

Psychological Literature

We have identified in Table 1 the following structural factors in the psychological literature: home language background, family generational status, teacher expectations. Based upon our review of the literature, we make the following general observations regarding the association between the Chicano family and educational outcomes.

Home language background. Many Chicano children live in households where Spanish is spoken in varying degrees. One result is that Chicano children enter the school—a primarily English-speaking domain—with varying degrees of language skills and abilities in English. In the selection and sorting processes of the school, Chicano children identified as Spanish speakers are assigned to bilingual education classrooms or classrooms that offer supplementary instruction in English while reinforcing the home language (Spanish). The tracking of Chicano children into these types of programs results in educational paths that are difficult to change. In the end, Chicano children are tracked into educational paths with limited educational opportunity. In particular, these educational paths prevent Chicano children from engaging in everyday discourse with their English-speaking classmates that, in turn, would enable Chicano children to acquire the sociolinguistic codes expected in the school.

Family generational status. Each generation of Chicano families has its own unique set of socio-cultural experiences that are associated with educational outcomes. Although they share a cultural background, each generation competes for educational outcomes. In general, increased generational presence in the U.S. is associated with higher educational outcomes. In particular, increased generational presence in the U.S. is associated with higher levels of English-language proficiency. Since English-language skills and abilities are instrumental in promoting one's educational outcomes, the English-language skills of the Chicano family are associated with children's educational outcomes.

Teacher expectations. In order to make "sense" of classroom activity, teachers create sets of expectations for students based on their status characteristics—sex, race, ethnicity, etc. (Dusek and Joseph, 1983; Eccles, 1983; Good, 1987). However, since status characteristics are not ascribed equal value by teachers, teachers lower their expectations for some students. Teachers often have lower expectations for Chicano student classroom performance because they perceive Chicano children as culturally and linguistically deficient. In turn, lowered teacher expectations promote lowered educational outcomes in Chicano children.

CONTEXTUAL FACTORS

Sociological Literature

From the sociological literature, we have identified three contextual factors that affect Chicano student performance: parental acculturation, parental teaching styles, and mother's role in the schooling process. Based on the research literature, we make the following observations regarding the role of contextual factors in the association between the Chicano family and educational attainment.

Parental acculturation. Chicano parents' acculturation to U.S. society is closely associated with their children's educational outcomes. The closer Chicano parents approximate in their behavior and lifestyle the sociocultural orientations of U.S. society, the more their children enhance their expected educational outcomes. As Chicano parents structure a household to reflect the sociocultural orientations of U.S. society, children in the household expect to attain comparable levels of institutional participation of mainstream (white) persons in U.S. society. One of those expectations is comparable educational outcomes. Interestingly, a residual effect of approximating Anglo culture is a loss of Chicano values and cultural orientations.

Parental teaching styles. Chicano families in which parents emphasize independent problem-solving and open discussion tend to have children that continue their education beyond high school. The emphasis on problem-solving and open discussion is compatible with the competitive and independent learning environment children find in school and classroom. As a result, Chicano parents are perceived by their children as knowledgeable about the schooling process. Consequently, an important link is established between Chicano parents and the school that is vital to the educational outcomes of Chicano children.

Mothers' Role

In general, mothers spend a larger proportion of their household time than fathers in shaping the learning experiences of children. Mothers in Chicano families are more instrumental than fathers in promoting educational aspirations in children. Regardless of their educational background, mothers in Chicano families are effective in mediating their children's interaction with the school. In most cases, mothers in Chicano families become effective brokers between the home and the school. One result is that Chicano children perceive their mothers as active participants in the educational process. In addition, Chicano children perceive their mother's participation in the educational process as a source of support for their progression through the educational process. As a result, children in Chicano families that perceive their mothers as active participants in the educational process tend to progress further in the educational process.

The contextual factors we have identified in the sociological literature suggest that certain family dynamics in the Chicano family are instrumental in promoting educational aspirations and outcomes. The contextual factor *acculturation*, for example, reflects the association between participation in U.S. society and cultural knowledge. If a high degree of acculturation to U.S. sociocultural orientations is indicative of a person's increased participation in U.S. society, then one by-product of participation is access to a larger share of cultural knowledge for U.S. society. In turn, access to cultural knowledge produces a "fund of knowledge" that allows persons and their families to believe that they can be active and meaningful participants in society —especially in school (Velez-Ibanez and Greenberg, 1992a, 1992b; Moll et al., 1992).

We have noted that parental teaching style is crucial in providing children with the necessary cognitive skills to mediate their participation in school. A mismatch between parental teaching style and cognitive skills promoted in the classroom, for example, increases the probability that a child will not attain full participation in the classroom. Given that mothers in Chicano families play an active role in shaping their children's educational aspirations, it is likely that mothers in Chicano families may be in a position to change the perception Chicano children have of being "isolated" in the educational process. That is, mothers in Chicano families can play a strategic role in reducing their children's perceived isolation in the participatory culture of the school and classroom.

Psychological Literature

In Table 1 we have identified three contextual factors from our review of the psychological literature: achievement motivation, self-concept, prosocial behavior. The salient nature of these factors in the

Chicano family and their association with educational attainment can be summarized as follows.

Achievement motivation. Chicano children are characterized as having a low need for achievement. The perception by teachers of this low need for achievement results in a lack of achievement and poor academic performance.

Self-concept. Chicano students have negative or lower self-concepts than white students. The perception by teachers of Chicano students as having a negative self-concept results in their exclusion from the participatory activities of the classroom important to the acquisition of cognitive skills.

Prosocial behavior. Chicano families socialize their children to be cooperative and interdependent. In contrast, the school encourages competition and independence. This mismatch results in poor academic performance and fewer years of educational attainment.

Research on the constellation of contextual factors in the psychological literature has identified differences between Chicano and white students. Chicano students, in general, tend to have a negative or lower self-concept of ability, and lower achievement expectations than white students. In particular, Chicano students tend to have a cooperative prosocial behavior orientation toward achievement and motivation whereas white students tend to have a competitive prosocial behavior orientation. The difference in prosocial behavior orientations has been used to explain Chicano student's poor academic performance and lack of educational attainment. However, this explanation does not account for within group variability in academic performance and educational attainment. There are some Chicanos who are academically successful. As a result, explanations that focus on culture and socialization practices have been criticized as no more than a mechanism for stereotyping entire groups.

CONCLUDING REMARKS

Even though a tremendous overlap exists between the sociological and psychological literature regarding the study of educational outcomes and the Chicano family, there are distinct differences. First, the sociological literature examines the relationship of the Chicano family to educational outcomes as derivative of a structured social process. Consequently, the sociological literature focuses on the need for society to maximize the potential of its institutions, such as education, to alter personal identity by adapting them to meeting the needs of persons. In contrast, the psychological literature focuses on the need to alter personal identity in order to change structured expectations in society.

Secondly, the sociological literature identifies educational change as a probable outcome if social institutions undergo a "radical" transformation—such as, the complete transformation of a structure of opportunity that equates social benefits with social class position. In contrast, educational change in the psychological literature is a process of structural adaptation in which persons are responsible for altering their own position in the structure of opportunity. For example, the emphasis on cooperative learning is not intended to change educational outcomes. Rather, cooperative learning facilitates the adaptation of the person to instructional activities that may not be directly linked with educational outcomes. As such, cooperative learning appears to work because it looks like part of the structured instructional process in the school.

THE MICRO-MACRO LINK

There is a need for closer examination of the link between micro (e.g. contextual) dimensions of individual performance and macro (e.g. structural) dimensions of social behavior. Such an examination would coordinate areas of research focused on a unit of analysis in order to create a framework that utilizes the empirical knowledge to examine the "social reality" of Chicano education. One cannot assume that structural change will eventually occur in society for Chicano students by ignoring the need to develop effective techniques for promoting the identity of Chicano persons in a structured social process. One may, for example, regard cooperative learning as an instructional vehicle for enhancing the educational opportunity of Chicano students. But is this enough for them to be able to use educational outcomes as a means for changing their unequal position in U.S. society? Is cooperative learning an instructional vehicle that reinforces, rather than alters, the mismatch between Chicano cognitive orientations and school expectations?

Finally, our review of the sociological and psychological literature has identified some intriguing linkages between micro and macro dimensions. The link between generational presence in the U.S., home language background, and educational outcomes is an intriguing one.

On the surface, the link is linear: increased generational presence promotes English-language speaking that enhances educational outcomes. Could there be mitigating factors in the Chicano family for this link? Under what conditions is the link not observable? Is it possible that increased generational presence in the U.S. and English-language speaking does not always result in increased educational outcomes for Chicanos?

REFERENCES

Achor, Shirley and Aida Morales. 1989. "Chicanas holding doctoral degrees: Social reproduction and cultural ecological approaches." *Anthropology and Education Quarterly* 21:269-287.

Aguirre, Adalberto, Jr. 1979. "Intelligence testing and Chicanos: A quality of life issue." *Social Problems* 27:186-195.

Alvirez, David and Frank Bean. 1976. "The Mexican American family." Pp.271-292 in Charles Mindel and Robert Habenste (eds.), *Ethnic Families in America: Patterns and Variations.* New York: Elsevier.

Baca-Zinn, Maxine. 1979. "Chicano family research: Conceptual distortion and alternative directions." *Journal of Ethnic Studies* 7:59-71.

Bronfenbrenner, Uri. 1979. *The Ecology of Human Development.* Cambridge, Massachusetts: Harvard University Press.

Buriel, Raymond and Desdemona Cardoza. 1988. "Sociocultural correlates of achievement among three generations of Mexican American high school seniors." *American Educational Research Journal* 25:177-192.

_____ and Evangelina Saenz. 1980. "Psychocultural characteristics of college bound and noncollege bound Chicanos." *Journal of Social Psychology* 110:245-251.

Chapa, Jorge. 1990. "Minorities and the college graduating class of 2010." Paper written for the Governing Boards of Universities and Colleges, Washington, D.C.

_____ and Richard Valencia. 1993. "Latino population growth, demographic characteristics, and education stagnation: An examination of recent trends." *Hispanic Journal of Behavioral Sciences* 15:165-187.

Coleman, James. 1987. "The relation between school and social structure." Pp.177-204 in Maureen Hallinan (ed.), *Social Organization of Schools*. New York: Plenum Press.

Cromwell, Richard and Richard Ruiz. 1982. "The myth of macho dominance in decision making within Mexican and Chicano families." *Hispanic Journal of Behavioral Sciences* 1:355-373.

Delgado-Gaitan, Concha. 1992. "School matters in the Mexican-American home: Socializing children to education." *American Educational Research Journal* 29:495-513.

_____. 1988. "The value of conformity: Learning to stay in school." *Anthropology and Education Quarterly* 19:354-381.

_____ and Martha Allexsaht-Snider. 1992. "Mediating school cultural knowledge for children: The parent's role." Pp.79-95 in Howard Johnston & Kathyrn Borman (eds.), *Effective Schooling for Economically Disadvantaged Students*. Norwood, New Jersey: Ablex Publishing Company.

_____ and Henry Trueba. 1991. *Crossing Cultural Borders: Education for Immigrant Families in America*. London: Falmer Press.

_____ and Denise Segura. 1989. "The social context of Chicana women's role in children's schooling." *Educational Foundations* 3:71-92.

Dusek, Jerome and Gail Joseph. 1983. "The bases of teacher expectancies: A meta-analysis." *Journal of Educational Psychology* 75:327-346.

Eccles, Jacquelynne. 1983. "Expectancies, values and academic behaviors." Pp. 75-146 in Janet Spence (ed.), *Achievement and Achievement Motives: Psychological and Sociological Approaches.* San Francisco: W.H. Freeman.

Fligstein, Neil and Roberto Fernandez. 1982. "Educational transitions of whites and Mexican Americans." *ERIC Document ED 246 162.*

Gandara, Patricia. 1982. "Passing through the eye of the needle: High achieving Chicanas." *Hispanic Journal of Behavioral Sciences* 4: 167-179.

Garcia, Homer. 1985. "Family and offspring language maintenance and their effects on Chicano college students' confidence and grades." Pp. 226-243 in Eugene Garcia and Raymond Padilla (eds.), *Advances in Bilingual Education Research.* Tucson: University of Arizona Press.

Good, Thomas. 1987. "Two decades of research on teacher expectations: Findings and future directions." *Journal of Teacher Education* 38:32-47.

Laosa, Luis. 1989. "Social competence in childhood: Toward a developmental socioculturally relativistic paradigm." *Journal of Applied Developmental Psychology* 10:447-468.

_____. 1984. "Social policies toward children of diverse ethnic, racial, and language groups in the United States." Pp. 1-109 in Harold Stevenson and Alberta Siegel (eds.), *Child Development Research and Social Policy* (vol. 1). Chicago: University of Chicago Press.

_____. 1983. "Parent education, cultural pluralism and public policy: The uncertain connection." Pp. 331-345 in Ron Haskin and Diane Adams (eds.), *Parent Education and Public Policy.* Norwood, NJ: Ablex Publishing Corporation.

_____. 1982. "School, occupation, culture and family: The impact of parental schooling on the parent-child relationship." *Journal of Educational Psychology* 74:791-827.

_____. 1980a. "Maternal teaching strategies in Chicano and Anglo-American families: The influence of culture and education on maternal behavior." *Child Development* 51:759-765.

_____. 1980b. "Maternal teaching strategies and cognitive styles in Chicano families." *Journal of Educational Psychology* 72:45-54.

_____ and Ronald Henderson. 1991. "Cognitive socialization and competence: The academic development of Chicanos." Pp.164-199 in Richard Valencia (ed.), *Chicano School Failure and Success: Research and Policy Agendas for the 1990s*. New York: Falmer Press.

Macias, Reynaldo. 1993. "Language classification of language minorities: Chicano and Latino students in the 1990s." *Hispanic Journal of Behavioral Sciences* 15:230-257.

Manaster, Guy, Janson Chan, and Randa Safady. 1992. "Mexican American migrant students' academic success: Sociological and psychological acculturation." *Adolescence* 27:123-136.

Martinez, Estella. 1988. "Child behavior in Mexican American/ Chicano families: Maternal teaching and child-rearing practices." *Family Relations* 37:275-280.

Martinez, Marco. 1986. "Family socialization among Mexican Americans." *Human Development* 29:264-279.

McKee, Nancy. 1989. "Learning and earning: Education and well-being in a Texas border barrio." *Urban Education* 24:308-322.

Mehan, Hugh. 1992. "Understanding inequality in schools: The contribution of interpretive studies." *Sociology of Education* 65:1-20.

Moll, Luis, Cathy Amanti, Deborah Neff, and Norma Gonzalez. 1992. "Funds of knowledge in teaching: Using a qualitative approach to connect homes and classrooms." *Theory into Practice* 31:132-141.

National Council of La Raza. 1991. *State of Hispanic America 1991: An Overview.* Washington, D.C.: National Council of La Raza.

Paisano, Edna. 1992. "Selected social and economic characteristics for the American Indian, Eskimo, and Aleut populations for selected areas: 1990." Presented at the meeting of the Census Advisory Committee on the American Indian and Alaska Native, Asian and Pacific Islander, Black and Hispanic Populations for the 1990 Census, November, Phoenix, Arizona.

Romo, Harriett. 1984. "The Mexican origin population's differing perceptions of their children's schooling." *Social Science Quarterly* 65:635-650.

Stryker, Sheldon and Richard Serpe. 1983. "Toward a theory of family influence in the socialization of children." Pp.47-71 in Alan Kerckhoff (ed.), *Personal Change over the Life Course.* Greenwich, CT: JAI Press.

Trueba, Henry. 1991. "From failure to success: The roles of culture and cultural conflict in the academic achievement of Chicano students." Pp.151-163 in Richard Valencia (ed.), *Chicano School Failure and Success: Research and Policy Agendas for the 1990s.* London: Falmer Press.

U. S. Bureau of the Census. 1992. *The Asian and Pacific Islander Population in the United States.* Washington, D.C.: U.S. Government Printing Office.

_____. 1991a. *The Hispanic Population in the United States: March 1990.* Washington, D.C.: U.S. Government Printing Office.

_____. 1991b. *The Black Population in the United States: March 1990 and 1989.* Washington, D.C.: U.S. Government Printing Office.

_____. 1982. *Persons of Spanish Origin by State: 1980.* Washington, D.C.: U.S. Government Printing Office.

Valencia, Richard, Ronald Henderson, and Richard Rankin. 1985. "Family status, family constellation, and home environmental variables as predictors of cognitive performance of Mexican American children." *Journal of Educational Psychology* 77:323-331.

Velez-Ibanez, Carlos and James Greenberg. 1992a. "Schooling processes among U.S. Mexicans, Puerto Ricans, and Cubans: A comparative, distributive and case study approach." ERIC Document ED 347 022.

_____. 1992b. "Formation and transformation of funds of knowledge among U.S.-Mexican households." *Anthropology & Education Quarterly* 23:313-335.

Wiley, Terrence. 1989-1990. "Literacy, biliteracy and educational achievement among the Mexican-origin population in the United States." *NABE: The Journal of the National Association for Bilingual Education* 14:109-127.

Williams, Norma. 1990. *The Mexican American Family: Tradition and Change.* Dix Hills, New Jersey: General Hall.

Zinn, Maxine. 1979. "Chicano family research: Conceptual distortions and alternative directions." *Journal of Ethnic Studies* 7:59-71.

The Price They Pay for the Places They Live: A Case Study of the Association of Educational Achievement and Aspirations with Residential Incongruence Among Middle-Class Black Adolescents

Janet Hope

A positive association between family status and the educational aspirations and achievements of black children is well established in the literature (Dawkins, 1981; Harvey and Kerin, 1978; Mickelson, 1990). Also well established is that unlike their white, middle-class counterparts, a substantial proportion of black, middle-class families finds it necessary to reside in neighborhoods inconsistent with their socioeconomic status (Massey et al., 1987; O'Hare et al., 1991). This paper examines the differences in the college aspirations and academic performance of two groups of black, middle-class, high school students: those living in poor quality neighborhoods; and those living in neighborhoods that are consistent with their families' middle-class socioeconomic status.

THE LITERATURE

Social Class and Educational Aspirations

The association between family socioeconomic status and educational aspirations has been found to operate in at least two ways. First, people's locations in the socioeconomic hierarchy dictate to a great extent their life conditions by determining the share and quality of goods and services to which they have access. In turn, this affects their goals and expectations for the future. Second, through the process of socialization, social class membership produces the appropriate personal characteristics that influence behavior (Borus, et al., 1980; Tidwell, 1989). It is, therefore, reasonable to suggest that the socioeconomic status of black adolescents determines their academic achievement as well as how they perceive their academic opportunities.

Social Class and Neighborhood Quality

Generally, as their socioeconomic status increases, so does the ability of most people to reside in neighborhoods consistent with such status. However, this does not apply equally to all races. Several studies have found that because of enduring barriers some middle-class blacks find access to the more desirable residential areas denied them and that they are much more likely than middle-class whites to live in poor-quality neighborhoods inhabited by people of lower social and economic status than their own (Erbe, 1975; Massey et al., 1987; O'Hare et al., 1991).

Neighborhood Quality and Educational Aspirations

Prior work suggests that the higher the socioeconomic status of a neighborhood, the more likely its adolescent residents are to aspire to college (Hollingshead, 1949; Jencks and Mayer, 1990; Labovitz, 1974). More than thirty years ago Rogoff (1962) suggested that part of the differing levels of achievement and aspirations existing in children from similar family backgrounds could be explained by differences in community settings. Turner (1964) also found that such aspirational differences were attributable in part to the status of the neighborhoods in which students live. The association between residential neighborhood and adolescent aspirations appears to operate in several ways. First, environmental characteristics can and do shape the ways in which people behave (Andrews, 1986; Fisher, 1982; Huckfeldt, 1983; Jencks and Mayer, 1990). Second, community norms, expectations and values influence the decisions and choices people make (Bowser, 1991; Brook et al., 1989; Labovitz, 1974; Scott, 1983). For example, how does the community view a college education? Is it the expected next step after high school, or is it a rare occurrence? Is it held in high regard, disparaged or viewed as unimportant? Is it generally considered to be beyond the reach of a neighborhood's residents, or is it viewed as easily attainable? Third, in poor-quality neighborhoods, obtaining a college degree may be seen as a means of escape. One's surroundings in such cases may provide an impetus for achievement and a foundation for college aspirations that does not exist in better-quality neighborhoods (Bowser, 1991). Fourth, adolescents' attitudes are shaped to a great extent by their interaction with friends (Huckfeldt, 1983). Willie (1990) suggests that in poor black neighborhoods, peers shape adolescents' lives as much as do any other aspects of community life. Studies in the late 1950s and early 1960s reported similar findings (see, for example, Sewell and Armer, 1966). However, they do not indicate if this is also the case in more affluent black neighborhoods.

What reasons exist for suspecting that the effects of residential quality might override the effects of family socioeconomic status in determining adolescent educational aspirations? Early work suggests that the offspring of high-status parents who live in low-status neighborhoods may not achieve and aspire academically at the levels one would expect, given their parents' educational and socioeconomic levels (Wilson, 1959; Wilson, 1967). However, later work is somewhat skeptical about the amount of variance one may actually attribute to socioeconomic context. Hauser and Featherman (1976) and Hauser et al. (1983), for example, found the relationship to be smaller than Wilson's work had indicated, a position supported by the research of Jencks et al. (1983).

Unfortunately, two major problems exist with prior work in this area. First, there is not enough of it. Second, previous studies often had measurement problems that make it difficult to distinguish between neighborhood effects and socioeconomic effects. These problems clearly point to the need for studies that are able to measure neighborhood effects independent of socioeconomic status.

In addition, one very important aspect of the link between communities and the aspirations and achievement of its young residents remains insufficiently explored: the impact of the *small primary neighborhood* versus the community as a whole. To date, the immediate neighborhood has been found to be related to academic performance only insofar as it constitutes the environment for family life and by its attracting families who share personal characteristics and attitudes towards education (Boocock, 1980). In part, the lack of research on small, primary neighborhoods arises because it has been difficult to know precisely how to identify the appropriate level at which to conduct such an examination (Osterman, 1991). If one designates too large an area as a neighborhood (as most of the early research has done), then capturing variation is difficult (Osterman, 1991). But, if one concentrates on too small an area, it is all too easy to become mired in detail.

DATA AND METHODS

The Sample

The respondents are 257 black, middle-class, senior high school students of both sexes who were in attendance at a predominately black, inner-city high school on one day in October of 1988. The school is located in a mid-sized city in the southeastern United States.

For most people, the term "inner-city school" suggests a school located in a city's poorest section, staffed with the worst teachers in the system, whose all-black student body is drawn from the most deprived neighborhoods in the area. The achievement levels of students at such a school are notoriously low, the drop-out rates high, and students whose parents were able to do so have long since left the area, leaving behind those from the most economically, socially, and educationally disadvantaged backgrounds. In several ways, these stereotypes do apply to this particular school. A large percentage of its students are from disadvantaged homes; it is part of a city school system that generally tends to do poorly by its students; at least 94.1% of its student body is black; and it is geographically located in an inner city. The resemblance to the stereotypical "inner-city school" ends there, however.

This school was built in 1935 in the heart of a thriving black, middle-class community. For many years, it was considered one of the leading high schools in the region, black or white. This school enjoys a strong sense of continuity with the past because many of the grandparents and parents of current students were themselves students there. It also enjoys considerable support from the community in which it is located. In addition, from their responses to open-ended questions in this research, these respondents are clearly proud to be students at the school.

Furthermore, some students actually zoned for other high schools choose to attend this one. At the time the data for this study were gathered, approximately 12% had the option of attending other schools. They attend this particular school in part because of family ties, but also because some parents believe quite strongly that their children would not receive the "nurturing" they receive at the school anywhere else. By this, they mean that at this school students' black heritage is an integral part of the learning experience and not something taught in addition to everything else, and that students are given the opportunity to develop as black leaders.

Today, although the neighborhood in which the school is located retains much of its middle-class stability, the areas from which its students are drawn vary considerably in quality. For example, it is not unusual for a relatively short street in this city to contain railroad tracks, a major intersection and industrial businesses on one block, small, wooden shacks and crumbling older houses on another, more substantial and better-kept older houses on a third, and fairly modern and well-tended homes on a fourth. The differing characteristics of its students' residential neighborhoods make this school especially suitable for a study of the association of residential quality and educational aspirations and achievement.

The research reported here was guided by several hypotheses:

1. (a) That significant differences in academic aspirations exist between middle-class, black students who live in poor quality neighborhoods and middle-class, black students living in neighborhoods of a quality consistent with their socioeconomic status.

(b) That the percentage of middle-class, black students living in poor-quality neighborhoods who aspire to college is significantly lower than the percentage of middle-class, black students living in good-quality neighborhoods who aspire to college.

2. (a) That significant differences in academic grades exist between middle-class, black students who live in poor-quality neighborhoods and middle-class, black students living in neighborhoods of a quality consistent with their socioeconomic status.

(b) That the academic grades of middle-class, black students living in poor-quality neighborhoods are significantly lower than the academic grades of middle-class, black students living in neighborhoods of a quality consistent with their socioeconomic status.

Data Collection

Data collection was accomplished in two stages:

Stage one. The students were administered a 55-question instrument which was a part of pre-test procedures for a proposed national study of adolescents. Its primary purpose was not to obtain information on the academic aspirations of these high school students, but rather to assess their ability to answer various types of questions. Nonetheless, for the most part, the questions did lend themselves well to this study.

Stage two. From the questionnaires, 644 different residential addresses were obtained. Following verification of the actual street names and block numbers through the use of the local zip code directory, this translated into 402 different blocks and 258 different streets on which one or more of the respondents lived.

The first step in the data-gathering procedure for this portion of the research began in September 1990 and involved searching the city and county directories at the public library to obtain the following information:

a) The number of structures on each block.
b) The number of single family homes, duplexes or apartments (three or more units).
c) The number of retail, industrial or manufacturing businesses; the number of churches and schools.
d) The names of householders.
e) Whether the properties were owned or rented.
f) If the householders were retired.
g) If the householders were employed, and if so, the nature of their occupations.
h) The presence of railroad tracks.
i) If the block is on a major thoroughfare.

Next, a search of the public records at the County Tax Assessor's office produced the following additional data:

j) The square footage of every residential building on each block.
k) The latest (1986) assessed value of each residence.
l) The score on the Tax Assessor's "Quality Index."

m) The number of bathrooms at each residence.
n) If a block was located in a public housing project.
o) If the block was located in the city.

For each block, the proportion of single family homes, duplexes, apartment buildings, retail businesses, manufacturing businesses and churches or schools was calculated as were the percentage of owner-occupied versus renter-occupied residences, the average assessed property value, the average residential square footage, the average quality index score, and the average number of bathrooms.

Coding the occupations of the householders was accomplished by the use of the Total Socioeconomic Index (TSEI) of Stevens and Cho (1985). This index contains socioeconomic scores for 1980 occupational codes and gives a measure of occupational prestige, which is particularly useful for this study because it is derived from the income and educational attributes of the **total** 1980 labor force, rather than from the 1980 **male** labor force alone. The large percentage of female-headed households in this study makes this consideration especially important. In addition, Stevens and Cho (1985) consider their classification schemes preferable to alternative methods of classification in that they allow for the description and interpretation of socioeconomic distances between occupations.

In those cases where I was able to obtain the occupations of the householders, they were assigned the appropriate TSEI score. House-holders were coded as missing when occupational information could not be obtained or when they were retired. Those blocks for which occupational codes for 50% or more of the residents could not be obtained were coded as missing. An average TSEI score was obtained by summing all available scores for a block and then dividing by the number of householders on that block for whom I had occupations. In this manner, 41 percent of the residential blocks were assigned average TSEI scores.

The Variables

The dichotomous dependent variable, **educational aspirations**, records a desire to attend college or not. Controls are those variables which prior research has consistently identified as being associated with the educational aspirations of adolescents. **Gender, grade level, age and social class** were included.

Respondents with a parent possessing an undergraduate degree or better were assumed to be middle class. Those whose parents had some college or who had attended a vocational school were assigned to the upper lower class and those with a high school diploma or lower were assumed to be lower class.

Prior work has associated high **academic grades** in school with aspiring to a college education (Hauser, 1971; Hout and Morgan, 1975; Kerckhoff and Huff, 1974; Wilson and Portes, 1975). Grades here are self-reported on a scale ranging from 0 (mostly Ds or lower) to 9 mostly As) in three subject groupings: science and math; English and writing; history and social studies. Self-reported grades as a measure of academic achievement have been successfully used in prior studies (see for example, Davies and Kandel, 1979; Wilson and Portes, 1975) and are generally accurate and reliable substitutes for actual grades.

"Joiners" and "doers" have been identified as achieving better academic grades and aspiring to higher levels of education than those who do not participate in various activities (Haensly et al., 1986; Hauser, 1971; Rehberg, 1968; Yarworth and Gauthier, 1978). The extent of **membership in clubs and organizations** was ascertained by respondents, indicating on a list of school-related clubs and organizations in which of them they had participated during the current and/or preceding school year.

Athletic participation in high school is positively related to college aspirations, especially for males (Rehberg, 1968; Otto, 1975). The extent of respondents' participation in sports was established in the same way as for clubs and organizations.

Prior research indicates that the less **alienated** students feel from their schools, the higher their educational aspirations (Ekstrom et al., 1986; Slaughter, 1987). Responses to the following four Likert-type questions were summed: 1) I feel close to the people at this school; 2) I feel like I'm part of this school; 3) I am happy to be at this school; 4) I have a lot of school spirit. The higher the score the more alienated the respondent.

A **neighborhood quality** score was assigned to each residential block. Scores range from a low of 14 to a high of 44. For ease of analysis, the index was collapsed into four categories: blocks with a score of less than 21 were given a poor quality rating; those between

21 and 28 were given a fair quality rating; those with scores of 29 to 36 were given a good rating; and those with scores of 37 to 44 were classified as very good quality. Students living in poor-quality neighborhoods accounted for 17.5 percent of the total; 29.6 percent of the respondents lived in fair-quality neighborhoods, 34.2 percent in good-quality neighborhoods and 18.7 percent in very good-quality neighborhoods.

RESULTS

Table 1 displays selected background characteristics by residential quality. For a clearer comparison, poor and fair-quality neighborhoods were grouped together as were good and very good neighborhoods.

Even this initial analysis produces interesting differences between the two groups. For example, the mean age, mean grade level, and mean number of years at the school of students from good/very good neighborhoods are slightly higher than the means for students from poor/fair neighborhoods. This suggests that middle-class students living in poor neighborhoods do not stay in school as long as do middle-class students from better residential areas. Also of interest is the finding that only 45.5 percent of the middle-class students living in poor areas live with both parents, as opposed to the 64.7 percent of middle-class students from the better areas who have both parents at home. This finding adds strength to the idea that the absence of fathers is a major reason that middle-class students reside in inferior neighborhoods in the first place.

Interesting differences are also noted in the extent of club memberships and sports participation. Students from good neighborhoods are more involved in school clubs and organizations than are those from poorer areas. However, the reverse is true for participation in sports. One possible explanation for the latter finding could be that students from the poorer neighborhoods see sports as a way "up" whereas those from higher-quality areas see education as the way to advance. Alternatively, students from poorer areas may simply be involved in sports at school because no such facilities exist in their neighborhoods. It is also clear from a simple comparison of the mean academic grades of these middle-class students that both boys and girls from good neighborhoods have higher grades than those from poor neighborhoods. The same is true of their college plans.

Table 1

Characteristics of Middle-Class,
Black High School Students
Living in Two Types of Neighborhoods

	Poor/Fair Quality (N=121)	Good/Very Good Quality (N=136)
Background Characteristic:		
Mean Age	15.7 (1.3)	15.9 (1.3)
Mean Grade	10.2 (1.1)	10.6 (1.3)
Mean Years at this School	1.4 (1.6)	1.6 (1.3)
% male	44.7	50.7
% female	55.3	49.3
% living both parents	45.5	64.7
% with employed mothers	80.9	85.6
Academic performance, involvement, and college aspirations:		
Mean academic grade*	5.1 (1.4)	5.7 (1.4)
For boys	4.7 (1.8)	5.4 (1.4)
For girls	5.4 (1.6)	6.0 (1.2)
Mean no. memberships	2.0 (1.8)	2.4 (2.0)
Mean no. sports	1.3 (1.7)	1.1 (1.5)
Mean Alienation Score**	3.8 (1.9)	3.7 (1.8)
% aspiring to college	68.1	82.9
Boys	64.1	76.8
Girls	79.1	86.6

* Range= 0 (mostly Ds) to 9 (mostly As)
** Range= 0 (not at all alienated) to 6 (highly alienated)

Note: Standard Deviation in parentheses.

Table 2 reports college aspirations by residential neighborhood in more detail. Middle-class girls living in poor quality neighborhoods are twice as likely not to aspire to college as they are to have college plans. Similar results apply to the boys living on poor quality blocks, although the ratio, at 1.3 to 1, is less dramatic. Both boys and girls living in the remaining types of neighborhood are at least three times as likely to plan on college than not, with the ratios for girls being considerably larger than for boys.

Table 2

The College Aspirations of Black High School Students
Living in Four Types of Neighborhoods
(Ratios in parentheses)

| | Planning on College | | | |
| | Boys | | Girls | |
	Yes	No	Yes	No
Neighborhood Quality:				
Poor	9	12 (1/1.3)	8	16 (1/2)
Fair	26	7 (3.7/1)	37	6 (6.2/1)
Good	34	11 (3.1/1)	36	7 (5.1/1)
Very good	19	5 (3.8/1)	22	2 (11/1)
N	(88)	(35)	(111)	(23)

The results contained in this table suggest that middle-class students living in the poorest-quality areas suffer considerably diminished aspirations. It also appears that the aspirations of students in fair-quality neighborhoods more closely resemble those of students from good and very good areas than they do the aspirations of students from poor-quality blocks.

Table 3 reports academic grades by residential quality. No clear linear pattern is evident from this table, which is partially explained by the small number of students from very good neighborhoods. When these students are excluded from the analysis, the linear relationship between grades and the other three neighborhood types becomes much clearer. The largest percentage of C/D grades are earned by both boys and girls from poor neighborhoods, while the largest percentage of A/Bs are earned by students from good neighborhoods.

Chi Square tests reveal that these results are statistically significant for the table as a whole as well as for the boys. There is, however, no significant difference in the grades of the girls by residential neighborhood. In other words, their grades are not suppressed as much as are the boys'.

Logistic regression indicates that neighborhood quality is positively and significantly associated with college plans when controlling for both achieved and ascribed characteristics. The size of the standardized coefficient is large. Table 4 contains the results of this analysis.

Table 3

The Academic Grades of Middle-Class, Black High School Students
by Neighborhood Quality

| | Academic Grades | | | | | |
| | Boys | | | Girls | | |
Residential Quality:	A/B	B/C	C/D	A/B	B/C	C/D
Poor	7.2	16.7	30.4	17.5	15.0	41.7
	(2)	(12)	(7)	(7)	(12)	(5)
Fair	17.9	31.9	21.7	25.0	35.0	25.0
	(5)	(23)	(5)	(10)	(28)	(3)
Good	57.1	34.7	17.4	35.0	32.5	35.0
	(16)	(25)	(4)	(14)	(26)	(3)
V. Good	17.9	16.8	30.4	22.5	27.5	8.3
	(5)	(12)	(7)	(9)	(14)	(1)
N	28	72	23	40	80	12

Chi-Square:
  Neighborhood quality/academic grades - all Rs 13.85*   df=6
  Neighborhood quality/academic grades - boys   13.15*   df=6
  Neighborhood quality/academic grades - girls   6.46   df=6

*** p<.001
 ** p< .01
  * p< .05

Table 4

Predicting Black Adolescents College Aspirations
from Neighborhood Quality[1]

Independent Variables	
Residence:	
Neighborhood Quality	.213**
Ascribed Characteristics:	
Being male	-.079
Grade level	-.035
Achieved Characteristics:	
Academic grades	.308***
Memberships	.377***
Sports Participation	.013
Alienation from school	-.078
N	257

[1] Standardized Logistic Regression Coefficients

*** $p < .001$
** $p < .01$
* $p < .05$

In an effort to see how the predictors of college aspirations differ among the three neighborhood types, logistic regressions for three separate subgroups were performed. Table 5 contains these results, which show that the predictors of college aspirations for adolescents living in poor-quality neighborhoods (Model 1) differ from those for adolescents from good-quality (Model 3) and fair-quality (Model 2)

Table 5

Predictors of Black Adolescent College Aspirations
by Block Quality

Independent Variables	1 Poor Quality Block (N=45)	2 Fair Quality Block (N=76)	3 Good Quality Block (N=136)
Ascribed:			
Being male	-0.011	-0.092	0.144
Grade level	-0.016	-0.088	-0.069
Achieved:			
Academic grades	0.265*	0.236*	0.390***
Memberships	0.427**	0.331**	0.323*
Sports participation	0.009	0.027	0.080
Alienation from school	-0.361**	0.049	0.042

Test differences:
Model 1 vs. Models 2 and 3   Chi-square = 7.51** df=1
Model 2 vs. Models 1 and 3   not significant
Model 3 vs. Models 1 and 2   not significant)

[1] Standardized Logistic Regression Coefficients
*** p<.001 (2-tailed test)
** p<.01   (2-tailed test)
* p<.05   (2-tailed test)

neighborhoods. This difference is significant at the .01 level. A black
adolescent from a poor-quality neighborhood will aspire to college if
his or her academic grades are good, and the adolescent is active in

clubs and organizations and is not alienated from school. Teenagers from both good and fair-quality blocks aspire to college if they have good grades and are active in clubs and organizations. These two predictors cross all neighborhood boundaries.

DISCUSSION

This study clearly demonstrates that at this particular school a large number of middle-class respondents live in residential neighborhoods not commensurate with their family socioeconomic status and that such residential incongruence negatively affects their college aspirations and academic achievement. Furthermore, the number of middle-class residents so affected is large. Almost two-thirds of these misplaced middle-class families are headed by women who, by virtue of their levels of education, belong in the middle class, but who nonetheless find themselves residing in lower-status neighborhoods. The largest factor contributing to the lack of mobility of these middle-class families appears to be the absence of fathers. A close look reveals that of the 104 respondents who do not live with their fathers, 58.7 percent reside on poor and fair-quality blocks. Of the 153 who do live with their fathers, only 39.2 percent live on lower-status blocks. When the total absence of any adult male is considered, 63.7 percent of middle-class, male-absent respondents are found to live on poor and fair-quality blocks.

Clearly middle-class black families who stay in poor-quality neighborhoods pay dearly in terms of their children's lack of achievement and loss of aspirations. What is unclear from these data is exactly how this occurs. One may speculate that these findings are attributable in large part to the economic circumstances responsible for keeping such families in lower-quality settings in the first place. That is, students whose middle-class families have been unable to find their way to good-quality neighborhoods may not view the possibility of a college education with much confidence. One might also suggest several other explanations. For example, the negative influences of other neighborhood residents may be to blame for these students' lack of educational ambition. Or, perhaps, tensions arising from the inconsistency between status and residence may manifest themselves in lower aspirations. Alternatively, reduced aspirations may arise from the simple absorption of prevailing attitudes and expectations of the neighborhood.

Middle-class black families who reside in poor and fair neighborhoods not only suffer because they do not live in areas commensurate with their social class but also suffer in terms of the decreased educational aspirations of their children. This study also identifies several interesting questions. Are middle-class students living in inferior neighborhoods at greater risk of dropping out of school than their counterparts from better residential areas? What factors contribute to the noticeable gender differences in academic performance? Why is girls' academic performance not affected by the quality of their residential neighborhood to the same extent as boys' performance? Future research should address these issues.

REFERENCES

Andrews, Howard J. (1986). "The effects of neighborhood social mix on adolescents' social networks and recreational activities." *Urban Studies* 23:501-517.

Boocock, Sarane Spence. (1980). *Sociology of Education: An Introduction*. (2d ed.) New York: University Press of America.

Borus, M., J. Crowley, R. Rumberger, R. Santos, and D. Shapiro. (1980). *Findings of the National Longitudinal Survey of Young Americans, 1979*. (Youth Knowledge Development Report 2.7). Washington, D.C.: U.S. Government Printing Office.

Bowser, Benjamin P. (ed.). (1991). *Black Male Adolescents: Parenting and Education in Community Context*. New York: University Press.

Brook, Judith S., Carolyn Nomura, and Patricia Cohen. (1989). "A network of influences on adolescent drug involvement: Neighborhood, school, peer and family." *Genetic, Social and Psychology Monographs* 165:123-145.

Davies, Mark and Denise B. Kandel. (1979). "Parental and peer influence on adolescents' educational plans: Some further evidence." *American Journal of Sociology* 87:363-387

Dawkins, Marvin P. (1981). "Mobility aspirations of Black adolescents: A comparison of males and females." *Adolescence* 16:701-710.

Ekstrom, Ruth B., Margaret E. Goertz, Judith M. Pollack, and Donald A. Rock. (1986). "Who drops out of high school and why? Findings from a national study." *Teachers' College Record* 87:356-373.

Erbe, B. (1975). "Race and socioeconomic segregation." *American Sociological Review* 40:801-813.

Fisher, Claude. (1982). *To Dwell Among Friends*. Chicago: University of Chicago Press.

Haensly, Patricia A., Ann E. Lupkowski, and Elaine P. Edlind. (1986). "The role of extracurricular activities in education." *The High School Journal* 69:110-119.

Harvey, Michael G. and Roger A. Kerin. (1978). "The influence of social stratification and age on occupational aspirations of adolescents." *Journal of Educational Research* 71:262-266.

Hauser, R.M. (1971). *Socioeconomic Background and Educational Performance*. Washington, D.C.: American Sociological Association, Rose Monograph Series.

Hauser, R.M. and Douglas K. Anderson. (1991). "Post-high school plans and aspirations of Black and White high school seniors." *Sociology of Education* 64:263-277.

Hauser, R.M. and D.L. Featherman. (1976). "Equality of schooling: Trends and prospects." *Sociology of Education* 49:99-120.

Hauser, R.M., Shu-Ling Tsai, and William H. Sewell. (1983). "A model of stratification with response error in social and psychological variables." *Sociology of Education* 56:20-46.

Hollingshead, A.B. (1949). *Elmtown's Youth.* New York: Wiley & Sons.

Hout, Michael and William R. Morgan. (1975). "Race and sex variations in the causes of the expected attainment of high school seniors." *American Journal of Sociology* 81:364-395.

Huckfeldt, R. Robert. (1983). "Social contexts, social networks and urban neighborhoods: Environmental constraints on friendship choice." *American Journal of Sociology* 89:651-669.

Jencks, Christopher, James Crouse and Peter Mueser. (1983). "The Wisconsin Model of Status Attainment: A National Replication with Improved Measures of Ability and Aspiration." *Sociology of Education* 56:3-19.

Jencks, Christopher and Susan Mayer. (1990). "The social consequences of growing up in a poor neighborhood: A review." In Michael McGeary and Lawrence Lynn (eds.), *Inner City Poverty in the United States.* Washington, D.C.: National Academy Press.

Kerckhoff, Alan C. and Judith L. Huff. (1974). "Parental influences on educational goals." *Sociometry* 37:307-27.

Labovitz, Eugene M. (1974). "Fulfillment of college aspirations." *Pacific Sociological Review* 17:379-397.

Massey, Douglas S., Gretchen A. Condran, and Nancy A. Denton. (1987). "The effect of residential segregation on Black social and economic well-being." *Social Forces* 66:29-56.

Mickelson, Roslyn A. (1990). "The attitude-achievement paradox among Black adolescents." *Sociology of Education* 63:44-61.

O'Hare, William P., Kelvin M. Pollard, Tayma L. Mann, and Mary M. Kent. (1991). "African Americans in the 1990s." *Population Bulletin* 46 (1):1-40.

Osterman, Paul. (1991). "Welfare participation in a full employment economy." *Social Problems* 38:475-484.

Otto, L.B. (1975). "Extracurricular activities in the educational attainment process." *Rural Sociology* 40:162-176.

Rehberg, J. (1968). "Participation in interscholastic athletics and college expectations." *American Journal of Sociology* 73:732-740.

Rogoff, N. (1962). "Local social structure and educational selection." In A.H. Halsey, et al. (eds.), *Education, Economy and Society.* New York: Free Press.

Scott, Richard R. (1983). "Blacks in segregated and desegregated neighborhoods: An exploratory study." *Urban Affairs Quarterly* 18:327-346.

Sewell, William H. and J. Michael Armer. (1966). "Neighborhood context and college plans." *American Sociological Review* 31:159-168.

Slaughter, Diana T. (1987). "The home environment and academic achievement of Black American children and youth: An overview." *Journal of Negro Education* 56:3-20.

Stevens, Gillian and Joo Hyun Cho. (1985). "Socioeconomic indexes and the new 1980 census occupational classification scheme." *Social Science Research* 14:142-168.

Tidwell, Romeria. (1989). "Academic success and the school dropout: A minority perspective." In G.L. Berry and J.K. Asamen (eds.), *Black Student: Psychosocial Issues and Academic Achievement.* Newbury Park, CA: Sage Publications.

Turner, R.H. (1964). *The Social Context of Ambition.* San Francisco: Chandler.

Willie, Charles V. (1990). *The Family Life of Black People.* Columbus, Ohio: Chas. E. Merrill Publishing Co.

Wilson, Alan B. (1959). "Residential segregation of social classes and aspirations of high school boys." *American Sociological Review* 24:836-845.

_____. (1967). "Educational consequences of segregation in a California community." *U.S. Commission on Civil Rights, Racial Isolation in the Public Schools.* Washington, D.C.: U.S. Government Printing Office.

Wilson, K.L. and A. Portes. (1975). "The educational attainment process: Results from a national sample." *American Journal of Sociology* 81:401-418.

Yarworth, J.S. and W.J. Gauthier Jr. (1978). "Relationship of student-self concept and selected personal variables to participation in school activities." *Journal of Educational Psychology* 70 (3):335-344.

Marital Status and Birth Outcomes: Toward an Understanding of Race and Ethnic Differences

Stan L. Albrecht and Leslie L. Clarke

INTRODUCTION

While infant mortality rates in the United States have declined dramatically over the past century, substantial differences remain in patterns among different subgroups of the population. For example, the once widely accepted assumption that advances in medical care and improved living conditions would narrow the inverse relationship between socioeconomic status and mortality has simply not been reflected in the data (see, for example, Antonovsky and Bernstein, 1977; Brooks, 1975; Markides and Barnes, 1977; Markides and McFarland, 1982; Moss and Carver, 1992), despite the fact that several studies conducted in the 1950's and 1960's suggested that the historical inverse association was on the decline (see, for example, Donabedian, Rosenfeld, and Southern, 1965; Stockwell, 1962; Willie, 1959). The clear message from the last two decades of research is that while overall infant mortality rates have experienced significant improvement, there remain important challenges associated with the effort to bring the life chances for children born to more disadvantaged groups in line with the more advantaged.

While race and socioeconomic status variables are certainly not unrelated, it is important to note that the gap between black and white infant mortality has not experienced any significant decrease, either, in recent years. For example, Shin (1975), in a study of southern states observed that, overall, the gap between black and white rates did not decrease over the three-decade period of 1940-1970. A number of more recent studies demonstrate that nonwhite babies continue to have a significantly higher probability of dying than do white babies with the rate remaining approximately twice as high for blacks as for whites (Alexander and Cornely, 1987; Cramer, 1987; Gee, Lee, and Forthofer, 1976; Geronimus, 1987; Geronimus and Bound, 1990; Hummer, 1993; National Center for Health Statistics, 1992; Sappenfield et al., 1987; Yankauer, 1990). Rates for Hispanics are generally similar to those for non-Hispanic whites, despite the fact that their socioeconomic circumstances as a group would more closely resemble that of blacks (Becerra et al., 1991; Cramer, Bell, and Vaast, 1991; Forbes and Frisbie, 1991; Frisbie and Bean, 1993; Gee et al., 1976; Hummer, Eberstein, and Nam, 1992; Moss and Carver, 1992; Powell-Griner, 1988; Rogers, 1984, 1989a).[1]

A substantial body of research is now available indicating the major socio-demographic and biological conditions that are associated with infant mortality. Eberstein and Parker (1984) summarize this literature as falling into several broad categories: (1) socioeconomic and racial/ethnic factors noted above; (2) other social influences, including family stability, illegitimacy, and rural-urban or metropolitan-nonmetropolitan residence; (3) demographic factors, including population size, density, age of mothers, mean length of birth intervals, and birth order; and (4) health influences, including physician density, birth weight, hospital births, nutrition, prenatal care, and medical technology.[2]

In their effort to sort out the relative importance of these variables, and in an attempt to identify the types of programs that might both further improve infant life chances overall and the life chances of those in the most-at-risk categories more particularly, several researchers suggest that attention must move from a primary focus on traditional medical techniques to a broader examination of the social issues involved (see, for example, Antonovsky and Bernstein, 1977; David and Collins, 1991; Hummer, 1993; Williams et al., 1994). We will build on this effort by focusing on family structure as a variable that may become increasingly important in explaining infant mortality and life chances. While increasing attention has been paid recently to family structural variables, how important they are independently or how they operate in conjunction with other variables is as yet unclear.

Specifically, in this paper we will focus on the relative importance of marital status because of the recent emergence of what appears to be, at least at first glance, an anomalous finding—that marital status may operate differently in explaining black infant mortality than in explaining white or Hispanic infant mortality. The broader sociocultural context in which the mother and infant are immersed will be discussed in our effort to understand this phenomenon. To more fully assess the relative importance of marital status, we will also report the effect on birth outcomes of other key variables, including age, education, and the nature of the prenatal care received by the mother.

MARITAL STATUS AND INFANT MORTALITY

Eberstein, Hummer, and Nam (1990) have recently noted that the consensus among researchers has been that out-of-wedlock births have substantially elevated risks of infant death, though the magnitude of marital status differentials varies somewhat by cause of death. In their study of a population of non-Hispanic whites, they observed that increasing the proportion of unmarried by one standard deviation implied an increase in deaths from infections, delivery complications, and SIDS of 21-24 percent. As has been the case for other studies, the most important intermediate variable in their analysis was birth weight, and being unmarried was associated with lower birth weights of infants.

Gee et al. (1976) found that next to birth weight, legitimacy status was the most important factor associated with neonatal mortality. While nonwhite infants continued to have an above-average risk of neonatal mortality in the absence of the legitimacy status effect, the unadjusted risk was reduced by 25 percent. Powell-Griner (1988) also reports a net effect of out-of-wedlock birth on mortality, though she notes that unmarried status confers more of a disadvantage among the offspring of white-collar than blue-collar women. Powell-Griner (1988:464) speculates that "Unmarried blue-collar women may be able to increase their resources through the assistance of their families and public programs, and may thereby attain resources similar to those of their married peers." Among white-collar women, on the other hand, the resources of married women may far exceed those of unmarried women despite any assistance from kin-based networks for the latter group. Her overall conclusion, however, is that the risk of mortality is substantially elevated for babies of single mothers.

Cramer (1987) has suggested that while blacks, unwed mothers, and mothers of low socioeconomic status are all higher risk groups for infant mortality, marital status *per se* may not be an independent risk factor because babies born to unwed mothers may experience higher neonatal mortality because their mothers are disproportionately young, black, and high school dropouts. If this is the case, the effect of marital status may operate quite differently for some population groups than for others.

In support of this contention, an emerging body of data suggests that illegitimacy may have different consequences for black than for white or Hispanic birth outcomes. For example, Berkov (1981) found the association between marital status and infant mortality to be much stronger among whites than among blacks. More recently, Cramer (1987:303) has reported from his analysis of California data that black infant mortality does not vary by mother's marital status, while among Anglos and Hispanics, the rate is higher among unmarried than married mothers. When controlling for race and age, he found that among Anglos and Hispanics, risk is greater for single mothers, whereas among blacks, risk is somewhat greater for married mothers. When controlling for interactions in his data, for blacks under age 20 the odds of an infant death were 50 percent higher if the mother is married than if she is not married.

Eberstein, Nam, and Hummer (1990) similarly found that when looking at birth outcomes with controls for race and marital status, the race/ethnicity x marital status interaction indicated that black infants with unmarried mothers had a lower than expected mortality. Our basic question is whether or not this finding can be replicated in another research setting and when controls are introduced for other important explanatory variables.

DATA AND METHODS

The data used in this study are from vital statistic birth and infant death certificate records for the State of Florida. Information on all births in the state in 1987 (N=176,635) and all infant deaths in 1987 (N=1,853) and 1988 (N=1,929) were used to analyze a full-year cohort of births and the deaths that occurred among these infants.

Death certificate data were linked to the birth certificate data to obtain a greater range of information for analysis than is available on either record independently. For example, the linked records provide maternal and medical care characteristics, available only on the birth records, to understand the predictors of infant death. The Florida birth and death records were linked using an algorithm which included mother's and infant's names (actual and soundex), Social Security number, county of residence, sex of the infant, and race as matching characteristics. A successful match rate of 93 percent was achieved, a rate that did not vary significantly by race/ethnic group. This match rate compares to the match rate of 97.8 percent achieved by the National Center for Health Statistics in the linking of national birth and infant death certificate data (NCHS, 1992). A total of 1,557 death records were linked to the 1987 birth records of which 1,006 were neonatal deaths (i.e., the death occurred in the first 28 days of life).

After linking these data and omitting cases with missing information on the variables of interest, the population sizes were 110,749 non-Hispanic whites, 36,651 non-Hispanic blacks, 18,838 Hispanic whites and 3,947 Hispanic blacks.[3] A total of 6,450 births (3.65 percent) were deleted due to missing values or racial/ethnic characteristics other than black, white and Hispanic. Of these infants, 4,816 non-Hispanic blacks, 6,463 non-Hispanic whites, and 1,116 Hispanic whites, and 359 Hispanic blacks were born weighing less than 2500 grams. The respective low birthweight rates for these racial/ethnic groups were 13.1, 5.8, 5.9 and 9.1. The number of neonatal deaths for this sample were 323 for non-Hispanic blacks, 456 for non-Hispanic whites, 80 for Hispanic whites, and 18 for Hispanic blacks. The respective neonatal mortality rates were 9.0, 4.0, 4.0 and 5.0 per 1,000 live births.

From the linked records, a set of maternal sociodemographic variables and medical care utilization measures that are known to be important predictors of infant health and survival were selected. Three infant outcomes, including birth weight, neonatal mortality, and infant mortality were included in the analysis as dependent variables, though just the first two are reported here.[4] These variables and their measurement are described below. Table 1 reports the distribution of the cases on each variable.

Measures

Maternal race and ethnicity were measured using two variables on the birth certificate record: mother's race and mother's origin. Women who reported their origin as one of the Hispanic groups (e.g., Cuban,

Table 1

Percentage Distributions
of Study Variables by Race/Ethnicity

	Race/Ethnic Group			
			Hispanic	
	White[1]	Black[1]	White	Black
	(N=110,749)	(N=36,651)	(N=18,838)	(N=3,947)
Marital Status				
Single	14.9	66.1	20.9	54.0
Maternal Age				
<16	0.5	3.5	0.8	0.5
16-19	9.8	21.7	10.1	5.3
20-24	28.5	33.9	29.7	19.1
25-29	33.6	23.7	32.3	32.3
30-34	20.4	12.7	18.9	27.7
35-39	6.2	3.8	6.9	11.8
40+	0.8	0.6	1.3	3.3
Maternal Education (Years)				
0-8	2.4	3.8	14.4	46.4
9-11	16.1	29.5	16.6	18.3
12	41.3	43.9	33.5	23.2
13+	40.2	22.7	35.5	12.1
Residence				
SMSAs >750,000	23.1	31.5	72.5	63.0
SMSAs 500,000-749,999	18.9	22.7	6.8	18.3
SMSAs 50,000-499,999	37.9	30.8	12.9	14.1
Non-metro Areas 10,000-50,000	12.1	7.9	4.7	4.3
Non-metro Areas <10,000	8.0	7.1	3.1	0.4
Public Prenatal Care				
Yes	15.1	37.2	13.3	27.8

table continues

Table 1 (continued)

| | Race/Ethnic Group | | Hispanic | |
| | White[1] | Black[1] | White | Black |
	(N=110,749)	(N=36,651)	(N=18,838)	(N=3,947)
Prenatal Visits				
0-6	10.8	26.3	12.7	14.7
7-19	85.1	70.9	86.1	85.1
20+	4.1	2.7	1.2	0.3
Parity				
First Birth	45.6	35.0	42.4	25.3
Plural Birth	2.2	2.4	2.1	2.0
Congenital Malformation	1.8	3.5	4.0	8.0
Complication of Pregnancy	9.6	10.6	7.3	8.5
Reproductive Risk	2.7	4.3	2.5	8.3
Baby's Gender				
Female	48.7	50.0	48.5	48.9
Low Birthweight	5.8	13.1	5.9	9.1
Neonatal Mortality	4.0	9.0	4.0	5.0

Note: [1] The white and black categories do not include any
individuals of Hispanic origin.

Puerto Rican) were categorized as Hispanics. These women were further categorized by race into white Hispanic and black Hispanic categories. Those not reporting Hispanic origin were coded by race as white or black. Women who reported an "other" racial/ethnic group included Asians, Native Americans, and Alaskan Natives. These groups were excluded from this analysis because of their small sample size. The final sample sizes, after deleting missing values were 110,749 non-Hispanic whites, 36,651 non-Hispanic blacks, 18,838 Hispanic whites and 3,947 Hispanic blacks.

The key family structural characteristic of concern in this analysis is mother's marital status. This variable was categorized as married and not-married for the analysis. While it would have been desirable to differentiate between never-married and divorced/separated respondents in the analysis, this additional delineation was not possible with this data set. The highest percentage of single women delivering during 1987 was found among non-Hispanic black women, at 66.1 percent, followed by Hispanic black women at 54 percent. White populations had markedly lower rates of single marital status at delivery—with 14.9 percent for non-Hispanic white women and 20.9 percent for Hispanic white women.

Maternal age was reclassified into categories based on an assessment of the bivariate relationships between age and low birthweight and age and neonatal mortality. Age categories that maximized the homogeneity of risk of the two outcomes were first created: younger than 16, 16-19, 20-39, 40 and older. Although the data were examined by racial/ethnic groups, the same age categorizations were determined to be appropriate across the different groups. The largest of the four categories (20-39-year-olds) was subsequently divided into four groups: 20-24, 25-29, 30-35, 35-39, resulting in seven age categories. The different racial/ethnic groups had comparable age distributions with the exception of non-Hispanic blacks, who tended to be younger and Hispanic blacks, who tended to be older. Approximately 33 percent of the births were to women age 25-29. Hispanic blacks had higher rates of births to older women (30 and above), while black non-Hispanics have higher rates for the younger age groups. Figures on teenage births are comparable to national rates of 10.9 percent among whites, 23.6 percent among blacks, and 16.6 percent among all Hispanics (National Center for Health Statistics, 1992).

Maternal education was categorized into four levels: fewer than nine years of education, 9-11 years of education (i.e., not a high school graduate), 12 years of education, and more than 12 years. These levels were selected based on an analysis of the association between education and low birthweight, and education and neonatal mortality. The category of 12 years of education was selected as the reference category. The distribution of births by education shows that a larger proportion of black births are to women with fewer than 12 years (33.3 percent) than is true for white women (18.5 percent). This is similar to national trends in 1984-1986 of 32.6 percent and 17.7 percent, respectively (Singh, Forrest and Torres, 1989).

The utilization of prenatal care was measured by the number of prenatal care visits the mother obtained during pregnancy. This variable has been reported in several studies to be associated with low birthweight and neonatal mortality (Institute of Medicine, 1988; Moore et al., 1986). Empirical analysis of the Florida birth certificate data suggested a significantly increased risk of neonatal mortality among infants whose mothers obtained fewer than seven prenatal visits or more than 19 visits. In light of this relationship, we collapsed prenatal visits into three categories: 0-6 visits, 7-19 visits, and 20 visits or more. In the analysis, the 7-19 visit category is excluded as the reference category. The proportion of women with fewer than seven prenatal visits ranged from 10.8 percent among whites to 26.3 percent among blacks. Approximately 85 percent of non-Hispanic white, Hispanic white and Hispanic black women received at least seven prenatal visits and no more than 19. This lower utilization of care among blacks and Hispanics is consistent with U.S. data.[5]

In addition to these variables, other measures were included to control for the effects of important maternal sociodemographic or medical factors. These included residence of mother (measured with a five-category indicator of population size and adjacency to a metropolitan area); maternal use of public (i.e., versus private) prenatal care; parity (first birth versus second or greater); plural birth (singleton versus non-singleton); presence of congenital malformation of the infant (yes or no); complications of pregnancy (yes or no); previous fetal or infant death labeled as "reproductive risk" (yes or no); and the sex of the infant. These variables were selected as control variables based on literature which affirms their role in influencing birth outcomes (Eisner et al., 1979; Institute of Medicine, 1985). The distributions of these variables are also included in Table 1.[6]

Analysis

To determine the impact of maternal marital status on birth outcomes, logistic regression models were estimated which included all of the variables described above. Models predicting low birthweight (less than 2500 grams versus 2500 or more) and neonatal mortality (death at 28 days or younger versus no death less than 28 days) were estimated for each of the racial/ethnic groups. The coefficients and odds ratios from these models were then compared to identify important patterns in the role of marital status on birth outcomes across racial/ethnic divisions.

FINDINGS

Low Birthweight Models

Table 2 presents the results of estimating the low birthweight model for each racial/ethnic group. The top number presented in each column is the unstandardized coefficient; the number in parentheses is the odds of a low weight birth associated with that category, relative to the excluded category (as noted by a dash in place of the coefficient). The data indicate a significant relationship of single marital status with the risk of low birthweight for blacks, whites, and both Hispanic groups. Being single increases the odds of a woman having a low birthweight infant by approximately 30 percent (odds ratios of 1.33 for white and 1.31 for black non-Hispanics and 1.25 and 1.19 for white and black Hispanics). This finding is generally consistent with existing literature: legitimacy status clearly has an important effect on birth outcomes as measure by infant birthweight. For three of the racial/ethnic groups which indicate statistical significance, our data suggest that unmarried status confers a distinct birthweight disadvantage for the infant. The coefficient for Hispanic blacks was not significant.

Maternal age has a rather different impact on the risk of low birthweight across the racial/ethnic groups. The sign and magnitude of the coefficients for non-Hispanic whites and blacks are similar across all age groups, with the exception of the 40 and older age group. At ages younger than 19, non-Hispanic mothers experience reduced risk of low birthweight. The risks of low birthweight increase at ages 20-24 and continue upwards with increasing age, with odds as high as 1.47 for white women aged 40 and older. These findings are consistent with contemporary literature which has argued that, contrary to earlier re-

Table 2

Coefficients (and Odds Ratios)
from Estimating Low Birthweight Models
by Race/Ethnic Group

	Race/Ethnic Group			
			Hispanic	
	White[1]	Black[1]	White	Black
	(N=110,749)	(N=36,651)	(N=18,838)	(N=3,947)
Intercept	-4.15	-3.07	-3.70	-3.56
Marital Status				
Single	0.29**[3]	0.27**	0.22**	0.17
	(1.33)	(1.31)	(1.25)	(1.19)
Maternal Age				
<16	-0.34*	-0.16	0.05	0.01
	(0.71)	(0.85)	(1.05)	(1.01)
16-19	-0.17**	-0.15**	0.08	-0.25
	(0.84)	(0.86)	(1.09)	(0.78)
20-24	0.18**	0.25**	0.00	-0.08
	(1.19)	(1.28)	(1.00)	(0.92)
25-29[2]	--	--	--	--
	(1.00)	(1.00)	(1.00)	(1.00)
30-34	0.32**	0.19**	0.14	-0.07
	(1.38)	(1.20)	(1.16)	(0.93)
35-39	0.38**	0.39**	0.32*	-0.01
	(1.47)	(1.47)	(1.38)	(0.99)
40+	0.38**	0.18	0.54*	-0.37
	(1.47)	(1.20)	(1.72)	(0.69)
Maternal Education (Years)				
0-8	0.31**	0.10	-0.12	0.16
	(1.37)	(1.10)	(0.89)	(1.18)
9-11	0.22**	0.20**	-0.00	0.39*
	(1.25)	(1.23)	(1.00)	(1.48)
12	--	--	--	--
	(1.00)	(1.00)	(1.00)	(1.00)
13+	-0.25**	-0.22**	-0.19*	-0.14
	(0.78)	(0.80)	(0.82)	(0.87)

table continues

Table 2 (continued)

	Race/Ethnic Group			
			Hispanic	
	White[1]	Black[1]	White	Black
	(N=110,749)	(N=36,651)	(N=18,838)	(N=3,947)

Residence				
SMSAs > 750,000	--	--	--	--
	(1.00)	(1.00)	(1.00)	(1.00)
SMSAs 500,000-749,999	-0.02	-0.23**	0.12	-0.02
	(0.98)	(0.80)	(1.13)	(0.98)
SMSAs 50,000-499,999	-0.06	-0.12**	-0.09	-0.14
	(0.94)	(0.88)	(0.91)	(0.87)
Non-metro Areas				
10,000-50,000	-0.25**	-0.41**	-0.37*	0.44
	(0.78)	(0.67)	(0.69)	(0.64)
Non-metro Areas < 10,000	-0.07	-0.29**	-0.26	-0.04
	(0.93)	(0.75)	(0.77)	(0.96)
Public Prenatal Care				
Yes	0.05	-0.10**	-0.16	-0.10
	(1.05)	(0.91)	(0.85)	(0.90)
Prenatal Visits				
0-6	1.18**	1.06**	1.05**	1.05**
	(3.25)	(2.88)	(2.87)	(2.86)
7-19	--	--	--	--
	(1.00)	(1.00)	(1.00)	(1.00)
20+	0.08	0.00	0.36	-3.85
	(1.09)	(1.00)	(1.44)	(0.02)
Parity				
First Birth	0.42**	0.22**	0.32**	0.40**
	(1.52)	(1.25)	(1.38)	(1.49)
Plural Birth	2.96**	2.82**	2.93**	2.19*
	(19.33)	(16.74)	(18.69)	(8.98)
Congenital Malformation	1.41**	0.82**	0.76**	0.46*
	(4.10)	(2.28)	(2.15)	(1.58)
Complication of Pregnancy	1.20**	0.95**	0.95**	0.74**
	(3.31)	(2.59)	(2.58)	(2.10)

table continues

Table 2 (continued)

| | Race/Ethnic Group | | | |
| | White[1] (N=110,749) | Black[1] (N=36,651) | Hispanic | |
			White (N=18,838)	Black (N=3,947)
Reproductive Risk	0.45**	0.53**	0.56**	0.62**
	(1.57)	(1.70)	(1.75)	(1.86)
Baby's Gender				
Female	0.28**	0.20**	0.17**	0.37**
	(1.32)	(1.23)	(1.18)	(1.44)

Notes: [1] The white and black categories do not include any individuals of Hispanic origin.

[2] The reference category for each variable is presented by dashed lines.

[3] The top number represents the unstandardized beta; the bottom number is the odds ratio.

* p < .05
** p < .01

search, young maternal age *per se* does not increase the risk of low birthweight (Geronimus, 1987). In fact, young age appears to have a protective effect for women younger than 19 years of age. The low birthweight findings for Hispanic women generally show no significant relationship with age, net of the other variables. At ages 35-39 and 40 and older, however, white Hispanic women have a significantly increased risk of low birthweight; the odds, relative to women aged 25-29, are 1.38 and 1.72, respectively.

As the data in Table 2 indicate, maternal education is an important predictor of low birthweight. Non-Hispanic women who do not graduate from high school have odds 22-36 percent higher than high school graduates to have a low weight birth. Non-Hispanic women and Hispanic white women with some college education are significantly less likely to deliver a low birthweight baby (odds .78, .80, .82, respectively). The coefficient for black Hispanic women did not reach statistical significance.

The residence variables present an interesting impact primarily upon non-Hispanic black births. Black women in areas smaller than the largest grouping (SMSAs with more than 750,000 persons) enjoy significantly lower risks of low birthweight, with odds ratios between .67 and .88. Both non-Hispanic and Hispanic white women also had significantly reduced odds of a low weight birth if they lived in nonmetropolitan areas of 10,000-50,000 persons.

The remaining variables in Table 2 served primarily as controls in the examination of the impact of the demographic variables on low birthweight. What is notable about these numbers is the significant detrimental effects of few prenatal visits on low birthweight. Women who receive fewer than six prenatal visits are almost three times as likely to have a low birthweight infant, regardless of racial/ethnic group. The impact of this insufficient care appears to be greatest for non-Hispanic white women (odds 3.25). The adequacy of prenatal care is generally assumed to serve as a proxy for income levels and social risk. Women who receive inadequate prenatal care are more likely to poor and uninsured (Poland, Ager and Olsen, 1987) and from unstable family conditions with little social support (Harvey and Faber, 1993).

The coefficients for the parity, plurality and other medical risk conditions show typical patterns of increasing rates of low birthweight in the presence of one or more of these risk factors. Plural births are risky for women of all race/ethnicities, but especially for white women.

Neonatal Mortality

Table 3 presents the coefficients and odds ratios from the logistic regression models predicting neonatal mortality for each of the four racial/ethnic groups. These data indicate significantly greater diversity in the impact of marital status and maternal age across race/ethnic lines. Specifically, as has been implied in other recent studies, being a single mother significantly reduces the odds of a neonatal death among the infants of non-Hispanic black women, while this variable increases the risk of neonatal mortality among white women.

This finding is interesting for at least two reasons. First, single marital status has long been believed to have deleterious effects on maternal health and, subsequently, on infant health and survival because of the potential absence of financial or other support from the infant's father. Consistent with the more recent literature, however, our

Table 3

Coefficients (and Odd Ratios)
from Estimating Neonatal Mortality Models
by Race/Ethnic Group

	Race/Ethnic Group			
			Hispanic	
	White[1]	Black[1]	White	Black
	(N=110,749)	(N=36,651)	(N=18,838)	(N=3,947)
Intercept	-6.51	-5.54	-6.28	-6.89
Marital Status				
Single	0.03[3]	-.043**	0.09	0.10
	(1.03)	(0.65)	(1.09)	(1.11)
Maternal Age				
<16	1.19**	0.09	1.33	-5.43
	(3.27)	(1.10)	(3.77)	(0.00)
16-19	-0.11	-0.11	0.31	-4.75
	(0.89)	0.90)	(1.36)	(0.01)
20-24	0.10	0.17	0.26	-0.01
	(1.11)	(1.18)	(1.30)	(0.99)
25-29[2]	--	--	--	--
	(1.00)	(1.00)	(1.00)	(1.00)
30-34	0.12	0.27	0.71*	1.03
	(1.13)	(1.31)	(2.04)	(2.81)
35-39	0.45*	0.52	0.46	1.75*
	(1.57)	(1.68)	(1.58)	(5.75)
40+	0.23	-0.02	1.47*	-3.42
	(1.26)	(0.98)	(4.35)	(0.03)

table continues

Table 3 (continued)

	White[1] (N=110,749)	Black[1] (N=36,651)	Hispanic White (N=18,838)	Hispanic Black (N=3,947)
		Race/Ethnic Group		
Maternal Education (Years)				
0-8	-0.50	-0.20	-0.04	-0.72
	(0.61)	(0.82)	(0.96)	(0.49)
9-11	-0.18	-0.15	-0.17	0.63
	(0.84)	(0.86)	(0.84)	(1.89)
12	--	--	--	--
	(1.00)	(1.00)	(1.00)	(1.00)
13+	0.03	0.02	0.03	-0.12
	(1.03)	(1.02)	(1.03)	(0.89)
Residence				
SMSAs > 750,000	--	--	--	--
	(1.00)	(1.00)	(1.00)	(1.00)
SMSAs 500,000-749,999	0.11	0.03	0.24	0.30
	(1.12)	(1.03)	(1.28)	(1.35)
SMSAs 50,000-499,999	0.27*	0.17	-0.23	0.61
	(1.31)	(1.19)	(0.79)	(1.85)
Non-metro 10,000-50,000	-0.44*	-0.76**	-0.31	0.22
	(0.65)	(0.47)	(0.73)	(1.25)
Non-metro Areas < 10,000	0.10	0.09	-5.30	-4.08
	(1.10)	(1.09)	(0.01)	(0.02)
Public Prenatal Care				
Yes	-0.37*	-0.13	0.24	-0.62
	(0.69)	(0.88)	(1.27)	(0.54)
Prenatal Visits				
0-6	1.91**	2.05**	1.69**	1.89**
	(6.77)	(7.78)	(5.44)	(6.63)
7-19	--	--	--	--
	(1.00)	(1.00)	(1.00)	(1.00)
20+	-0.23	-0.10	-4.93	-2.87
	(0.80)	(0.90)	(0.01)	(0.06)

table continues

Table 3 (continued)

	White[1] (N=110,749)	Black[1] (N=36,651)	Hispanic White (N=18,838)	Hispanic Black (N=3,947)
Parity				
First Birth	0.05	0.65**	0.57*	1.36*
	(1.05)	(1.92)	(1.78)	(3.88)
Plural Birth	1.76**	1.20**	1.04*	1.16
	(5.80)	(3.32)	(2.84)	(3.20)
Congenital Malformation	2.88**	2.11**	2.02**	0.88
	(17.74)	(8.28)	(7.54)	(2.40)
Complication of Pregnancy	1.19**	.074**	0.99**	0.56
	(3.30)	(2.09)	(2.70)	(1.75)
Reproductive Risk	1.16**	1.13**	-0.02	0.30
	(3.19)	(3.09)	(0.98)	(1.35)
Baby's Gender				
Female	-0.19*	-0.43**	-0.39	-0.18
	(0.82)	(0.65)	(0.67)	(0.83)

Notes:

[1] The white and black categories do not include any individuals of Hispanic origin.

[2] The reference category for each variable is presented by dashed lines.

[3] The top number represents the unstandardized beta; the bottom number is the odds ratio.

* $p < .05$
** $p < .01$

results suggest that single motherhood among black women may operate quite differently than is the case for other racial/ethnic groups. We will elaborate on some possible explanations for this below. Secondly, these findings suggest that despite the strong functional relationship between low birthweight and neonatal mortality, maternal marital status operates on these outcomes quite differently. While being single increases the risk of a low birthweight infant among black women, once born, these infants have a *lower* probability of dying in the first 28 days of life than do white or Hispanic infants. Our data also reflect less of a protective function for being married for whites than has generally been reported in the literature; the odds of losing an infant in the neonatal period is only marginally increased for white women (odds 1.03).

Turning to young maternal age, we see that being younger than 16 has no significant impact on the odds of a neonatal death for blacks or Hispanics, but it does for non-Hispanic white women (odds 3.27). It appears that the protective effect of young age on birth outcomes is contained primarily in the ability of young women to have babies of normal birthweight; once born, the infants of young black and Hispanic women have no greater or lesser chance of survival than do infants born to older women. Age does, however, have a significant impact on the risks of neonatal mortality. Hispanic black women aged 30-34, and Hispanic white women 35-39 have increased odds of a neonatal loss.

As with the low birthweight models, limited education and few pre-natal visits have consistent effects across racial/ethnic groups. However, the impact of low educational attainment is insignificant for all groups, suggesting that the major effect of education occurs during the prenatal period, i.e., to impact birthweight. The impact of prenatal care is significant and large in magnitude. Women who obtain fewer than seven prenatal visits are more than five times as likely to lose their infants in the first 28 days of life than are women who receive 7-19 visits. The impact of insufficient prenatal care is greatest for non-Hispanic black women: the odds of a neonatal death are 7.78 times greater than for women who obtain 7-19 visits.

Adding Birthweight to the Mortality Model

Because of the frequently observed finding that the most important determinant of neonatal mortality is infant birthweight, we added this variable to the mortality model to determine its effect on the relationships between race and neonatal mortality. Table 4 summarizes the coefficients produced from the estimation of race-specific neonatal mortality models when birthweight is included as an endogenous variable. When these coefficients are compared to those from the neonatal mortality models that do not include birthweight we see that the effects of

Table 4

Coefficients (and Odds Ratios)
From Estimating Neonatal Mortality Models
by Race/Ethnic Group

	Race/Ethnic Group			
			Hispanic	
	White[1]	Black[1]	White	Black
	(N=110,749)	(N=36,651)	(N=18,838)	(N=3,947)
Intercept	-6.41	-5.69	-6.88	-6.77
Marital Status				
Single	-0.09[3]	-0.45**	-0.20	-0.26
	(0.92)	(0.64)	(0.82)	(0.78)
Maternal Age				
<16	1.02*	-0.09	0.95	-4.72
	(2.78)	(0.91)	(2.59)	(0.01)
16-19	0.13	-0.08	0.31	-4.93
	(1.13)	(0.92)	(1.37)	(0.01)
20-24	0.00	-0.13	-0.14	-0.36
	(1.00)	(0.88)	(0.89)	(0.70)
25-29[2]	--	--	--	--
	(1.00)	(1.00)	(1.00)	(1.00)
30-34	-0.14	0.14	0.51	0.74
	(0.87)	(1.15)	(1.67)	(2.10)
35-39	0.32	0.06	0.36	1.08
	(1.37)	(1.06)	(1.44)	(2.95)
40+	-0.24	-0.33	1.04	-4.70
	(0.78)	(0.72)	(2.82)	(0.01)
Maternal Education (Years)				
0-8	-0.55	-0.03	0.63	-1.09
	(0.58)	(0.97)	(1.87)	(0.34)
9-11	-0.20	-0.13	0.03	0.50
	(0.82)	(0.88)	(1.03)	(1.66)
12	--	--	--	--
	(1.00)	(1.00)	(1.00)	(1.00)
13+	0.02	0.04	0.44	-0.52
	(1.02)	(1.04)	(1.56)	(0.60)

table continues

Table 4 (Continued)

| | Race/Ethnic Group | | | |
| | | | Hispanic | |
	White[1] (N=110,749)	Black[1] (N=36,651)	White (N=18,838)	Black (N=3,947)
Residence				
SMSAs >750,000	--	--	--	--
	(1.00)	(1.00)	(1.00)	(1.00)
SMSAs 500,000-749,999	-0.07	0.16	0.13	0.65
	(0.93)	(1.18)	(1.14)	(1.91)
SMSAs 50,000-499,999	0.31*	0.29	-0.05	1.85*
	(1.37)	(1.34)	(0.95)	(6.37)
Non-metro 10,000-50,000	-0.05	-0.29	0.20	2.83*
	(0.95)	(0.75)	(1.22)	(17.02)
Non-metro Areas <10,000	-0.03	0.31	-6.85	-2.97
	(0.97)	(1.36)	(0.00)	(0.05)
Public Prenatal Care				
Yes	-0.12	0.04	0.73	-1.19
	(0.89)	(1.04)	(2.07)	(0.30)
Prenatal Visits				
0-6	0.67**	0.95**	.09	0.55
	(1.95)	(2.59)	(1.09)	(1.73)
7-19	--	--	--	--
	(1.00)	(1.00)	(1.00)	(1.00)
20+	-0.16	0.17	-5.70	-2.82
	(0.86)	(1.19)	(0.00)	(0.06)
Parity				
First Birth	-0.28*	0.37*	0.13	0.83
	(0.76)	(1.44)	(1.13)	(2.29)
Plural Birth	-0.16	-0.19	-1.20*	-0.45
	(0.85)	(0.82)	(0.30)	(0.64)
Congenital Malformation	2.23**	1.18**	1.47**	-0.49
	(9.34)	(3.27)	(4.37)	(0.61)
Complication of Pregnancy	0.11	-0.08	0.43	-0.81
	(1.11)	(0.93)	(1.54)	(0.44)
Reproductive Risk	0.62**	0.50*	-0.89	-0.55
	(1.86)	(1.65)	(0.41)	(0.58)

table continues

Table 4 (Continued)

	White[1] (N=110,749)	Black[1] (N=36,651)	Hispanic White (N=18,838)	Hispanic Black (N=3,947)
Baby's Gender				
Female	-0.39**	-0.55**	-0.64*	-0.72
	(0.68)	(0.58)	(0.53)	(0.49)
Baby's Weight (Grams)				
0-1499	5.30**	4.38**	6.43**	6.10**
	(199.82)	(79.79)	(618.71)	(445.38)
1400-1999	2.80**	1.73**	2.39**	3.16*
	(16.53)	(5.64)	(10.87)	(23.54)
2000-2199	1.78**	1.01*	3.03**	-3.08
	(5.92)	(2.76)	(20.60)	(0.05)
2200-2499	1.41**	0.54	2.25**	2.40*
	(4.11)	(1.72)	(9.50)	(11.02)

Notes:
[1] The white and black categories do not include any individuals of Hispanic origin.
[2] The reference category for each variable is presented by dashed lines.
[3] The top number represents the unstandardized beta; the bottom number is the odds ratio.

* $p < .05$
** $p < .01$

maternal marital status change somewhat. The impact of single marital status for non-Hispanic whites becomes non-significant; the Hispanic coefficients remain non-significant. An important change in these data can also be seen in the prenatal care coefficients. The magnitude of the effects of inadequate prenatal care on neonatal mortality diminishes by nearly two-thirds when birthweight is added to the model, rendering the impact of inadequate prenatal care non-significant for Hispanics.

These findings suggest that the family structure variables have relatively little impact on neonatal mortality directly but have a significant impact indirectly through their association with birthweight (see Table 2). They also indicate that the effects of prenatal care on neonatal death operate primarily through low birthweight; for Hispanics the effect is exclusively through birthweight.

Consistent with our earlier observations, single marital status had a protective effect for black women, regardless of their age. Specifically, among blacks, single women were significantly less likely to lose their infant in the first month of life than were married women. The protective effect of single marital status for black women was maintained even when birthweight was controlled.

DISCUSSION

Our findings, building upon recent observations by Cramer (1987) and Eberstein, Nam, and Hummer (1990), suggest an interesting and anomalous relationship between race, marital status, and neonatal mortality. Net of other important factors that are associated with neonatal death, single marital status was found to be associated with significant reductions in neonatal mortality among non-Hispanic black women. This relationship did not hold for white or Hispanic women of either racial group. The interaction with age for blacks suggests, additionally, that the finding cannot be explained away by noting that unwed mothers are disproportionately young.

The protective effects of single marital status on neonatal mortality among blacks is particularly surprising because the same relationship was not found between single marital status and low birthweight, despite the fact that low birthweight is the predominant cause of neonatal death. The data indicate that black, white, and Hispanic single women had significantly increased risks of a low birthweight infant, net of the same controls included in the neonatal mortality models. The fact that this does not carry over to neonatal mortality for blacks would generally be contrary to expectations because low birthweight has long been associated with increased risks of neonatal death and because black women are two times as likely as white women to deliver a low weight infant. If black women have greater probabilities of delivering a low weight infant, and these infants are at significantly increased risk of neonatal death relative to normal weight infants, and single marital status among black women increases the risk of a low weight infant, we should expect that single marital status among blacks would, accordingly, increase the risks of neonatal death.

How, then, do we explain a finding that has now been replicated in at least three studies? Though what follows remains speculative (and will remain so until studies that address the issue very specifically are completed), it does provide a possible explanation that is consistent with the growing literature on the importance of family structure in explaining a variety of different outcomes.

While most analysts and policy makers have typically begun with the assumption that childbearing outside the context of marriage is a nonnormative life event, this assumption might simply be inappropriate in some cases and may not actually correspond to the childbearing preferences of women and their families in some sociocultural contexts (Burton, 1990). Hamburg (1980), for example, has argued that teenage childbearing reflects an alternative life-course strategy in some cultural subgroups and may be a response to certain developmental, social, and economic forces that are specific to the setting (see also Stack, 1974). In such a context, Burton (1990:124) suggests that "early childbearing may be perceived as a viable option that fosters individual growth, family continuity, and cultural survival in an environment in which few other avenues for enhancing development are available."

What all of this suggests is that among some groups, childbearing outside the context of marriage has actually become the norm (Geronimus, 1987). As Wu and Martinson (1993) recently demonstrate, demographically, a first premarital birth is now the modal fertility pattern for recent cohorts of black women. This pattern is less common for Hispanics and much less common for whites.

To the extent that nonmarital births are normative, such a course is seen as neither a major social or personal calamity and the baby's presence can both improve the self-image of the mother and improve her opportunities for financial, psychological, and other support from those around her (Ryan and Schneider, 1978:1197). Informal family support structures exist to encourage the young mother and assist her with childcare and other parenting needs and to protect her from the stigmatization that frequently occurs in other settings (St. John and Rowe, 1990). Out-of-wedlock and teenage motherhood in such a context can be an adaptive strategy that is consistent with social expectations and the extended family household can often more than not meet the needs that might otherwise be met by the presence of a spouse.[7]

This suggests that the normative aspect of nonmarital childbearing can have obvious effects on successful birth outcomes. The presence of a support structure that looks out for the pregnant woman and that is available to help meet her most pressing economic, nutritional, and other needs, can have a significant difference on life opportunities. Furthermore, remaining single can provide a protective function that might be removed with marriage. As noted by Geronimus (1987:264), the young woman who marries "will not have the benefit of parental authority and guidance to attenuate the potentially harmful effects of their immaturity on the health of their unborn children."

Finally, we should note that the findings for the Hispanic population are important both in those instances where they differ from the non-Hispanics and in the observed differences between the two Hispanic racial groups. These differences affirm that race and ethnicity are distinct, but overlapping, categories that must be considered when assessing their impact on health outcomes. In terms of single marital status, the Hispanics of both racial groups had somewhat similar coefficients to the non-Hispanic whites, but the impact was only significant for white Hispanics. It is important to note here that the small sample of black Hispanics may be responsible for the general lack of significance among the independent variables for the low birthweight and neonatal mortality models. Significant associations with the risks of having a neonatal death were only noted for black Hispanics aged 35-39, those with fewer than seven prenatal visits, and those having a first birth. In each of these cases, the odds were notably higher than for most other groups.

CONCLUSIONS

Clearly, studies are needed that will specifically address the nature of the role played by alternative family structures in affecting things like birth outcomes. We have emphasized the role that is attributed in the literature to the extended black family. However, Hispanic women are also much more likely to live in extended families than are whites (see Angel and Tienda, 1982; Beck and Beck, 1989; Farley and Allen, 1987), yet their pattern of birth outcomes is much more similar to that of whites than that of blacks. How and why might the extended family be operating differently in these different racial/ethnic settings?

The presence of a protective relationship between single marital status and neonatal death among blacks suggests that important variables associated with single marital status and neonatal mortality remain uncontrolled in the research models that have been reported to this point. The specific role of alternative family structures in affecting birth outcomes clearly requires additional research attention. However, we must emphasize an important caution that has been suggested by others. There is great diversity in the black population, as there is among other racial and ethnic groups, and there is no monolithic culture among blacks that leads to the observed higher rates of unmarried childbearing (Bumpass and McLanahan, 1989). Some subgroups of the population show much greater propensities for this than others—for example, those living in central cities, in single-parent households, and so on. We must keep this fact clearly in mind as we attempt better to understand what is happening. And, it is particularly important to keep this in mind if we remember that one of the primary reasons for additional research in this area is to attempt to address the observation we noted at the beginning: that health and life chances of individuals born in this country continue to be significantly affected by social class and racial/ethnic factors.

Our findings add to the puzzle that confronts policy development. If, as Geronimus (1987) has convincingly argued, it is not teenage childbearing as such that contributes to high black infant mortality rates, but the fact that black teenagers reflect a combination of other important risk factors associated with poverty and lower socioeconomic status, then programs that focus specifically on teenage pregnancy will have little overall impact. Our findings suggest that just as teenage pregnancy among blacks may not be the most critical issue, neither is marital status, particularly if one is interested in improving something like birth outcomes. This suggests that what is needed may be ways to support the black social family, even when it does not show the "normative" pattern of husband and wife living together with their offspring.

NOTES

[1] The negative health-related consequences of minority and lower socioeconomic status are, of course, reflected in a broad range of indicators in addition to measures of infant mortality. For example, Williams, Lavizzo-Mourey, and Warren (1994:31) have recently noted that one of the most clearly established findings in social epidemiology is the relationship between SES and health. Simil-

arly, Lieu, Newacheck, and McManus (1993) have summarized a large body of research on race and ethnicity by noting that despite overall worse health status, minorities have fewer health care services than whites and this inequity persists across income levels and is present even for patients with chronic illness. (See also, Blendon et al., 1989; Keil et al., 1992; Williams, 1990).

[2] We should note that while birth weight is included in the variables listed by Eberstein and Parker, several studies have demonstrated that most of the other variables that have been found to be important impact infant mortality primarily through their effect on birthweight. Birthweight clearly remains the one single most important predictor of infant mortality.

[3] As noted by a reviewer of the previous draft of this manuscript, race and Hispanic origin (ethnicity) are distinct concepts that result in overlapping categories—i.e., both black and white racial groups include persons of Hispanic and non-Hispanic origin. Because of this, we have chosen to cross-tabulate race and Hispanic origin in the analysis to derive four categories: non-Hispanic whites, non-Hispanic blacks, Hispanic whites, and Hispanic blacks.

[4] Several researchers have argued for the importance of examining cause-specific determinants of death in studies of infant mortality (see, for example, Eberstein, Nam and Hummer, 1990; Hummer, 1993; Rogers 1989b). While some findings indicate rather complex relationships among different biological and social factors and specific causes of death for different ethnic groups (Eberstein et al., 1990; Rogers 1989b), Hummer (1993) has recently shown that the racial gap in infant mortality is very similar for both endogenous and exogenous causes. Thus, while there may be some rather important racial and ethnic differences by specific cause, the overall pattern between the groups remains basically the same. We have chosen not to include cause-specific rates here because race/ ethnic differences in cause are less central to our purposes than are the specific effects of marital status on overall birth outcomes. Additionally, because our indicator is neonatal rather than infant mortality, exogenous causes of death—and, hence, differences in

endogenous and exogenous causes—should be somewhat less important than may be the case in studies of infant mortality.

[5] Adequacy of prenatal care has typically been addressed in the literature through using one or the other of two measures, either the Kessner or the Kotelchuck indices. Neither of these indices was used in this analysis due to the poor quality of gestational age data available in the data set. Gestation age data were missing for more than 20 percent of the birth records available from the Division of Vital Statistics in 1988. Imputation of missing gestational age data during the original creation of the linked data set was attempted but determined to be too inaccurate. Thus, the number of prenatal visits and the trimester of entry into care were the best available measures of prenatal care use. Preliminary analyses of the data indicated an insignificant effect of trimester of entry so this variable was omitted from the analysis. Prenatal care visits was retained as a measure of medical care use during pregnancy, but should not be considered a measure of prenatal care adequacy.

[6] Quality checks were performed on all of the variables included in the data set. Out-of-range values were excluded based on information from various sources, including *Guidelines for Prenatal Care* (American Academy for Pediatrics and the American College of Obstetricians and Gynecologists, 1983) for the infant characteristics. The following values were considered to be out of range and were consequently set to missing: mother's age less than 10 or over 50, more than 49 prenatal visits, mother's education more than 26 years, parity of more than 20, and the plurality greater than 4. Additional details on the creation of the data set are available from the University of Florida Institute for Health Policy Research in the report "The Evaluation of the Impact and Cost-Effectiveness of Florida's Improved Pregnancy Outcome Program."

[7] If we shift the perspective to the black male, several studies have noted that among the poor, particularly, black men's wages are insufficient to support a family. As a result, the possibility of a pre-maritally pregnant black teenager marrying into an economically stable family environment is extremely limited and acts to reduce

the potential economic returns to marriage for her (Darity and Myers, 1986-87; Hogan and Kitagawa, 1985; Wilson, 1987). From this economic perspective, there are some very serious disadvantages associated with marriage, and this has contributed to the emergence of matrifocal family patterns that reflect the reality of existing economic conditions (Geronimus, 1987; Stack, 1974).

REFERENCES

Alexander, G.R. and D.A. Cornely. 1987. "Racial disparities in pregnancy outcomes: The role of prenatal care utilization and maternal risk status." *American Journal of Preventive Medicine* 3 (5):254-261.

American Academy for Pediatrics and the American College of Obstetricians and Gynecologists. 1983. *Guidelines for Prenatal Care.* Elk Grove Village, IL and Washington, D.C.: American Academy for Pediatrics and the American College of Obstetricians and Gynecologists.

Angel, R. and M. Tienda. 1982. "Determinants of extended household structure: Cultural pattern or economic model?" *American Journal of Sociology* 87:1360-1383.

Antonovsky, A. and J. Bernstein. 1977. "Social class and infant mortality." *Social Science and Medicine* 11:453-470.

Beck, R.W. and S.H. Beck. 1989. "The incidence of extended households among middle-aged black and white women: Estimates from a 5-year study." *Journal of Family Issues* 10:147-168.

Becerra, J., C.J.R. Hogue, H.K. Atrash, and N. Perez. 1991. "Infant mortality among Hispanics: A portrait of heterogeneity." *JAMA* 265:217-221.

Berkov, B. 1981. "Does being born out of wedlock still make a difference?" Paper presented at the Annual Meeting of the Population Association of America, Washington, D.C.

Blendon, R., L. Aiken, H. Freeman, and C. Corey. 1989. "Access to medical care for black and white Americans." *JAMA* 261:278-281.

Brooks, C.H. 1975. "The changing relationship between socioeconomic status and infant mortality: An analysis of state characteristics." *Journal of Health and Social Behavior* 16 (3):291-303.

Bumpass, L. and S. McLanahan. 1989. "Unmarried motherhood: Recent trends, composition, and black-white differences." *Demography* 26 (2):279-286.

Burton, L. 1990. "Teenage childbearing as an alternative life-course strategy in multigeneration black families." *Human Nature* 1:123-143.

Cramer, J., K. Bell, and K. Vaast. 1991. "Race, ethnicity, and the determinants of low birthweight in the U.S." Paper presented at the Annual Meeting of the Population Association of America, Washington, D.C.

Cramer, J.C. 1987. "Social factors and infant mortality: Identifying high-risk groups and proximate causes." *Demography* 24 (3):299-322.

Darity, W. and S.L. Myers. 1986-87. "Public policy trends and the fate of the black family." *Humboldt Journal of Social Relations* 14:134-164.

David, R.J. and J.W. Collins. 1991. "Bad outcomes in black babies: Race or racism." *Ethnicity and Disease* 1:236-244

Donabedian, A., L.S. Rosenfeld, and E.M. Southern. 1965. "Infant mortality and socioeconomic status in a metropolitan community." *Public Health Reports* 80:1083-1094.

Eberstein, I.W. and J.R. Parker. 1984. "Racial differences in infant mortality by cause of death: The impact of birth weight and maternal age." *Demography* 21 (3):309-317.

Eberstein, I.W., C.B. Nam, and R.A. Hummer. 1990. "Infant mortality by cause of death: Main and interaction effects." *Demography* 27 (3):413-430.

Eberstein, I.W., R.A. Hummer, and C.B. Nam. 1990. "Sociodemographic influences on infant mortality: Direct and indirect effects." Paper presented at the annual meeting of the American Sociological Association, Washington, D.C.

Eisner, V., J.V. Brasic, M.W. Pratt, and A.C. Hexter. 1979. "The risk of low birthweight." *American Journal of Public Health* 69 (9):887-893.

Farley, R. and W.R. Allen. 1987. *The Color Line and the Quality of Life in America*. New York: Russell Sage Foundation.

Forbes, D. and W.P. Frisbie. 1991. "Spanish surname and Anglo infant mortality: Differentials over a half-century." *Demography* 28:639-660.

Frisbie, W.P. and F.D. Bean. 1993. "The Latino family in comparative perspective: Trends and current conditions." Paper presented at the Center for Studies of the Family's 20th Annual Conference: Race/Ethnic Families in the United States, Provo, UT (October).

Gee, S.C., E.S. Lee, and R.N. Forthofer. 1976. "Ethnic differentials in neonatal and postneonatal mortality: A birth cohort analysis by a binary variable multiple regression method." *Social Biology* 23 (4):317-325.

Geronimus, A.T. 1986. "The effects of race, residence, and prenatal care on the relationship of maternal age to neonatal mortality." *American Journal of Public Health* 76 (12):1414-1421, December.

————. 1987. "On teenage childbearing and neonatal mortality in the United States." *Population and Development Review* 13 (2):245-279.

Geronimus, A.T., and J. Bound. 1990. "Black/white differences in women's reproductive related health status: Evidence from *Vital Statistics*." *Demography* 27 (3):457-466.

Hamburg, B.A. 1980. "Teenagers as parents: Developmental issues in school-age pregnancy." In E. Purcell (ed.), *Psychopathology of Children and Youth: A Cross Cultural Perspective*. New York: Josiah Macy, Jr. Foundation.

Harvey, S.M. and K.S. Faber. 1993. "Obstacles to prenatal care following implementation of a community-based program to reduce financial barriers." *Family Planning Perspectives* 25 (1):32-36.

Hogan, D.P. and E.M. Kitagawa. 1985. "The impact of social status, family structure, and neighborhood on the fertility of black adolescents." *American Journal of Sociology* 90 (4):825-855.

Hummer, R.A. 1993. "Racial differentials in infant mortality in the U.S.: An examination of social and health determinants." *Social Forces* 72 (2):529-554.

Hummer, R.A., I.W. Eberstein, and C.B. Nam. 1992. "Infant mortality differentials among Hispanic groups in Florida." *Social Forces* 70:1055-1075.

Institute of Medicine. 1985. *Preventing Low Birthweight*. Washington, D.C.: National Academy Press.

_____. 1988. *Prenatal Care: Reaching Mothers, Reaching Infants*. Washington, D.C.: National Academy Press.

Keil, J.E., S.E. Sutherland, R.G. Knapp, and H.A. Tyroler. 1992. "Does equal socioeconomic status in black and white men mean equal risk of mortality?" *American Journal of Public Health* 82:1133-1139.

Lieu, T.A., P.W. Newacheck, and M.A. McManus. 1993. "Race, ethnicity, and access to ambulatory care among U.S. adolescents." *American Journal of Public Health* 83:960-965.

Markides, K.S., and D. Barnes. 1977. "A methodological note on the relationship between infant mortality and socioeconomic status with evidence from San Antonio, Texas." *Social Biology* 24 (1):38-44.

Markides, K.S., and C. McFarland. 1982. "A note on recent trends in the infant mortality-socioeconomic status relationship." *Social Forces* 61 (1):268-276.

Moore, T.R., W. Origel, and T.C. Key. 1986. "The perinatal and economic impact of prenatal care in a low-socioeconomic population." *American Journal of Obstetrics and Gynecology* 154:29-33.

Moss, N. and K. Carver. 1992. "Explaining racial and ethnic differences in birth outcomes: The effect of household structure and resources." Paper presented at the Annual Meeting of the Population Association of America, Denver, CO (May).

National Center for Health Statistics. 1992. *Health United States, 1989*. Hyattsville, MD: U.S. Department of Health and Human Services, Public Health Service.

————. 1991. *Public Use Data Tape Documentation: 1988 National Maternal and Infant Health Survey*. Hyattsville, MD: U.S. Department of Health and Human Services, Public Health Service.

Poland, M.L., J. Ager and J.M. Olsen. 1987. "Barriers to receiving adequate prenatal care." *American Journal of Obstetrics and Gynecology* 157:297-303.

Powell-Griner, E. 1988. "Differences in infant mortality among Texas Anglos, Hispanics, and blacks." *Social Science Quarterly* 69:453-467.

Rogers, R. 1984. "Infant mortality among New Mexican Hispanics, Anglos, and Indians." *Social Science Quarterly* 65:876-884.

————. 1989a. "Ethnic differences in infant mortality: Fact or artifact?" *Social Science Quarterly* 70:642-649.

————. 1989b. "Ethnic and birth weight differences in cause-specific infant mortality." *Demography* 26:335-343.

Ryan, G.M. and J.M. Schneider. 1978. "Teenage obstetric complications." *Clinical Obstetrics and Gynecology* 21 (4):1191-1197.

Sappenfield, W. M., J.W. Buehler, N.J. Binkin, C.J. Hogue, L.T. Strauss, and J.C. Smith. 1987. "Differences in neonatal and postneonatal mortality by race, birth weight, and gestational age." *Public Health Reports* 102 (2):182-191.

Shin, E.H. 1975. "Black-white differentials in infant mortality in the South." *Demography* 12 (1):1-19.

Singh, S., J.D. Forrest, and A. Torres. 1989. *Prenatal Care in the United States: A State and County Inventory*, Volume One. New York: The Alan Guttmacher Institute.

St. John, C. and D. Rowe. 1990. "Adolescent background and fertility norms: Implications for racial differences in early childbearing." *Social Science Quarterly* 71 (1):152-162.

Stack, C. 1974. *All Our Kin*. New York: Harper and Row.

Stockwell, E.G. 1962. "Infant mortality and socioeconomic status: A changing relationship." *Milbank Memorial Fund Quarterly* 40:101-111.

University of Florida. ND. "The evaluation of the impact and cost effectiveness of Florida's improved pregnancy outcome program." Gainesville, FL: Institute for Health Policy Research.

Williams, D.R. 1990. "Socioeconomic differences in health: A review and redirection." *Social Psychology Quarterly* 53:81-99.

Williams, D.R., R. Lavizzo-Mourey, and R.C. Warren. 1994. "The concept of race and health status in America." *Public Health Reports* 109:26-41.

Willie, C.V. 1959. "A research note on the changing association between infant mortality and socioeconomic status." *Social Forces* 37:221-227.

Wilson, W.J. 1987. *The Truly Disadvantaged*. Chicago: University of Chicago Press.

Wu, L.L. and B.C. Martinson. 1993. "Family structure and the risk of a premarital birth." *American Sociological Review* 58:210-232, April.

Yankauer, A. 1990. "What infant mortality tells us." *American Journal of Public Health* 80:653-654.

Family Bonds and Adolescent Substance Use: An Ethnic Group Comparison

*Gabe T. Wang, Stephen J. Bahr,
and Anastasios C. Marcos*

INTRODUCTION

During the past two decades there has been a significant increase in the quantity and quality of research on substance use. However, there has been relatively little study of substance use among ethnic groups. The available research has tended to focus on African Americans living in large, urban areas, and there has been less attention to substance use among other ethnic groups or among non-urban populations. The growing body of research that has emerged has tended to be descriptive and atheoretical (Rebach et al., 1992). Few theories of drug abuse account for the special circumstances of different ethnic groups, and few researchers have attempted to explain ethnic variations in drug use (Tucker, 1985).

If we are to understand adolescent substance use it is essential to study adolescents in different ethnic groups. The number of adolescents in ethnic minority groups has been increasing rapidly in the United States. In some American cities, ethnic minority adolescents have become the majority of the youth population. It is projected that by 1995 about 30 percent of all American youths will be ethnic minorities (Davis and Stiffman, 1990).

Our knowledge of adolescent substance use is based primarily on data from white adolescents. To what extent can data from whites be generalized to other ethnic groups? The answer to this question would require a systematic comparison of substance use among various ethnic groups and white adolescents. A number of researchers have described patterns of substance use within different ethnic groups but only a few have compared models which explain substance use (Barnes and Welte, 1986b; Maddahian et al., 1985; Rebach et al., 1992; Tucker, 1985).

The purpose of this research is to compare the drug use of adolescents from four ethnic groups and whites. A simple explanatory model is developed and tested within each of the five groups. The five groups studied are (1) African Americans, (2) American Indians, (3) Asian Americans, (4) Hispanic Americans, and (5) white Americans.

ETHNICITY AND DRUG USE

The population of the United States is undergoing a transition from a predominantly white population to a diverse group of ethnic minorities. The proportion of the population that was minority grew from 14.9 percent in 1960 to 25 percent in 1990 (O'Hare, 1992).

Ethnicity is a social category which is based on an individual's identification with a particular social group. Ancestry, national origin, language, and religion are some of the social characteristics that define ethnicity.

African Americans are the largest ethnic group in the United States and in 1992 they comprised 12 percent of the population. In 1950 African Americans were 75 percent of the minority population in the United States, but this decreased to less than 50 percent by 1992. This change was due primarily to the immigration of large numbers of Hispanics and Asians into the United States. African Americans tend to be concentrated in the south, the east coast, and California (O'Hare, 1992).

The second largest ethnic group is Hispanics who in 1992 made up almost 10 percent of the population. Hispanics are defined as people from a Mexican, Puerto Rican, Cuban, Central or South American or other Spanish culture or origin. By the year 2010 the number of Hispanics is expected to surpass the number of African Americans (O'Hare, 1992). Hispanics tend to be concentrated in the southwest, particularly in California, Arizona, New Mexico, and Texas, but there are also significant numbers of Hispanics in Florida and in the New York and Chicago metropolitan areas.

During the eighties the fastest growing ethnic group in the United States was Asian Americans, whose population more than doubled during the decade. In 1992 Asians comprised about 3 percent of the total U. S. population. They tend to be concentrated on the west coast, especially in California, in the northeast, and in Florida (O'Hare, 1992).

American Indians are the smallest of the four ethnic groups in this study and they comprised only 0.7 percent of the total population in 1992. American Indians tend to be concentrated in the western states, especially in California, Arizona, and New Mexico (O'Hare, 1992).

Bachman et al. (1991) examined ethnic differences in the adolescent use of alcohol, cigarettes, marijuana, and cocaine. They reported that the prevalence of use was lowest among Asian American youth and highest among American Indians. African American adolescents consistently reported lower rates of use than white youth. Hispanics typically had higher rates than African Americans but slightly lower rates than whites. Maddahian et al. (1985) found that Asians had the highest proportion of alcohol abstainers while Hispanics, African Americans, and whites were virtually equal in the proportion of non-users. However, of alcohol users, Asians also had the highest percentage at 37 percent, compared to 28 percent for whites, 21 percent for Hispanics, and only 10 percent for African Americans.

In a study of adolescent alcohol use, Barnes and Welte (1986b) reported that whites and American Indians had the highest prevalence of drinking, followed by Hispanics, African Americans, and Asian Americans. Among those that drank, American Indians had the highest and African Americans the lowest proportion of heavy drinkers (see also, Welte and Barnes, 1987).

Caetano (1984) compared African Americans, whites, and Hispanics in northern California. Hispanics had the highest rate of frequent, heavy drinking. Noting that most research had been conducted in urban areas, Chavez et al. (1986) studied drug use among Hispanics in small towns. They observed that Hispanics had higher rates of use than whites. They also found that the small-town youth had higher rates of use than a national sample of youth. In a Wyoming comparison of Hispanics and whites, Cockerham and Alster (1983) reported that Hispanics were more likely than whites to be frequent users of marijuana.

Beauvais et al. (1985) reported that American Indians had higher usage rates than youth in other ethnic groups. The differences were most striking for alcohol, marijuana, stimulants, and inhalants.

Some evidence exists that ethnic groups tend to be overrepresented in substance abuse problem behaviors. For example, Oyemade (1990) reported that a majority of crack users admitted to hospitals and treatment centers were low-income minorities.

In sum, two conclusions can be drawn from existing research on drug use by ethnic groups. First, in virtually all of the research Asian Americans had the lowest usage rates for all drugs. American Indians, on the other hand, tended to have the highest rates of drug use (Beauvais and LaBoueff, 1985; Harford, 1985). Several researchers reported that Hispanics had higher usage rates than whites, while others found them to be similar to whites (McRoy et al. 1985). African Americans tended to have less overall use than all other groups except Asians. However, there was some evidence that African Americans may be overrepresented among problem users of drugs such as cocaine and heroin (Brunswick and Messeri, 1986; Meddis, 1989).

The second conclusion is that there has been a lack of ethnic-specific research which attempts to explain ethnic variations in drug use, especially when controls are applied (Tucker, 1985; Rebach et al., 1992). The lack of research has resulted in misconceptions about substance use among minority adolescents. For example, the findings of Welte and Barnes (1987) contradicted many common-sense notions concerning drinking among minority youth. As a result, some programs designed for treating minority adolescents may be ineffective because they are based on misconceptions. Oetting et al. (1988) have pointed out that some programs based on commonly believed ideas may fail because they are based on misunderstandings.

PREDICTIVE FACTORS

We turn now to a discussion of several factors that have been found to be associated with adolescent drug use. After a general review of the literature, we will develop our model and discuss its applicability to adolescents in ethnic groups.

In an extensive review of the literature, Hawkins et al. (1992) identified families, schools, and peers as important groups that influence the drug use of adolescents. It is within these three groups that adolescents learn attitudes and values about the use of alcohol and other drugs (Brook et al., 1989; Rapoport, 1989).

Family

The family is a key factor in the development of alcohol and drug abuse. However, there is conflicting data about how and the extent to which the family influences the risk of adolescent drug abuse. On the one hand, some researchers have found that the family influences are weak relative to peer and school factors. For example, Krohn (1974) reported a negative zero-order correlation between adolescent involvement with parents and adolescent marijuana use. That correlation became negligible when amount of association with drug-using friends was controlled. In their longitudinal study, Elliott et al. (1985) observed that adolescent family involvement had a modest, negative impact on involvement with delinquent peers but had no direct effect on the level of drug use. Several other scholars have reported findings consistent with the conclusion that family bonds and other family characteristics do not have direct effects on level of adolescent drug use (Johnson et al., 1987; Akers and Cochran, 1985; Kandel et al., 1976; Marcos et al., 1986).

Other researchers have contended, however, that parent-adolescent bonds may have a significant, direct influence on adolescent drug use. Hundleby and Mercer (1987) examined the role of family and friends in the use of alcohol, tobacco, and marijuana among over 2000 adolescents. They found that although drug use by friends was the most predictive of all measures, family characteristics contributed substantially and uniquely to the variance in adolescent drug use. Parental affection, concern, and involvement were particularly important.

In a review of existing literature, Glynn (1981) concluded that adolescent drug use is influenced by both parents and peers. Family bonds were found to discourage use of alcohol, marijuana, and other illicit drugs. Hawkins et al. (1992) identified low bonding to family as a risk factor in adolescent drug use. The findings from a number of other studies suggest that the strength of parent-child bonds has a significant influence on the amount of adolescent drug use (Barnes et al., 1986; Brook et al., 1983; Chassin et al., 1986; Coombs and Landsverk, 1988; Coombs and Paulson, 1988; Coombs et al., 1991; Delgado, 1990; Dembo et al., 1985; Johnson and Padina, 1991; Kandel et al., 1978; McKay et al., 1991; Oyemade, 1990; Vicary and Lerner, 1986).

Several explanations are possible for the inconsistencies in these findings. First, in some studies the measurement of family variables has been inadequate, such as using marital disruption as an indicator of family bonds. For example, Ellickson and Hays (1992) used living in a single-parent home as a measure of weak family bonds without measuring those bonds directly. A direct measure of family bonds would be more valid than using a structural characteristic as an indicator of bonding. Second, some of the studies with adequate measures of family bonds have not examined peer influences. For example, Smart et al. (1990) observed that adolescents from families with extremely low or high bonds were more vulnerable to drug abuse but they did not include peer influences. Without including peer influences, it is impossible to estimate the relative importance of peer and family factors. Third, conceptualization of family variables has been inadequate. Hawkins et al. (1992) have identified family drug behavior, family management practices, family conflict, and low family bonding as four different family variables associated with adolescent substance abuse. Distinguishing among these different types of family variables is important.

In this research we examined family bonding as a predictor of adolescent drug use. Family bonding refers to the amount of attachment and involvement among family members. As discussed above, a number of researchers have found that low bonding is associated with increased risk of adolescent drug abuse (Hawkins et al., 1992).

Available research, though sparse, suggests that family bonds are associated with adolescent drug use among ethnic groups. Gilbert (1989) and Coombs and Landsverk (1988) reported that the quality of parent-child relationships affected alcohol use patterns of Hispanic adolescents. Similarly, Oetting et al. (1989) suggested that the family is an important factor in preventing substance abuse among American Indian youth.

Education

Low commitment to school was also one of the variables identified by Hawkins et al. (1992). Adolescents who are committed to school tend to be less likely to abuse alcohol and other drugs than adolescents who are not committed to school (Delgado, 1990; Hawkins et al., 1985; Krohn et al., 1983). A desire to attend college, greater time spent on homework, feeling that grades are important, and liking school have been found to be associated with lower levels of drug involvement (Johnston et al., 1985; Johnston et al., 1993; Kelly and Balch, 1971).

Low satisfaction with school was related to greater severity of drug use, especially in females (McBride et al., 1991). Oetting et al. (1989) concluded that school failure increased the risk of substance use among American Indians.

Peers

Numerous researchers have documented the powerful influence of peers on adolescent drug use. Available data indicate that the single best predictor of adolescent drug use is the extent to which one associates with other adolescents who use drugs (Barnes and Welte, 1986a; Brook et al., 1990; Dielman et al., 1991; Elliott et al., 1985; Hawkins et al., 1992; Jaquith, 1981; Johnson et al., 1987; Kandel, 1986; Kandel and Andrews, 1987; Kaplan et al., 1984; Krohn, 1974; Kumpfer and Turner, 1990; McBride, 1978; McBride et al., 1991; Needle et al., 1986; Newcomb and Bentler, 1986; Orcutt, 1987). Longitudinal studies have indicated that association with peers who use drugs usually precedes actual drug use (Kaplan et al., 1984; Elliott et al., 1985). Farrell and Danish (1993) suggested that there may be reciprocal influences between peers and drug use and that the influence of peers on drug use may not be as strong as commonly assumed. Studies of ethnic groups are consistent with the above findings (Gilbert, 1989; Oetting et al., 1988).

Theoretical Model

Existing literature indicates that low family bonding, low educational commitment, and having close friends who use drugs tend to be associated with adolescent alcohol and drug abuse. A diagram of these relationships is shown in Figure 1. Although this model is consistent with much of the existing literature (Hawkins et al., 1992), it is not known how the strength of these predictors may vary among different ethnic groups. Our purpose in testing this model was to estimate how well it predicts substance use in each of the groups. We are particularly interested in the relationship of family bonds to adolescent drug use.

We found only one existing study in which this type of ethnic comparison was reported. Catalano et al. (1992) examined initiation to drug use among a sample of 919 Asian American, African American, and white students in the fifth grade. Attachment to parents had a significant

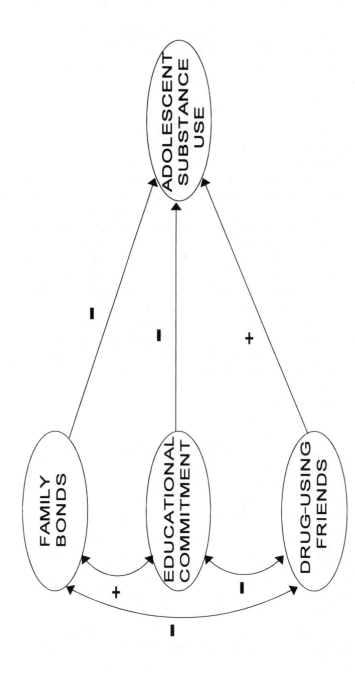

FIGURE 1. HYPOTHESIZED MODEL OF ADOLESCENT
SUBSTANCE USE

association with substance use among the African American youth but not among the white or Asian youth. Parental monitoring of friends was a significant factor only among African Americans. These data indicate some family predictors appear to operate differently among African Americans than among whites or Asians. Catalano et al. (1992) studied only fifth graders at early initiation. The present study was designed to make comparisons among older adolescents.

METHODS

Sample and Data Collection

The data used for this study were taken from a sample of high school students collected in Utah during 1989. A multi-stage cluster sample was used to sample schools and classrooms within schools. A comparison of the sample with the school population of the state showed that it was representative in terms of ethnic status, gender, age, and region.

The questionnaire was administered to all students in attendance on the day of the survey. In order to encourage students to be truthful, the survey was voluntary and anonymous. A nonexistent drug was included in the questionnaire to detect overreporting, and only 1.7 percent of the students reported that they had taken it. This indicates that intentional overreporting was minimal. All students who reported taking the nonexistent drug were excluded from the analyses.

Nonresponse rates to drug use questions were less than one-half of 1 percent and were similar to nonresponse rates on other types of questions. This indicates that there was not underreporting caused by intentional skipping of questions.

Test-retest data were also collected from 149 junior and senior high school students in four schools not included in the sample. Ten items on drug use were included in two different questionnaires administered one week apart. Ninety-four percent of the responses at Time 2 were identical to those at Time 1. This shows that junior and senior high school students are able to respond consistently over time to drug-use questions.

The prevalence rates obtained from the seniors in our sample were similar to those obtained in a national sample of high school seniors (Johnston et al., 1989). Overall, the evidence suggests that high school students' responses to drug use questions are sufficiently reliable and valid to be used to test theoretical models.

The proportion of each ethnic group in the sample was similar to the proportion in the population of Utah. However, it is very different from the distribution of ethnic groups in the United States because Utah has a low proportion of African, Asian and Hispanic Americans, but a higher than average number of American Indians. The total sample included only 0.9 percent African Americans, 3.8 percent Hispanics, 1.5 percent Asians, and 4 percent American Indians. Because the total sample size was large (27,291), there were sufficient cases in each group for comparisons and our major purpose was comparative and not to describe the population.

The total sample used in this analysis was 4,921 students. Table 1 shows the distribution of the sample by ethnic group, age, and gender.

Table 1

Description of Sample

	Sample Size	Percent of Sample	Percent Female	Mean Age
African American	191	3.9	46.0	15.2
American Indian	1051	21.4	49.4	15.0
Asian American	392	8.0	48.0	15.2
Hispanic American	962	19.5	50.1	14.8
White*	2325	47.2	50.5	14.9
Total	4921	100.0	49.8	14.9

*The 2325 whites were a 10 percent random sample of the 23721 white adolescents who completed the survey.

In each of the groups females were about half of the respondents. The age distributions of the ethnic groups were similar.[1] The 2,325 white adolescents were a 10 percent random sample of the total white adolescents who completed the survey. A sub-sample of white students was used in order to decrease the difference between the size of the white sample compared to the ethnic groups. This technique did not change the comparison and estimation of the coefficients.[2] We used all the available cases in the analysis of the ethnic groups.

Measurement and Analytical Methods

Table 2 shows the items used to measure each of the constructs in the model. In order to make comparisons, we constructed an overall measure of substance use. Scales measuring use of tobacco, alcohol, and other drugs were each used as an indicator of overall *substance use*.

As a preliminary step in the data analysis, one-way analysis of variance was used to compare the five groups on substance use. To test our model we used LISREL, the structural equation program developed by Joreskog and Sorbom (1989). Initially, we conducted a confirmatory factor analysis to determine if the measurement models were similar for each of the five ethnic groups. Each of the groups had the same pattern of factors or latent variables as expected.

In the next step we used multiple-group structural equation modeling (Joreskog and Sorbom, 1989) to compare the white adolescents with each of the minority adolescents. Invariance tests were used to determine which parameters of the minority groups were significantly different from the comparable parameters of the white adolescents. For a more detailed discussion of LISREL, see Joreskog (1969), Bollen (1989) and Bollen and Long (1993).

An initial test of the model in Figure 1 revealed that for each of the groups, the coefficient between family bonds and drug use was not significant, net of the other variables. Therefore, the model was recomputed with that coefficient omitted. Having developed a LISREL model for the five groups, the next step was to conduct multi-group invariance tests using LISREL to find out the similarities and differences between white adolescents and adolescents from each of the other groups.

Table 2

Measurement of Variables

Family Bonds (Attachment to parents; amount of family involvement)
(1) In your free time away from home, does your mother or father know where you are?
(2) How well do your parents know your best friends?
(3) Do you enjoy doing things with your family?
(4) Do you remember any special things your family has done together that were lots of fun, such as trips, holidays, or other activities?

Educational Commitment (Extent of school involvement; desire for more education)
(1) How important is it to you to get good grades in school?
(2) About how much time do you spend on school work outside of class each day?
(3) What grades do you receive in school?
(4) What are your educational expectations?

Number of Drug-Using Friends
(1) How many of your best friends drink beer, wine, or liquor regularly?
(2) How many of your best friends have used marijuana?
(3) How many of your best friends have taken other drugs for non-medical reasons?

Substance Use (Scale scores from Tobacco, Alcohol, and Other Drugs used as indicators)
(1) *Tobacco* (mean of the following 3 items)
    (1) If you have ever used any tobacco products (cigarettes, cigars, pipes, chewing tobacco, snuff), when was the last time?
    (2) On how many of the past 30 days have you used any tobacco products (cigarettes, cigars, pipe tobacco, chewing tobacco, snuff)?
    (3) During the past 30 days, about how many cigarettes did you smoke a day?
(2) *Alcohol* (mean of the following 8 items)
    (1) If you have ever had beer, wine, or liquor to drink, when was the last time?
    (2) How often during the past 30 days did you drink beer, wine, or liquor?
    (3) On how many of the past 30 days have you had beer to drink?
    (4) When you drink beer, about how many beers do you usually have?
    (5) On how many of the past 30 days have you had wine or wine coolers to drink?
    (6) When you drink wine or wine coolers, about how many glasses or drinks do you usually have?
    (7) On how many of the past 30 days have you had liquor?
    (8) When you drink liquor, about how many drinks do you usually have?

Table continues

Table 2 (continued)

(3) *Other Drugs* (mean of the following 8 items)

    (1)   If you have ever used marijuana, when was the last time?

    (2)   On how many of the past 30 days have you used marijuana?

    (3)   During the last month, about how many marijuana cigarettes did you smoke a day, on average?

    (4)   How recently did you use marijuana or hashish on a daily basis for at least a month?

    (5)   If you have ever used amphetamines without a doctor telling you to take them, when was the last time?

    (6)   On how many of the past 30 days have you taken amphetamines without a doctor telling you to take them?

    (7)   If you have ever used cocaine, when was the last time?

    (8)   On how many of the past 30 days have you used cocaine?*

*The number of response categories ranged from 4 to 7, depending on the item. A copy of the questionnaire may be obtained by writing the authors.

RESULTS

The results of the one-way analysis of variance are presented in Table 3.[3] For all three measures of substance use, Hispanic, African American, and American Indian adolescents reported higher levels of use than white or Asian adolescents. Asian and white adolescents did not differ significantly on any of the three types of use. On alcohol use, American Indians were significantly lower than Hispanics and African Americans. For "other drugs," American Indians were significantly lower than African Americans.

Table 4 is a summary of the invariance tests among the independent variables. In a comparison of family bonds and educational commitment (C1 of Table 4), none of the differences was significant, which indicates that correlation between family bonds and educational commitment was the same across all groups.

Table 3

Mean Use of Tobacco, Alcohol, and Other Drugs
by Ethnic Group
(Standard Deviations in Parentheses)*

Ethnic Group	Tobacco	Alcohol	Other Drugs	Sample Size
African American	.927 (1.486)	1.141 (1.198)	.446 (.959)	191
American Indian	.912 (1.301)	.793 (1.039)	.300 (.679)	1051
Asian American	.416 (.986)	.560 (.873)	.166 (.503)	391
Hispanic American	.757 (1.212)	1.150 (1.090)	.326 (.675)	961
White American	.513 (1.089)	.620 (.936)	.150 (.465)	2324
Total Sample	.654 (1.185)	.776 (1.020)	.229 (.594)	4918

* Each variable was computed by taking the mean of the items in the scale (See Table 2 for a description of the items). For all three drugs, the Scheffe test showed that Asian Americans and whites were significantly lower than African Americans, American Indians, and Hispanic Americans. Asians and whites did not differ significantly on any drug. In addition, the alcohol use of American Indians was significantly lower than the alcohol use of African Americans and Hispanics. For "other drugs," Indians were significantly lower than African Americans.

Table 4

Summary of Invariance Tests of Correlations
among Family Bonds, Educational Commitment, and
Number of Drug-Using Friends

Correlations Among	Chi-Square Differences between Whites and				Degrees of Freedom
	Hispanic Americans	African Americans	American Indians	Asian Americans	
C1. Family bonds & ed. commitment	0.54	0.47	0.41	1.36	1
C2. Family bonds & drug-using friends	5.31*	7.94*	16.81*	3.04	1
C3. Ed. commitment & drug-using friends	5.41*	4.90*	26.35*	0.01	1

* Difference is statistically significant at .05 level.

A comparison of family bonds and number of drug-using friends (see C2 of Table 4) revealed no significant difference between white and Asian American adolescents. However, the differences between white adolescents and each of the other ethnic groups (Hispanic, African American, and American Indian) were significant, which indicated that the strength of the correlation between family bonds and drug-using friends was significantly different for Hispanics, African Americans, and American Indians compared to whites.

The third set of invariance tests (C3 of Table 4) showed that the correlation between educational commitment and number of drug-using friends was the same for white and Asian adolescents. However, for Hispanic, African American, and American Indian adolescents, the correlation was significantly different.

Next, we tested the overall invariance of the structural coefficients relating the independent and dependent variables, again comparing whites to each ethnic group. For the association between educational commitment and substance use, the differences between whites and Hispanic Americans and between whites and Asian Americans were not significant (see S1 of Table 5). However, the negative association between educational commitment and adolescent substance use was significantly stronger among African Americans and American Indians than among whites.

Table 5

Summary of Invariance Tests of Structural Coefficients
Relating Educational Commitment and Number of
Drug-Using Friends to Adolescent Substance Use

Correlations Among	Chi-Square Differences between Whites and				Degrees of Freedom
	Hispanic Americans	African Americans	American Indians	Asian Americans	
S1. Ed. Commitment on Substance Use	3.63	8.14*	9.57*	0.33	1
S2. Drug-Using Friends on Substance Use	7.54*	8.82*	6.55*	2.48	1

* Difference is statistically significant at .05 level.

The strength of the relationship between number of drug-using friends and adolescent substance use was the same for white compared to Asian American adolescents, but differences between whites and each of the other groups were statistically significant (see S2 of Table 5).

Having conducted invariance tests systematically between whites and each of the ethnic groups, we tested our model on the five groups simultaneously using LISREL multi-group analysis. Table 6 reports the goodness of fit indices, root mean square residuals, and explained variances for each of the five groups as well as the overall chi-square ratio for the five-group comparison.

Table 6

Overall Model Comparison
Among Five Groups

Ethnic Group	Goodness of Fit Index	Root Mean Square Residual	Explained Variance
African American	.91	.09	.47
American Indian	.97	.05	.57
Asian American	.93	.06	.68
Hispanic American	.96	.05	.71
White American	.97	.03	.73

Overall Chi-Square = 1315.78
Degrees of Freedom = 344
Chi-Square Ratio = 3.8

The model has reasonably good fit within each ethnic group; the goodness of fit indices rangd from .91 (African Americans) to .97 (whites and American Indians) and the overall chi-square ratio is only 3.8 which is small for such a large sample. However, the fit of the model is somewhat better for white and Hispanic Americans than for the other groups; and the model has the poorest fit among African Americans.

The structural coefficients among the latent variables were standardized to a common metric among the five groups to allow comparisons and are shown in Figure 2. The structural coefficients between family bonds and educational commitment are strong for all groups and suggest that within each of the five groups, a high level of family bonding tends to be associated with a high commitment to education by adolescents. Since the association between family bonds and educational commitment is not significantly different for any group, this parameter is constrained to be equal in the final model and therefore, in Figure 2 it is exactly the same for each group. Without this constraint the parameters would vary slightly among the groups. The associations between family bonds and drug-using friends, and between educational commitment and drug-using friends are smaller for African Americans and American Indians than for the other three groups. Although educational commitment is negatively related to number of drug-using friends for each of the ethnic groups, the correlation is strongest for Asian (-.44), white (-.41), and Hispanic (-.29) adolescents, and weaker for American Indian (-.13) and African American (.13) adolescents. Comparatively speaking, the correlation between family bonds and number of drug-using friends is strongest for whites (-.54), moderate for Asians (-.44) and Hispanics (-.40), and small for American Indian (-.27) and African-American (-.18) adolescents.

The effects of educational commitment on adolescents' substance use are strongest for African American adolescents (-.38), moderate for American Indians (-.31) and Hispanic Americans (-.24), and weakest for white (-.17) and Asian American (-.13) adolescents. Adolescents who are committed to their education are less likely to use drugs, particularly among African Americans and American Indians. The effects of drug-using friends on adolescent substance use are strong among all groups; this association is strongest among Asian (.91) and white (.78) adolescents and weakest for the African American (.49) adolescents.

DISCUSSION

The model in Figure 2 is based on the integration of social control and social learning theory proposed by Hawkins et al. (1992). Among all five groups, there was a strong association between number of close friends who used drugs and the risk of drug use. Through friends adolescents may learn how to use substances and may feel social pressure to experiment with various substances.

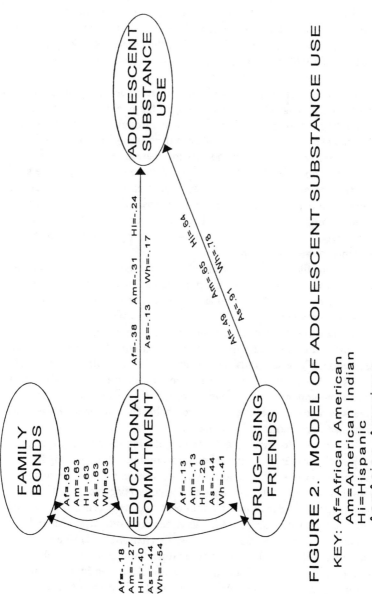

FIGURE 2. MODEL OF ADOLESCENT SUBSTANCE USE

KEY: Af=African American
Am=American Indian
Hi=Hispanic
As=Asian American
Wh=White

Educational commitment had a modest, negative association with the risk of drug use, although the strength of this association varied among the different groups. When adolescents were committed to education and involved in school activities, they were less likely to have close friends who used drugs and less likely to use substances themselves.

Although there appeared to be no direct influence of family bonds on adolescent substance use among any of the five ethnic groups, family bonding had important indirect effects through its association with educational commitment and number of drug-using friends. If there was low bonding to their families, adolescents were more likely to associate with drug-using friends and, consequently, were more likely to use substances themselves. On the other hand, adolescents who were attached to their families were less likely to have close friends who used drugs and therefore, were less likely to use substances themselves. Similarly, if adolescents were bonded to their families, they were more likely to be committed to education.

Overall, the adolescents from each of the five groups were similar in that the variables in the model predicted substance use well. Family bonds and educational commitment appear to be two protective factors for adolescents while having friends who use drugs is a risk factor.

There were three striking similarities among the groups: (1) After controlling for other variables, none of the groups showed a significant association between family bonds and adolescent substance use. (2) Among all five groups, there was a strong, positive association between educational commitment and family bonds. (3) Among all five groups, there was a strong positive association between number of drug-using friends and adolescent substance use.

There were four striking differences among the ethnic groups: (1) The association between family bonds and number of drug-using friends was significantly smaller among African Americans and American Indians than among whites, Asian Americans, or Hispanics. (2) The association between educational commitment and drug-using friends was significantly smaller among African Americans and American Indians than among whites, Asian Americans, or Hispanics. (3) The negative association between educational commitment and adolescent substance use was stronger for African Americans and American Indians than for Hispanics, whites or Asian Americans. (4) The impact of having drug-using friends on adolescents' substance use was less among African Americans than among the other groups.

These findings suggest that family bonds may be more important for whites, Hispanics, and Asian Americans than for others in terms of reducing the chance of having drug-using friends. And the impact of having close friends who use drugs would appear to be stronger among whites and Asians than among the other groups. Thus, family and peers may be particularly important in reducing drug use among whites and Asians. However, educational commitment would appear to be more important for African Americans and Indians than the other groups in reducing the risk of drug use. Although white and Asian American adolescents reported less association with drug-using friends than did the African American adolescents, associating with drug-using friends had a stronger effect on substance use for white and Asian American adolescents than for African American adolescents.

This research indicates that strengthening family bonds, increasing educational commitment, and reducing association with drug-using friends may decrease the risk of substance use for adolescents in all five of the groups. However, strengthening educational commitment may have the strongest direct effect on the African American adolescents, a moderate direct effect on Hispanic and American Indian adolescents, and a weak direct effect on Asian and white American adolescents.

Why did these ethnic differences occur? To answer this question it may be useful to explore the social context within which minority groups live. For example, if one lives in an environment where drug use is common and drugs are plentiful, perhaps close friends are less important. One becomes aware of and exposed to drugs whether or not one's close friends use drugs. On the other hand, the situation is very different among adolescents who live in an environment where drug use is less common, anti-drug messages are prevalent, and the average adolescent does not use drugs. In such an environment adolescents would not become exposed to drugs unless they became acquainted with friends who introduced them to drugs. Thus, in a relatively drug-free environment becoming a friend to a drug user may be a critical factor.

Ethnic groups living in poor, urban areas might be somewhat more likely to live in an environment where drug use is common, and hence, the influence of having drug-using friends may be somewhat less. Similarly, in such a social context having strong family bonds might be less likely to shield one from associating with friends who use drugs. Hawkins et al. (1992) suggested that social context may have an important influence on drug use but noted that the social context of drug use has not been studied extensively. The findings in this study suggest that social context should be a high priority in future research.

The findings from this study may not generalize to other adolescents because the data were collected in a western state in which there were relatively small numbers of ethnic minorities. Nevertheless, the findings add to our knowledge of drug use among ethnic groups. Research in other geographical areas needs to be conducted to confirm the generalizability of the findings and examine how social context may explain these results.

NOTES

[1] A one-way analysis of variance, with the Scheffe test of significance for the various pairs of means, revealed that none of the mean ages were different except Asians were significantly older than the Hispanics.

[2] We computed many of the results reported on the entire sample of white adolescents. The findings were the same as those reported here from the 10 percent sample.

[3] A Scheffe test was used to compare each of the pairs of mean. It adjusts the alpha level when multiple comparisons are made, so that the significant differences are accurate and not simply the artifact of several comparisons.

REFERENCES

Akers, R.L. and J.K. Cochran. 1985. "Adolescent marijuana use: A test of three theories of deviant behavior." *Deviant Behavior* 6:323-346.

Bachman, J.G., J.M. Wallace Jr., P.M. O'Malley, L.D. Johnston, C.L. Kurth, and H.W. Neighbors. 1991. "Racial/ethnic differences in smoking, drinking, and illicit drug use among American high school seniors, 1976-89." *American Journal of Public Health* 81 (3):372-377.

Barnes, G.M., M.P. Farrel, and A. Cairns. 1986. "Parental socialization factors and adolescent drinking behaviors." *Journal of Marriage and the Family* 48:27-36.

_____. and J.W. Welte. 1986a. "Adolescent alcohol abuse: Subgroup differences and relationships to other problem behaviors." *Journal of Adolescent Research* 1 (1):79-94.

_____. and J.W. Welte. 1986b. "Patterns and predictors of alcohol use among seventh through twelfth grade students in New York State." *Journal of Studies on Alcohol* 47 (1):53-62.

Beauvais, F. and S. LaBoueff. 1985. "Drug and alcohol abuse intervention in American Indian communities." *International Journal of the Addictions* 20 (1):139-171.

Beauvais, F., E.R. Oetting, and R.W. Edwards. 1985. "Trends in drug use of Indian adolescents living on reservations: 1975-1983." *American Journal of Drug and Alcohol Abuse* 11:209-229.

Bollen, K. A. 1989. *Structural Equations with Latent Variables*. New York: Wiley.

Bollen, K.A. and J.S. Long. 1993. *Testing Structural Equation Models*. Newbury Park, California: Sage Publications.

Brook, J.S., D.W. Brook, A.S. Gordon, M. Whiteman, P. Cohen. 1990. "The psychosocial etiology of adolescent drug use: A family interaction approach." *Genetic, Social, and General Psychology Monographs* 116 (Whole No. 2).

Brook, J.S., C. Nomura, and C. Patricia. 1989. "A network of influences on adolescent drug involvement: Neighborhood, school, peer, and family." *Genetic, Social, and General Psychology Monographs* 115 (1):123-145.

Brook, J.S., M. Whiteman, and A.S. Gordon. 1983. "Stages of drug use in adolescence: Personality, peer, and family correlates." *Developmental Psychology* 19:269-277.

Brunswick, A.F. and P. Messeri. 1986. "Drugs, life style and health." *American Journal of Public Health* 76:52-57.

Caetano, R. 1984. "Ethnicity and drinking in Northern California: A comparison among whites, Blacks and Hispanics." *Alcohol and Alcoholism* 19:31-44.

Catalano, Richard F. and Diane M. Morrison. 1992. "Ethnic differences in family factors related to early drug initiation." *Journal of Studies on Alcohol* 53 (3):208-217.

Chassin, L., C.C. Presson, S.J. Sherman, D. Montello, and J. McGrew. 1986. "Changes in peer and parent influence during adolescence: Longitudinal versus cross-sectional perspectives on smoking initiation." *Developmental Psychology* 22:327-334.

Chavez, E., F. Beauvais, and E.R. Oetting. 1986. "Drug use by small town Mexican American youth: A pilot study." *Hispanic Journal of Behavioral Science* 8:243-258.

Cockerham, W.C. and J.M. Alster. 1983. "A comparison of marijuana use among Mexican-American and Anglo rural youth utilizing a matched set analysis." *International Journal of the Addictions* 18:759-767.

Coombs, R.H. and J. Landsverk. 1988. "Parenting styles and substance use during childhood and adolescence." *Journal of Marriage and the Family* 50:473-482.

Coombs, R.H. and M.J. Paulson. 1988. "Contrasting family patterns of adolescent drug users and nonusers." *Journal of Chemical Dependency Treatment* 1 (2):59-72.

Coombs, R.H., M.J. Paulson, and M.A. Richardson. 1991. "Peer vs. parental influence in substance use among Hispanic and Anglo children and adolescents." *Journal of Youth and Adolescence* 20 (1):73-88.

Davis, L.E. and A.R. Stiffman. 1990. *Ethnic Issues in Adolescent Mental Health.* Newbury Park, California: Sage Publications.

Delgado, M. 1990. *Hispanic Adolescents and Substance Abuse: Implications for Research, Treatment, and Prevention in Ethnic Issues in Adolescent Mental Health.* Edited by Stiffman and Davis. Newbury Park, California: Sage Publications.

Dembo, R., G. Grandon, R.W. Taylor, L. La Voie, W. Burgos, and J. Schmeidler. 1985. "The influence of family relationships on marijuana use among a sample of inner city youths." *Deviant Behavior* 6:267-286.

Dielman, T.E., A.T. Butchart, J.T. Shope, and M. Miller. 1991. "Environmental correlates of adolescent substance use and misuse: Implications for prevention programs." Special Issue: Environmental factors in substance misuse and its treatment. *International Journal of the Addictions* 25 (7A-8A):855-880.

Ellickson, P.L. and R.D. Hays. 1992. "On becoming involved with drugs: Modeling adolescent drug use over time." *Health Psychology* 11:377-385.

Elliott, D.S., D. Huizinga, and S.S. Ageton. 1985. *Explaining Delinquency and Drug Use.* Beverly Hills, California: Sage Publications.

Farrell, A.D. and S.J. Danish. 1993. "Peer drug associations and emotional restraint: Causes or consequences of adolescents' drug use?" *Journal of Consulting and Clinical Psychology* 61:327-334.

Gilbert, M.J. 1989. "Alcohol use among Latino adolescents: What we know and what we need to know." Pp. 35-53 in B. Segal (ed.), *Perspectives on Adolescent Drug Use*. New York: Haworth Press.

Glynn, T.J. 1981. "From family to peer: A review of transitions of influence among drug-using youth." *Journal of Youth and Adolescence* 10:363-383.

Harford, T.C. 1985. "Drinking patterns among black and non-black adolescents: Results of a national survey." Pp. 276-291 in E.M. Freeman (ed.), *Social Work Practice with Clients Who Have Alcohol Problems*. Springfield, Illinois: Charles C. Thomas.

Hawkins, J.D., R.F. Catalano, and J.Y. Miller. 1992. "Risk and protective factors for alcohol and other drug problems in adolescence and early adulthood: Implications for substance abuse prevention." *Psychological Bulletin* 112:64-105.

Hawkins, J.D., D.M. Lishner, R.F. Catalano, M.O. Howard. 1985. "Childhood predictors and prevention of adolescent substance abuse." Pp. 75-126 in C.L. Jones and R.J. Battjes (eds.), *Etiology of Drug Abuse: Implications for Prevention*. NIDA Research Monograph No. 56, DHSS Publication ADM 85-1335. Washington, DC: U.S. Government Printing Office.

Hundleby, J.D. and G.W. Mercer. 1987. "Family and friends as social environments and their relationship to young adolescents' use of alcohol, tobacco, and marijuana." *Journal of Marriage and the Family* 49:151-164.

Jaquith, S.M. 1981. "Adolescent marijuana and alcohol use." *Criminology* 19:271-280.

Johnson, R.E., A.C. Marcos, and S.J. Bahr. 1987. "The role of peers in the complex etiology of adolescent drug use." *Criminology* 25: 323-340.

Johnson, V. and R.J. Padina. 1991. "Effects of the family environment on adolescent substance use, delinquency, and coping styles." *American Journal on Drug and Alcohol Abuse* 17:71-88.

Johnston, L.D., P.M. O'Malley, and J.G. Bachman. 1985. *Use of Licit and Illicit Drugs by America's High School Students, 1975-1984*. Rockville, Maryland: National Institute of Drug Abuse.

Johnston, L.D., P.M. O'Malley, and J.G. Bachman. 1989. *Drug Use, Drinking, and Smoking: National Survey Results from High School, College, and Young Adult Populations, 1975-1988*. Rockville, Maryland: National Institute on Drug Abuse.

Johnston, L.D., P.M. O'Malley, and J.G. Bachman. 1993. *National Survey Results on Drug Use from Monitoring the Future Study, 1975-1992, Volume I, Secondary School Students*. Rockville, Maryland: National Institute on Drug Abuse.

Joreskog, K.G. 1969. "A general approach to confirmatory maximum likelihood factor analysis." *Psychometrika* 34:183-202.

Joreskog, K.G. and D. Sorbom. 1989. *LISREL 7: A Guide to the Program and Applications*. Chicago: SPSS Inc.

Kandel, D.B. 1986. "Processes of peer influence in adolescence." Pp. 203-288 in R. Silberstein (ed.), *Development as Action in Context: Problem Behavior and Normal Youth Development*. New York: Springer-Verlag.

Kandel, D.B. and K. Andrews. 1987. "Processes of adolescent socialization by parents and peers." *International Journal of the Addictions* 22:319-342.

Kandel, D.B., R.B. Kessler, and R.Z. Marguiles. 1978. "Antecedents of adolescent initiation into stages of drug use: A developmental analysis." *Journal of Youth and Adolescence* 7:13-40.

Kandel, D.B., D. Treiman, R. Faust, and E. Single. 1976. "Adolescent involvement in legal and illegal drug use: A multiple classification analysis." *Social Forces* 55:438-458.

Kaplan, H.B., S.S. Martin, and C. Robbins. 1984. "Pathways to adolescent drug use: Self-derogation, peer influence, weakening of social controls, and early substance use." *Journal of Health and Social Behavior* 25:270-289.

Kelly, D.H. and R.W. Balch. 1971. "Social origins and school failure: A reexamination of Cohen's theory of working class delinquency." *Pacific Sociological Review* 14:413-430.

Krohn, M.D. 1974. "An investigation of the effect of parental and peer associations on marijuana use: An empirical test of differential association theory." Pp. 75-89 in M. Reidel, and T.P. Thornbery, (eds.), *Crime and Delinquency: Dimensions of Deviance.* New York: Praeger Publishing.

Krohn, M.D., J.L. Massey, W.F. Skinner, and R.M. Lauer. 1983. "Social bonding theory and adolescent cigarette smoking: A longitudinal analysis." *Journal of Health and Social Behavior* 24 (4):337-349.

Kumpfer, K.L. and C.W. Turner. 1990. "The social ecology model of adolescent substance abuse: Implications for prevention." *International Journal of the Addictions* 25:435-463.

Maddahian, E., M.D. Newcomb, P.M. Bentler. 1985. "Single and multiple patterns of adolescent substance use: Longitudinal comparisons of four ethnic groups." *Journal of Drug Education* 15 (4):311-326.

Marcos, A.C., S.J. Bahr, and R.E. Johnson. 1986. "Test of a bonding/association theory of adolescent drug use." *Social Forces* 65:135-161.

McBride, D. 1978. *Parental and Peer Influences on Adolescent Drug Use.* Rockville, Maryland: National Institute on Drug Abuse.

McBride, A.A., G.W. Joe, and D.D. Simpson. 1991. "Prediction of long-term alcohol use, drug use, and criminality among inhalant users." *Hispanic Journal of Behavioral Sciences* 13 (3):315-323.

McKay, J.R., R.T. Murphy, T.R. Rivinus, and S.A. Maisto. 1991. "Family dysfunction and alcohol and drug use in adolescent psychiatric inpatients." *Journal of the American Academy of Child and Adolescent Psychiatry* 30 (6):967-972.

McRoy, R.G., C.T. Shorkey, and E. Garcia. 1985. "Alcohol use and abuse among Mexican-Americans." Pp. 229-241 in E.M. Freeman (ed.), *Social Work Practice with Clients Who Have Alcohol Problems*. Springfield, Illinois: Charles C. Thomas.

Meddis, S. 1989. "Drug arrest rate higher for Blacks." *USA Today*. Dec. 20, p. A-1.

Needle, R., H. McCubbin, M. Wilson, R. Reineck, A. Lazar, and H. Mederer. 1986. "Interpersonal influences in adolescent drug use—the role of older siblings, parents, and peers." *International Journal of the Addictions* 21:739-766.

Newcomb, M.D. and P.M. Bentler. 1986. "Frequency and sequence of drug use: A longitudinal study from early adolescence to young adulthood." *Journal of Drug Education* 16:101-120.

Oetting, E.R., F. Beauvais, and R. Edwards. 1988. "Alcohol and Indian youth: Social and psychological correlates and prevention." *Journal of Drug Issues* 18 (1):87-102.

_____, R.W. Edwards, and F. Beauvais. 1989. "Drugs and Native-American youth." Pp. 1-34 in B. Segal (ed.), *Perspectives on Adolescent Drug Use*. New York: Haworth Press.

O'Hare, W.P. 1992. *America's Minorities—The Demographics of Diversity*. Population Bulletin 47 (4):1-46. Washington, DC: Population Reference Bureau, Inc.

Orcutt, J.D. 1987. "Differential association and marijuana use: A closer look at Sutherland (with a little help from Becker)." *Criminology* 25:341-358.

Oyemade, U. 1990. "The role of family factors in the primary prevention of substance abuse among high risk black youth." In L.E. Davis and A.R. Stiffman (eds.), *Ethnic Issues in Adolescent Mental Health*. Newbury Park, California: Sage Publications.

Rebach, H.W., C.S. Bolek, K.L. Williams, and Russell, R. 1992. *Substance Abuse Among Ethnic Minorities in America: A Critical Annotated Bibliography*. New York: Garland Publishing, Inc.

Rapoport, T. 1989. "Experimentation and control: A conceptual framework for the comparative analysis of socialization agencies." *Human Relations*, 42 (11):957-973.

Smart, L.S., T.R. Chibucos, and L.A. Didier. 1990. "Adolescent substance use and perceived family functioning." *Journal of Family Issues* 11:208-227.

Sutherland, E. 1939. *Principles of Criminology*. Philadelphia: J.B. Lippincott.

Tucker, M.B. 1985. "U.S. ethnic minorities and drug abuse: An assessment of the science and practice." *International Journal of the Addictions* 20:1021-1047.

Vicary, J.R. and J.V. Lerner. 1986. "Parental attributes and adolescent drug use." *Journal of Adolescence* 9:115-122.

Welte, J.W. and G.M. Barnes. 1987. "Alcohol use among adolescent minority groups." *Journal of Studies on Alcohol*, 48 (4):329-336.

CONTRIBUTORS

Most of the papers included in this volume were originally presented at a conference on Racial and Ethnic Families in the United States. The conference was supported by the Dean's office of the College of Family, Home and Social Sciences, and was organized by Cardell Jacobson with the aid of Norene C. Petersen. Mrs. Petersen prepared the complete manuscript for copy-ready publication; she is the administrative assistant for the Center for Studies of the Family and prepares all manuscripts for publication that appear in the journal *Family Perspective.*

ADALBERTO AGUIRRE, JR. is Professor of Sociology at the University of California-Riverside.

STAN L. ALBRECHT is Professor in the Department of Health Policy and Epidemiology at the University of Florida.

HOWARD M. BAHR is Professor of Sociology at Brigham Young University.

KATHLEEN S. BAHR is Assistant Professor in Family Science at Brigham Young University.

STEPHEN J. BAHR is Professor in the Department of Sociology and the Center for Studies of the Family at Brigham Young University.

FRANK D. BEAN is the Ashbel Smith Professor of Sociology and Director of Graduate Training Programs in Demography at the Population Research Center at the University of Texas.

MARILOU C. LEGAZPI BLAIR is an Assistant Professor in the School of Social Work at the University of Oklahoma.

SAMPSON LEE BLAIR is an Assistant Professor in the Department of Sociology at the University of Oklahoma.

ANNA Y. CHAN received a Master's degree in Family Studies at the University of Utah.

LESLIE L. CLARKE is Research Assistant Professor in the Department of Obstetrics and Gynecology and an Associate Research Scientist in the Institute for Health Policy Research at the University of Florida.

KENNETH L. CLINTON, JR. is Professor of Sociology at East Texas State University.

W. PARKER FRISBIE is Professor of Sociology and Director of the Population Research Center at the University of Texas at Austin.

MONICA D. GRIFFIN is a Ph. D. candidate in sociology at the University of Virginia.

ANTHONY C.R. HERNANDEZ is an Assistant Professor of Psychology at Arizona State University West.

GREGORY HINCKLEY is a graduate student in sociology at Purdue University.

JANET HOPE is Assistant Professor of Sociology at the College of St. Benedict/St. John's University in Minnesota.

TRINA L. HOPE is a Ph. D. candidate in sociology at the University of Arizona.

CARDELL K. JACOBSON is Professor of Sociology at Brigham Young University

CAROLYN G. JEW is a graduate student in sociology at Brigham Young University.

VIVIAN Z. KLAFF is Professor of Sociology at the University of Delaware.

ANASTASIOS C. MARCOS is an Associate Professor in the Department of Sociology at The American College of Greece, Athens, Greece.

KATHERINE MCDADE is Associate Professor in the Department of Sociology at Pacific Lutheran University.

ROBERT E. PARKER is an Associate Professor in the department of Sociology at the University of Nevada, Las Vegas.

VÂNIA PENHA-LOPES is a graduate student in sociology at New York University.

KAE SAWYER completed a Master's degree in sociology in 1993 at Brigham Young University and completed the Inter-university Program for Chinese Language Studies in Taipei in 1994.

KEN R. SMITH is a Professor in the Department of Family and Consumer Studies at the University of Utah.

YANICK ST. JEAN is Assistant Professor of Sociology at the University of Nevada, Las Vegas.

ROBERT STAPLES is Professor in the Graduate Program in Sociology at the University of California-San Francisco.

JOSEPH (JAY) H. STAUSS is Professor of American Indian Studies and Family Studies at the University of Arizona. His tribal affiliation is the Jamestown Band S'Klallam in Sequim, Washington, and he is the Director of the Indian Studies Department at the University of Arizona.

GABE T. WANG is Assistant Professor of Sociology at Morehead State University.

CAROL WARD is an Assistant Professor of Sociology at Brigham Young University.

LARRY E. WILLIAMS is Professor of Sociology at Midwestern State University.

DEBORAH S. WILSON is an Adjunct Professor of Sociology at Utah Valley State College. She is also a Captain in the United States Army National Guard.

LISA WYATT is a graduate student in sociology at the University of Oklahoma.

YAN YU is a Ph. D. candidate in sociology at Florida State University.

Author Index

Subject Index